THE LAST UNTOLD STORY
OF THE BEATLES

JEM ROBERTS

CANDY JAR BOOKS · CARDIFF
2021

The right of Jem Roberts to be identified as the
Author of the Work has been asserted by them in accordance
with the Copyright, Designs and Patents Act 1988.

Copyright © Jem Roberts 2021
Fab Fools

Editor: Shaun Russell
Editorial: Will Rees
Cover by Steve Beckett

Printed and bound in the UK by
Severn, Bristol Road, Gloucester, GL2 5EU

ISBN: 978-1-912535-74-3

Published by
Candy Jar Books
Mackintosh House
136 Newport Road, Cardiff, CF24 1DJ
www.candyjarbooks.co.uk

For my dear Mum & Dad, Lindy & George –
For never having the slightest interest in The Beatles.

And in ever-loving memory of NEIL INNES.
"Fab Fools – we're all one, y'know?"

ABOUT THE AUTHOR

Jem Roberts was born in Ludlow, studied at Aberystwyth University, gained his first professional writing gig as a teenager reviewing Nintendo games, and has over twenty years of publishing toil under his belt. Love for *I'm Sorry, I Haven't a Clue* led to his first officially authorised book, *The Clue Bible*, in 2009, and a lifetime's obsession meant that the ultimate guide to *Blackadder* had to follow, with 2012's *The True History of The Black Adder*.

In 2014 he became Douglas Adams' official biographer, with *The Frood* marking his third release from Preface Publishing. *Soupy Twists!* – the officially authorised Fry & Laurie story – came from Unbound in 2018, and the following year *Tales of Britain*, from the same publisher, became the first full British folktale anthology to be released in over forty years – the author also performs British folktales all over the world, under the moniker of Brother Bernard. As a performer, he has inflicted noises on audiences from Edinburgh to Glastonbury Festival, solo and with his troupe, The Unrelated Family.

JEMROBERTS.COM

BY THE SAME AUTHOR

The Clue Bible – The Fully Authorised History of I'm Sorry, I Haven't a Clue (Preface 2009)

The True History of The Black Adder (Preface 2012)

The Frood: The Authorised Biography of Douglas Adams (Preface 2014)

Soupy Twists! The Official Fry & Laurie Story (Unbound 2018)

Tales of Britain (Unbound 2019)

LIVING IN HOPE

The desire to see this book created came not with peace and love, but a kind of righteous indignation, that a great monument of our culture demanded to be seen from a neglected angle – a silly one. For me, devotion to The Beatles has long displaced any form of religion, which means my shelves groan, moan and sag with Beatle books, and I eventually decided enough was enough, and unless the two remaining Knights of Rock were going to have further bashes at putting out their own stories, there wasn't much Beatle-ish left unsaid, and worth buying a book about, let alone writing one.

But then, as my career as comedy historian mutated, through official chronicles of British institutions like *I'm Sorry, I Haven't a Clue, Blackadder, The Hitchhiker's Guide to the Galaxy* and *A Bit of Fry & Laurie,* the realisation hit me – The Beatles weren't just the greatest rock and roll band of all time, they were one of Britain's greatest *entertainment* exports to the rest of the world, and particularly when it came to my area – comedy.

In retelling this well-loved legend once again, a certain knowledge of the facts of The Beatles Story must be assumed from you all for the ensuing pages – to expend too much tree on the young Beatles' family tragedies, or trudge through the 'Get Back' sessions in daily detail, would be obtuse, so if you want the details of how much it cost to pay off certain lovechild claimants, or what kind of maracas were used on 'A Day In The Life', Mark Lewisohn is your guide. It's impossible at this stage to write a Beatle book without standing on the shoulders of a whole crowd of giants, but Lewisohn is the most gigantic of them all, and although I had sworn off buying more Beatle books, Mark is the exception to that rule. That said, as the great chronicler agreed with me, when you see this well-worn tale through a red-nose-tinted filter, the glowing branch-lines of the comedic history of The Beatles make the familiar seem startlingly fresh.

Though publishers were blinded by the over-abundance of books on the band for many years, this crucial volume finally came to be thanks to the passionate support of a number of wiser Beatlemaniacs, and there are debts of thanks to be paid first to Kevin Eldon, for his stirring opener (not to mention the massive and fascinating thesis which was Draft 1), plus fabulous *Beano* artist Steve Beckett, Peta Button, Barnaby Eaton-Jones, Paula Clarke Bain, Jason Hazeley, Mark Lewisohn, Darrell Maclaine-Jones, Roger McGough, Joe McGrath, Adam Newell, Trevor Peacock, Phil Pope, Shaun Russell, Will Rees and everyone at Candy Jar Books, Huw Spink of @Teatlemania, Jeff Walden and everyone at the BBC Archives, Tim Worthington – and above all, Denise Hoelandt, for the magical mystery tour.

Incidentally, the original plan was to launch this book on the 60th anniversary of The Nerk Twins' shows at The Fox & Hounds, Caversham (so close to that cultural historian's mecca, the BBC archives), and though obvious tragedy prevented this jolly evening of silly Beatles and Rutles tunes, thanks to Kevin and all at the pub for trying. Maybe the 61st?

Also, extra gratitude goes to Vicky Holmes at the University of Leicester and the Orton estate for use of an extract from *Up Against It* (Orton Collection, University of Leicester, MS 237/3/8/1).

All those who helped nudge this book into existence – you are my very pal. Everyone else – you're a grotty nit.

Special thanks must go to Graeme Garden for doing his best to intercede for us with his old flatmate Eric Idle, but the ultimate response of 'Tell them not to wait up' seemed regrettably final. On the other hand, the line-up for the 2019 Rutles live tour were warmly welcoming, so cheers to Dave Catlin-Birch, Phil Jackson, Mickey Simmonds, Rutling Ken Thornton, and of course, the glorious John Halsey. Above all, however, the most encouragement for this book's existence came from our hero, Neil Innes – his spirit, his kindness, his scorn for the short-sightedness of the publishing Powers That Be.

This book would not be here had he not offered his support – more than one interview, perhaps even an afterword. Neil shared with his dear friend Terry Jones the misfortune of being, in showbiz terms, so unusually and genuinely nice, fans always had to be hyper-careful never to take advantage of their happiness to help, both being such busy creative forces, so constantly dogged for their approval by so many fans and freaks for so many causes. But when told of this campaign, Neil vehemently insisted that the comedic Beatles story deserved to be told, even if it was to inevitably put him at the centre of the narrative – 'You stupid publishers, you don't know what you're missing!' We spoke a few (all too few) times, and he left us all before we could complete his full involvement, and clear up all those grey areas – unfinished words. To make this book a tribute to Neil Innes, his genius, his art and his humanity, is only the smallest balm for his loss. But now, the story is told.

This magnificent octopus' garden has been so long in the pipeline, in 2011 I made the crucial preliminary move of contacting none other than Sir George Martin for his thoughts on a comedic Beatle odyssey, hoping to quiz him about his trailblazing in the world of audio comedy, and was delighted to receive a reply, no matter what the verdict. He tactfully explained, 'When they first hit the world of entertainment and particularly in the US, they were able to give pretty "smart ass" answers to the most obvious questions, but in print they are not so funny. For instance, when an interviewer asked Ringo about his hair style and said "what do you call it?" Ringo replied "Fred". I hope you understand what I mean... while I would like to read a book that you have written on the subject, I very much feel it would be very difficult to get off the ground.' The great man was certainly right on the final point, hence these extensive acknowledgements, but this equivocal mix of encouragement and discouragement has not tempted me from this path.

Was Sir George right? Or does the momentary wit of his old friends work on the page, with only the ghost of that Beatle charm which could turn the bluntest barb into a bon mot? In truth, not always, no – but the story of how that charm and humour turned a talented musical combo into the twentieth century's greatest entertainment phenomenon remains untold, and we can't have that. Just remember Martin's words, and as you read on, reflect that these comic moments live on through that indefinable group charisma of John, Paul, George and Ringo, a charm which few of us ever experienced in person, and which we can now only sense second-hand, and envy those who were really there, back when they was Fab Fools.

JEM ROBERTS Spring 2020

GOT TO BE A JOKER

KEVIN ELDON

I was born ninety days before the beginning of the sixties. Brand new Beatles music permeated my early years. Lucky kid. Every couple of months or so some freshly-minted Fab sonic wonder would come spilling out of the radio, doing its beautiful thing, ringing me like a bell. I loved their music from the off. It was, however, a while before I realised just how *funny* The Beatles were.

Now. Before we get properly started, since you're going to be reading a lot about that particular subject in this book, allow me to pose a question in four easily digestible parts:

Were they? Actually? Funny? The Beatles?

Well, as we all know, humour is a very subjective thing. With that in mind, if the Beatles never moved *your* gob in a generally upwards direction then perhaps it's best you put this book down. Yes, step away from the book. Try another one perhaps. May I recommend *Van Morrison: The Laughter Years*?

...

Have they gone? ... Good. So, yes. The answer is The Beatles *were* funny. Obviously.

It was only when TV channels started regularly showing *A Hard Day's Night* and *Help!* in my early teens that I started properly appreciating their humour. Even though The Beatles were acting out lines and scenarios created for them by other people, their own personal sparkle shone clearly through. In retrospect *Help!*, I would argue, is not really a terribly accurate depiction of their funniness. It's drenched in a self-conscious 'wackiness'. As far as *A Hard Day's Night* is concerned though, credit has to go to screenplay writer Alun Owen for delivering a pretty credible facsimile of the bouncy buzz of Beatle banter.

A little later, in the mid-'70s, I started catching reruns of the early to mid-period Beatles media interviews. They really made an impact on me. You know the ones I mean – usually in grainy black and white, the lads would be jammed together in a corner somewhere, four shaggy-haired youths hemmed in by a phalanx of microphones, cameras, lights and journos. Chaos! Everyone would have a fag on and the questions would be fired at them, relentlessly, endlessly, questions, questions, questions, and they would parry and they would thrust and they would dance elegantly around them. Those riotous jousts are still a delight to behold.

I mention these interviews specifically because I think they give a pretty good insight into The Beatles' overall innate playfulness.

It's quite hard now to fully appreciate just what a lungful of fresh air those media encounters must have been at the time. If you look at any interviews with pop stars up until then they're generally steeped in soporific blandness. The order of the day seemed to be a degree of condescension from the interviewer and a 'know your place' deference from the interviewees. The very first Beatles interviews saw them falling roughly into line with the established template, giving pretty staid answers to unimaginative questions. However, it wasn't long before they were undermining and subverting the process, as much to keep themselves amused as anything else. It's still a joy to watch them at work – dodging questions, holding their own conversations, confusing their interrogators with non-sequiturs and generally enjoying themselves almost as much as when they played music together. In fact their 'riffing', picking up on each other's cues and commenting on and embellishing each other's contributions, always strikes me as a sort of spoken version of musical jamming. Indeed, just as each one of them contributed in his own specific way to their collective sound, in a similar way, whether it was the benign cheerfulness of Paul, the child-like drollery of Ringo, the bone-dry irony of George or John's keen sense of the absurd, they each had their own distinctive comedic identity which fed into and formed their collective funniness.

The Beatles hit the big time pretty well-armed against fame's disorientating effects and the chief weapon in that armoury was their sense of humour. But it wasn't all lovable cuteness. They were gentle but persistent piss-takers. Their cheekiness was the antithesis of the stale 'aw shucks' humility of pop stars up until then. That was not The Beatles' style. It certainly wasn't Lennon's. Here was cheekiness often verging on impertinence. Many of their male interviewers provided a sharp contrast to the bright young men they were interviewing. These baggy interrogators looked and sounded even older than they were; all jowls, brogues and tweed jackets, and they expected a certain amount of default respect from the younger generation. What they mostly got from Lennon, though, was a delightfully knowing facetiousness. It was an attitude that would have been very familiar to many of the teachers who had taught him through his school years. With John leading the naughty boy charge, the others were only to happy to follow if not with quite the same degree of relish. That always struck me as very funny. The confidence it was done with. The enjoyment of it. A bit of status subversion will always get a giggle.

For all the smart one-liners and upbeat badinage, it's a fallacy to say that every single interview was a jamboree of dazzling one-liners. From quite early on they made no effort to hide their complete lack of interest or enthusiasm when questions were nonsensical or trite. As the pressure of Beatlemania grew, they could even be pretty curt when things got too idiotic. And who could blame them? Still, even in a more irritable frame of mind, the gags were never far way.

Of course, these interviews, as you will see in this fine tome, weren't the whole story. The Beatles were funny in many ways, in different scenarios, both individually and collectively, in public and, tellingly, in private. Studio outtakes reveal endless quips, daft voices, surreal flights of fancy, and just general nuttiness. They weren't just putting it on for show. It was simply how they were.

Writing this, I got to thinking – *why* were they funny? And immediately the 'Explaining Comedy' klaxon sounded. Deconstruction of comedy is always a joyless and usually fruitless business. A few things do come to mind, though, if you'll indulge me for a sec. They all possessed lively, creative, open minds, they had the musicality of comedy, its rhythm and timing, and of course it's a major part of the Scouse make-up to go for the laugh whenever possible. They gave terrific deadpan too. They were no strangers to the ironic understatement. But that's probably enough of the attempts at forensic dissection. The nuts and bolts of what's funny are damn hard if not impossible to neatly sum up with any real precision. Why were The Beatles funny? Probably the best answer I can offer to that question is:

They just *were*.

The Beatles often used their humour to attempt to deflate the hysteria. Maybe as they watched the world around them going loony tunes they knew, unconsciously or otherwise, that the moment they started taking the madness seriously they'd be mad themselves. None of them got out of the storm completely unharmed. The downside of their dizzying journey was that there were episodes of depression, frustration, grief, anger and loneliness. I'd like to think that as well as making the fun times even more fun, their humour helped ease some of the downers and even occasionally played a part in pulling them clear. One thing I personally know for sure is that, as well as their music, their humour has lit up my life.

Sometime in late 1975 I borrowed a (double) album from Dave Roberts across the road. The cover had a cartoon on it of a dog playing a harmonica. It was called *The History of the Bonzos*. I humbly offer Dave a huge apology all these years later. I never returned that album. Bad teenage Kevin! I owe you Dave, I really do. On those two 33-inch discs was a wonderful collection of wildly different songs in every style going: rock, surf, blues, psychedelia, country and western, trad jazz, you name it. They all had one shared element, and that was that they were absolutely hilarious. Even the booklet within was funny. I'll never forget the picture of the band, a gaggle of twenty-something long haired bohemians sitting together in a ragged gang. What catches the eye is that one of the figures has a vertically extended forehead, madly painted eyes and no arms. In front of them is a sign which reads 'Can you spot which student has taken a mind-expanding drug?'

I listened to those songs endlessly.

It was only two or three years later when who should burst onto the scene but an alternative version of The Beatles from a parallel universe where the cosmic comedy dial was cranked up several notches. The Rutles. Parody? Homage? Both. Executed with a joyful, affectionate and very deft panache. The one thing in common between the two? Mr Neil Innes.

I spent many, many hours listening to Neil's stuff. I was a proper fan. And so it happened that eventually I got to meet him. And kept meeting him. I even got to perform live with him a couple of times on some Rutle and Bonzos songs. As if this wasn't already more than enough for a wide-eyed fanboy, I finally had the honour of actually recording some music with him. Lucky kid indeed.

At the time of writing it's more than a year since Neil's death. His absence is still a presence in me, a palpable ache. It will always sadden me that he wasn't able to hang around a while longer, watch his grandkids grow a bit more and enjoy a few more years with his beloved Yvonne and his sons Miles, Luke and Barney. When I remember Neil I think, of course, of the brilliant musician and lyricist who gave us many wonderful, funny and beautiful songs. I remember the man who not only hung out with The Beatles and went on to parody them so lovingly but who also made amazing contributions to the joy that was Monty Python. There's so much brilliant work I could mention. But even more than all that, when I remember Neil I remember his gentleness, kindness and wit, all of which flowed so easily from him. It was his default setting. Having bloomed into artistic fruition during the hippy years he never lost the notion that love is all important. But this wasn't empty, shallow idealism. He spoke out passionately and wittily about causes he believed in as well as those he thought were bullshit. Admirably, his positivity remained intact despite having been done some fairly grievous wrong over the years by a handful of greedy showbiz operators. He was simply a bigger and better man.

I'll always treasure the times we spent sitting in the pub, chatting about this, that and everything else. He truly was a lovely man. Neil would always say hello and goodbye with a big, warm hug. I'll miss those hugs.

Enjoy this book. The music of The Beatles is essentially joyous. Much of it is suffused with their humour. The same goes for Neil's work. Humour, when it comes from a positive place, energises. It heals misery. It encourages hope. It brightens up the dark corners of our minds.

Enough said!

KEVIN ELDON
Actor, comedian, George Martin impersonator.

CHAPTER ONE

A LAFF AND A SHOUT

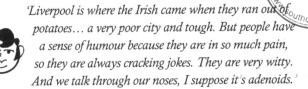

'Liverpool is where the Irish came when they ran out of potatoes… a very poor city and tough. But people have a sense of humour because they are in so much pain, so they are always cracking jokes. They are very witty. And we talk through our noses, I suppose it's adenoids.'

'At a very early age I was the only kid in class who knew how to spell "phlegm".'

'There are three teams in Liverpool – and I support the other one.'

'People in Liverpool don't move very far, you know.'

As a wise scouser once wrote, being born in Liverpool 'carries with it certain responsibilities', and these duties are naturally distilled in the majority of Liverpudlians, wherever they live; even though in many ways the two at the top of the list are strange bedfellows. Firstly, coming from Liverpool stereotypically carries with it a fierce and often unfairly maligned sentimentality – a passion for home enriched by a vast tapestry of eternally-held grudges, historical wrongs against the region remembered with the utmost prejudice (as any Liverpudlian vendor of *The Sun* would tell you). But of absolute equal importance to every Merseyside native happy to align themselves with the cultural cliché is the apparent opposite spirit – of laughter, loopiness, and of coping with any suffering thanks to a large helping of 'The Craic' – or alternatively, 'a Laff'. The other cliché of Liverpool life – the footie – need not detain us much. Paul is a mild Evertonian, Ringo favours the Arsenal, but the boys rarely expressed any passion for sport, least of all John.

In his disjointed memoir *As Time Goes By*, Beatles press guru Derek Taylor reminisced, '"Laff" is a great Liverpool word… it's a highly prized commodity, a laff, especially in Liverpool where there's hardly anything to laff at unless you laff at all the sadness and poverty. On Saturday nights in the old days the best night out was what you called "a laff and a shout"… if you woke up the next morning and could only remember a fraction of what had happened, you knew it had been a good night out.'[1]

THE LIDDYPOOL CRAIC

Despite the now popular Gaelic spelling, 'crack' – raising the spirits with jocular sharing of news and gossip – is a British term, popular in Scotland and the North of England, which made it over the Irish sea and fused with the universally agreed notion of Éire charm, the gift of the gab that came with kissing the Blarney stone, to become an irresistible part of Gaelic lore, before being shipped back to Blighty. In times of hardship, even in the darkest industrial slums, the ability of folk to enjoy the craic was a community touchstone, a burning coal in the fire of British humour, that Dunkirk Spirit and the stiff upper lip, lazily claimed as a unique virtue by Brits the Empire over. Therefore, just as a port like Liverpool was a musical conduit, with Black American culture washing up on the banks of the Mersey and clashing with the native folk tradition, the city was also a mixing bowl for strains of humour, Irish immigration blending whimsical jocularity with the innate deadpan dryness of North West England.

A legend has grown of a certain Irish lad from County Down called Jack Lennon, who toured the United States with the vaudeville troupe Robertson's Colored Operatic Kentucky

Minstrels before settling back in Liverpool, and fathering many children, including a son, Alfred. The boot-polish-smeared musicians, touring the provinces with the least sophisticated musical entertainment around, would have been, in their racist way, largely goofing around to raise laughs. As the Lennon family's version of this story has been disproved by dogged researchers, it's moot whether anyone in John Lennon's family tree really had any meaningful toe in show business before him, but there would be nothing unique in Vaudeville and Music Hall providing an escape for impoverished Lancastrians. Young Alfred Lennon was put in an orphanage after the death of Jack, and at the age of fifteen he passed an audition to join children's Music Hall act Will Murray's Gang, headed up by a celebrated female impersonator who had toured with pre-fame Charlie Chaplin. The young rebel ran away with this troupe, hoping to make a living getting laughs, but sadly Alf was sent back home when the tour reached Glasgow, and whipped for his cheek.

North West England almost had a monopoly on mood-boosting madcap silliness in the early 20th century, with Lancashire (if we include the historical county's twin cities, Manchester and Liverpool) the home of Music Hall stars like Harry Weldon and George Formby Sr, and as Music Hall mutated into Variety, their successors on stage, radio and silver screen George Formby Jr, Gracie Fields, Frank Randle, Robb Wilton, Jimmy Clitheroe, Arthur Askey, Norman Evans, Will Hay, Tommy Handley, Ted Ray, Al Read, Deryck Guyler and even – given the traditional siting of the town of Ulverston – one of Britain's greatest ever comedy exports, Stan Laurel. Although the equally grimy and tough Scottish port of Glasgow has a rich roster of historical comic talent, no other region of Britain comes close comedically, London included – though the capital, of course, would be where the talents of most of these artists ultimately took them, down south to share that weird, deadpan Lancashire humour with the rest of the country, if not the world. The next generation along would provide further stars in Knotty Ash's Ken Dodd, Wilton-inspired Mancunian Les Dawson, Oldham's Eric Sykes, and Eric Bartholomew from further up the Lancastrian coast in Morecambe, who would take his stage name from the town and team up with young Yorkshire hoofer Ernest Wiseman to embark on their own comedy careers on the Variety circuit, and in working men's clubs up and down the land, billed as 'Morecambe & Wise'.

As our four heroes took their first bows in the years 1940-43 and Liverpool raged under a barrage of Nazi bombardment, morale boosting for the troops and the nation was a notably Lancastrian duty – Formby and Fields twanging ukes in the cinema, and on the radio, the biggest popular hits were *Band Waggon* starring the Dingle-born 'big hearted' quipster Arthur Askey, and above all, Toxteth native Tommy Handley's *It's That Man Again* or *ITMA*, the most successful British radio comedy of all time. Their accents may have had the harshest edges knocked off for the BBC, but these two wartime comics, plus Ted Ray, star of later hit *Ray's A Laugh* (and uncle of one of Paul's first girlfriends), were the first famous scousers of the new era of Light Entertainment (LE), and Liverpool was becoming famous nationwide not just for its port, but its daft wit. This is rarely taken into account in any retelling of The Beatles Story – to most of their initial audience, these four boys came from the land of 'footballers and comedians', and deadpan humour.

These wartime hits, however, made little impression on The Beatles in their infancy – the real comedy bug was yet to bite. Although there are an array of moments in 20th century history which commentators can claim to be 'the birth of modern comedy', from the debut of satirical revue *Beyond the Fringe* to the opening of London's first Comedy Store, a comfortably leading contender for the moment involves the meeting of four demobbed eccentrics – a London-Irishman, a Welsh tenor, an itinerant half-Jewish Yorkshireman and a quasi-Peruvian – in a small Westminster pub called Grafton's (Now The Grafton Arms). A spreading firmament of talented British ex-servicemen were finding their way in the post-WWII entertainment business, perhaps gaining experience at the legendary Windmill Theatre in between nude tableaux, and making connections and gaining tiny wireless credits which would power the coming decades of

4

comedy in every medium – but for all the ground broken by myriad humorists in this time, the forming of The Goons, Spike Milligan, Harry Secombe, Peter Sellers and Michael Bentine, under the benevolent eye of producer and publican Jimmy Grafton in the late 1940s, released a surreal comic energy totally unlike anything else in British culture hitherto. Chief scripter Milligan's unpredictable Irish logic, Sellers' outrageous silly voices (honed on *Ray's a Laugh*) and an explosive soundscape which took the BBC's burgeoning experimentation with radio sound effects to an unimagined new level, were just some of the ingredients which made their wireless series *The Goon Show* a life-changing addiction for a whole generation of British kids.

The programme was a slow-burner, however, and it wasn't until the second or third series in 1952 that the gang's audio antics had a new convert, in twelve-year-old John Lennon. Before this eureka moment, Lennon's memories of humour tended to be family-based. Despite his parents' traumatic split when he was five years old, he recalled Alf making him laugh by changing the lyrics to popular songs, and above all, his mother Julia Stanley was John's first comic hero: 'My mother was a comedienne and a singer. Not professional, but, you know, she used to get up in pubs and things like that. She had a good voice. She could do Kay Starr...' Always known for a lacerating comeback to any barb, Julia was the jester of a large family of sisters, and her son treasured memories of her wandering around with underpants on her head, playing comic songs on the banjolele. 'She was gay, witty and full of fun,' her sister Mimi recalled, 'She never took life or anything seriously. Everything was funny...' But once Auntie Mimi took charge of the boy, of course, home life was less filled with laughter.

Lennon was however a voracious reader, not least of comics smuggled to him under Mimi's nose by his Uncle George, like *The Beano* and *The Dandy* – as were most British children, the other three Beatles included; no institution informed British children's ideas of cheeky anarchy like the comic-strip output of Scottish publishers DC Thompson, and young McCartney was only slightly facetious when he told the *NME* that his ambition was to appear in *The Dandy*. That's what this generation of lads had to make them laugh – comics, practical jokes, and maybe the odd trip to the circus when it was in town – John certainly had a life-long love of the circus, and clowning. Perhaps above all, though, the subversive, apple-scrumping Lennon lad loved Richmal Crompton's rebellious schoolboy William Brown, and the topsy-turvy world of Lewis Carroll. 'I was passionate about *Alice in Wonderland* and drew all the characters. I did poems in the style of *Jabberwocky*. I used to *live Alice*, and *Just William*. I wrote my own William stories, with me doing all the things.' Not content with soaking up stories and cartoons, the lonely boy was soon creating his own. 'It started back in my schooldays. Three people I was very keen on were Lewis Carroll, James Thurber and the English illustrator, Ronald Searle. When I was about eleven I was turned onto these three. I think I was about fifteen when I started 'Thurberising' the drawings.' Searle remains celebrated in the UK for his depictions of school rebellion in *St. Trinians* and *Molesworth*, whereas the American cartoonist and writer Thurber popularised a simple line-drawing style, allied to surreal captions, which are clear influences on Lennon's own scribbles.

One of Lennon's first schoolmates at Dovedale Primary shared memories of a less than cerebral lad, young Jimmy Tarbuck remembering, 'If ever there was a scrap in the schoolyard, John was likely to be involved. And I'll always remember the way he looked at you. His glasses had really thick lenses, the kind we called bottle-bottoms. At school, we used to have this thing, if you were out for trouble with another kid you'd say "Are you lookin' at me?" But John's lenses were so thick, you could never tell if he was looking at you or not.'[2] When Lennon reinvented himself as a teddy boy in later years, Tarbuck would avoid him altogether, but The Beatles' eventual promotion of Liverpool into the coolest place on the planet did Tarbuck no harm in the '60s, when he became one of the top mainstream comedians in Britain.

Many of young John's early comic inspirations were shared by his bandmates, with Paul and little brother Mike just as bedazzled by *Alice* – though the McCartneys earn extra comedy geek credits, having received Robb Wilton's autograph after attending a Liverpool Empire show as lads. The extended

McCartney family took the business of 'laffs' further than private japes, his father Jim spreading sunshine in the inter-war years with his own Jim Mac's Jazz Band (once also a minstrel group, 'The Masked Marauders'). 'I grew up steeped in that Music Hall tradition,' Paul said. 'My father once worked at the Liverpool Hippodrome as a spotlight operator. They actually used a piece of burning lime in those days which he had to trim. He was very entertaining about that period and had lots of tales about it.' When he was still young, Paul's cousin Bett married local stand-up comedian and entertainment professional Mike Robbins, whose experience and Butlin's connections were to play a key role in turning Paul on to showbiz – Mike liked to say, 'Variety is dying, and my act is helping to kill it.' The holiday camps founded by Billy Butlin in the 1930s have forever been a by-word for the cheesiest family entertainment, with red-coated hoofers falling in swimming pools and yodelling over the serving of chicken in a basket, but they did provide an apprenticeship for a very select few future stars, not least Irish comedian Dave Allen. Robbins' stints as a Redcoat and emcee in camps in Filey on the east coast and Pwllheli in North Wales were early splashes of showbiz for Paul and little Mike, and they lapped it up. As Paul entered his teens, Bett and Mike would begin their own showbiz dynasty with the arrival of comedians-to-be Ted and Kate Robbins.

Back home in Wavertree, the large and jovial Harrison family's two-up-two-down rang with private jokes – with the gawky, cheeky, banjolele-plucking George Formby always the favourite: 'Those George Formby songs were always in the back of me life', our George told Russell Davies in 1991, attending that year's Formby Fan Club meeting in Blackpool, uke in hand. 'They were either being played in the background or my Mother was singing them when I was three or four.'[3] The family's first flirtation with showbiz came when bus driver Dad Harry began to compere union socials for work, where he allegedly managed to kick off the career of one of Liverpool's greatest comedic sons, who would stand at the bar with gigantic buck teeth and crazy hair awry, having his mates in stitches. As Harry told Hunter Davies, 'One of the earliest comedians we launched was Ken

Dodd. We'd seen him at the club, having a drink, and we knew he was very funny, but he was always too nervous to go on stage. But he eventually went on. He did this act, "The Road to Mandalay", with shorts on and one of those pith helmets. It was a riot!'[4]

Back home, youngest son George revelled in the era's comic songs, the cornier the better. 'I don't understand people who say, "I only like rock 'n' roll," or "I only like the blues" or whatever. Even Eric Clapton says he was influenced by "The Runaway Train". As I said in my own book *I Me Mine*, my earliest memories are things like "One Meatball" by Josh White... I would say that even the crap music that we hated – schmaltz records like "I'm A Pink Toothbrush, You're A Blue Toothbrush" – even that had some kind of influence on us, whether we like it or not. All that is in me somehow, and is capable of coming out any any point. It shows in the comic aspect of some of our songs, like the middle of "Yellow Submarine".'[5] As the family moved to Speke, some of the more sonically complex musical releases all too easily dismissed as 'novelty singles' (as if 'novelty' can only be a pejorative term) were likely to include Parlophone productions crafted by ambitious record producer George Martin – a working class Londoner demobbed from the RAF and trying to get ahead in the snobbish world of gramophone recordings.

Martin's own quirky productions (such as 'Nellie The Elephant', future Beatles song publisher Dick James singing the theme to children's TV show *Robin Hood* or 'Experiments With Mice', Johnny Dankworth's 1956 recording of 'Three Blind Mice' in a variety of jazz styles) gave the young producer a gradual self-education in creating ear-arresting, effects-filled sound productions. 'Sound effects were always a key ingredient in these humorous records, and we were forever having to improvise,' Martin recalled. 'For instance, there was a record I made with Michael Bentine, on one track of which he did a send-up of a horse show, a skit on the jingoism of English commentators. Obviously we needed horse noises, and we had a couple of whinnies on tape which we put in from time to time. But most of the sound effects consisted of me patting my hand on a piano stool... People have their own ideas of what things should sound like.'[6]

It's true that 'novelty song' could become a term of abuse, and although much has been written about Lonnie Donegan's nonchalant incitement of the skiffle movement which inspired The Beatles and their entire musical generation in Britain, the cheeky singer's tongue-in-cheek style, so different from the snarling appearance of America's early rock-and-rollers, did quickly turn him from an inspiration to another name on the Variety treadmill, performing sub-Music Hall singalong numbers like 'Does Your Chewing Gum Lose Its Flavour (On the Bedpost Over Night)?' and 'My Old Man's A Dustman' for the Pye label. The US folk song 'Rock Island Line', however, cribbed from Lead Belly, which had made John and his little friends' ears perk up in 1956, was a number built around a hoary old gag about a train driver smuggling pig iron by claiming to be carrying 'pigs'. When George and Paul got tickets to see Donegan play, joshing with their hero as they got his autograph, the show they enjoyed was packed with laughs.

Martin's novelty output for Parlophone would earn six of his productions places on the classic children's song collection *All Aboard*, but they were soon to be joined by the producer's first truly anarchic, world-changing sonic collaboration with a gang of bright young talents as he set to work, translating *The Goon Show* to record. George Martin loved The Goons – in the 1950s, everyone who wasn't boring loved The Goons, even wee Richie Starkey had the wireless madness of Eccles, Bluebottle, Seagoon and co to turn to in his lonely childhood bouts of hospitalisation. John acknowledged, 'We were the sons of *The Goon Show*. We were of an age. We were the extension of that rebellion, in a way.'[7]

'LOVE THESE GOON SHOWS!'

'I was twelve when the Goon Shows first hit me. Sixteen when they were finished with me,' Lennon wrote in a *New York Times* review of a Goon script book in 1972, keen to turn his adopted compatriots onto the classic comedy. 'Their humour was the only proof that the world was insane... what it means to Americans I can't imagine (apart from a rumoured few fanatics). As they say in Tibet, "You had to be there."' He added, 'like all my generation I was really drawn to The Goons. In many ways they influenced The Beatles as much as rock 'n' roll – Elvis and Little Richard. They were, to my generation, what we were to the next... Hipper than the hippest and madder than "Mad", a conspiracy against reality. A coup d'etat of the mind!'[8]

Despite John's unique article, the comedy universe created by Milligan and co has remained a supremely British institution, and indeed, now that the youngsters who frothed with excitement when listening to every new episode are all long past retirement age, even within the UK the Goons have become an odd, esoteric rosetta stone in the history of British comedy, more celebrated for the generations of artists the gang inspired than for their own surreal ingenuity, which has become an acquired taste. When you consider that those artists include not just The Beatles but all of Monty Python and even Comedy Godfather Peter Cook (who would feign illness at public school just to enjoy every episode uninterrupted) that's unsurprising, but although hosts of passionate Goon devotees remain at large – uber-fanboy Prince Charles for one – they should understand it's no slight against the show to suggest that its jokes and catchphrases are not quoted in the 21st century with a tenth of the regularity of Monty Python; somehow that fresh fizzy foolishness which enraptured a whole generation of comedy ears in the 1950s has not progressed from its post-WWII bubble into lasting popular cultural currency. Nonetheless, Beatle fans who find the boys' studio chat in outtakes and bootlegs confounding could see a number of bulbs lighting up with even a casual listen to the BBC programme – when introducing Chuck Berry's 'I Got to Find My Baby' on radio show *Pop Go The Beatles*, John ad-libbed with a gobbledegook-ish 'Don't know where she's been, pardon, hello? Love these *Goon Show*s!'

By the time our teenage heroes became hooked on the series, *The* ('Highly Esteemed!') *Goon Show* had progressed from a rudimentary madcap format featuring what Spike called 'a loose assembly of hungry young comics' initially titled *Crazy People,* and Bentine had peeled off to develop his own weird whimsy. The self-contained half-hours which evolved always centred on the same group of familiar characters, principally obnoxious boy scout Bluebottle ('You dirty, rotten swine, you have deaded me!'), flatulent Major Bloodnok, villainous Grytpype-Thynne, geriatric Henry Crun (all Sellers) plus Minnie Bannister and the supremely dumb Eccles (both Milligan) and finally the squeaky everyman, Neddie Seagoon (Secombe). Each week's story, heavily laden with mind-stretching developments conveyed to the fans via ever-more ambitious sound effects, was almost invariably obsessively rooted in Milligan's wartime experiences – making the show a sustained attack on authority and pre-War ideas of respect for the establishment which gladdened millions of young hearts, instilling a social rebellion in British youth like nothing which came before it. All society needed now was the end of conscription, and a brave new world awaited. Just as the show's crucial musical element (jazz standards courtesy of Max Geldray and the Ray Ellington Quartet, give or take a spot of rockabilly) remained largely oblivious to the changing styles of the decade, the arrested development of Seagoon and friends kept them eternally in the 1940s, unchanging audio comic book heroes – which was just as the delighted fans loved it. Above all, of course, the mix of jazz, surreal non-sequiturs, snark and risqué gags tended to totally bemuse or irritate the older generation, which is almost a prerequisite for any decent youth movement. The Goons created their own irreverent revolution, each twist and turn unpredictably bizarre, and above all, compared to their comedy contemporaries, they were unpolished, and genuinely anarchic. For every truly arresting surreal concept, the modern ear may be assaulted by a now-unacceptable smattering of racial impersonations, or the crummiest schoolboy howlers, but it's impossible to wipe our cultural memory now and hear these shows in context, for the cultural dynamite that they were, any more than anybody can ever truly hear The Beatles 'for the first time' ever again.

Some years before Elvis hollered into their adolescent

consciousnesses, The Beatles were hooked on *The Goon Show*, little guessing how Spike and Peter would influence their own careers – particularly away from the wireless. George Martin was only a few years into his own career as head of EMI's Parlophone label, already in pole position as the most innovative record producer in the country, when he chased up the Goons – the plummy voice and grave appearance of this classically-trained musician belied his simple North London roots, and incorrigible sense of fun. He'd had a taste of radio performance himself, playing his own *Prelude* on BBC programme *Navy Mixture* in 1946, on the same show as young comedian Lieutenant Jon Pertwee, who was keen for Martin to join his comic troupe in the Department of Naval Entertainments, but George remained true to the RAF.

Once his real career was underway, early artists to come under Martin's politely patrician producing powers included jazz hero Humphrey Lyttelton, decades before legendary Radio 4 panel game antidote *I'm Sorry, I Haven't a Clue* made 'Humph' a comedy icon, and their 1956 hit 'Bad Penny Blues' was to provide an identifiable blueprint for 'Lady Madonna' twelve years later. Martin's first real comic collaboration, however, came in 1952 with witty polymath Peter Ustinov, a comedy improvisor eons ahead of his generation. 'At that time, Peter was the *enfant terrible* of British actors, our answer to Orson Welles,' Martin recalled in his memoir *All You Need Is Ears*. 'Because he was always amusing people with his funny little pieces of mouth-music and so on, we decided to make a double-sided single, "Mock Mozart" and "Phoney Folk Lore". The first was a mini-opera done in three minutes by Peter, and I labelled it "The voices and noises of Peter Ustinov".'[9] The productions involved extensive multi-tracking for Ustinov to play all the parts, and the experiment paid off, becoming a huge seller. 'I had already started trying to get "between the cracks" of the other labels, by doing things that nobody else had tried, or dared to try... I knew I had to make a mark in some way, and my only plan was to find a way of making records that other people weren't making. Ones that would sell. And the way I chose was to go into comedy, because no one was doing it. People were doing it in the States – Stan Freberg, Bob

Newhart – but there was nothing in England to speak of. And it seemed to work.'[10] Even George's first attempt at pop stardom centred on a comedy legend – Jim Dale was an ambitious songwriter and performer, landing Parlophone a respectable Number 2 in December 1957, 'Be My Girl', before he joined the *Carry On* cast. Despite the cheap and cheeky film series being as defining a part of British culture in the '60s as Beatlemania, there are next to no Beatle lines to draw to the *Carry On* canon, besides the inclusion of a brief classical choral parody of 'She Loves You' in 1967's *Carry On Don't Lose Your Head.*

'Things that nobody else had tried' was a perfect description of Martin's first production to feature Sellers, that other vocally chameleonic Peter. George's colleague the celebrated composer Ron Goodwin had cooked up a quirky children's sci-fi confection with lyricist Ken Hare, 'Jakka and the Flying Saucers', about a space boy and his five-legged dog. Sellers' amusingly Churchillian appearance as a wise planet stood him in good stead when he and Milligan approached Martin a couple of years later, keen to translate their radio stardom to the hit parade, with a scheme to record a truly awful version of 'Unchained Melody' in 1955. The three had a ball in the studio sending up the previous year's biggest hit, with squawking vocals and unnecessary ukulele, but when EMI insisted on formal permission from the song's publishers before release, the raspberry they received inspired Spike and Peter to storm off to George's sworn adversaries at Decca, who had a huge hit with the first Goonish single, 'I'm Walking Backwards For Christmas', followed by 'The Ying Tong Song' (bought by teenager John alongside 'Hound Dog'). Martin was crestfallen, feeling that he and The Goons were a match made in heaven, and he was hugely relieved to find both Spike and Peter quick to return. 'Happily we all soon got together again, and I made my first record with Spike, a work of minor importance called "You've Got To Go Ow". It was a resounding failure... Everything we ever turned our hands to seemed to end in disaster. Perhaps that's why we became such good friends – so much so, that when he got married for the second time, which was during this period, he asked me to be his best man.'[11]

The Goons weren't only expanding into vinyl territory, however – translating their wireless madness onto television became a dream, which wasn't ever to come true with total success. One night in 1955, Sellers was tuned to the all-new commercial channel when he happened upon a one-time-only broadcast called *The Dick Lester Show*. Young American director Richard Lester had been living in the UK for some years, helping to train TV directors in the best US techniques, and on this occasion an emergency slot required an ad-libbed half hour headed by Lester, abetted by scouse trainee director Alun Owen, who also acted, but was shortly to begin flexing his muscles as a writer. The content of this show is forgotten by all, but the next morning Sellers discovered Lester's phone number and gave him a call, saying, 'Either that's the worst television programme that I have ever, ever seen or I think you're onto something that we are aspiring to', to which Lester replied, 'Well, if there's a choice, could it be the latter?' The programme the pair managed to hammer together over lunch, *The Idiot Weekly Price 2d,* received no input from Milligan for its first half hour besides the name – the nearly-forty-year-old wireless madman Spike had pooh-poohed the project, cynically claiming that his imagination could not be caught in the TV net... that is until he watched the pilot episode going out, whereupon he showed up at the next meeting with a full running order for episode two, without any acknowledgement of his initial prejudice.

Spike, Peter and Richard would explore together the limits and potential of TV comedy throughout 1956, performing live in a series of series, *A Show Called Fred* being followed by *Son of Fred*. Only this last run was broadcast as far away as Liverpool and could possibly have been seen by any Beatle, whether on their own family TV sets or with friends, but as Milligan's scripts gained confidence and became more unintelligible, ratings dipped and the experiment was halted weeks before any intended finale. Besides, Lester recalled, doing the TV and radio shows at the same time was taking its toll on Spike's mental health: 'The man was on the most massive tranquillizers. Any of Spike's daily medication would have put a troop of horses out.'[12]

It was hard to keep Spike down, though. Not long after these series aired on ITV, the BBC took a huge step towards acknowledgement of the growing teenage audience with the launch of *Six Five Special* at the start of 1957, conceived and produced by impresario Jack Good. Besides the skiffle and jiving on offer, comedy was always part of the programme's magazine format, headed by Good's old school friend and double act partner Trevor Peacock – a diminutive, eccentric actor who would go on to write early rock numbers for larksome cockney combo Joe Brown & The Bruvvers, plus 'Mrs Brown, You've Got A Lovely Daughter' for Herman's Hermits, both published by Good. Peacock's TV troupe regularly featured Milligan, plus Bernie Winters, the more ambitious half of a much maligned comedy double act with his brother Mike.

The Goons' luck on vinyl finally changed in this same year, George Martin scoring a minor hit with Sellers' husky rendition of an old music hall number, the skiffle-fuelled cockney knees-up 'Any Old Iron' (or as Paul had it in *Yellow Submarine*, 'Any Old Einstein'), backed with 'Boiled Bananas and Carrots'. Nobody could capture madness on microphone like the Parlophone boss, and the label's reputation as the funniest in the music business just kept growing, with much of the Goon-ish experimentation bolstered by the huge success of *At The Drop of a Hat* – the first of two recordings of hit live shows by Flanders & Swann, a musical comedy duo who had started out performing witty numbers like 'The Hippopotamus Song' at Oxford. Martin became as adept at capturing comedy from live performance as he was crafting it in the studio, and Sellers' modest successes boded well for a full album, which Martin had to fight the dreary EMI bosses tooth and nail to greenlight – getting his own back by prophetically entitling it *The Best of Sellers*. The disc featured sketches by Denis Goodwin & Bob Monkhouse and Frank Muir & Denis Norden – most notably the latter's deadpan travelogue 'Balham – Gateway to the South'.

'The technique with Peter,' Sir George wrote, 'was to make amusing records which the public would like to listen to time and time again. I tried very hard not to make the side-splitting kind of

15

funny record including a lot of heavy jokes, because they tend not to last for more than a couple of hearings. Once you know the joke, you know what's coming. But you can go on enjoying the way Irene Handl says "a bottle of Borjolais" instead of "Beaujolais", and you can always find something new to chuckle about in the little noises and gurgles she makes while being goosed by Peter. The humour would bear repetition simply because there were combinations of words that stuck in the mind.'[13]

The McCartney boys knew Sellers' first album almost by heart, and Paul insisted that their copy of *Songs for Swingin' Sellers* was worn out with replaying. There's no further solid evidence that the other Beatles personally owned any more of these records at the time, but that they heard, and enjoyed the musical output of The Goons as produced by George Martin is beyond doubt. And they knew that when a record with that famous £ sign in the centre was placed on a radiogram turntable, laughs were likely to follow. Paul added, 'The other thing about it was that it wasn't just comedy, there was good music in it, and you know, things like "Right Said Fred", "Goodness Gracious Me", it was groovy for those times.'[14]

1D OR THE VICAR'S HEAD

Of course, by the time these records were in the shops, the lives of all four young musicians had been re-routed more dramatically than ever before by the spring 1956 arrival of Elvis Presley's 'Heartbreak Hotel' – a humourless song that stoked the nascent musicianship of skiffle into full-blown rock 'n' roll obsession for a whole generation of kids, The Quarrymen included. That John was the leader of this group was never in doubt, and his sense of humour could not have been more central to his powerbase: 'I was the King Pin of my age group. I learned lots of dirty jokes very young; there was this girl who lived near who told me them.'[15] With Spike and co's madness being regurgitated in every schoolyard in Britain, John was one of those who took his love for The Goons further, and started to craft his own comedy to make his friends chuckle.

Being 'a character' was one way of achieving some sort of local fame, as McCartney once recalled, 'There were millions of characters in Liverpool. I lived about a half-hour from the centre and I remember there was a great guy got on the bus once. All he did was recite comedians' names to himself on the packed bus: "Tony Hancock! Hahaha haaa! Tommy Cooper! Hahaha…" He was just talking to himself but by the time he got off, the bus was just heaving. Then there was a guy walking along thinking he had a parrot on his shoulder, "Hello! Pretty Polly!" and there was no parrot there.'[16] Lennon was already a notable eccentric in his corner of the Liverpool suburbs, sighted at an early garden fete at the Salvation Army home in Woolton, Strawberry Field, dressed as a monk dispensing insane prophecies to anyone who cared to listen. Fancy dress was a silly preoccupation for all four Beatles, and Paul in particular would get many a kick from wandering around in public in false moustaches, at the height of Beatlemania – and maybe even to this day. John confided in Hunter Davies, 'We did all think of disguises, so we could get around. George and I went through customs in long coats and beards thinking no one would recognise us, but they all did. Paul was the best. He pretended to be a weird photographer, coming out with a lot of psychological gibberish. He even fooled Brian… We were on the way to Wembley once in the van. We wrote on a piece of paper, "Which way to Wembley?" We spoke in a foreign language and pointed to a map of Wales. Everybody went mad putting us right… I miss playing soft jokes on people. I used to do it on trains, go into people's compartments and pretend to be soft, or in shops. I still feel an urge to do that, but you can't. It would be "Beatles Play Tricks"…'[17]

John's experiments with print humour provided a more permanent glimpse into his comedic ambitions, and he'd rattle away producing nonsense on his big old Imperial typewriter at Menlove Avenue, and even had a piece of pleasing doggerel printed in school magazine *The Quarry*, presumably after a master had confiscated the scrap of paper:

*

The wandering hermit Fred am I,
With candlestick and bun
I knit spaghetti apple pie,
And crumbs do I have fun
I peel the bagpipes for my wife,
And cut all negroés hair
As breathing is my very life,
To stop I do not dare.

John's less respectably self-produced school rag *The Daily Howl* was handed round schoolyards with glee, each scrap now worth an incredible fortune. 'One of my earlier efforts at writing was a "newspaper" called "The Daily Howl",' he recalled. 'I would write it at night, then take it to school and read it aloud to my friends; looking at it now it seems strangely similar to *The Goon Show*! Even the title had "highly esteemed" before it!'[18]

Filled with jokes and cartoons, though no comic strips, 'The Daily Howl' was a news spoof which at his most productive, Lennon could fire out several times a week. One school chum lucky enough to giggle through many a copy, Bill Turner, reminisced to *Mersey Beat* magazine, 'at the time, Davy Crockett was all the rage and one of his poems was "The Story of Davy Crutch-Head"... Forever Wigan Pier kept cropping up, mainly in a story called "A Carrot In A Potato Mine", and the mine was at the end of Wigan Pier. One of his favourite cartoons was a bus stop scene. I remember he wrote under the sign, which said "Bus Stop", "Why?" And he had a flying pancake at the top of the cartoon, and below it there was a blind man wearing glasses leading along a blind dog – also wearing glasses.'[19] Even as a kid two years younger than Lennon, George Harrison was aware of these gag-packed rags, recalling, 'John had a gift for writing and drawing and speaking – particularly funny stuff. He had a book which he wrote when he was at Quarry Bank called *The Daily Howl*. It was quite big, the size of a *Beano* annual. It was a kind of newspaper with little jokes and cartoons – schoolboy humour, but really good and nicely illustrated. He was good at all that.'[20]

Packed with egregious misspellings, non-sequiturs and namechecks of then popular celebrities like magician David Nixon, monocled misanthrope Fred Emney and Professor of Gobbledegook Stanley Unwin, John's comic also heavily featured a preoccupation with 'cripples', and race-based daft gags which are a challenge to comfortably contextualise seven decades on. The fake periodical, supposedly priced '1d or the Vicar's Head, ½d to the Vicar' would get passed around, earning the weird author tons of teenage kudos. The pages which have survived to this day, complete with excessive use of commas and numerous coloured-in cartoons which were as clearly influenced by Spike Milligan's style of line-drawing as the jokes were influenced by The Goons, reveal a mix of simple gags and in-jokes very much of the time, even when not overtly offensive to 21st century sensibilities:

'WEATHER REPORT. Today it will be Muggy. Flowed by Tuggy, Weggy, Thurggy and Friggy. Yesterday it was wet. It was the rain that did it.'

'Have you got dandruff of the foot, making the lumbago in your ear start throbbing in your head, causing baldness? You're one of many, sonny…'

'VOTES FOR CRETINS'

'News about Firework Night (Fred's birthday). The sad news has just come through that only 80 people above the age of 76 were killed. Most of the spoilsports just lost their sight, and maimed for life. And it wasn't for want of trying.'

'Our late editor is dead, he died of death, which killed him. His wife married again, the day he died, and sold his possessions which he owned. She said she was sure that it was the way he would have wanted it. The photos underneath, which are below, are Polly photo's, taken by a parrot at

Lewissesisessis… es. These photos are given by kindly permission of Mrs Williams of Bootle.'

'The kindly Vicar of a parish, has kindly donated a kind donation, which he kindly decided to kindly donate to the SOCIETY for the Prevention of Standing on Toadstools. But it is found that the treasurer of the S.P.T.T. has run away to Garston, he went on the (booze) bus.'

'This book contains only the work of J.W. Lennon, with additional work by J.W. Lennon, and a helping hand given by J.W. Lennon, not forgetting J.W. Lennon.

Who is this J.W. Lennon? Here are some remark by a few famous Newspapers.

"A good book better" – J.W. Lennon of the Daily Howl

"This book has many good uses and should go down well" – The Sanitary Journal

"Yes" – Fred Emney Fan Club Magazine

"(Belch!)" – Garston Herald.[21]

Some of these gags, including the sick desire to kill maximum OAPs on 5th November and numerous mocking asides of Winston Churchill, would be recycled in different forms, but this level of subversion was tolerated by teachers, some of whom enjoyed confiscated copies as much as the kids for whom they were created.

The personal heartbreak suffered by both Lennon and McCartney in these years has been documented time and again, but if anything the loss of their mothers darkened the black humour they shared more than ever before, as well as bringing the pair of budding songwriters closer together. As we shall see, the system of private jokes within the band would be one of the crucial secret elements that kept them sane in the eye of the storm of Beatlemania. And for young men in any era, that more often than not means transgressive humour, the more offensive and outrageously sick the better.

John had famously invited Paul to join the group for wholly musical reasons after their first fateful meeting at the Woolton Village Fete in '57, but he may have been just as impressed and disconcerted by the newbie's skills as a writer and a clown as he was by his musicality. Little George Harrison's quickness with a dry one-liner to complement his combative streak also tightened the tie between the three of them, when Paul brought the youngest of his Liverpool Institute pals into The Quarrymen, but McCartney's prodigious talents were more instantly apparent. Where Lennon's school reports had been a series of exasperated condemnations from teachers, McCartney had always done rather well at school, following in some famous footsteps, as Arthur Askey recalled to Roy Plomley on *Desert Island Discs* in 1980: 'In the early '60s I was doing a show for the BBC called *Pop In*, where they played records, and a long-haired boy came up to me and said, "Excuse me, sir, I went to the same school as you did in Liverpool." I said, "Oh, the Liverpool Institute?" He said, "Yes, there's four of us from Liverpool, and two of us went to the Institute... we play guitars and sing our own songs, we're quite well known in Germany, I think we'll make it here." I said, "Oh good for you, what do you call yourselves?" He said, "The Beatles." I said, "The what?"... I immediately thought of cockroaches and things, as you would in those days. I said, "Oh, that's a silly name, son, you'll never get anywhere in show business with a name like that. I should certainly change that." And who was that? My dear friend, Paul McCartney. And he said he sat at the desk that I sat at – I must have been a vandal as a kid, I carved my initials on the desk – A.A. – and he said they looked on it as a sort of shrine. So there you are, two geniuses on the same seat!'[22] Sitting at that very school desk Askey had called his forty years earlier, wee McCartney major once wrote a cute, prize-winning essay on the 1953 Coronation, and was tipped by some teachers to eventually join them in the profession. 'I had the greatest teacher ever of English Literature, called Alan Durband, who was a leading light in the Everyman Theatre, when Willy

Russell and everybody were there,' Paul reminisced with Barry Miles. 'He'd actually written a ten-minute morning story for the BBC, so I respected this guy.' But Paul soon proved to his new friend that he was anything but a teacher's pet, and unlike other Quarrymen, who often felt the acid spray of Lennon's invective without having the wit to fire anything back in retaliation, the fifteen-year-old could return, if not top, the Lennon brand of loony cheek.

This even extended to allowing McCartney to experiment with co-writing comedy as well as pop songs, including a parody of TV series *White Hunter*, 'On Safairy With Whide Hunter', which was 'written in conjugal' and ended up in print many years later. 'He would show me what he'd been typing,' McCartney recalled. 'I would sometimes help him with it. We would sit around giggling, just saying puns really, that's basically what it was; "In the early owls of the Morecambe", I remember, "a cup o-teeth" was one section that was in the typewriter when I was around there. But I would like all that and I was very impressed. He was a big Lewis Carroll fan, which I was too. In my view two of John's great songs, "Strawberry Fields" and "I Am the Walrus", both come from "Jabberwocky".'

With no kind of religious rubbish tolerated amongst the gang, blasphemy was a Lennon staple – he quickly responded to the death of Pope Pius XII in 1958 by drawing a cartoon of the late pontiff rattling the locked gates of Heaven with indignation, and the crucifixion became a cartoon fixation, with Christ's suffering being heckled with the single word – 'EXHIBITIONIST!' – and his holy slippers being set neatly at the base of his cross. These thrillingly wicked urges inspired John and Paul to attempt to write a play together, vaguely remembered by the latter decades later as a kind of early take on *Jesus Christ Superstar*-cum-*Waiting For Godot*. 'We sat down with another exercise book, and tried to write a play involving a Christ figure called Pilchard. The whole idea was that he was not going to appear. We only got two pages, but I can remember it quite clearly. There was the mother and the young daughter of the family sitting at home in a kind of John Osborne suburban

22

parlour setting, and they're talking. Suddenly, "knock knock, knock" comes on the door. "Who's that?" "Harold." "Oh my God, it's not him again, is it?" Then he walks in, "Oh, hello." Enter left, unwanted Harold. And he's trying to laugh it off because he'd heard them say, "Oh no, not him again." He comes in making polite Pinterish conversation. He says, "Where's Pilchard?" "Oh, he's upstairs praying again." And we were going to have this character: the person upstairs who never comes in, and the play is just people talking about him and his terrible crisis. "Oh, our Pilchard, you know, he's taken a turn. He's born again, and he really thinks he's the Messiah. He's upstairs praying." This was the way it was going to go but we couldn't figure out how playwrights did it. The question was, do they work it all out and then work through the chapters or do they just write a stream of consciousness like we were doing? In which case, that was a fairly hard way to do it, because we ran out on the second page."[23] "Since I left school I've written little essays about a character called Small Sam, and off-beat things about Liverpool,' John told the *NME*. 'I even had a bash at writing a serious play with Paul... It all fell through in the end, but we aim to do at least one big play or musical together. That's our ambition – a West End production with our own words and music.'

The lads also tried recording their own audio comedy, mutual pal Derek Hodkin bringing a tape recorder round to the McCartney house at Forthlin Road, where John, Paul and Mike joined him in improvising what he called 'an hour of repartee, jokes, laughs, practice songs, and quite a few ribald remarks about my French girlfriend', which has naturally not survived. The idea of Lennon & McCartney not using rare access to tape recording to capture their growing musical skills seems perverse, but there's no denying that music was what consumed them, although even when they got a chance to capture their sound, they were still liable to take up precious tape with comic riffing. Recorded in the McCartney bathroom in 1960, the bluesy Lennon & McCartney original 'You'll Be Mine' featured Paul's ridiculously bombastic crooning spoofing The Ink Spots, decades before Vic Reeves invented 'club-style singing', and a drawled middle-eight of Milliganesque grotesquery from John:

My darling, when you brought me that toast the other mornin'
I looked into your eyes, and I could see that National Health eyeball
And I love you, like I've never done… before!

This rough collective were known to be good for a laff, showing up for gigs in their 'twat hats' (pink caps which begged for the invention of the term 'metrosexual') and once performing as 'The Rainbows', their stage festooned with stolen cabbages and a workman's lamp. At one party, a drunken John dealt with one old dear determined to hog the piano for a singalong by pouring a pint over her head and crying, 'I anoint thee David!' That his victim apparently let the lad get away with it must be testament to the charm young Lennon could switch on when necessary. It was amazing what the rogue could get away with, with a cheeky grin and innocently waggled eyebrows.

John was well aware of the Lancashire comedy heritage they all shared, but Paul brought with him an all-rounder attitude to entertainment, a spirit of variety that teased a layer of gold lamé behind the rough leather – they could all rock hard, but on top of that, McCartney was a glorious ham, a Butlin's-coached clown who had watched the Redcoats geeing up audiences as a child. If a fuse blew down in the sweaty depths of The Cavern and all was plunged in darkness, trainee electrician George would head off to fix it while Lennon & McCartney formed a double act, the latter crying 'Come forth, Quasimodo!' as the former 'cripped' his way horrendously onstage, trousers stuffed with newspaper, lisping 'How about I come fifth?', or they would fill in time with a lampoon of radio quiz show *Have a Go* and the Yorkshire vowels of its presenter, Wilfred Pickles, or throw in impersonations of Morecambe & Wise or Arthur Lowe as Leonard Swindley in *Coronation Street,* or vamp the theme to the commercial for Sunblest bread, or the strangulated melody which presaged Gerry Anderson puppet show *Torchy The Battery Boy*. The odd dig at the city's first national pop star Frank Ifield was also welcome, as

Paul and he jealously shared a girlfriend at the time. The boys could work the room, with a grin for the girls (including avid fan Sue Johnston, née Wright, who would go on to work for Brian Epstein before embarking on an acting career packed with beloved comedy roles crowned by *The Royle Family*'s Barbara Royle) and a gag for the lads (who could otherwise have easily resented the band's effect on their girlfriends), beyond the wit of most other bands on the scene, no matter how wacky their approach. Sometimes Paul's holiday-camp eagerness to please could earn the disdain of the others, with one memorable attempt to ape Elvis singing 'Are You Lonesome Tonight?' causing John and George to collapse with mocking laughter, deriding any apparent bid from Paul to become the thing so sneered at by Peter Sellers on disc, 'an all-round entertainer'.

The leader of the group, Paul recalled, was the best at plumbing the comedic depths: 'John used to do the spastic impersonations on stage a lot. He had a habit of putting a clear plastic bag on his foot with a couple of rubber bands. Brian wouldn't like it... We used to think certain words were very funny that out of teenage nervousness made us laugh: "cripple", "hare-lip", "cleft palate", "club foot" – when a guitar came out, a Club 40, we used to call it a Club-Foot. A sign on the way down to London used to make us howl: "Cripples crossing". We used to think it was a place rather than an event... it was so sort of terrifying we had to laugh. A lot of what we did was based in that. And that was the kind of thing that separated us from other people. It meant we had our own world. A world of black humour and of nervousness at other people's afflictions. The way we got through our lives was laughing at them.' 'John was allergic to cripples,' George added. 'You could see he had a thing about them; I think it was a fear of something. You can see in all our home movies, whenever you switch a camera on John, he goes into his interpretation of a spastic. It's not very nice to be afflicted, so John had this thing that he'd always joke about it. I think the reality was too much for him... After a while, we used to call even normal people "cripples", because most people are crippled in a way... Like John wrote, "One thing you can't hide, is when you're Crippled Inside."'[24]

Much has been written and groaned about the Lennon fixation with cripples and the handicapped, from the point of view of a horrified modern society which naturally finds it hard even to hear the long outdated term 'spastic', let alone the euphemism 'soft'. Aping the handicapped is a Lennon trait it's impossible to ignore; John's painful distorted mugging accompanied by exaggerated stiff-legged stage-stamping was a tic which even the greatest world fame imaginable could hardly knock out of him. Paul's dad Jim complained, 'Toleration IS very important. They would laugh at people with infirmities, as kids do. I'd explain to them how THEY wouldn't like it.'[25] As many lads do, John would eventually develop beyond his youthful taste for the extremely sick, appearing at the 1972 'One To One' benefit concert in New York to raise money for local children with disabilities, and as early as 1968, he protested to Hunter Davies, 'I suppose I did have a cruel humour... Liverpool is full of deformed people, the way you have them in Glasgow, three-foot high men selling newspapers... I suppose it was a way of hiding your emotions, or covering it up. I would never hurt a cripple. It was just part of our jokes, our way of life.'[26] Later in life, he went further: 'I don't think I'd know a spastic from a Polaroid lens. I'm not hung up about them. When I use the term "spastic" in general conversation, I don't mean to say it literally. I feel terrible sympathy for these people, it seems the end of the world when you see deformed spastics, and we've had quite a lot of them in our travels... it's always the mother or nurse pushing them on you. They would push these people at you like you were Christ, as if there were some aura about you that would rub off on them... When we would open up, every night, instead of seeing kids there, we would see a row full of cripples along the front. When we'd be running through, people would be lying around. It seemed that we were just surrounded by cripples and blind people all the time, and when we would go through corridors they would all be touching us... I have to laugh, or I'd just collapse from hate. They'd line them up, and I got the impression The Beatles were being treated as bloody faith healers. It was sickening. It was sort of the "in joke" that we were supposed to cure them... I mean, we felt sorry for them, anybody would, but it was awful.'[27] Neil Aspinall would apparently resignedly indicate the arrival of each evening's visitors with a bleak 'Okay guys, spastic time...'

Having been through so much so young, John's attitude to using humour as a way to combat suffering, both of others and his own, seems encapsulated by another personal observation he made about death, discussing the loss of Epstein with *Rolling Stone* scribe Jan Wenner: 'There is a sort of little hysterical, sort of "hee, hee, I'm glad it's not me!" or something in it, the funny feeling when somebody close to you dies. I don't know whether you've had it, but I've had a lot of people die around me.'[28] The suffering young John felt was inflicted on him by the world became repackaged as a kind of snarling piss-take, both on stage and in print, the darkness of their shared clandestine humour bringing the three most talented Quarrymen closer than ever, even while in song, the more simplistic words of 'LOVE LOVE LOVE' would be taking 'Just John' and his pals to the much-promised 'toppermost of the poppermost' – no matter how thick with sarcasm the repetition of that pep-talking ambition was intended to be.

PURPLE HEARTS AND TOILET SEATS

The musical trial of fire experienced by John, Paul, George and (separately) Ringo in the seedy clubs of Hamburg's Reeperbahn from the late summer of 1960 onwards is infamous, but the sheer hilarity of their first real taste of freedom out there is a crucial part of the story. The pressures of eight-hour-plus sessions at The Indra, The Star Club and elsewhere, surviving on booze and pills, young lads making the most of a youth which their elders had been forced to lose to National Service, resulted in outrageous pranks and piss-taking they wouldn't have dreamt of back home in Liverpool, at any age.

Back in the spring, John and Paul had hitched down to the Reading suburbs to once again take inspiration from Paul's showbiz cousin-in-law Mike Robbins, who was running a pub called the Fox & Hounds with Bett and their young family, and allowed the two teenagers to perform a couple of weekend music shows under the screamingly silly moniker 'The Nerk Twins' – 'nerk' being a neologism popular among the more madcap of British comic strips – as they sucked up showbiz wisdom from the landlord. The two naughty lads, who earned their gig by washing up, were on the verge of their greatest rite of passage, but life in Liverpool for the art school near-drop-out Lennon and his two schoolboy chums was hardly innocent even then – the older lad already lived a bohemian life in scuzzy student digs at Gambier Terrace with his best pal Stu Sutcliffe and (occasionally) his far more well-to-do girlfriend Cynthia, and Paul and George were regular visitors.

The budding quartet of John, Stu, Paul and George even dipped a toe into the growing poetry scene in Liverpool, which would become celebrated nationwide and draw the attention of Mike McCartney. The fledgling four-piece jammed along to back up visiting Beat poet Royston Ellis, who had taken a fancy to George when he spied him in Allan Williams' club the Jacaranda, and in between sucking benzedrine out of Vicks inhalers, the poetic collective would jaw through the night on the ways in which rock 'n' roll could do so much more than just inspire kids to dance and scream. A distinct, horizontally dour humour pervaded this early explosion of scouse poetry, and young sardonic versifiers like Adrian Henri, Roger McGough and John Gorman welcomed Mike – at first credited as 'Mike Blank' but soon to spare his big brother blushes by taking the moniker 'McGear' – into their comedy troupe The Liverpool One Fat Lady All Electric Show. Mike was otherwise employed as a hairdresser, working alongside Tarbuck and actor Lewis Collins, but this was an interesting new world for him, and an odd snub for Paul, as Gorman has always claimed he turned down The Beatles' offer to provide music for an inaugural arts festival at the newly-opened Everyman Theatre. In time, McGough, Gorman and McGear would congeal under the banner of The Scaffold, and forge their own pop careers in Paul's wake. 'The only way to survive was to choose a theatrical comedy concept. If I had chosen pop music I'd be dead by now,' Mike told avid Beatleologist Geoffrey

Giuliano. 'We played the Cavern, but we didn't go down too well because they were used to pop groups, and we'd come on spouting poetry and bloody comedy.' McGear nevertheless knew his brother's band had talent beyond the toe-tapping, and insists, 'John was a great comedian, a natural... he was the heavy one and Paul was a very good feed. Two good comedians. But then Ringo's a very funny guy as well... Liverpool life is the best apprenticeship in the world, because our families are virtually goldmines of upbringing. Without that grounding I doubt very much whether the Beatles would have stayed at the top for so long or kept their sanity when all about them so many died. Of course an enormous contribution to that longevity was their sense of humour. They always say in Liverpool: you've got to have a sense of humour to survive.'[29]

With drummer Pete Best added to the line-up, the newly-named Beatles were let further off the leash as autumn arrived, and they began their punishing rock and roll baptism in the land long maligned by the British as being entirely without a sense of humour. Some of the tales of how these speed-raddled blister-defying minstrels expressed their new-found freedom have been scaled back in time – no, Paul now assures us, John didn't actually urinate on any nuns from the roof, and if any of them felt the odd spot of splashback, it was purely accidental. John did actually make his own priest costume – religious fancy dress being something of a habit – and gave insane sermons to the uncomprehending German passers-by in a bad Indian accent. But yes, John was receiving head in a Star Club toilet cubicle when Horst Fascher turned a hose on the horny couple, and sent Lennon out onto the stage wearing just his pants and a toilet seat around his head, roaring that it was fitting as the crowd were 'a shower of shite' anyway. And yes, he did moon the audience, at least once.

The all-night sets, free booze and copious 'purple heart' speed pills which kept the boys going fuelled all manner of daft excess. Challenging the British view of German mirthlessness, Paul recalled, 'They made fun of us because our name, The Beatles, sounded very like the German "peedles" which means "little willies". "Oh, ze Peedles, ha ha ha!" They loved that. It appealed directly to the German sense of humour, that did.' In response, there was no limit to the Nazi references and salutes the scousers could hurl at their audiences, McCartney introducing a performance of 'Besame Mucho' as 'a special request for Hitler!' Just to be playing well-rehearsed rock numbers for eight-hour shifts would be tough enough, but engaging with the crowd (including, bizarrely, Malcolm Muggeridge) as funny frontmen was every bit as important, with the constant need to 'Mach shau'. 'In those old Cavern days,' John recalled, 'half the thing was just ad-lib; what you'd call comedy. We just used to mess about, jump into the audience, do anything.'[30] Their hosts began to identify this band of leathery fools as 'The Verrüchte [Crazy] Beatles'.

There was, however, one odd Beatle out in this crazy line-up – or rather two, though the first issue was solved when shy Stu Sutcliffe fell in love with Astrid Kirchherr and decided to quit the group to follow his artistic bent in Germany. 'I couldn't speak English when I met The Beatles, so I learned it from them,' Astrid said. 'It was difficult to pick up their jokes at first. But I loved their humour, and I loved the English language, which was so much funnier and more precise than German.'[31] Even Stu's tragically early death didn't stop the comic turns – for The Beatles' first gig of their last Hamburg run, not long after being told the heartbreaking news, John was said to have over-compensated for his grief by turning up at the Star Club dressed as a cleaning lady limping along with a plank, knocking over the drums and diligently scrubbing Paul's armpits as he tried to marshal the crowd. Stu's absence, however, only highlighted the problem with Pete. He had his own merry memories of the German stints: 'We were just five fellows having a good time. We did daft things all the time. John had a pair of Long John underpants, as it was getting very cold with winter drawing on. George bet him ten marks that he wouldn't go out, wearing them and nothing else. He went out in the street, just in his Long Johns, with sun specs on and read the *Daily Express* for five minutes. We watched him, killing ourselves laughing.'[32] But, besides his side-splitting attempt to burn the Kaiserkeller by pinning condoms to the wall of their digs with Paul and setting them alight, few stories of Pete's larks in Germany have survived.

The infamous and undeniably spineless replacement of Best with Starr at the drums is one of the most well-worn edit points in The Beatles story, but seen through the prism of the band's humour, it perhaps seems more necessary and inevitable than ever. He could hold the backbeat – admittedly not as skilfully as Rory Storm & The Hurricanes star Ringo, but musically Best had always kept the band together, and had the ability to learn with his bandmates' growing ambitions. There's no question Best's exit could not have been more problematic, given his gaggle of voluble adoring fans, his knowledge of the band's numbers, the effort he and his mother Mona had put into promoting the careers of all four of them, giving them gigs at The Casbah and fighting with dodgy promoters on their behalf (not to mention the fact that indispensable roadie and driver Neil Aspinall had fathered little baby Roag Best with best friend Pete's mum); it all made the ejection of the hard-working drummer seem far more trouble than it was worth. But the reason that Pete Best absolutely *had* to go if The Beatles stood a chance getting anywhere near the 'toppermost of the poppermost' was that he just wasn't daft enough.

'Mean, moody and magnificent' was Pete's style, exemplifying the kind of teen-bait that British pop had been trading in for years, with acts like Billy Fury (Ringo's one-time classmate Ronald Wycherley) and Marty Wilde, curling lips at the command of Larry Parnes, as lampooned by Peter Sellers on his second album, *Songs For Swingin' Sellers,* in the Frank Muir & Denis Norden sketch 'So Little Time'. This skit, with Sellers playing all roles, put George Martin in the control room of the first pointed pastiche of a new wave in music, while the track 'Puttin' On The Smile' was a lampoon of Lonnie Donegan's skiffle business ('Rock Island Line' had far outsold Martin's own attempt at a skiffle hit with The Vipers, so revenge was sweet). The LP also provided the producer's first run-in with traditional Indian instruments like the sitar, the start of a fumbling education which was extended in the next year's collaboration between Sellers and Sophia Loren (resulting in 'Goodness Gracious Me', a blacked-up hit publicising their new movie *The Millionairess,* which reached the dizzy heights of Number three).

'So Little Time' exposed the angry young pop stable of Parnes cipher Major Rafe Ralph – Clint Thigh, Matt Lust and Twit Conway, plus combos The Fleshpots and The Muckrakers:

NANCY: …What does it feel like to suddenly find yourself a teenage idol?

TWIT: Well, er, it don't make much difference really, I mean – I was idle before I was a teenager.

MAJOR: Heh! No, no, what the lad is trying to say, Miss Lisbon, is that success has not spoiled him. He is still the same Twit he always was. Right, lad?

TWIT: Er, yeah, that's what I shoulda said, yeah.

MAJOR: Of course it's what you should have said! Now don't be nervous, lad! Just remember your lessons on how to answer press questions. Just bear in mind what you've been told to say.

NANCY: Well, Twit, do you want to stay a rock and roll singer all your life? I mean, what is your ultimate ambition?

TWIT: Er – we are just good friends.

MAJOR: That is the answer to another question! Remember? The answer to this one is: I want to become an all-round…

TWIT: Oh yeah! Er – I want to become an all round…

MAJOR: (*sotto voce*) Entertainer!

TWIT: Er – entertainer, yeah. Um, my dream is one day to play Old Vic in Shakespeare.

NANCY: Oh how sweet! You are fond of Shakespeare?

TWIT: …Er – we are just good friends.[33]

This kind of sizzling tosh wasn't John, Paul and George's style at all, and with the best will in the world, Pete never fully got the lads' weird humour, happy though he was to goof around when John and co were all off on one. It's true that jocular rockers weren't a rarity in the Liverpool scene at that time, Gerry Marsden quite the cheeky chappie as he fronted his band The Pacemakers, but there was something about Butlin's star Ringo – shining with jewellery, no stranger to the gold lamé suit and big grin for the grannies during his 'Starr Time' showpieces, well trained by the holiday camp entertainer life he would eventually depict on screen in *That'll Be The Day* over a decade later. Richie Starkey was already a hit with the others for his laconically delivered singular turn of phrase, packed with malapropisms and linguistic misconnections helped along by a poor education, which he admits in the *Anthology:* '"Tomorrow Never Knows" was something I said, God knows where it came from. "Slight bread" was another: "Slight bread, thank you." John used to like them most. He always used to write them down.'[34]

A legend persists that Ringo was not the first 'Starr' to be approached to join The Beatles – a local lad called Freddie Fowell had taken the stage name himself as he fronted his band The Midniters, who were to be briefly pursued by Brian Epstein before signing with Joe Meek. Freddie Starr was to eventually find fame as a broad, anarchic comic, winning the popular vote on *Opportunity Knocks* a decade later, but the story of John approaching him to be in the band has been embroidered over the years, not least by the man himself – it is true, however, that Ringo occasionally sat in with The Midniters, until accepting the call to become a Beatle.

'Ringo was a star in his own right in Liverpool before we even met,' Lennon insisted years later. 'He was a professional drummer who sang and performed and had "Ringo Starr-Time" and he was in one of the top groups in Britain, but especially in Liverpool, before we even had a drummer. So Ringo's talent would have come out one way or the other as something or other. I don't know what he would have ended up as, but whatever that spark is in Ringo that we all know but can't put our finger on – whether it's acting, drumming or singing I don't know – there is something in him that is projectable and he would have surfaced as an individual.'[35] With a quick shave and a brush-down of the fringe, Ringo fell in with The Beatles' clowning as well as their rhythm, giving the other three a glimpse of what it could be like to have a quartet without a weak corner, four funny performers each able to hold their own, and all greeting the crowd with a smiling panache, rather than hunkering down behind the skins and providing nothing but a beat. Plus, McCartney had a fellow crowd-pleasing showman on his side, for when Lennon and Harrison decided to take the piss out of his slick excesses on stage.

John, Paul and George were aware of this imbalance even before Brian Epstein crept down to the Cavern to survey their act, but his assistant Alistair Taylor recalled Pete's drag on the showmanship of McCartney and the madness of Lennon being apparent from the start: 'They looked completely out of control. I could see Brian's eyes widen with amazement as they yelled and swore at their audience between songs... Since that fateful visit, I have wondered exactly what it was that Brian saw in this loud and dirty pop group. I remember saying years later to Paul that they sounded as if they only knew five chords. He replied, "Do you mind? We only knew three!"... From the very first time we saw them, John, Paul and George had a jokey rapport both on stage and off that Pete clearly did not share. He was a terribly nice fella but he would be sulking when the other three were laughing.'

'I was immediately struck by their music, their beat, and their sense of humour on stage,' Epstein wrote. 'They were very funny; their ad-libbing was excellent.' However, one of the first things the new manager urged on his charges, as part of the smartening up of their image, was that John should refrain from 'cripping' on stage – a promise barely kept at all by the pig-headed rebel. Stagecraft was certainly a preoccupation of the young NEMS store manager, and had been from infancy, when dreams of making it in the theatre had first been planted in his head by Pamela Brown's children's book *The Swish of the Curtain*. He had entertained his cosily well-off Jewish Liverpudlian family with infant entertainments, for which he even created his own programmes, and he became a regular at Liverpool's Playhouse and Royal Court theatres. Although he dutifully played his part in the family business, selling furniture in the city's poshest outlets, Brian's failure to get ahead at RADA down in London (where he enrolled just after the graduation of bigwigs Peter O'Toole and Albert

Finney) left him with an unsated penchant for the stink of the proverbial greasepaint.

Were The Beatles in particular need of the slick (albeit untested) management of the local celebrity at this point? Views vary, but the existing regime must have been doing their best, as the band's gigs only seemed to be on the up – in October 1961 they played the Albany Cinema, Maghull, just north of Liverpool, although top of the bill that night was that protégé of Harry Harrison, Ken Dodd, starting his own journey to national fame. Brian had heard about The Beatles because they were already by then the best band in Liverpool, local heroes who had been encouraged to create their own legend by have-a-go editor Bill Harry, who had been at school with Lennon. On the second page of the inaugural issue of Harry's teen paper *Mersey Beat* in July 1961, the same brand of John Lennon doggerel which had earned him so much cred at school and art college appeared under the title 'Beatcomber', named in tribute to the 'Beachcomber' humorous columns. The famous 'Being A Short Diversion On The Dubious Origins Of Beatles' had a little input from George:

> Once upon a time there were three little boys called John, George and Paul, by name christened. They decided to get together because they were the getting together type. When they were together they wondered what for after all, what for? So all of a sudden they grew guitars and fashioned a noise... Many people ask what are Beatles? Why Beatles? Ugh, Beatles, how did the name arrive? So we will tell you. It came in a vision – a man appeared on a flaming pie and said unto them, 'From this day on you are Beatles with an "A".' 'Thank you, mister man', they said, thanking him.[36]

There are very few rock bands capable of creating their own legends in such a comically nonsensical way, their very genesis a jumble of laughs – the extract would be re-used for the press as the band's fame grew, Paul laughing with one interviewer, 'John came up with the name Beatles one night. And he sort of explained how it was spelled with an "E-A", and we said, "Oh yes, it's a joke!"' And there was loads more where that daftness came from, too – one night at the Jacaranda, Harry enquired whether Lennon had any writing ambitions, and was astonished to be immediately handed a fresh scrap of strangulated pastoral nonsense:

Owl George ee be a farmer's lad, with mucklekak and cow
'Ee be the son of 'is owl Dad, but why I don't know how
One day maybe he marry be, to Nellie Nack the Lass
And we shall see what we shall see, a-fucking in the grass...
And so I go rambling on with a hey nonny nonny no...[37]

...And there were at least a couple of hundred similar scraps of scribbled and thump-typed pieces the young editor was welcome to publish in his hip new paper. Though some made it into print, the sad sequel to this story was the spot of tidying carried out by Harry's fiancé Virginia one day, which saw over two hundred and fifty Lennon originals accidentally thrown into the bin – John reportedly wept on her shoulder when told the news.

So it's wrong to see Epstein's professional stewardship of the band as a stroke of luck for the boys – whether cleaned up or as is, Brian knew a good thing when it lured him down into a sweaty cellar. Perhaps it's less surprising than it sounds that McCartney chose the first proper meeting to agree on Epstein's management in December 1961 to make a subtle power play, making everyone wait around forever while he took a leisurely bath at home. When news of his slow progress filtered back, Epstein grumbled, 'This is disgraceful. He's going to be very late', to which Harrison casually responded, 'Late, yes... but very clean.'

FOUR BOYS WHO SHOOK THE WORLD

Having signalled his skill at capturing live sophisticated Oxbridge wit with Flanders & Swann, George Martin was a shoo-in to helm the first official record of the greatest revue of all time, *Beyond the*

Fringe, in the late spring of 1961. The show's seed had been sown in late 1959 by the artistic director of the Edinburgh Festival, Robert Ponsonby, who wanted to head off Fringe events by creating his own – and when Louis Armstrong proved an impossible booking, he allowed his assistant John Bassett to forge ahead with arranging a comedy revue in his stead, made up of the finest student comics from both Oxford and Cambridge in recent years. Hence the celebrated meeting of practising doctor Jonathan Miller and his Cambridge Footlights successor Peter Cook with Oxford graduates, medieval scholar Alan Bennett and hot little jazz pianist Dudley Moore, to iron out a satirical sketch show which would change all of their lives. *Beyond the Fringe* debuted in Edinburgh that August, and Martin, already acquainted with Moore via shared jazz circles, diligently flew up to Scotland to catch a performance well in advance. By the time EMI's mobile recording van pulled up in Cambridge to capture the show on its way to its epic London run (the eventual release nonetheless being labelled a London recording), the quartet's bleak bite had ruffled enough establishment feathers to ensure notoriety. As the largely student punters – quite probably including John Cleese, Tim Brooke-Taylor, Bill Oddie and Graham Chapman – settled in for that evening's entertainment, the producer captured an audience ambience which he would later find useful for the very start of *Sgt Pepper's Lonely Hearts Club Band*. Nobody there quite guessed what they were in for, nor how far the ripple of these satirical barbs would reach – by the time the revue's immense popularity earned it a run on Broadway, the New York press raised eyebrows by hinting at a 'British Invasion!'

Martin had been aiding Sellers and others in recording quietly subversive audio comedy for some years by this point, reflecting numerous cracks which presaged trickles through the dam of the British culture of deference throughout the 1950s, the rise of the 'Angry Young Man' – or rather, 'Person' – with John Osborne and Shelagh Delaney in the theatre, directed by Joan Littlewood with her eye for social satire, plus moody monochromatic cinema masterpieces like *Saturday Night, Sunday Morning,* which gave rise to 'kitchen sink' realism – a temporary artistic levelling of Britain's indestructible class system perpetrated by those who grew up with war and rationing, and had had enough. The Cambridge contingent of *Beyond the Fringe* may have been more well-bred, but Moore and Bennett were genuine working class voices, and the stark staging of their sketches certainly felt allied to the broader establishment-thumping movement.

It was, however, the other pair who were invited by Milligan and Sellers to form a one-off quartet on record, with a very obtuse Parlophone release masterminded by Martin. For reasons taken to their graves, two years after *The Goon Show* proper ceased broadcasting in 1960, the two elder statesmen of comedy decided to record a spoof of five-year-old war movie *Bridge on the River Kwai* ('You saw the film, you read the book. Now feel the suit as you heard it on the new wide stereophonic phonograph. Here it is, as nature never intended!'). Milligan recycled a five-year-old *Goon Show* script, 'The African Incident', co-written with Larry Stephens and packed, of course, with embarrassing 'ethnic' voices, besides Sellers' excellent Alec Guinness impression. No matter what the quality, Cook and Miller simply basked in the pleasure of performing with their comedy heroes. Sadly, the meeting of these two comic worlds did not result in an explosion of comic chemistry, despite all Martin's attempts to make up for the lack of a live audience by pulling all the atmospheric tricks in the book, and diverting bilge such as Cook's intro: 'It was 1962 in England, but still only 1943 in Japan. Such was the great difference in teeth between these two great religions…' In fact, the creaky resultant release, *Bridge on the River Wye*, is mainly famous for the producer's herculean achievement in deftly cutting out every single 'K' sound when 'Kwai' was uttered in the recording, after EMI got cold feet about spoofing the film too closely – hence the unintended tribute to the Welsh river.

For more class-clashing satirical bite, George was shrewd to snap up the seemingly whimsical satirical songwriting team of Ted Dicks & Myles Rudge – attuned to the delivery of loveable comic actor Bernard Cribbins, in 1962 they scored a palpable hit with 'The Hole In The Ground', in which a workman confronts a bowler-hatted management type, and ends up burying him in the hole he was digging. This was followed up by a further inventive novelty 'celebrating' the antics of the British worker, 'Right Said Fred' – another future children's favourite which made good use of Martin's mastery of audio scene-painting.

Cribbins' releases reached the Top Ten, but that long-desired Number One for Parlophone came from a differently whimsical quarter. While in Cambridge watching *Beyond the Fringe*, George was over the moon to be informed that top of the hit parade at that time was 'You're Driving Me Crazy', by eccentric ironic jazzers The Temperance Seven, the vanguard of an oft-forgotten British musical movement which greatly coloured the 1960s and beyond – 'British Rubbish'. While many British students were picking up washboards and guitars in the 1950s, a weird coterie were manhandling sousaphones, bassoons, tubas and worse, harking back to an inter-war jazzamaniac spirit, with lashings of the musical mayhem of comedy combo Spike Jones and his City Slickers. Lennon and co weren't the only art school musicians headed for fame, and a gang from Chelsea formed in late 1955 spent the latter half of the decade building up quite a following as The Temperance Seven, playing jazz standards with a slightly ironic bent.

Synchronous with these syncopators were The Alberts, of whom Martin was to say, 'This country has eccentric people, here and there. And I guess they are the most eccentric of the lot.' Formed by fancy-dress-loving jazzers Tony and Dougie Gray, who brought in esteemed oddball artist 'Professor' Bruce Lacey to add pizzazz, The Alberts' outlandish surreal events mixed outrageous ragged jazz with Lacey's troupe of garish bubble-blowing automatons, exploding camels and theatrical tricks, marking them out as something truly new – part hot jazz band, part Dada-ist knockabout comedy outfit. An affinity with Goonish humour landed The Alberts regular spots on both Bentine's and Milligan and Sellers' TV outings where, despite Lennon's overtly anti-jazz attitudes, their bizarre approach to entertainment (or was it even entertainment?) may have caught the odd Beatle eye or ear. When producing his friend Harry Nilsson in the early 1970s, Lennon christened one recording line-up 'The Masked Alberts Orchestra'.

Jazz man Dick Lester was very at home with the loony stylings of this new 'British Rubbish' approach, and booked The Temperance Seven to appear in his first feature, cheap musical *It's Trad, Dad!* Since the TV work had ended, Lester carried on shooting commercials, until, with the help of Bruce Lacey, Spike, Peter and others, he spent a couple of Sundays in 1959 having a little fun with one of Sellers' new toys: 'a 16mm Paillard Bolex, which was the best small 16mm camera that was available at the time,' Lester recalled, 'and he wanted to try it out. So he came over and we had dinner and we started just ad-libbing jokes...' The loose collective Lester convened was complemented by actor friends including rotund Australian Leo McKern and lantern-jawed Liverpudlian Norman Rossington, and the tiny company headed out into the nearest field to see what visual gags they could capture on monochrome celluloid. Lester continues, 'it was just what one grabbed, as you can imagine. The whole thing cost £70 in all.' 'It all started because Spike and I once said we wanted to experiment in visual humour,' Sellers added. 'We got as many friends together as we could and went and found a field. That was all we had – friends, a field, a roll of film. We shot ideas, that was all, and linked them together.'[38] From the moment a top-hatted McKern ranged his telescope over the fields to discover David Lodge scrubbing the grass clean to a backing of trad jazz and birdsong, to the conclusion in which Graham Stark is slowly beckoned into close-up just to be punched in the face, this short was nothing but an exercise to attempt all the corniest non-sequitur visual gags that were impossible on radio and record. The resulting eleven minutes of frivolity was nearly entitled *Chickens*, but became known as *The Running Jumping & Standing Still Film*, and its silliness tickled Sellers so much he managed to get it shown first at Edinburgh, and then San Francisco movie festivals, and eventually it even garnered an Oscar nomination. As each participant took it in turns to become hot, the film was kept in circulation, and in those days of myriad shorts shown at fleapits, it was certainly a favourite with John, Paul and George when they would while away the time between each day's gigs hanging out at The Tatler cinema in Church Street, Liverpool 1, smoking and snacking their way through the usual cartoons, newsreels and oddities.

Lester and Martin were the two figures of supposed authority marshalling these manifold criss-crossing comedic and musical talents, but they were not close, George writing, 'He is the sort of person who, at a nightclub or a party, will go to the piano in the corner and play his idea of jazz to amuse people. He plays jazz piano tolerably well, and he gave me the impression that he considered me inferior to him musically.' Martin worked to capture the daft essence of both The Alberts and The Temperance Seven on vinyl, and the latter's Number One was the culmination of years of experimentation and hope. The producer had a sideline in composing film music, and besides providing the theme to Leslie Phillips crime farce *Crooks Anonymous,* the soundtrack for 1963 musical *Take Me Over* was Martin's work, putting The Temperance Seven in the centre of the action, but the film failed to echo the success of the band's single.

Parlophone was hungry for musical hits, and the boss was in real need of hit makers: 'I wanted to have something that would be easy to make, instead of the difficulty of making comedy records, because comedy records were hard work! You had to get the right material, the right script, the right artist, and so on... When I said that I was willing to listen to anything, it was absolutely true. The comedy records had been fine, and had begun to put Parlophone on the map. But I was looking, with something close to desperation, for an act from the pop world. I was frankly jealous of the seemingly easy success other people were having with such acts, in particular Norrie Paramor, my opposite number on Columbia, whose artist Cliff Richard was on an apparently automatic ride to stardom...' Despite this ambition, the Parlophone boss was proud to wear his laurels as the country's top producer of audio comedy – in March 1962 he was invited to give a lecture at the Blackpool Festival of Live and Recorded Music, entitled 'Humour on Record'.

A blow struck against his pop rival was just around the corner thanks to another comedy development – David Frost may have been correctly criticised for riding Peter Cook's coattails when he graduated from Cambridge in '62, but he certainly swung into action on them with vim, and one of his first jobs was with ATV, researching the music business for an edition of topical programme *This Week*. He lunched with Martin and received all sorts of dirt on the practice of producers giving themselves unearned songwriting credits – naming Paramor in particular. Although *This Week* never acted on the information, Frost developed Martin's testimony into a tirade on his breakthrough show *That Was The Week That Was* (*TW3*) towards the end of the year. Ned Sherrin – as key a figure within Britain's cultural revolution as any big name dropped hitherto – had spearheaded a way of wrangling some of the momentum of *Beyond The Fringe*'s success onto TV screens, with Frost as his grinning figurehead. The programme's two infamous series from November 1962 onwards form an epic saga in their own right, and the embarrassment of George Martin's nemesis caused an early stir as the 'Satire Boom' continued to resound. Of course, no label but Parlophone was considered for the record release of *TW3* highlights, and the single of Millicent Martin's jazzy TV theme.

Peter Cook himself had been banjaxed to learn that while he had been performing *Beyond the Fringe* in New York, 'the bubonic plagiarist' Frost had made himself the star of the satirical revolution he had kicked off back home. But even a young entrepreneur like Cook could not keep too many plates spinning – before the move to Broadway he had opened London's first satirical nightclub, The Establishment, an extremely chic (and claustrophobically popular) venue in Greek Street. Before 1968, the Lord Chamberlain still censored any theatre presentation, and so although cabaret abounded throughout the capital, The Establishment could offer satirical comics absolute creative freedom, and Cook oversaw the formation of a resident comedy team made up of his Footlights co-performers including Johns Bird and Fortune, plus Jeremy Geidt and Eleanor Bron, a sensitively cerebral performer who came from a terribly well-to-do North London family, but who had technically been prevented from full Footlights membership due to the circumstances of her gender – a source of shame for the club not remedied until Eric Idle's presidency in 1964. The Alberts were given a residency in the club too, and visiting guest star Lenny Bruce took such a shine to them he arranged for a US tour which must have stretched many an American idea of what constitutes 'entertainment'.

Establishing The Establishment was a titanic ambition for Cook, but the joy of realising it was not long-lasting, the doors remaining open for only three years. However, besides being the hallowed site of so many moments of comedy history, with satirical magazine *Private Eye* blooming from an upper floor, and comedy careers made, revived and broken on its tiny cabaret stage, one other detail of the club's history is less well known. One of the club's many doormen was a young Liverpudlian called Ivan Vaughan – the very pal who had introduced Paul to John back in 1957. With such an old chum on the door – born on the very same day – it proved irresistible for twenty-year-old Paul McCartney to make a far more sophisticated journey south than when he was half of The Nerk Twins. In October, he hitched to London with his girlfriend Celia Mortimer (she was just seventeen), and though the couple arrived too late to enjoy the comedy, they were happy to dance the night away in the hottest club in Britain. Lewisohn has it that this was the evening McCartney began to piece together 'I Saw Her Standing There', lending 18 Greek Street, Soho a rock heritage to complement its comedy one.

If Paul ever caught up with The Establishment cabaret, it may well have been on vinyl – as a Parlophone release, it should almost go without saying. In fact, it was while immersed in the production of an LP starring The Establishment cast that George Martin received a phone call from publisher Syd Coleman which hinted of a four-piece combo from Liverpool whose songwriting skills could mark them out as worth at least a brief meeting. Apparently unaware or at least unbothered that Epstein had apologetically led the nervous Beatles on wild goose chases for some time by this point, Martin set so little store in the band's recommendation he chose to hand their session at Abbey Road on 6 June to his assistant Ron Richards, until something in 'Love

Me Do' compelled Richards to summon his boss from the canteen, and everyone repaired to the control room for a playback. The Beatles' nerves were all over the place, McCartney perturbed as to why they'd been given 'the comedy guy' as producer, but the dashing Martin was keen to reassure them, 'If there's anything you're not happy about, just speak up.' Nineteen-year-old Harrison was the one who dared to take the leap and retort, 'Well, I don't like your tie for a start.'

In any biopic, this would be the moment for an unbearable beat, an awkward moment registering the looks of genuine consternation from the other Beatles, after all their misery getting to this auspicious point – besides, Martin's tie was brand new, from Liberty's, red and black with horses on it, and he was rather fond of it. However, in his memory, it wasn't like that at all, and he instantly 'fell about the place' laughing, with swift and relieved backing from everyone else in the control room. 'There was a moment of *ohhhh*, but then we laughed and he did too. Being born in Liverpool you have to be a comedian',[39] Harrison later recalled, and engineer Norman Smith added, 'It cracked the ice, and for the next fifteen to twenty minutes The Beatles were pure entertainment. When they left, George and I just sat there saying, "Phew! What d'you think of that lot, then?" I had tears running down my face.' Martin was subsequently told, however, that as soon as he was out of earshot, John and Paul were aghast at George's daring, horrified that their chance may have been blown.

'Even though they had nothing really behind them, they were still fairly irreverent even in those days,' Sir George was to say, 'which I loved, I like a bit of rebel in people, and I liked their sense of humour – after all, that was my main stock-in-trade too, and I guess they quite liked what I'd been doing with Peter Sellers and The Goons.'[40] Just as they had been bonded together by laffs, and had caught Epstein's eye with on-stage tomfoolery, it was humour, once again, which put The Beatles on the next rung of their ladder to the toppermost. Martin's colleagues presumed that 'The Beatles' was another Goonish joke of George's, but they were to be shown otherwise. 'I was very conscious that they exuded a tremendous field of magnetism,' Martin added, 'They had great charisma. When I first signed them, it wasn't because they could write great songs... They had that wonderful, electric vibrancy which made me happy, and I knew it would make everyone else happy too... they made you feel good, to be with them. And, er, I thought their music was rubbish!'[41]

A HAIRDO NAMED ARTHUR

United by this camaraderie and humorous bond, the cautious development of The Beatles' recording careers with George Martin of course centred strongly on the musical, capturing the live voodoo of the group's performances at The Cavern, sans expletives and Arthur Lowe impersonations. Martin and Parlophone obviously remained committed to their outrageously silly output too – in 1963, The Alberts had a long-running surprise hit with their West End Variety show *An Evening of British Rubbish*, and George naturally tried to capture it on disc, even calling the band in to the studio to attempt an audience-free recording. Ultimately, EMI would spike the LP's release on the basis of Bruce Lacey's cover art, which distorted the Union Jack in a way deemed most unpatriotic – fourteen years before the company released The Sex Pistols' similarly adorned 'God Save The Queen', which rankled with Lacey forever more. It's a shame that Martin's recording has never come to light, not least for the inclusion in the show's line-up of a singular talent, Ivor Cutler, a wee bald bespectacled Jewish Glaswegian teacher who was making a quiet name for himself as a poet and writer/performer of the most facetiously unusual skits and short songs, about things like flies, teeth and egg meat. For now, the years of experience Martin had racked up exploring the boundaries of sonic invention in the name of comedy was to have little relevance to The Beatles' recordings, excepting the way in which it gave the producer a singularly free attitude to experimentation. But it was outside of the studios that The Beatles' final arrival on the national pop scene, bolstered by their own Number One record on second attempt, would begin to highlight the four lads' comedy chops.

Peter Sellers' rock and roll sketch had drummed into the boys exactly how they did not want to sound when faced with the press, but none of them had to try too hard to impress interviewers with their natural scouse wit and charm. In their first radio interview, with Merseyside hospital station Radio Clatterbridge, the biggest laugh came once again from George, after the others began listing relations who lived nearby, when he threw in a sarcastic 'I know a man in Chester!' 1962 saw a growing number of promotional chats with local journalists and radio presenters – in Harrogate, this included a future comedy star in young Gordon Kaye, who would add an E to his name before finding fame as René in WWII sitcom *'Allo 'Allo*. Harrison would later sum up the image they began to get across as 'Wacky Moptops, cheeky chappies, y'know, just sort of "Oh hello then, how you doing?" like on the cartoon Beatle things, with little jokes and stuff… Very naive, very sincere, charming but a bit thick.'[42] In Doncaster at the end of the year, the boys had a few moments with Australian DJ Dibbs Mather before a show, which showed that Lennon's poetry was still catching on:

Q:	It's said, John Lennon, that you have the most 'Goon-type' humour of the four Beatles.
JOHN:	Who said that?
Q:	I think I read it in one of the newspapers.
JOHN:	You know what the newspapers are like.
Q:	I don't know. What are they like?
JOHN:	Wrong.
Q:	(*Laughs*) This is going wrong… I want to get a nice 'Personality' bit.
JOHN:	I haven't got a nice personality.
Q:	Is this evidence of Goon-type humour?
JOHN:	No, I don't think I really have Goon-type humour. That's just an expression people use… (Takes crumpled paper from his pocket, reads) 'Dressed in my teenold brownsweaty I easily micked with crown at NevilleClub, a seemy hole. Soon all but soon people acoustic me

saying such thing as "where the charge man?"'... I'm turning it over ... 'All too soon I notice boys and girls sitting in hubbered lumps smoking hernia and taking odeon and getting very high. Somewhere only four foot three high, but he had Indian Hump which he grew in his sleep.'... things like that just help me keep sane.[43]

1963, however, would turn this rising tide of merry chats into a tsunami of coverage, in the year that the tabloid-friendly term 'Beatlemania' was coined. Epstein employed Lancashire journalist Tony Barrow to offer a more sensible press voice for the band. The liner notes Barrow provided for The Beatles' first releases were hardly laff-a-minute, but could lunge into the daft: 'When, in a generation or so, a radio-active, cigar-smoking child, picnicking on Saturn, asks you what the Beatle affair was all about – "Did you actually *know* them?" – don't try to explain all about the long hair and the screams! Just play the child a few tracks from this album and he'll probably understand what it was all about. The kids of AD 2000 will draw from the music much the same sense of well being and warmth as we do today.'[44] When it came to the band's own hype duties, although all four tended to be on their best behaviour at first, their irreverence when faced with the press was never wholly controllable.

The rookie manager was building a stable of very jolly 'all-round entertainers' by now, soon including Liverpool acts Gerry and the Pacemakers and good-time giggling Cavern cloakroom attendant Cilla Black, while his star turns were zooming around the country on tour rubbing shoulders with the kind of heroes they would once have approached for autographs, including Roy Orbison and showbiz legend and gigantic influence Little Richard. Not that the experience was remembered too fondly by Richard, with the incorrigible Lennon's sense of humour showing scant respect for a rock and roll legend: 'Heavens, that John was pure misery! If I would have had a stick, I think I might have beat him with it. He would do horrible things, like get you in a little room, pass gas and run out and lock you in. Oh my, I can still smell it.'[45]

Similar irritation was experienced by a less revered trailblazer of the period, the now disgraced Australian children's entertainer and artist Rolf Harris, whose links to The Beatles included having George Martin produce his 1961 hit 'Sun Arise' (recreating the sound of the didgeridoo with a bank of double-basses), and even covering the 1964 novelty hit 'Ringo For President'. Epstein favoured Harris as a well-equipped compère, and he shared a number of bills with The Beatles, including their first Christmas Show. 'One night while I was on, John was standing in the wings, and had somehow got hold of a live mike,' Harris told Philip Norman. 'With everything I said, his voice would come booming over the PA: "Is that right, Rolf? … Are you sure about that, Rolf?" It fair knocked me through a loop. As soon as I came off, The Beatles went on, so I had to wait to the end of their show to have it out with John but I was still so mad, I was spitting chips. I said, "Look, if you want to fuck up your own act, that's your prerogative, but don't fuck up mine." John just turned on the charm: "Ooh, look, Rolfie's lost his rag…" Being angry with him was like trying to punch away a raincloud.'[46] Rolf was also the presenter of radio special *From Us To You* at the end of '63, and recalled, 'I was sent to interview The Beatles and my hands were shaking so much I could barely flick the switch on the tape recorder. I shoved the mike in John's face and said, "Well, do you like spaghetti then?" Fortunately for me, they all fell about the place… buoyed by their enthusiasm, I pulled out a crumpled song sheet and announced, "I've got something for you boys." I had written a new version of "Tie Me Kangaroo Down Sport" with a verse for each of them. When I asked them if they'd like to sing it with me, they responded with a deafening "*Yes!*"'[47] Altered lyrics on this one-off collaboration included 'Keep the hits coming on, John', 'Prop me up by the wall, Paul' and 'Don't ill-treat me pet dingo, Ringo!' as the presenter wobbled his wobble board and encouraged the band to throw in trademark 'Woooh!' sounds – one of a number of clichés the public quickly picked up on as the band's popularity boomed.

From Us To You – The Beatles' own radio special – was the culmination of a year of wireless antics. The odd TV spot had also come along by 1963, but it was on radio that The Beatles really began to share their daft personalities between songs, first as guests in shows like *Teenager's Turn* or *Here We Go*, and before long as favourite turns on the top pop show *Saturday Club*, a magnet for teenage ears every Saturday morning for a whole generation. Under Martin's patronage, they were cutting classic tracks with tongue nowhere near cheek – for the lamented Decca audition, they had peppered 'Sheik of Araby', cribbed from tour buddies Joe Brown & The Bruvvers, with cries of '*Not 'alf!*' in tribute to DJ Alan 'Fluff' Freeman, and each '*cha-cha-BOOM!*' of 'Besame Mucho' also had the tang of vaudeville about it. As for their live rendition of 'Tequila' – in which John would offer alternative shouts of '*Heil Hitler!*' or simply '*TITS!*' at inappropriate junctures – that was never considered for recording. Besides the dash of cuteness of Ringo singing about 'Boys', and despite the shared humour producer and band were still gleefully discovering together, the first Beatles albums offer passion, and charm, but a distinct tight rein on laffs, and none of the spoofing spirit of 'You'll Be Mine' all those years earlier. The cheeky additions of '*ooh la la*' to their half-hearted attempt at 'How Do You Do It?' may have helped Martin accept that The Beatles weren't going to lend their name to other people's tin-pan-alley offerings, but further musical piss-taking was held in check for the ensuing chain of love-filled pop hits and earnest covers. Let off the leash on radio, however, they could throw in numbers like 'Three Cool Cats', a Leiber/Stoller mini-drama allowing for audio 'cripping' from John as the boys took their turn as each cat, or send themselves up with discordant medleys of their smash hits, far more in the daft spirit of the Cavern lunchtime shows.

The boys' rapport with avuncular but game presenter Brian Matthew quickly began to fizz, and by the end of spring 1963 they were made house band on their own series for the BBC's Light Programme service, *Pop Go The Beatles*, complete with a Merseybeat nursery rhyme theme tune. With new presenters Lee Peters ('Pee Litres') or Rodney Burke as the voice of Auntie Beeb,

The Beatles played host to an array of guest bands, helping to establish themselves as the premier outfit in pop. Between tracks they would still quite sheepishly approach the mic to introduce the next song as coming from 'the very first LP in 1822', to read out a fan letter or spoil a song dedication to 'Di, Gus, Wizz, Wack, and all at the form upper third in Hemel Hempstead' while the other three barracked laffingly from behind. And of course, they would introduce themselves:

RINGO: I'm Ringo and I play the drums.
PAUL: I'm Paul and I play the, erm, bass.
GEORGE: I'm George and I play a guitar. (*Whistle*)
JOHN: I'm John and I too play guitar, sometimes I
            play the fool.[48]

There was hardly much room for comic invention in the pop show formats, and the boys never wasted any time with prep, given their breakneck schedules as their touring spilled out over the British shores. But back home in Blighty, resident on stage at London's Playhouse Theatre where many *Goon Shows* had been recorded, and where the next generation of comics would soon start creating bedlam in the name of *I'm Sorry I'll Read That Again*, the boys could audibly relax and take themselves anything but seriously for a bit.

On the subject of *ISIRTA*, while 1963 was the ultimate year of arrival for The Beatles, the successors to Peter Cook's generation in the Cambridge Footlights were just beginning their own tour. Cleese, Brooke-Taylor, Oddie, Kendall, Hatch and others would go on to make *ISIRTA* the youth comedy hit of the '60s, and *Cambridge Circus* would land the gang in Broadway in a stage of 'The British Invasion' which predated any US knowledge of The Beatles. These public-school-educated postgraduate wits specialised in bizarre and corny jokes, harking back to music hall in a way which displeased their American promoters, and in desperation to form a completely new show before their New York opening, director Humphrey Barclay put word out to the alma mater for any material lying around. He was overjoyed to be offered a silly musical squib performed in a Pembroke College smoker, 'I Want to Hold Your Handel', which mashed up Beatles and choral song with the cast in angelic apparel and hairy Beatle wigs. This idea, which may well constitute the first spoof of the band professionally performed, was provided by first year student and fashionably early Beatles fan Eric Idle. The sketch's inclusion, however, didn't prevent the show from closing unfashionably early.

Probably the strongest hook the general public had on The Beatles for comic purposes at first was their hair (thur hurr), and soon, as every newspaper realised they had to have maximum Beatle coverage every day, the country's favourite new sensation started to make regular print cartoon appearances – four near-indistinguishable mop-topped gnome figures pottering about causing mayhem wherever they played. The Conservative cabinets headed by PMs Harold MacMillan and Alec Douglas Home were caricatured in wigs and Pierre Cardin suits, cynically trying to attract votes from 'the younger generation', or begging the band to stand as Tory candidates, because 'after all, you've never had it so good!' The national obsession with the Fab hairdos led to so many interminable questions that it was the main topic which fired up The Beatles' sarcasm:

Q:	How do you feel about teenagers imitating you with Beatle wigs?
JOHN:	They're not imitating us because we don't wear Beatle wigs.
Q:	What do you call that hairstyle you're wearing?
GEORGE:	Arthur.
Q:	Can you ever go anywhere unnoticed?
PAUL:	When we take off our wigs.
Q:	Where'd you get the idea for your haircuts?
JOHN:	Where'd you get the idea for yours?
Q:	Do you wear wigs?
JOHN:	If we do they must be the only ones with real dandruff!
Q:	Where do your hair-dos originate from?

GEORGE:	Our scalps.
Q:	How do you sleep at night with your hair so long?
JOHN:	Well when you're asleep at night you don't notice.
Q:	What's the biggest threat to your careers: the atom bomb or dandruff?
RINGO:	The atom bomb. We've already got dandruff.

After hair, next on the cliché list was how much money the band were raking in, and what they would do 'when the bubble burst'. Ringo's sincere aspiration to run a chain of hairdressing salons was even sent up in the BBC documentary *The Mersey Sound*, which filmed the drummer out of his depth at a barber's. The lack of invention shown by most journalists was a drag, but the wry replies maintained the gushing position held by Maureen Cleave in the *Evening Standard:* 'They are bound together by their hair, their music and their jokes… apart from laughing, their main occupation is music.' The *Daily Mirror* echoed the approval: 'You have to be a real sour square not to love the nutty, noisy, happy, handsome Beatles… The Beatles are whacky. They wear their hair like a mop – but it's washed, it's super-clean. So is their fresh young act.' Lennon's summation of the quick-fire wit they had to put into play as the questions just kept coming was less approving: 'We were funny at press conferences because it was all a joke! They'd ask joke questions, so you'd give joke answers. But we weren't really funny at all. It was just Fifth-Form humour, the sort you laugh at at school. They were putrid.'[49]

John further undermined the cliché of himself as the acidic Beatle early on, pointing out to the *NME* that his reputation was 'very useful. A lot of slimy little reporter types seem to fear me. It's fantastic. I didn't work for the title of the vicious Beatle, the biting Beatle, the one with the rapier wit. It's a load of crap. But it is handy being tagged like this. When I meet intelligent and hip people I have to be on my toes not to disillusion them. The people who have fallen for my image and publicity go to Paul, which I think is funnier still. Paul can be very cynical and much more biting than me when he's driven to it. 'Course, he's got more patience. But he can carve people up in no time at all, when he's pushed. He hits the nail right on the head and doesn't beat about the bush, does Paul' 'The Beatles were asked the stupidest and most basic of questions,' their first press officer Tony Barrow added. 'What happened was, whenever they were asked an awkward question, and they felt they were backed up into a corner, they very often fought their way out of that corner by going for the laugh line... that would get them off the hook, also make the journalist look pretty much a fool for asking such a daft question, but it did mean that the press conferences more and more turned into straightforward variety shows, vaudeville, with an audience... great roars of laughter and applause at the "turn"! The earliest joking was a direct result of nervous reaction to sweaty-palmed press conference situations, the rest taking their cue from John Lennon, the most accomplished – and cynical – satirist amongst the quartet.'[50]

Real comedy 'turns' were far from exempt from the desire to bask in the Fab glory, and some of TV's biggest names were thrilled to appear alongside the band. They could be funny without the aid of comics too, John joshing with an overly charmed Dusty Springfield on *Ready Steady Go* about his scabs, deflecting her giggling adoration, and merrily marring the band's mimed performance by scratching his nose mid-song. The band's second big TV booking in May saw them entertaining the kiddies live on *Pops and Lenny*, a lost BBC programme starring camp lion Lenny, created by Lancashire ventriloquist Terry Hall, and even joining the hairy star in a sing-a-long of 'After You've Gone' at the show's close. But the first human comedians to nab a Beatle guest spot were eternally derided light entertainers Mike & Bernie Winters, presenters of North Country ABC Television's *Big Night Out* Variety show. The brothers – gawky Bernie and straight Mike – were from North London, but welcomed the boys up to Didsbury Studios, while being reportedly miffed that the gangs of screaming girls weren't for them. A kind of prototype Ant & Dec, the Winters brothers have been wedged firmly in the history of Variety as the dire flip-side of Morecambe & Wise, but the explosion-packed wackiness of the Winters' ITV Variety show did put The Beatles in front of the cameras in comedic sketch situations for the first time – usually centred on Bernie's bewigged belief that he was much better than John, Paul, George or Ringo.

As the band's popularity ballooned ever further, the slowly burgeoning teen pop scene in British TV provided ample scope for them to perform their hits, mimed or otherwise, but as The Beatles and their management were effectively creating the pop-rock business as they went along, the fact was these four lads were now part of 'show business', and in Britain, that meant variety, defined by Andrew Loog Oldham as 'a world of regimented entertainment, summer seasons and pantomime', and any band who weren't able to charm with their instruments down and get involved with the fun would only get so far. 'We'd sometimes get booked on variety bills,' Paul said. 'I remember a comedian called Derek Roy once introduced us, a poppy-eye English comedian who was now fallen on hard times, and the only way I knew of him was from a comic called *Radio Fun*, when I'd been a little kid… in it were people like Frank Randle… they used to have a terrible time because the audience only wanted to see us. They did not want to listen to the ramblings of a demented old comedian. But we also had people like Dave Allen, who was just starting off. He was very good. Dave could handle it, he was irreverent, knew how to do this kind of stuff.'

Another pop-themed opportunity for the band to shine was the BBC's *Juke Box Jury*, the still-missed panel show in which celebrities voted the latest chart single a hit or miss. John had made a solo appearance in June 1963, but his constant rubbishing of every song offered up – particularly Elvis' 'Devil in Disguise' – did not endear him to audiences very much. The duff appearance wasn't helped by airing amid news reports of John punching Bob Wooler in the face at Paul's 21st birthday party back home, allegedly because of Wooler's cracks about what John and Brian had been getting up to on their recent Spanish holiday. Paul had encouraged his kid brother to perform with The Scaffold for the event, as the outfit were finding their feet, but the punch-up made a bigger impression. When all four Beatles starred in their own special *Juke Box Jury* five months later, they would be on better behaviour.

You knew you had made it in 1963 when you found yourself on the independent station's pride and joy – Val Parnell's *Sunday Night at the London Palladium*, the bastion of glamour and talent. That very year, Jimmy Tarbuck wowed the crowds with his scouse charm, and two years later would take over as compère, but when The Beatles made their first appearance on 13 October, long thin hoofer Bruce Forsyth's capable hands were on the steering wheel. Even given the great year the band had enjoyed, the scenes of hysteria which clogged up the streets around the London theatre were unimagined, triggering equally hysterical front pages the next day spreading the 'Beatlemania' meme further and further. Brucie absolutely wound the situation up for all he was worth from the very start of the show, stepping on stage in full Beatles costume and the inevitable wig to disappoint the expectant young crowd. Also on the bill was veteran comic-loving crooner and Eric Morecambe plaything Des O'Connor, who shuddered: 'I went on just before they did and had six minutes for my act, I could barely hear myself! I knew the audience wanted me out of the way as soon as possible so I made jokes and sang bits of Beatles songs. When I heard Paul warming up on bass behind the curtain, I cut my act short by two minutes.'

Faced with the wall of screaming, Lennon went into full 'cripping' mode throughout, stamping his feet with rubber legs as Paul gamely tried to introduce 'Twist & Shout', but besides one link where all four attempted to introduce a song at the same time, there was little messing around in their tight spot. After the last chord, the whole cast returned to the stage as it rotated its weight of grinning, waving talents and the familiar theme played out. This must have been a life-defining thrill for the theatre-adoring Brian Epstein, his boys the darlings of this revered London stage – but was it also what Lennon was thinking when he said, 'You have to completely humiliate yourself to be what The Beatles were'?

He would be more prepared in November when the showbiz honour took its next step up, to the very height of British variety

– supremo impresario Bernard Delfont had booked them to top the bill at that year's *Royal Variety Performance*. The attendance of HRH The Queen Mother with Princess Margaret did not deferentially tone down the white-hot scream-saturated bedlam of Beatlemania, and few of the other acts could get by without making some reference to the performers everyone was waiting for, especially compère Max Bygraves. Besides Burt Bacharach and Marlene Dietrich, Eric Sykes & Hattie Jacques, diminutive comic Charlie Drake held his own, and if any stars deserved second billing to The Beatles, it was Steptoe & Son. The rag and bone men sitcom had only launched on the BBC the previous year, created by Spike Milligan's colleagues at Associated London Scripts, Ray Galton & Alan Simpson, but as portrayed by tiny wiry Irish actor Wilfrid Brambell as 'dirty old man' Albert Steptoe, with Harry H Corbett as Son Harold, they had already wheedled their way into public affections, and a Royal audience.

Besides a rather unfair crack at large singer Sophie Tucker from Paul, the group seemed uncharacteristically stolid throughout their wild set, until the very end, where instead of the usual request for noise to accompany 'Twist & Shout', John took to the mic with his best 'Just William' innocent look, bit his lip, and announced:

JOHN: For our last number I'd like to ask your help. Would the people in the cheaper seats clap your hands, and the rest of you, if you'd just rattle yer jewellery…

Of course, it didn't at all faze the Queen Mother, who afterwards charmingly replied to McCartney's meek admission that they were playing Slough the next day with a beaming 'Oh, that's just near us!' But the way the caustic, angry, farting, rebellious John Lennon had faced down the Queen's closest kin and played court jester, licenced to mock, thumbing his nose at the riches of the British upper classes, standing in the spotlight of the opulent Prince of Wales theatre, was what made the news the next day, and all of Britain was nattering about the cheek. There was nothing ad-lib about the moment: Alistair Taylor recalled all four Beatles playing around with lines – 'throw yer tiaras in the air', 'wave yer crown' – but the joke was to echo through the ages, and at least Brian could be relieved that John didn't go through with his very real threat to add a 'fucking' before 'jewellery'. Lennon, as ever, played the moment down: 'I cracked a joke on stage. I was fantastically nervous, but I wanted to say something to rebel a bit, and that was the best I could do.'[51]

There was still much more to pack in before their flight to America in the New Year, and they already knew a movie was agreed upon to start shooting in early 1964, but The Beatles' incredible year, which saw them finally rise to that much-mocked poppermost pedestal in British entertainment, was capped by a cheeky gag and a theatre-filling roar of rapturous laughter. As the UK's greatest stars, they were going to have to learn to take it as well as dishing it out, though – that year's festive charts saw the band's own hits joined by the sugary snark of comedian Dora Bryan's 'All I Want For Christmas Is A Beatle', a novelty record which Dora was always proud to announce was voted the worst single of 1963.

Despite all their successes, George Martin was happy to tell the boys, 'Success hasn't changed you. You're still the arrogant, self-opinionated bastards that you always were!' Looking back at the breakthrough of 1963, George Harrison mused, 'I think that was an important part of The Beatles – people associate humour with us. When all the new bands first came out, Gerry and the Pacemakers and others, nobody could tell who was who... Even if you had a hit you needed something else to carry you. The Beatles actually were very funny, and even when our humour was transposed to New York, or somewhere else, it was still great. We were just being hard-faced really, but people loved it... Everyone in Liverpool thinks they're a comedian. Just drive through the Mersey Tunnel and the guy on the tollbooth will be a comedian. We've had that born and bred into us. And in our case the humour was made even stronger by the fact that there were four of us bouncing off one another. If one dried up somebody else was already there with another fab quip.'[52]

– CHAPTER TWO –
IN THEIR OWN WRITE

 'You know the way people begin to look like their dogs?
Well, we're beginning to look like each other!'

'The way we work is like, we just whistle.
John will whistle at me and I'll whistle back at him.'

 'MBE really stands for Mr Brian Epstein.'

'Beatles, women and children first!'

Before drawing the deep breath preparatory to wowing America on *The Ed Sullivan Show*, there were exciting TV bookings to honour back home – one in particular causing the most excitement in the group, performing with Morecambe & Wise in their ATV comedy show. Eric & Ernie had by this point become regular faces on Sullivan's coast-to-coast talent showcase, but unlike The Beatles, Eric's devotion to home and their hard-won fanbase meant that Hollywood stardom would never come the pair's way, even if their eventual unequivocal place as Britain's most beloved comedy duo was to be a great consolation.

An odd comedy reunion was to come before the meeting of Britain's top band with Britain's top double act, however, when Granada's *Late Scene Extra* trained its cameras on Ken Dodd in conversation with the boys, mediated by Irish TV veteran Gay Byrne – the first presenter ever to introduce The Beatles on TV.

Dodd had developed a singular addiction to provoking titters since his debut, and worked his rear-end off to become one of Liverpool's rising stars years before the band formed. By 1962 he boasted his own radio show, co-scripted by one of Liverpool's greatest gagsmiths, ex-market trader Eddie Braben, who would become key to Morecambe & Wise's rise to the very top of LE several years later. The Beatles had guested on Dodd's Variety show back in September (albeit after Gerry and the Pacemakers) and though the boys hadn't taken part in any scripted japes, Dodd and his team, including Scottish actor John Laurie, formed their own Merseybeat group, 'The Doddles', in the guests' honour, which mainly involved banging on buckets and howling.

Their combined Mersey chemistry was clearly a coup for late night TV, but that said, the fifteen-minute studio item teaming the toothy eccentric with the young pop stars, while studded with flashes of hilarity, did also have some of the hallmarks of a slightly strained conversation between acquaintances in a trapped lift. What the archive footage shows is that The Beatles were witty responders to journalists, but if the producer hoped their madness would flow spontaneously, they were mistaken, and the interview's success relied heavily on Ken and occasionally Gay geeing the bemused boys along amid the former's improvised flights of fancy about jam butties and writing a musical about Charles II for them. Perhaps the best gag of all was George's suggestion that if the comic wanted an 'earthy name' on joining the group, he should go for 'Ken Sod'. The subject was steered onto the topic of musicians and comics, and dangerously close to sincere territory:

KEN:	I've seen you do comedy as well – John, you do some, er… very good lines, that one about rattling their jewels, that was very good, that, I've used it since…
JOHN:	You owe me five bob.
KEN:	But you do clowning yourselves – would you in time work gags into your act?
JOHN:	I don't know… most of our gags are made

	up, and they either die, or we keep 'em if they go down well. That jewel thing we thought of the night before, y'know.
GAY:	It certainly went down well, didn't it?
KEN:	So you'd like to do a bit more comedy?
JOHN:	Yeah, but it's so hard, isn't it? (*Grins at Ken*)
PAUL:	It'll be easier when we get him in the group, though, we'll leave it all up to him then.
KEN:	Yeah, I'll be the one in the baggy pants...[53]

GET OUT OF THAT!

On 2 December, the Beatles finally got to join Eric & Ernie in front of the TV cameras with a live audience, for their much-anticipated comedic clash – although the episode would not air until April, a very long time in Beatle terms. The duo's writers Sid Hills & Dick Green had concocted a barrage of mutual abuse not that distinct from Mike & Bernie Winters' own patter, but the delivery of Morecambe in particular, with Wise in charge, could raise any material to new heights.

Having been included on *The Beatles Anthology* programme and audio releases, these skits will be known to many Beatlemaniacs off by heart, but to most listeners not from the UK, the significance of this meeting between two British entertainment icons was lost. Though fifteen years older than the Beatles, this was still a relatively youthful Morecambe & Wise in their first burst of nationwide success. Some traditional elements of their act were already in place by 1963 – Ernie's 'short fat hairy legs' and Eric's pincer movement cry of 'Get out of that!' – but it was only after their successful switch to the BBC at the end of the '60s (and largely thanks to Eddie Braben's scouse wit-packed scripts) that Morecambe & Wise's drubbing of celebrity guests would become the lynchpin of their show.

This turned out to be their only chance to rib the UK's greatest group – with the last strains of 'I Want To Hold Your Hand' ringing out, the best little straight man of the century stepped forward to bask in The Beatles' charismatic glow:

ERNIE:	Boys! What I was thinking was, would you like to do a number with us? You know, we'd like to do a number together. (*They all nod along*) You fancy that? Great!
ERIC:	(*Squawks in triumph*) EEEY! It's The Kay Sisters, they've come! Great! Fabulous!
ERNIE:	The Kay sisters?! This is…
ERIC:	Have you dyed your hair?
ERNIE:	…This is The Beatles!
ERIC:	*'Ellooo, Beatles!* Where is he? There he is! Hello, Bongo! Hey!
ERNIE:	That's Ringo!
ERIC:	Oh, is he there as well? … oh dear. By golly!
ERNIE:	Boys! As you can gather this is Eric. Say hello to Eric.
PAUL:	Hello, Eric!
ERIC:	Hello, mate!
PAUL:	I remember you, you're the one with the short fat hairy legs!
ERIC:	No, no, he's the one with the short fat hairy legs. No, him.
GEORGE:	We're the ones with the big fat hairy heads. *Get out of that!*
ERIC:	He-hey! What's it like being famous?
JOHN:	(*Shaking hands with and eyeballing Eric*) Well, it's not like in your day, you know.
ERIC:	What? That's an insult, that is! You didn't expect that, did you?
ERNIE:	No!
ERIC:	What do you mean 'not like in my day'?
JOHN:	Well, me dad used to tell me about you, you know. (*Gestures 'yea high'*)
PAUL:	In the old days!
ERIC:	You've only got a little dad, have you? Yer dad used to tell yer? That's a bit strong, innit? Alright, Bonzo?
ERNIE:	That's Ringo!

61

ERIC:	Yeah, him as well. Get 'em off, Ern, they've done enough.
ERNIE:	What do you mean 'done enough'?
ERIC:	No, well I'm getting insulted now…
ERNIE:	No, look, what I was going to suggest was, let's do a number with the boys!
ERIC:	Oh yes! One that the dad will remember. That I used to do, with yer dad![54]

Eric in particular was a stickler for rehearsal right down the line, but the looseness which must have been a result of The Beatles' packed schedule did nothing to lessen the charm of this face-off. Every episode of this series ended with Eric failing to get across a filthy old gag – 'Two dirty old men sitting in deckchairs: one says "It's nice out", and the other says "Yes, I think I'll take mine out too!"' – and his invitation to John to give it a go before the credits rolled seemed to result in a spot of genuine Lennon subversion when he began 'These two old men sitting in a dirty deckchair…' and caused the hosts to crack up. Though the inclusion of an edited version of the appearance in *Anthology* may have seemed more bemusing than amusing to many fans around the world, to most Brits there remains no hyperbole in Ernie's announcement that 'we're gonna make history on television – for the first time we have Morecambe & Wise and The Beatles presenting to you that wonderful old-fashioned number, "On Moonlight Bay"', as everyone changed into striped minstrel jackets and straw boaters… bar Eric, of course, who threw on the now traditional wig and Beatle suit like Brucie and Bernie before him, for cries of 'Twist and Shout!' (plus Gerry & The Pacemakers' 'I Like It!') throughout the crooned golden oldie: one for the grannies. Here were six 'all-round entertainers' indeed, entertaining each other in front of the cameras.

Nothing quite exemplified this – or indeed, tweaked Lennon's spleen – as much as *The Beatles Christmas Show*, which opened at Finsbury Park's Astoria Cinema on Christmas Eve, and ran until 11 January. As any Brit knows, this is pantomime season, and so Brian's theatrical urges pushed what could have been a straightforward pop gig into panto territory, with silly skits, audience participation, and all the gender-bending jolly dressing up the season demanded. Again, The Beatles were famous before their time, making up the rock biz as they went, and it's hard to think of any other rock icons – Hendrix, Clapton, Bowie – who actually went so far as to *perform panto* for their fans (although Epstein did also book Gerry and the Pacemakers for *Babes In The Wood* at the Hanley Gaumont). 'We didn't like the idea of pantomime,' Harrison insisted, 'so we did our own show – like a pop show, but we kept appearing every few minutes, dressed up for a laugh.'[55] Neil Aspinall reflected, 'It was good that they could still get involved with shows like those funny little sketches at Christmas. For a rock 'n' roll band, it was amazing. That came from art school days and the rag night. They could still join in that sort of fun.'[56]

Old school friend and Fabs insider Tony Bramwell recalled, 'It was fun, being around them while the crazy and over-the-top ideas were bounced back and forth. It ended up a kind of cod "Perils of Pauline"… the audience went wild and wolf-whistled pretty George like crazy… It was all very loose with a great deal of ad-libbing when they forgot their lines or what part they were each playing.'[57] There was little call for anything but music, with support from Cilla, Rolf and the Barron Knights (jocular musicians happy to send up their hosts – their single 'Call Up The Groups' had imagined The Beatles being conscripted into the army), and the extra dose of silliness for the season never sat well with the boys, but they went along with the daft Victorian melodrama send-up, Harrison even accepting the female role in proper cross-dressing panto style. No surviving script has ever surfaced, but Tony Barrow recalled that the attempt to turn the country's favourite musicians into actors was not a high point: 'By proper theatrical standards the production was an awful mess. This was not the fault of those who were staging the show. There was ridiculously inadequate rehearsal time, the sketches involving The Beatles were an utter shambles and, in the event, dialogue was wholly obliterated by continuous screaming. This was the first time that The Beatles had tried to involve themselves in a "produced" stage presentation. They obtained little artistic satisfaction from the whole thing but the audiences went home pleased and, after all, these were the punters who had paid to be present... The Beatles were never much for rehearsing. That never really mattered as far as songs were concerned, but the fact that they were so bad at doing the sketches was an added extra for the show – it was organised chaos but it was very funny chaos.'[58] The *NME*'s report was even more forgiving: 'The Beatles are seen on four occasions through the show, which is good value in itself... The show has a clever opening with all the artists emerging from a helicopter to take their bow. The subsequent sketch with The Beatles in doctor uniforms (giving us the first ever glimpse of John Lennon wearing glasses on stage) was as weak as it was brief, but that hardly mattered as it gave a second glimpse of the Fab Foursome. The Beatles provided a further non-musical interlude by way of their "Sir Jasper" sketch, which was brilliant in both its conception and their performance of it. Fortunately someone had had the foresight to present the words they spoke on a screen behind them – for they couldn't possibly have been heard. At the display of the words "it is snowing", Ringo danced on stage wearing a grin we rarely see him with, scattering make-believe snow; as the villain of the plot John "Sir Jasper" in a cloak and top hat secured "Mrs" George Harrison adorned in a shawl and "her baby" to the railway line. But hero (of course) "Fearless Paul" McCartney saved George from the path of an on-coming train.'[59] 'Let's face it,' Paul admitted, 'they would have laughed if we just sat there reading the Liverpool telephone directory.'

Christmas was also marked by the first rudimentary stab at the annual tradition of The Beatles' Fan Club Christmas records – flexidiscs of seasonal greetings snatched between song recordings, which in its first instance wasn't much more comedic than the boys' usual reading out of fan mail on the radio. The discs were slight loss-makers for NEMS, but Epstein was happy to foot the bill in the season of goodwill – Tony Barrow had the original brainwave, and wrote the awkward bumph for the boys to read – or rather, send up mercilessly. 'Every year we'd take ten minutes of the session time and do nonsense like this,' Paul told

Miles, 'EMI was such a sort of funny place in those days. We thought of it in the same terms as the BBC: sort of huge monolithic corporation, but groovy with it. I remember when we went to the toilets, there was this old-fashioned bog roll, and on every sheet it had "PROPERTY OF EMI LTD" – what, they think someone's gonna nick it?'[60] Besides John and George's daft lyrics in their discordant carolling of 'Good King Wenceslas' and a sarcastic whistle of the national anthem on mentioning the *Royal Variety Performance*, the first flexi was the simplest fan service, but in years to come the boys grew sick of the robotic doling out of platitudes, and began to utilise George Martin's skill with soundscapes to record some very silly and unnecessarily adventurous audio comedy.

The idea of live subtitles amid the din of screaming fans came in handy once again for The Beatles' last appearance on *Sunday Night at the London Palladium*, alongside pals Alma Cogan and Dave Allen. Forsyth reminisced that the bosses were keen for the boys to show their comedic sides, but it wasn't easy: 'For The Beatles' second show, Val Parnell wanted more than three straight numbers. He was convinced there was something else we could do… it became apparent that if we tried to do anything extra with the band, anything that involved them speaking, no one would hear a word. Then an idea struck me. The audience might not be able to hear a word, but they could still see. So why don't I hold a visual conversation with the boys? Between their second and last song each of them could run on and offstage to grab different cue cards, introducing themselves and responding to questions.' The skit concluded with the whole band lining up to spell out the order, 'GET OFF YOU NIT'. Unabashed, Brucie continued, 'The routine was a big success. The Beatles had that fantastic attitude of being willing to give anything a go to inject some fun. I wish I'd worked with them more.'[61]

At last, with this midwinter foolery completed, the fateful moment came when The Beatles turned left at Greenland, and exploded in a shower of screaming and laughter on American soil. Ken Dodd had joshed that the boys were all aliens a few weeks earlier, but to their new audience, the wisecracking quartet could not have been more of a novelty, and a tonic. Never would their quick tongues and daffy cheek be more required, as a scrum of ravenous journalists, including their loudest advocate, New York DJ Murray the K, fired off less than welcoming questions about how much money they were planning to take from the US – and of course, inevitably, American barbers in particular:

Q:	Are you a little embarrassed by the lunacy you cause?
JOHN:	No, it's great… We like lunatics.
Q:	You're in favour of lunacy?
JOHN:	Yeah. It's healthy…
Q:	Liverpool is the…
RINGO:	It's the capital of Ireland.
PAUL:	Anyway, we wrote half of your folk songs in Liverpool.
RINGO:	Yeah, don't forget!
Q:	In Detroit Michigan, they're handing out car stickers saying, 'Stamp Out The Beatles.'
PAUL:	Yeah well first of all, we're bringing out a 'Stamp Out Detroit' campaign…
RINGO:	How big are they?
Q:	How many of you are bald, that you have to wear those wigs?
RINGO:	All of us.
PAUL:	I'm bald… Don't tell anyone, please.
JOHN:	And deaf and dumb, too…
Q:	What do you think your music does for these people?
RINGO:	I don't know. It pleases them, I think. Well, it must do, 'cause they're buying it…
PAUL:	We don't know. Really.
JOHN:	If we knew, we'd form another group and be managers.
Q:	What do you think of Beethoven?
RINGO:	Great. Especially his poems.

Two days later, on 9 February, their first appearance on Ed Sullivan's show would make history, without a single gag – or even a word from any of them – required. To a country in desperate need of cheering up in the aftermath of Kennedy's assassination in November, the sound and sight of the four smiling lads, a fully formed entertainment phenomenon, witnessed by seventy million viewers, was enough to win over most of the country, kids and adults, even though the closest thing to levity present was the added caption for John – 'SORRY GIRLS, HE'S MARRIED'. As they dipped their toe into the birthplace of rock and roll, with so few precursors to this madcap foursome, the US press stepped up the idea of the band as 'the new Marx Brothers', originally mooted by Maureen Cleave, which held little water, and John griped, 'when people start comparing us to the Marx Brothers, that's a load of rubbish! The only similarity is that there were four of them and there are four of us.'[62] Groucho himself did become a voluble fan, attending their Hollywood Bowl concerts on their second US visit (plus, in a roundabout way, he bequeathed his luxurious circular bed to Paul – via Alice Cooper – to complement the geodesic dome at McCartney's London home).

Photo opportunities allowed The Beatles to further communicate their zany side to America – staging a four-way knockout when visiting Cassius Clay, for instance – and the constant presence of the Maysles brothers filming the mini-tour for a documentary forced them to be 'on' for an exhausting amount of time, clowning around in hotel rooms and in transit. The resultant film is so in love with Paul he almost seems like the leader of the group, and he certainly shows the most insistent comic reflexes, flitting between silly voices from British RP to insincere US reporter to lobotomised northerner to caustic Welshman. He even entertains when on the opposite side of the spectrum, sitting back smoking a fag complaining, 'I'm not in a laughing *mood*, even', or reading through transcripts of their recent press event, deadpanning: '"We're all bald"... *funny*.'

The all-too-sudden return of this new sensation to their homeland seemed to traumatise American fans, triggering an outpouring of bandwagon-jumping tributes, spoofs and cash-ins of all kinds, before and after the first proper Beatles US tour later in the year. These discs were largely split into two broadly gendered camps, either yearning for the band's return, or warning them to keep well away from America, get a haircut and stop wearing such 'tight pants'. Dora Bryan's novelty single was to be joined by a deluge of far worse offerings, bland cash-ins called things like 'Beatle Walk' or 'Beatle Wig Party', and angsty love songs from Donna Lee's sappy 'My Boyfriend Got a Beatle Haircut', to Cher's debut 'Ringo I Love You YEAH YEAH YEAH!' The drummer had inadvertently scored a particular hit with an American public not typically noted for their support of the underdog, and his sad eyes and winsome grin inspired a disturbing number of bizarre tributes in a jumble of genres, from doo-wop to bluegrass to calypso. There were even Halloween novelty singles in the vein of 'The Monster Mash', such as Gene Moss' 'I Want To Bite Your Hand'. Scores of male pop acts launched desperate attempts to grab Beatle appeal, or mock the English interlopers, but the closest these bitter ersatz Fab tracks came to amusing was The Four Preps' 'A Letter to The Beatles':

...My girl wrote a letter to The Beatles, saying,
"Beatles, I'd give you anything, all of my true love."
But they wrote a letter back to her, saying,
"That ain't enough! You gotta send us 25 cents
For an autographed picture, $1 bill for a fan club card,
And if you send in right away you get a lock of hair
From a St. Bernard!"

Murray the K may have claimed 'Fifth Beatle' status, but other DJs were quick to get in on the act, and satirical record releases included one 'Ed Solomon' cheesily narrating a flying saucer invasion by The Beatles packed with song samples, while Casey Kasem released his only single (a strangely straight fan story, 'Letter From Elaina', backed by an orchestral 'And I Love Her') a few years before taking on the mantle of Scooby Doo's best friend Shaggy. America's deathless satire periodical *Mad* also began a long campaign of spiking the nation's Beatlemania, portraying mascot Alfred E Neuman in a Beatle wig very early on, but the makers never gave the impression that they were anything but huge fans, and their attention was rewarded with a cameo from a copy of *Son of Mad* in *A Hard Day's Night*, as read by fictional roadie Shake in the film's opening train sequence.

Despite the greatest surge forward in their story so far, The Beatles' return to chilly Blighty must have felt like business as usual, particularly the journey to *Big Night Out* for the second of three appearances. The returning heroes sailed up the Thames to the Teddington studios, George providing an Oxbridge Boat Race-style commentary as they went, only to burst through the wall at the top of the show, burnt and bedraggled like living Looney Tunes characters. They also performed in a quickie, smuggling suitcases of dollar bills past customs officers Mike and Bernie, and each got one line in a sketch which saw them becoming part of a six-piece band:

BERNIE:	I'll tell you something, I still believe that we are definitely the best group in the country, and we should definitely be on that *Thank Your Lucky Stars.*
PAUL:	Yeah, but maybe they wouldn't like us.
MIKE:	Wouldn't like us? You've got no confidence, of course they'd like us. Mind you, there is something wrong with the act.
RINGO:	Maybe it's our hair.
MIKE:	The hair's great! Noses, possibly.
BERNIE	Oh, he's started!... It's definitely the name, the name is definitely wrong for this group.
MIKE:	What's wrong with 'The Mike Winters Six'?
BERNIE:	It doesn't mean anything, it's 1964, we've got to be with it, Daddio, wow! You know, we need something earthy, something, a good name... what about 'The Beatles'?
GEORGE:	'The *Beatles*'? You're joking? Terrible!
MIKE:	That was good, George!... No, The Beatles,

	nah, it's not right, let's look at this thing scientifically – who's the top of the hit parade now?
BERNIE:	The top of the hit parade is whatsisname, Cilla Black.
JOHN:	Let's call ourselves Cilla Black then.
MIKE:	Tell you what, let's watch television.
BERNIE:	What's on?
MIKE:	You know what's on.
BERNIE:	It's that *Big Night Out*, innit? (*Everyone groans, John gives thumbs down*) Have you seen that show, with those two fellas who keep getting blown up? Absolute rubbish…
RINGO:	Cup of tea?
BERNIE:	That's right, make a cup of tea.
MIKE:	And I'll have some chocolate biscuits! (*The boys all file out*)
BERNIE:	Listen, we've got to get rid of those four fellas.
MIKE:	Why?
BERNIE:	Because they're holding me back, that's why![63]

The deliveries may have been stilted – John in particular crashing a laugh and performing his line like a Third Shepherd in an Infants' Nativity play – but maybe their next comedy outing would have a better script to perform.

FOUR BOYS IN THE WIND

Hardly anyone even remotely involved with the production of *A Hard Day's Night* has ever hinted at the film being anything but a breeze, and an intense pleasure, throughout its breakneck-rapid creation. Epstein was undeniably lucky to have responded to the attentions of United Artists, the most liberal and creative-friendly studio in Hollywood, but when the contracts were signed at the end of 1963, few of the suits felt it would be anything but a cash-in. Between ink meeting contract and 'action' being called, the newfound devotion of the US fans changed all that. The boys had avoided disaster when Epstein toyed with lending the band to feature in a British teen movie about unwanted pregnancy, *The Yellow Teddy Bears,* but now a deal was struck, the four-headed beast was adamant that they wouldn't appear in a typical Brit teen flick like Cliff Richard's *Summer Holiday* – all four Beatles loathed everything that had gone before in the mini-genre, and their addition to it had to be worthy of the band's unique success. John insisted, 'We'd made it clear to Brian that we weren't interested in one of those typical nobody-understands-our-music plots where the local dignitaries are trying to ban something as terrible as the Saturday night hop!'[64] Richard Lester recalled, 'I think the Beatles were more interested in not being like the other films than I was, because I don't think I'd seen that many of them. I did know, deep down inside me, that I wanted it to be as natural an experience for them as possible. And what was important was we tried to delineate their personalities, because there was always that sense, especially when being with them, that they were always four parts of one man – they were very protective, very close and very like each other. To help out, it was important to create artificially that George was mean, that Paul was the cute one, John was the cynic, and Ringo was up the back and unloved.'[65]

Lester called action on 2 March and wrapped on 24 April with only a few short weeks left for all the agonies of post-production before the twin premieres in London and Liverpool in July – all while honouring the modest £200,000 budget provided by producer Walter Shenson. He was abetted by some of the finest crew in the world, Associate Producer Denis O'Dell laughed, 'We managed to put together a crew of top-flight people for bottom-flight money.' Still, for a self-confessed 'kick-bollock-and-scramble' director, this was a supreme achievement which rewarded Dick with a fascinating career in cinema. Not that this was his first film, and it's always overlooked by Beatle historians how much practice Lester had already had in making musical comedy – his previous movie *The Mouse On The Moon* was the sequel to a Peter Sellers film with a whole host of beloved British comedy actors making up for the temperamental Sellers' absence, but 1962's *It's Trad, Dad!* (unfortunately AKA *Ring-a-Ding Rhythm*) had the most hackneyed (albeit tenuous) through-line of talented kids Craig Douglas and Helen Shapiro (pre-Beatle-supported tour) showing the fusty older generation that their jukebox-loving frothy coffee antics were alright really by 'putting on the show right here' and so on. Still, although the film wasn't funny (it featured Arthur Mullard), putting interesting monochrome pictures to the lesser loved songs of Gene Vincent, Chubby Checker, The Temperance Seven and others was as clear an audition for helming The Beatles' cinema debut as Shenson needed.

'They accepted me because I was a poor piano player and therefore they at least felt that I would understand where an 8-bar phrase should be and how I could cut round it,' Dick said, 'and they accepted Alun as the writer because he seemed to be able to produce a sound they could manage to do, and as they say pathetically, the rest is history.' On meeting the director of one of their favourite bits of cinematic goonery the previous autumn, the band's approval was no surprise, nor did they object to Dick's nomination of old mucker Alun Owen. True, Lennon was said to have squared up to the Welsh-Irish-Liverpudlian writer growling 'The trouble with you, Alun, is you're a professional scouser', but Owen's reply 'Better than being an amateur one, John' must have been an indicator of the right man for the job. 'The first person I thought of was Johnny Speight, one of the young writers from *Idiot's Weekly*,' Lester said, 'but he had since been writing a lot of successful television... Some of the other writers were Galton & Simpson who were writing *Steptoe & Son*, in which Wilfrid Brambell was Steptoe... and by then Alun Owen had written *No Trams to Lime Street*... I felt I could persuade The Beatles that he could write for them. Alun was an Irishman, a Welshman, from Liverpool – or wherever you like: "You tell me where you want me to be from, and I'll be from there."'[66]

In the *Idiot Weekly* days Owen appeared on-screen in lunatic duelling sketches with fellow comic writer John Junkin, a gag writer who had only been coaxed in front of the camera as a physically suitable stand-in for Eric Sykes, but would soon join Joan Littlewood's theatrical troupe and start a whole new career, while Alun made the opposite move, creating such a name for himself as a screenwriter that in 1961 three of his teleplays were published by Jonathan Cape. Although not unique in his ability to overhear the right conversations and present a story with the sparse naturalism of the age, Owen's ear for real-life dialogue was already a calling card, and he wrote in the book's introduction, 'The things I wanted to say were about the way people behave to each other, and I have tried to strike chords in the mind of the viewer. I am constantly trying to say, "It was like this when it happened. Not factually like this, but this was the climate, feel of the situation. Surely you remember something like it?"... The town I was brought up in is an active part of these plays. I think it is highly individual, but then everyone's hometown is, and Liverpool has the added advantage of a multi-racial population. It's a Celtic town set down in Lancashire. Its people have evolved an accent for themselves that they borrowed from their Irish and Welsh grandfathers. The problem of Identity, which is to me one of the greatest the twentieth century has produced, is exaggerated in Liverpool, and the exaggeration makes it dramatic.' The closest to a dry-run for capturing the Fab Four's characters Owen boasted was a respected half hour about a trio of sailors on shore-leave in Liverpool, *No Trams to Lime Street*:

CASS: Isn't it marvellous, eh! She's like the wink from a fancy woman! Liverpool... the Garden of Eden of the North... *(Looking at his watch)* Eh up, mustn't keep you waiting love... (*He blows a kiss out to the city. He skips off down the ship, down the stairs and along the corridor, kicking one door, slapping another. He thunders on Billy Mack's door. Shouting*). Billy Mack! William Mack Esq.! Go to the top of the class and fill up the inkwells! Billy Mack! Billy!

BILLY: (*Almost dressed, opening the door.*) Oh, for God's sake, Cass – you're like a big, soft kid!

CASS: First night home in Liverpool and you're not

	ready yet!
BILLY:	Some people have to work, like, for their living, y'know!
CASS:	Go on, you're only the Second Engineer on this rotten old tub – you're not on the Queen Mary, son!
BILLY:	If a job's worth doing…
CASS:	I know, it's worth doing well. Oh, change the needle… Anyroad, forget your work, Billy, we're home! Liverpool's waiting like a turkey dinner with stuffing. Grab your knife and fork and let's get stuck in… Which way d'y'want to go, son? Down Mill Street, down Park Road, or along the boulevard? Which tram-car?
BILLY:	You've done nothing but talk about Liverpool trams for the past two months.
CASS:	Go on! Y'know you can't wait to gerron a tram. Ooooh – them old bone rattlers! Umpty-umpty-umpty-ump! All the way down to Lime Street! 'Pass right down the car please! All change for Penny Lane!' (*Laughs*.)[67]

Having met the boys, Owen said, 'I had a couple of false starts trying to write a fantasy film, but quickly realised that nothing could compare with their own fantastic lives. They are *always* on the move… What I am doing is taking what I see in them and putting it down on paper. In fact, they emerge as four very different people. I want to give them things they want to do. They have a terrific joy in being alive and there is a great sense of fantasy in their humour. There is conflict in the script and in the way the boys send each other up.'[68] As the movie follows the band to Paris to observe them before their French fans, and it was instantly clear that The Beatles *were* the story. 'The film was writing itself in front of us', Lester said, 'It would have taken an idiot not to say "Let's do *this.*"' It was absolutely on a plate and it was inconceivable from the moment we started that it would be anything but that… we

74

knew the standard of acting experience, and the more we could give them situations that were familiar to them – like doing a press conference – the better the odds they would be able to carry it off moderately well. With just a bit of judicious editing.'[69]

Ringo recalled, 'Alun Owen came on part of our British tour, wrote down the chaos that went on all around us and how we lived, and gave us a caricature of ourselves. So *A Hard Day's Night* was like a day in the life; or really, two days and two nights of our life.'[70] Paul had seen Owen's work on TV and described it as 'like an early Bleasdale or Willy Russell. It was a sort of kitchen-sink Liverpool thing… So Alun was a good choice and Alun was from Wales, and it's often said that Liverpool is the capital of Wales, there are so many Welsh people there. Alun came and hung around with us for a few days, which was an idea we'd picked up from *Life* magazine… They'd hang with you and pick up on the feel then they'd go away and write the story and they always wrote something cool because they'd got our sense of humour or they saw we were tongue in cheek. It wasn't just a po-faced group and a handout, it was something more alive, and that was what we were about. Our whole gig was to shake down the temple with our native wit and our blunt remarks. Blunt northern humour! … So Alun picked up all the little things like "He's very clean, isn't he?" or we would tell him, "Oh, we met a guy the other day…" because we did actually meet a guy on the train who said, "I fought in the war for people like you." And it eventually found its way into the film… The more we told Alun, the more of us he'd get in it, which is always a good thing, it would just reflect back.'"[71] O'Dell recalled that Owen's first draft was too long and unwieldy, but Shenson estimated that the finished movie contained at best 5% genuine ad-libbing from the Beatles: 'I don't want to take anything away from Dick, who did a terrific job, but I don't think enough credit has been given to Alun's script. Everyone assumed we just got The Beatles together and winged it. Actually, the film was very tightly scripted and not improvised at all. So much of the idiom that became famous – like George's use of the word "grotty" for grotesque – were Alun's inventions.'[72] Tony Barrow adds, 'The Beatles were coming out with that kind of stuff all the way along the line, to their inner circle of business associates, buddies, pals and mates, so we were all used to that kind of thing, but their humour had not been exposed before in public to the same extent, and therefore there was this magnificent marriage of Owen... and The Beatles, it worked beautifully. A lot of the humour in the film was pure Beatles, and pure Liverpudlian. And there was this blurring of fact and fantasy... we don't know to this day whether those one-liners came from a Beatle or Alun's inventive brain.'[73] When Ringo re-used Alun's line that he was neither a mod nor a rocker, but a mocker, the line between fact and fiction became even more blurry.

Lester's mingling of a documentary style with unexpected stabs of madcap fantasy was the film's masterstroke – establishing early on that The Beatles were able to suddenly appear outside the train carriage fooling around on bicycles shouting 'Mister can we have our ball back?', and could slip from playing cards to performing a full band rendition of 'I Should Have Known Better' in a single cut gave the whole movie a necessarily heightened cartoonish feel, letting audiences know that anything could happen when the boys were around, and glib visual gags like George teaching Shake how to shave via the bathroom mirror, or John disappearing down the plughole after a barrage of Nazi U-Boat commander impersonations, would not feel out of place. 'The bit in the bathtub was spontaneous,' Lennon said at the time, 'The idea wasn't; they just ran it and I had to do whatever I thought of in the background. Quite a lot of it *is* spontaneous. There were a lot of ad-lib remarks, but in a film you don't get ad-lib because you've always got to take it eight times. You ad-lib something quite good and everybody laughs, the technicians laugh, and the next minute you're told to "take it again", so your "ad-lib" gets drier and drier until it doesn't sound funny anymore.' Perhaps the key moment in the film was also totally un-choreographed – having kept the band visually hemmed in for almost half the film, in low-ceilinged rooms, suddenly the boys find a fire escape, and with a cry of 'We're out!' were invited by Lester to 'run into this field and just be idiots'. The overhead shots of the four falling over each other and doh-si-doh-ing around the helipad in Thornbury playing fields was the closest the action came to *The Running Jumping & Standing Still Film*. Lester said, 'The anarchic qualities that Spike brought to surrealism, that willingness to fight against the establishment, is something else which we hope we have all tried to carry on.'[74]

The ultimate synopsis provided for The Beatles' first film ran: 'Once upon a time there were four happy Liverpool lads called Paul, John, George and Ringo and they played their music all over the country. Now, when they'd finished playing in one place they'd run to the nearest railway station and go on to a new place to play some more of their music, usually pursued by hundreds of young ladies… The show does well but as soon as it is finished, again it is the mad dash on to the next plane for the next show. The past thirty-six hours have been a hard day's night. The next thirty-six will be the same.' Or, as John put it, 'a car and a room and a room and a car and a cheese sandwich.' 'We want to put over their non-conformist, slightly anarchist characters. We want to present their almost Goon-like quality', Shenson reassured fans via the *NME*.

The band were complemented by a supporting cast naturally packed with talented comic turns, from PC Deryck Guyler to magician Derek Nimmo, plus stock posh patriarch Richard Vernon clashing with the boys on the train years before taking on the mantle of *Hitchhiker's* Slartibartfast, and minuscule cameos including regular Lester face John Bluthal as a thief, and future sitcom writing legend Jeremy Lloyd dancing with his then girlfriend, Charlotte Rampling. The key roles of fictionalised manager Norm went to Lester cohort and *Carry On* irregular Norman Rossington, with Mal Evans-a-like roadie Shake played by John Junkin, future star of corny sketch comedy *Hello Cheeky*, who had been encouraged by Lester to adopt a Liverpudlian brogue to win The Beatles' approval, despite being London-born. Both were naturally approving of their adored co-stars, Rossington particularly: 'I've never before met a bunch of characters who are so obviously interested in everything going on around them: always a smile for the lowlier characters on the film set, always a quick gag if there was any hold-up… I think Paul really was the most self-conscious one of the four in the earlier days. He'd clown around sometimes, but I thought he was hiding a little bit of embarrassment... Ringo is being made to be the dumb one of the four – like Harpo Marx of the Marx Brothers. He's doing very well indeed, but in a different way to the others.'[75] Norman recalled being stuck in a car with fans beating on the windows yelling the band's names, and Ringo responding by banging back shouting 'Cliff! Cliff!'

Junkin became particularly pally with George, recalling a time Harrison phoned the Junkin home, and John's mother's screech that there was 'a Beatle on the phone' inspired his father's assurance that he'd crush it with his shoe. When Junkin asked George about Mal, he was told 'He's our road manager – we've just come back from New York and the luggage is in Iceland.' The band, he insisted, 'were *good*... They weren't "Beatles" and I was an actor, we were all actors in a scene, playing off each other... so non-starry and so generous... they were six of the happiest weeks of my working life – and I got paid as well!'[76]

That no complaints were ever heard from the third supporting actor speaks volumes, fastidious professional Wilfrid Brambell being infamously hard to please, even only a couple of years into his new-found fame in *Steptoe* – of course, the observations that Paul's grandfather is 'very clean' are a direct reference to Harold Steptoe's legendary wails of 'You *dirty* old man!' 'I never know if I'm being sent up or taken for serious', he told the BBC for special 'Making Of' documentary *Follow The Beatles*, 'But they're marvellous!'

As a major recurring pain in the band's collective arses, prim little conman and 'mixer' John McCartney Sr carried whole sequences of the film, but an actor in a much smaller part, Welsh-Italian Victor Spinetti, was to forge a more lasting bond with The Beatles. Apparently John approached Victor, grinning, 'When Dick shouts action, the other actors jump up and become different people but you stay the same. Does that mean you're as terrible as we are?' 'The banter that I heard on my first day never stopped,' Spinetti enthused. 'Between takes, the Beatles didn't go to their dressing rooms like film stars. They sat behind the set, chatting away. I've made lots of films but I've only worked with two other people like that, Richard Burton and Orson Welles.' Although more than ten years senior to the boys, the puckish thesp, fresh from winning a Tony award in Joan Littlewood's hit musical *Oh What A Lovely War* (which was to be wrongly mooted as having Beatle input when transferring to film in 1969), spread a bonhomie which suited them well, Paul dubbing him 'the man who makes clouds disappear', and George insisting to him that 'You've got to be in all our films – if you're not me mum won't come and see them, because she fancies you.' He made the role of a paranoid TV director a stand-out spot in *AHDN*, and many years later, McCartney paid tribute, 'It was a kind of knack to get into our inner circle. And it was the knack of not being bothered, not thinking, "Ooh, I want to get into that inner circle!" Anyone who thought that couldn't get in! You could see, "Oh, they're trying too hard." Someone like Victor? He was just in anyway. Couldn't get him out!' 'You never knew what they were going to say or do', Victor said. 'They had to cut so many scenes. Honestly, if you could get all of the outtakes, you'd have another film… They sent each other up all the time. They'd say things like,[1] "Paul, you're the prettiest, you get out of the car first." As the lunatic director, I'd walk up to them and say, "You're late. You should have been at rehearsals ages ago!" John would say, "You're not a television director. You're Victor Spinetti acting as a television director!"'[77]

'He wasn't one for talking much, George, but when he did, he was either quietly witty or to the point. John may have been famous for his chat, but George, he was for the connoisseurs', Spinetti further regaled. When it comes to how the Fab Four performed in their cinema debut, Dick Lester was in agreement: 'I think the most accurate performer was George – he never attempted too much or too little, but was always right in the centre… he got out of the scene everything there was to get out of it… I think there was always a sense, and it was very easy to portray physically, that Ringo was the one up the back nobody looks at… and of course, he had a lugubrious expression permanently, and the ability to come up with the most asinine non-sequiturs; it was he that invented the title – and "Eight Arms To Hold You", which, thank god we didn't have to use that one! I always think of John as one of the three or four most interesting people I've ever met... he was unique, in that he suffered fools very badly: he was quick-witted, and quickly cynical. Hated pomposity, and hated people in authority who treated them as hired servants... he just said what he felt, and it was refreshing. With Paul, he was the most theatrical of them all, he had a girlfriend who was an actress... he loved the theatre, he loved "show business" as it were in a way that the other three really didn't... I think this was a disadvantage to him, in that I think in a way sometimes Paul tried too hard to act – in the nicest possible way, because he was always very willing and has remained a lovely guy. But had he been less enamoured with the trappings of cinema and theatre, he might have been a bit more relaxed.' Since moving in with the highly cultured Asher family (Jane and brother Peter having been child stars in *Robin Hood,* theme music produced by George Martin) Paul was indeed a regular theatre goer, which may have inspired his own solo sequence in *AHDN*. Each of the Beatles had their own 'moment', John's being only a fleeting daft duologue with Anna Quayle, and George deadpanning through a face-off with Kenneth Haigh's paranoid trend-setter, a definite highlight:

SIMON:	We'd like you to give us your opinion on some clothes for teenagers.
GEORGE:	Oh, by all means. I'd be quite prepared for that eventuality.
SIMON:	Well, not your *real* opinion, naturally. It'll be written out, and you'll learn it. Can he read?
GEORGE:	'Course I can.
SIMON:	I mean lines, ducky, can you handle lines?
GEORGE:	Well, I'll have a bash...
SIMON:	At least he's polite. Show him the shirts, Adrian. Now, you'll like these. You'll really 'dig' them. They're 'fab', and all the other pimply hyperboles.

GEORGE:	I wouldn't be seen dead in them. They're dead grotty.
SIMON:	Grotty?
GEORGE:	Yeah, grotesque.
SIMON:	(ASIDE) Make a note of that word and give it to Susan.[78]

Paul's own spot was to crop up as he searched for the missing Ringo, and featured him, with some irony, coaching young Isla Blair's over-acting (but very cute) Shakespearean actor on natural performance, a la *Hamlet,* to her disdain:

GIRL:	…That's not like a real person at all.
PAUL:	Aye, well, actresses aren't like real people, are they?
GIRL:	…What are you?
PAUL:	I'm a group. I mean, I'm in a group. Well, there are four of us, we play and sing.
GIRL:	I bet you don't sound like real people.
PAUL:	We do, you know. We sound just like us having a ball. It's fab.
GIRL:	Is it really fab, or are you just saying that to convince yourself?
PAUL:	What of? Look, I wouldn't do it unless I was sure of it. I'm dead lucky – I get paid for doing something I love doing. All this and a jam butty too!
GIRL:	I only enjoy acting for myself. I hate it when other people are let in.
PAUL:	Why? I mean, which are you, scared or selfish?
GIRL:	Why selfish?
PAUL:	Well, you've got to have people to taste your treacle toffee. No, hang on, I've not gone daft. You see, when I was little me mother let me make some treacle toffee one time in our back scullery. When I'd done it she said

to me, 'Go and give some to the other kids.'
So I said I would but I thought to meself,
'She must think I'm soft.' Any road, I was
eating away there but I wanted somebody
else to know how good it was so in the end I
wound up giving it all away... but I didn't
mind, cos I'd made the stuff in the first place.
Well... that's why you need other people, an
audience, to taste your treacle toffee, like.
Eh, does that sound as thick-headed to you
as it does to me?

GIRL: No. But I'm probably not a toffee maker.
How would you do those lines of mine?

PAUL: Well, look at it this way, I mean, when you
come right down to it, that girl, she's a bit of
a scrubber, isn't she?

GIRL: Is she?

PAUL: Of course... Look, if she was a Liverpool
scrubber... 'Eh, fella, you want to try pulling
the other one, it's got a full set of bells
hanging off it. Y'what? I know your sort, two
Cokes and a packet of cheese and onion
crisps and suddenly it's love and we're
stopping in an empty shop doorway. You're
just after me body and y'can't have it, so there!'

GIRL: And you honestly think that's what she
meant?

PAUL: Oh, definitely, it sticks out a mile, she's
trying to get him to marry her but he doesn't
want... well... I don't reckon any fellas ever
wanted to get married. But girls are like that,
clever and cunning. You've got to laugh.

GIRL: Well it's nice to know you think we're clever.

PAUL: And cunning.[79]

There weren't many sequences filmed which never made it
to the screen (one casualty of the edit was a traffic jam scene

featuring the boys' chauffeur, played by Frank Thornton, a comedy veteran who eventually found fame as Captain Peacock in *Are You Being Served?*), but Paul's 'moment' was one which hit the dust, Lester diplomatically claiming that 'Its pace was a little languid, and we felt it really didn't deserve to be in the film.' But as suggested by Paul's chat with the *NME* at the time, there was a huge difference between clowning around in front of a camera and delivering a script: 'We get up about five in the morning – it takes some doing. The film is going very well, though we never seem to learn our lines. The idea is that we are given our lines and are supposed to learn them that night for the following day, but it never works out like that. We all read them frantically in the car going down to the studio. A bit like school.' It's telling that the most successful solo sequence in the film came about due to Ringo's massive hangover, and lack of much dialogue to perform – the dejected drummer's sagging off was hailed as a worthy tribute to the days of silent comedy. 'I know people said I was okay in *A Hard Day's Night*,' he told the *NME*, 'but I had no idea what was going on. That little scene with the little boy on the canal that they said was good. I was stoned out of my mind when I did that. I had a real thick head. I'd been up all the night before. I just came on with me mac on, feeling dead weary. I couldn't hardly move. Dick had to shout everything at me. But it did turn out okay. That bit where I kicked the stone along, that was my gag!'[80] The teenage David Jaxxon (Janson) who shared Ringo's on-screen triumph was still recognisable thirty years later, as Hyacinth Bucket's unfortunate postman in *Keeping Up Appearances*.

YOU MIGHT WELL ARSK

If John's solo sequence was the briefest, that may have been a blessing, given his double duties that spring, when his first book hit the shops – a unique collection of jumbled words and freaky line-drawings – and suddenly he was required to be everywhere at once publicising it. *In His Own Write* had originally been posited by Paul as '*In His Own Write And Draw*', a torturous pun on keeping scraps of scribbling in a 'right-hand drawer', but in its truncated form certainly a safer title than John's preferred *The Transister Negro,* though perhaps no better than the other alternative, *Stop One and Buy Me*.

The deal to publish those scraps of paper Lennon kept about his person came about in the first flushes of Beatlemania. Jonathan Cape's literary director, Tom Maschler, had commissioned a Beatles cash-in from US journalist Michael Braun, and when Braun shared a few of Lennon's scribblings, Maschler decided to step up his ambitions, giving the mouthy pop star a unique opportunity to broaden the minds of teenybopper fans with the twisted contents of his imagination (albeit, the traditional celebrity author legend runs that Braun did not reveal Lennon's identity until Maschler had already registered interest). A contract for £1,000 was signed at the start of 1964, and by 23 March, copies were on sale. In typical myth-busting style, the new author shrugged, 'It's about nothing. If you like it, you like it; if you don't, you don't. That's all there is to it. There's nothing deep in it, it's just meant to be funny. I put things down on sheets of paper and stuff them in my pocket. When I have enough, I have a book. If I hadn't been a Beatle I wouldn't have thought of having the stuff published; I would have been crawling around broke and just writing it and throwing it away.'[81]

The publishing world was slower to understand the importance of Beatlemania than other industries, and Maschler goggled, 'They thought I was nuts! They thought it would sell for about a week to the fans, then sink. They wanted a photo of John on the front with a guitar, but I refused. It was just a nice, simple head shot. The first print was quite modest, just 25,000. But then the Sunday papers gave it a rave review, and so did the *Times Literary Supplement*. That was extraordinary. I think it sold 500,000 in that first year.'[82] In the US, first editions were emblazoned with the added inducement 'The Writing Beatle!' but Lennon threatened to tear up every copy if it wasn't removed.

That the *Melody Maker* would write 'Lennon is a remarkably gifted writer… often hilarious, clever and funny'[83] may have been no surprise, and it's not too controversial that celebrated author and progressive legal hero John Mortimer insisted that Lennon was the best English poet 'since W.H. Auden went soppy', but the *TLS* concluding that 'It is worth the attention of anyone who fears for the impoverishment of the English language and the British imagination' was something else, and respected American novelist Tom Wolfe expanded, 'He seems to take the general format for his stories, fables, playlets and poems from a British humorist named Spike Milligan. But the underlying bitterness of much of what Lennon writes about marriage and family life, for example, as well as his Joycean excursions into language fantasies, are something else altogether. The intimations of Joyce... are what have most intrigued the literati here and in England.' Lennon was typically dismissive, as expected of the rebel who insisted 'avant garde is French for bullshit', claimed reviews of his music noting its 'aeolian cadence' 'sounded like exotic birds', and responded to further praise about his use of onomatopoeia with 'Automatic pier? I don't know what you're on about, son.' But although he had long cited the influence of Carroll, Milligan, Searle and Thurber in his writings and cartoons, with Lear an afterthought, the Joyce comparison was new to him. He did once claim 'When I read James Joyce, it was like finding Daddy', but in more honest mode, he enlarged, 'When they said "James Joyce", I must have come across him at school, but we hadn't done him like I remember doing Shakespeare and I remember doing so-and-so... so the first thing I do is buy *Finnegan's Wake* and read a chapter, and it's great, y'know, and I dug it, and I felt as though he was an old friend, but I couldn't make it to the end of the book... He just didn't stop!'[84]

'There was never any real thoughts of writing a book,' he told the *NME*. 'It was something that snowballed. It started back in my school days. When I was about fourteen I remember they gave us this book in English Literature. It was Chaucer or some guy like him and we all thought it was a gas. Whenever the teacher got that book out we would all collapse. After that I started to write something on the same lines myself... There's a wonderful feeling about doing something successfully other than singing. I don't suppose the royalties will ever amount to much, but it doesn't matter.'[85]

Despite the tragic burning of so many Lennon originals, some of the first book's entries dated back to John's schooldays, and as with a fair few Beatle lyrics, the writer did not work in a vacuum, his friends being happy to throw in gags as they occurred to them. Paul even enjoyed co-writing credit for 'Whide Hunter', besides penning an introduction in the right spirit, albeit with a greater clarity to his humour than that of his very buddy and pal:

> 'At Woolton Village fete I met him. I was a fat schoolboy and, as he leaned an arm on my shoulder, I realised that he was drunk. We were twelve then, but, in spite of his sideboards, we went on to become teenage pals... Aunt Mimi, who had looked after him since he was so high, used to tell me how he was cleverer than he pretended, and things like that. He had written a poem for the school magazine about a hermit who said: "as breathing is my life, to stop I dare not dare." This made me wonder right away – "Is he deep?" He wore glasses so it was possible, and even without them there was no holding him. "What bus?" he would say to howls of appreciative laughter... There are bound to be thickheads who will wonder why some of it doesn't make sense, and others who will search for hidden meanings... None of it has to make sense and if it seems funny then that's enough. Paul McCartney, 1964. PS I like the drawings too.'[86]

Many years later, Harrison recalled, 'It was fun to be around John as we were feeding this comedy machine. He was funny then and the books are still great... Even our children find them just as much fun as we did.' Back in '64, George had a column about the Beatle life which was part-ghost-written by new 'insider', Liverpudlian journalist Derek Taylor, who was soon employed full-time by Epstein as press officer (before absconding for four years in the US working for the Beach Boys). With typical Taylor effusiveness, the Fab Four's most erudite fan wrote, 'With one bound copy of *In His Own Write* John was free! He had made a giant leap out of the box named "Pop Star". What a career move! ... His three comrades, to their undying credit, begrudged him none of it and gave him joyful support. But from then on John was "the literary Beatle" and the halo shines on to this day.'[87]

Some may suspect a patronising air of indulgence from the literary world, not wanting to rock the growing Beatle industry but accepting Lennon's work at face value – the freedom he enjoyed was a key part of his whole typewriter-thumping style, he admitted. 'I hardly ever alter anything. Because I'm selfish about what I write or big-headed about it. Once I've written it I like it and the publisher sometimes says, you know, shall we leave this out or change that and I fight like mad because once I've done it, I like to keep it. But I always write it straight off.'[88] John admitted at the time that now very familiar celebrity cry, 'I always set out to write a children's book', and presented as it was in a dreamy child-like format, designed by Robert Freeman, it's still impossible to imagine any subsequent teen pop idol getting away with a work like *IHOW*. Even at the time the perverseness and free-wheeling absurdism of these cartoons, mini-plays, poems and spoofs of books like *Treasure Island* and Enid Blyton's *Famous Five* series could have provoked a larger dose of public disapproval, with their acidic overtones and thoroughly expected obsession with cripples, spastics, bad-old-fashioned misogyny and wildly stereotyped racial minorities – the very first item, 'Partly Dave', features a 'coloured conductor' called Basubooo and ends '"But would you like your daughter to marry one?" a voice seem to say as Dave leapt off the bus like a burning spastic.' As for the cruel fate of 'Good Dog Nigel', the least said the better.

Textually, the nonsense poems remain perhaps the most successful element of the book, particularly 'Deaf Ted, Danoota, (and Me)' and 'I Sat Belonely', which was included in a BBC children's anthology for schools, while the other pieces remain gloriously frustrating in their typo-packed nihilism, shaggy dog stories told in a Stanley-Unwin-esque tangled tongue, glorifying in their lack of anything approaching a satisfying punchline:

*

87

Sad Michael

There was no reason for Michael to be sad that morning, (the little wretch); everyone liked him, (the scab). He'd had a hard day's night that day, for Michael was a Cocky Watchtower. His wife Bernie, who was well controlled, had wrabbed his norman lunch but he was still sad. It was strange for a man whom have everything and a wife to boot. At 4 o'clock when his fire was burking bridely a Poleaseman had clubbed in to parse the time around. 'Goodeven Michael,' the Poleaseman speeg, but Michael did not answer for he was debb and duff and could not speeg.

'How's the wive, Michael' spoge the Poleaseman

'Shuttup about that!'

'I thought you were debb and duff and could not speeg,' said the Poleaseman.

'Now what am I going to do with all my debb and duff books?' said Michael, realising straight away that here was a problem to be reckoned with.[89]

The cartoons may have been marketed in different ways over the years, but despite the massive initial sales, and being kept in print with different editions from generation to generation, Lennon's books have become only a minor part of the Beatles legend, and couldn't be more at odds with the default Lennon of love, peace and understanding – but this was the sense of humour of a pretty twisted lad in his mid-twenties, presented with absolute artistic freedom, to rail at the 'brummer strivers' who would never understand the contents of his mind. The more problematic elements are akin to the prose work of Spike Milligan in his later years, packed with hoary old sexist gags and gob-smacking racial stereotyping. However, 'Deaf Ted, Danoota, (and me)' did exclaim, *We fight the baddy baddies, / For colour, race and cree / For Negro, Jew and Bernie...*' and as Milligan was the man who gave McCartney the inspiration for 'Ebony and Ivory' with his motto, 'black notes, white notes, and you need to play the two to make harmony, folks!' it would be wrong to label either a harbourer of racial hatred. Despite his many painful missteps when it comes to race-based humour, Spike simply found all people funny, and particularly those who seemed out of the ordinary, new in the British soup of the latter half of the twentieth century, and Lennon inherited much of that attitude. There may be an element of *Derek & Clive*-style intent to shock in *IHOW*, but ultimately the offensive content of Spike and John's humour was, in intention, as guileless as Lennon's 'speech' when toasted at a Foyle's literary luncheon: 'Thank you very much, it's been a pleasure', which was mis-reported as 'You've got a lucky face', a spot of absurdity actually trotted out by John on TV a few days later. The author's non-speech was a disappointing failure to hold a posh audience entranced with Beatle wit, which he quite honestly put down to being 'scared stiff'. This was after all John striking out on his own without his three brothers, and he had a lot more fun publicising his book as part of the gang, particularly on Swedish TV, when George intervened halfway through one of John's child-like readings by tearing a chunk out of the book and saying he preferred that bit.

The Ringoism John nicked for the second sentence of the above story of course soon put in double duty as the title of their debut film (and its title song, written to order in a mad dash during post-production), which was otherwise floated as *'Beatles Number One'*, *'Moving On'*, *'Let's Go'* or *'It's a Daft Daft Daft Daft Daft World'*. Only a few weeks earlier they were embarking on their film careers on that train just outside London, filled as it was with past and future friends, Klaus and Astrid from Hamburg being in attendance as George flirted with 'schoolgirl' Pattie Boyd, a model spotted by Lester in one of his recent Smith's Crisps adverts, soon to be the first Mrs Harrison and inspire some of the greatest love songs of the century. The hectic few spring weeks of filming then took the boys to some of the least exotic corners of South London, concluding in a long shoot at the (sadly long demolished) Scala Theatre, which suited a number of sequences which saved time at Twickenham Studios, particularly of course for the orgasmic on-stage conclusion, with the band performing their hits to hundreds of manic fans (and child actor Phil Collins) over four days of screaming so incessant that one camera operator's back teeth were vibrated out of their sockets. From *Big Night Out* through to *Let It Be*, though, Twickenham would become the most important home of the band for all their on-screen projects. One of the first sequences, in which Ringo nearly kills a parrot with a mis-thrown dart, was filmed at the nearby Turk's Head, and with all footage in the can, a small crew stepped out onto the Twickenham pavements to record a quirky trailer, with all four boys sitting in prams fiddling with phones and typewriters.

Lester zipped through post-production with superhuman speed, The Beatles' skills at looping dialogue being helped by their experience with miming for TV shows, but the one sour note came from early executive mutterings about dubbing the band's natural scouse burrs so the average American could understand them, allegedly suggested by one cigar-chomper's wife. Lester was not the only creative to threaten absolute abandonment of the project if such a moronic scheme went ahead, Owen thundering, 'It's not been made for forty-year-old women in mink, it's been made for teenagers in Liverpool!' The first ever private US showing was in the presence of comic cinema legend Billy Wilder, who reportedly responded, 'I have no idea what that was about, but you're gonna make a lot of money.'

Despite Paul's fears that his hometown would resent their success, by 10 July there they were, stars of the biggest new comedy in the world at the Liverpool Odeon, and waving from the balcony of the town hall as the Liverpool Police Band played 'Can't Buy Me Love' and an ocean of ecstatic scousers – reportedly a quarter of the city's population – roared their pride in the boys... and Lennon returned their ovation with a Hitler salute. 'John got away with his Hitler bit on the balcony', Neil Aspinall smirked. 'Nobody seemed to pick up on it. John was always like that, a bit irreverent. Anybody in nerve-racking situations tends to do things to relieve the tension.'[90]

As with John's writings, finding a negative review was no easy task. The *Village Voice* in New York dubbed it 'the *Citizen Kane* of jukebox movies', the *Sunday Telegraph* wrote 'Its charm is unforced. Its humour is knobbily non-conformist' and Leonard Mosley in the *Daily Express* agreed: 'It's a mad, mad, mad, mad, mad film, man. Nothing like it since the Goons on radio and the Marx Brothers in the thirties.' There were no Oscar nods for any Beatles, but both Alun Owen and George Martin received nominations.

Dick Lester has never been anything but proud to have helmed the film, and says, 'I think the serious structure of *AHDN* was just the chronicling of what was a serious movement – the explosion of youth as a power in this country, the sudden gaining of confidence of an enormous section of England, which hadn't happened for a long time. The "angry young man" syndrome was that of a semi-soured cynical defeatism, where The Beatles told everybody you could do what they damn well like, just go out and do it! There's no reason why you can't do it. Although we did it in a light way, that seemed a marvellous thing to examine... The main thing was to let our energy and our enthusiasm go... I knew while we were filming, probably the second week, that one day in fifty-something years' time, if I fell under a bus and died the newspaper headlines would say, "Beatles director in death drama", no matter what else I did. And that has absolutely come out to be the way it's been. If I managed to produce the way I felt about them on the screen in a way that holds up, I'm just grateful. They were a marvellous part of my life.'[91]

MIDSUMMER MADNESS

While Lester was immersed in post-production, the Beatles were fooling around in what would ultimately become the closest the existing archives can get to seeing the band in full live panto mode. *Around The Beatles* went out across the ITV network on 6 May, the baby of Pop TV pioneer Jack Good, and Epstein set his super-human powers of persuasion to their extreme setting, to get all four boys dressed up for a Shakespearean skit performed in front of a live and delighted audience of fans – despite John's snarl, 'I hate Shakespeare, I don't care whether you should like him or not. I don't know if it's because of school or because it doesn't mean anything to me.'[92]

Despite their dislike of rehearsal, the boys arrived at Rediffusion's studios in Wembley at 11am two days running to piece together the programme's quirky opening item. Most of the hour was of course to be filled with live music from Epstein's finest, with Cilla, PJ Proby and others presaging a finale from the lads themselves, but Brian's dream meeting of theatre and pop was the focus of the concert, presented as it was 'in the round', to mark the 400th birthday of the world's greatest playwright by having his words spoken by the world's greatest musical group. Extra layers of theatricality were added by the careful selection of the preposterous performance of 'Pyramus & Thisbe' by the rude mechanicals led by Nick Bottom in Act 5 Scene 1 of *A Midsummer Night's Dream*. McCartney and Lennon portrayed the lovers, with Starr as Lion and Harrison playing Moonshine, complete with dog. It was a wily choice, the scene's joyously threadbare nature making up for any lack of thespian skills, though the planted rowdy cockney crowd's heckling cries of 'Go back to Liverpool!' and worse were harsher than the original Shakespearean barracking of Theseus and co:

PAUL: O, I fear my Thisbe's promise is forgot! And thou, O wall, O sweet and lovely wall, that stand'st between her father's ground and mine! O thou, O wall, O sweet and lovely wall, show me thy chink, to blink through with mine eye! But what see I? No Thisbe do I see. O wicked wall, cursed be thee…

JOHN: O wall, full often hast thou heard my moans, for parting my fair Pyramus and me! My cherry lips have often kissed thy stones…

PAUL: I see a voice: now will I to the chink, to spy and I can hear my Thisbe's face. Off to the chink, then, come along! (*Calls through* WALL) THISBE! *TH-IS-BE!*

JOHN: WOT?! My love, my love, thou art my love, I think.

PAUL: Wilt thou at Ninny's tomb meet me straight away?

JOHN: Ninny's tomb? Is that still open? Jolly good... (*Exeunt*)

RINGO: You ladies, you who fear the smallest monstrous mouse that walks the floor, may now perchance both quake and tremble here, when lion rough in wildest rage doth roar. (*Arrr!*) Then know that I, one Ringo the drummer, am. But if I was really a lion I wouldn't be making all the money I am today, would I?

GEORGE: This lantern doth the horned moon present... I the man in the moon do seem to be... look you, all that I have to say, is, to tell you that this lantern is the moon, you see; I'm the man in the moon; this thorn-bush here's my thorn-bush; and this doggy-woggy here's my dog. And if you don't wrap up, I'll give you a kick in the – the eye![93]

No transcription of this necessarily simplified extract, however, can quite convey the bedlam of The Beatles facing the noisy groundlings while mugging their way through the Bard's lines; Paul in particular – a natural for deluded luvvie Bottom – winked at the very idea of The Beatles attempting to perform the classics and John made up for his female role by performing every line in a gruff bass voice, with outrageous wig and blackened teeth. Once again, by playing the role which already displayed the maximum indifference, George came across best, but it simply didn't matter, as the whole burlesque was watertight in its amateurish, giggly, critic-proof sense of fun, concluding with the dead lovers ending not with '*I die die die!*' but '*Oh I do like to be beside the seaside...!*' John and Paul showed a new awareness of how to play up to the right camera, which must have come from the extra rehearsal time, and the patient support of two other actors – Andre Tayir, an American who had featured in *West Side*

Story and was choreographer for all Jack Good's *Shindig* shows, played Wall, and delivering the Prologue was Good's old buddy Trevor Peacock. 'They were surrounded, locked into rooms, so I wasn't able to mix very much,' he says. 'They knew we were playing Shakespeare, and they weren't daft, they were quite intelligent blokes. And they were *huge*, they didn't need this television show, but they said, "Well, we'll do it." I was there for a couple of rehearsals, Jack had got me in to do the introduction, and they seemed to have been practising! I said I hadn't had any breakfast, and Ringo offered me half of his. It was incredible, all these men had to do was push a button and get anything they wanted, it was like going to see the Lord Jesus... My first wife was going around saying "I kissed Ringo", but nobody believed her.' Peacock became the last actor alive to have tried to perform live scripted comedy with The Beatles, an odd job as part of a celebrated comedy career which reached its zenith – as with fellow Fabs co-star and Milligan sidekick John Bluthal – with a plum role in Richard Curtis' sitcom *The Vicar of Dibley* thirty years later.

McCartney enjoyed the experience enough to name his cat Thisbe in tribute, but Lennon's macho neuroses made this one spot of gender-neutral casting a definite one-off for him, judging by a following US radio interview:

Q: In the show you included some comedy but you were the only female...

JOHN: Look, I don't want any insinuations, mister. We was doing Shakespeare, and I had to be Thisbe, the girl... Because, y'know, if anybody likes dressing up more stupid than the rest, I enjoy doing it. I was asked to do it, 'cause they thought, 'cause I've got a deeper voice, you know, I do the girl bit, sort of *grrr*, all that bit.

Q: Do you like Shakespearean literature generally?

JOHN: As far as I'm concerned, Shakespeare's a drag...

Q: On the plane the other night, Ringo had a statement to make that he really enjoys doing comedy... He'd rather do that than play, he said. Do you feel the same way?

JOHN: Well he says that, but if he was doing comedy sketches every night, he'd be saying "I'd rather sing or play than do comedies." You know, it's just whatever you're not doing. But we enjoy, you know, messing around with Shakespeare, but, you know, we read him in school and that's enough.[94]

This was not the end of the band's post-movie mugging for cameras, however, with a final appearance alongside the Winters brothers on ITV, broadcasting from Lancashire's chilly seaside pleasure resort, in *Blackpool Night Out*. Only the audio of The Beatles' final set has survived, but besides the boys dressing up as dustmen, the show also made fun of Ringo's recent medical emergency with tonsillitis, which had required Jimmie Nicol to sit in for a run of shows in Australia: with Ringo ill in bed, the other three shouted rude instructions to surgeons Mike and Bernie, who closed by singing the drummer 'Rock-a-Bye Baby' in lieu of anaesthetic.

The rest of the summer was given over to the first proper US tour, *AHDN* earning plaudits afresh from American reviewers, so there were few further dalliances with comedy back home until John agreed to feature in a crafty new pilot for the BBC in November, *The Dudley Moore Show*, or rather, *Not Only... But Also*. Of all the *Beyond the Fringe* stars, Moore had been green-lit by the BBC as the perfect all-rounder to front his own comedy programme, mingling performances with his jazz band with comedy sketches, poems and guest items which would feature 'not only' Dudley, 'but also' talented friends. In no time at all, Dud's drafting in of Peter Cook to provide many of the laughs (famously splitting his EL Wisty mackintoshed philosopher into two to create the nasal know-it-alls from Dagenham, Pete & Dud) launched the two colleagues into double act territory, ultimately to become one of Britain's most beloved duos, with the 'But Also' denoting Cook specifically – or rather, Moore, with the tall, overbearing satirical wit easily dominating his loveable clown-like partner, putting his name before the ampersand.

When Lennon arrived at Wimbledon Common in November to make a film version of his poem 'Deaf Ted, Danoota, (and me)', however, it was Dud alone who accompanied him – besides his *AHDN* co-star, Norman Rossington. In fact, it was Rossington who had been booked first, and dared to venture that his Beatle pal might be a strong addition to the pilot's line-up. Directing and producing the show was a hitherto unmentioned cornerstone of the Goon-Beatle creative community, Glaswegian filmmaker Joe McGrath, who apparently earned the pique of Brian Epstein for booking his star behind his back, before settling the dispute on a fiver. Contemporary with Spike, Peter and Dick, Joe had started out on the art side of Lester's early TV experimentations, but by 1963 was producing and directing Michael Bentine's TV vehicle *It's a Square World*, and Muir & Norden sitcom *The Big Noise,* starring Bob Monkhouse as a pop DJ, alongside Rossington. Having long ago seen and enjoyed The Beatles at the Cavern, accompanied by Larry Adler, Joe's friendship with Dick Lester also placed him behind the scenes in the creation of *AHDN,* when he claims to have played a role in Ringo's stand-out moment: 'I wrote that scene, because Richard said to me, "We really need a sequence with "This Boy". Ringo goes missing and wanders down the river, a lonely boy…" I think I got something like fifty pounds for writing that. All those silent film jokes. Richard and I had a lot of discussion about Buster Keaton, and what Buster would do… They were funny lads, but as Eric Morecambe said, "We don't just make it up, y'know?"'

Having known Moore since his Oxford days, Joe it was who had proposed the very idea of *NOBA* in the first place, reviving a format tried out for his original TV directing course, and with a Beatle on board, McGrath's first TV creation looked like becoming a hit long before it aired. 'I got a phone call from John, he said, "I dig what you're doing." I said, "Oh? Do you wanna be in this new show with Pete and Dud?" He said, "Absolutely.

We're at the ABC Luton next week, come and see the show and we'll go for a drink." So I went with Norman Rossington, he and John were great friends, and when John came off, he was livid: "We don't even have to sing! We should just be miming!"' McGrath filmed Dud, John and Norman in Wimbledon's stark countrified surroundings in the style of TV arts show *Monitor*, the three of them cycling around, holding balloons, and swinging on trees (Norman causing John's contact lenses to shoot out when he pushed him too hard) until the one spoken line at the end, 'Sometimes we bring our friend Malcolm', revealing none other than Bruce Lacey, the freak connoisseur's freak, with 'MALCOLM' written on his forehead. With classical backing and slow-motion it was very unlike The Beatles' playtime in *AHDN*, but for the first time, John really seemed to be enjoying himself, away from the other three heads of the four-headed monster. 'I noticed when you were filming with John,' McGrath continues, 'he didn't care about where the camera was, he was completely himself, with no fear, he just got on and did it. Also, having been at art school, he had a very good ability to understand where he was in the frame, and visualise it in his head in the way maybe some of the others couldn't. But he never worried about his performance, or had any ego.' John's buoyancy carried over to the studio recording in front of a live audience later in the month, where Dudley linked together further highlights from *IHOW* performed alongside Norman and John, including elocution piss-take 'All Abord Speeching', 'Unhappy Frank' and a rendition of 'Good Dog Nigel' with added menace, thanks to the bloodhound in Lennon's arms trying desperately to escape. John also performed his own author biography to camera, more relaxed and confident – and pleased to get laughs – than he had ever seemed before:

JOHN: I was bored on the 9th Octover 1940 when,
               I believe, the Nasties were still booming us
               led by Madalf Heatlump (who only had one).
               Anyway they didn't get me. I attended to
               varicous schools in Liddypol. And still didn't
               pass-much to my Aunties supplies. As a

member of the most publified Beatles my and (P, G, and R's) records might seem funnier to some of you than this book, but as far as I'm conceived this correction of short writty is the best laff I've ever ready. God help and breed you all.[95]

Dancing away from the cameras with thumbs aloft after closing with 'The Wrestling Dog', this was a newly confident comedic John Lennon sans guitar – though McGrath suggests his relaxation may be due to the fact that he was so drunk he ended up dancing on the set's revolving stage with Una Stubbs, singing the theme to *Sunday Night At The London Palladium*. Lennon enjoyed the experience so much, he even turned up uninvited to a greasy London café for a further sketch, 'La Tour Gastronomique', featuring Barry Humphries. Although he's never visible onscreen, a Beatle presence was marked by an incongruous snatch of 'I'm A Loser' on the soundtrack.

Lennon said, 'One of the reviews of *IHOW* tried to put me in this satire boom with Peter Cook and those people that came out of Cambridge, saying, "Well he's just satirising the normal things, like the Church and the State", which is what I did. Those *are* the things that keep you satirising, because they're the *only* things.' But while David Frost happily basked in the delight of the satire boom, Cook & Moore's new show deliberately avoided all that, and when the pilot was reworked for broadcast just after the New Year, it was the start of one of the best comedy shows of the 1960s (sadly, with most Lennon-free episodes wiped forever by the BBC).

Despite the closure of the Establishment club, Cook remained the coolest comedian in a London whose swinging was only just beginning to build up momentum, and his dinner parties were legendary, with both John and Paul regularly invited. 'John became best friends with Peter,' Joe McGrath exaggerates. 'They used to meet up at the Zen restaurant in Hampstead. In fact, I remember Dudley saying, "I don't know what they have in common. Peter's stone deaf!" We would never allow Peter to sing, and he always wanted to, swinging the microphone around his head. That's why Dudley said to him, "I will *sing 'Now is the time to say Goodbye...'* and you *say* 'Goodbye!' Don't *sing* it, for God's sake!"' Cynthia Lennon recalled this meeting of minds in her 2005 book *John*: 'He and Peter hit it off immediately and became good friends. They shared an outrageous sense of humour and a fierce intelligence. Soon after they met Peter and his wife Wendy invited us to lunch. Their home in Hampstead was like something out of a glossy magazine, and as we walked in John and I glanced at each other apprehensively... The food was superb and we had our first taste of garlic – amazing, it was unheard-of in the Liverpool of our childhood. Dudley Moore was there too and as we sat around the table Pete and Dud fell into their comedy routine. John joined in, putting on his thickest Liverpool accent, and as we drank bottle after bottle of expensive red wine the afternoon descended into hilarity.'

This friendship naturally did not excuse Lennon or his fellow Beatles from satirical ribbing from *Private Eye*, the satirical periodical started in an office above Cook's club, of which he became proprietor within a few years of its first publication. October 1964 saw the first ever appearance in those pages of dumb pop group Spiggy Topes and the Turds, introduced by Maureen Cleavage – and though the catch-all rock industry spoof outfit went on to be as targeted at The Rolling Stones and others, there's no questioning which band first demanded the Turds' creation, and Lennon was a clear model for Spiggy. In June 1965, The Beatles also received the singular honour of featuring on *Private Eye*'s front cover, posing under the headline 'BEATLES TO GO ON VIETNAM PEACE MISSION', with PM Harold Wilson's speech bubble gloating, 'Good evening Mao Tse Tung! May I introduce my Commonwealth colleagues?' This was only to happen twice more, with a nude John and Yoko featuring on 1968's 'Special Revolting Issue' (Lennon's caption being a disappointingly trad 'It won't stand up in court' gag), and in 1970 McCartney's announcement of the band's split landed him the cover treatment, complaining 'I can't even afford to pay the BBC to plug my records!'

As another year of unceasing achievement closed, the by-now traditional seasonal duties came around – the Christmas flexi and live show, this year both dubbed 'Another...' Filling the bigger venue of the Hammersmith Apollo was no challenge, of course, especially with the likes of Freddie and the Dreamers and The Yardbirds in support, but that year's nods to 'panto' were such a drag, it became the last time they ever let themselves in for such an experience, openly admitting to (now disgraced) Chris Denning of Radio Luxembourg behind the scenes that it was 'lousy'. It couldn't have helped that compere and fellow performer was the ultimate (now disgraced) pop villain, Jimmy Savile. Producer Peter Yolland had claimed 'I'm changing the concept of pantomime', but had only three days with reluctant performers to perfect a sketch in which the boys wrapped up in furs to play Arctic explorers in search of the Yeti (who turned out to be Savile, triggering the now particularly unfortunate cry of 'BEHIND YOU!'). The *NME* lost no time in bursting Beatle bubbles all over the place when they complained, 'In the whole production The Beatles only appear in a weak opening scene, in which they are "delivered" as gifts from a Christmas tree, and two other weak sketches. In the first they appear as polar explorers captured by an abominable snowman. In the second these top world entertainers neither move, nor speak, nor sing. They're cast as waxwork dummies! Thank goodness for their singing spot.'[96] It's little wonder that when the idea of a third production was mooted the following year, George politely declined, saying 'Mr Epstein may have a Mr Epstein Christmas Show'.

That Yule's brief festive fan recording, meanwhile, was only *incrementally* funnier than the previous year's, with 'Little Drummer Boy' marching SFX accompanied by 'Jingle Bells' in the opening, and the pitter-patter of running feet at the end as the boys fade out, while even less care was taken over making any sense of Barrow's grubby print-outs. There was one bizarre aside which foxed Beatleologists for decades, while always making the lads fall about – Paul's '*Been for a – have we, Megan?*' – which turns out to be the carefully expurgated key line from an old scouse shaggy dog story at the expense of their Welsh neighbours. In this scally gag, there's this young lad who loves the girl next door but can't say a word to her, and he's ordered by his frustrated family to simply say the very first thing which comes into his mind the next time they meet. Almost immediately, he sees her coming up from the bottom of the garden, and bravely dares to ask the girl, *'Been for a shit, have we, Megan?'* – which explains Paul's broad Welsh accent as he skipped the operative word in the punchline. This secret spot of scatology aside, however, there was little to cause hilarity in the flexi except the odd ad lib, such as John answering Paul's assurance to fans 'We don't know where we'd be without you' with 'In the army!' George also took time to whet fans' appetites for what 1965 would bring. Discussing their debut cinematic comedy caper, he read, 'We're glad it turned out okay. The next one should be completely different. We start shooting it in February. This time it's gonna be in colour!' ('Green!' murmured John) '...It'll be a big laff, we hope!' Cue hysterical laughter from all four.

– CHAPTER THREE –
STILL THE SAME AS THEY WAS

'When you're drowning, you don't say, "I would be incredibly pleased if someone would have the foresight to notice me drowning and come and help me", you just scream!'

'Animation is not just for children – it's also for adults who take drugs.'

'The Beatles saved the world from boredom.'

'I like kids, I used to be one.'

'It's a comic book adventure; one long chase with Oriental church leaders who want to fill up their temples with sacrifices and mad scientists who want to blow up the world', Dick Lester revealed to the press, tellingly leaving out any mention of the Fab Four. Ringo was to add, 'It's basically a chase film, because I keep getting chased by all these lunatics. And my three pals save me!' while George snarked, 'I don't mind colour in a film if it doesn't mean dancing about in a red shirt, like in one of Cliff's. I don't like that.'⁹⁷

When filming began, The Beatles could have felt some degree of déjà vu, 1965 kicking off in much the same way as 1964, but *Help!* was to prove a vastly different experience to *AHDN*, generally in negative ways. Not that the boys were too bothered – since the hysterical evening in New York on the previous US tour in which Bob Dylan, amid answering the hotel phone with 'This is Beatlemania here!' to raucous giggles, had helped to make the whole band instant (and in some cases, life-long) devotees of cannabis, they had barely smoked a cigarette which contained only tobacco, and the whole experience was a haze of red-eyed laughter. 'It was very very funny', McCartney reminisced. 'The Beatles were about humour, we had a great humour between us. There was an "in" side to the track of humour that we would use as a protective thing, so with this on top of it, things were really hilarious. I remember walking round the suite, trying to get away from it all, closing the door behind me without realising George Harrison had walked step by step with me, so I thought I'd lost him, turned around, and he's in the room with me. "Ohhh! This is hilarious. I can't handle it!" It was like the funniest bloody dream going.'[98]

EIGHT ARMS TO HOLD YOU

Some said that Epstein had good tax reasons for visiting Nassau in the Bahamas, but McCartney maintained that the four boys just picked two holiday destinations they'd never been to, and so they touched down on New Providence Island in expectation of tropical paradise, only to find it freezing cold as they were put into thin shirts and told to act warm, and their second movie got underway. They also fancied a go at skiing, and so Obertauern in Austria was to be the even colder second port of call. With the addition of the more homely third location of Salisbury Plain (sadly only *near* Stonehenge, at Knighton Down, rather than having The Beatles play within the ancient monument itself) Dick Lester essentially had the ingredients for three distinctly aesthetically pleasing music videos, making the most of the switch to colour, in need of only some kind of plot to knit them together.

The director had of course been developing the new film for some time already, and crowbarred in the Bahamas with little difficulty. As Alun Owen did not return, for unspecified reasons, Lester looked to unexpected quarters for his screenplay this time. 'The first idea I came up with when we started playing around with it was that Ringo was getting edgy at the constrictions of fame. And when drunk in a bar, he says to a stranger he has befriended that he wishes he could end it all – just not wake up – because he can't take any more. And the man said, "I have a friend who does that sort of thing. You'd never know it, he's highly professional"… And Ringo wakes up the next morning and remembers this and then panics and calls the boys… it turned out that Philippe de Broca had made a film called *The Man from Rio*, and their sequel was called *The Chinese Gentleman from China*. It's that exact idea and they were shooting it at that time… It was based more on Ringo getting antsy and edgy. So it at least it started as a continuation of *AHDN*.'[99] Joe McGrath has a slightly different story: 'I did a rough synopsis, because Richard asked me, and he said, "It should be some kind of murder or mystery story", and I had read this story by Edgar Allen Poe, *The Suicide Club*, where a guy pays somebody to kill him, then realises he doesn't want to be killed, but by that time it's too late because the murderer's now gonna kill him. I gave this idea to Richard, stolen from Poe, and he said "That's a good idea", and went away, and I got paid for it. And I thought that when he got back to me, I'd write the screenplay.' Despite this never happening, McGrath's treatment would mutate into the Bernard McKenna TV comedy and movie *The Odd Job* many years later.

Lester's basic concept, of Ringo in peril, was given to France-based American Marc Behm, who had only freshly turned pro as a jobbing screenwriter, due to the success of Stanley Donen's screwball comedy thriller *Charade*, which he had co-written. Behm's own preoccupations tended towards the fantastical thriller, with a dash of magical realism, and he delivered a preposterous plot which saw Starr doomed to a bloody living sacrifice thanks to a sacred ruby-red ring sent to him by a fan, which is maniacally prized by both an Eastern death cult and a ruthless British scientist. The parallel international success of another British cultural export, United Artists' James Bond series, was also very consciously used as inspiration for an eccentric globetrotting caper capable of serving up the most important part – the songs. The sci-fi-tinged screenplay quickly delivered by

Behm being judged too dry and bereft of the British idiom, let alone Owen's finely tuned Beatle-ese, Dick then brought in his favoured playwright, Charles Wood, who had pleased Lester with the adaptation for his latest film, sex comedy *The Knack*, but who in all honesty had no more comedic chops than Behm, having a preoccupation with military plots which would culminate in his opus, TV drama *Tumbledown*, in 1988. Lester said, 'The dialogue was much more complex because we were working with almost a surreal writer in Charles Wood, who was a wordplay specialist, and so there were lots of plays on words going on, which they could all manage – I mean, John was writing books in this style.'[100] However, besides the facetious repetition of 'famous' throughout, there was little in the league of Ringo's drums 'looming large in his legend', or any of Owen's carefully observed linguistic treats. What the second Beatles movie did have in spades was madcap action, more in line with Lester's Goonish early work. 'We didn't want to do a colourised *AHDN*,' Lester said, 'we couldn't show them in their private life, which would be the most logical extension to it, because that was by then certainly X-rated... so if we can't show them in their public life, or private life, they have to become, if you like, passive recipients of an outside plot or an outside threat, brought on by a weakness within themselves... We chose to do a Pop Art fantasy within which we could play around with the state of Britain in 1965 and Harold Wilson's white-hot modern society... if the film seems innocent, we can all plead guilty – the songs were great and filming them was sheer pleasure.'[101]

Getting underway with no confirmed title besides '*Beatles Production 2*' (though Shenson considered it '*The Day The Clowns Collapsed*', John suggested '*High-Heel Knickers*' and George was all for '*Who's Been Sleeping In My Porridge?*'), the shivering Beatles were far from alone in the Bahamas. Beginning filming with the plot's denouement was a perfect example of just how less straightforward the experience would be second time around, and the plot demanded the many different factions hunting Ringo to be present. There was early talk of Peter Sellers playing a role, but he allegedly refused to play second fiddle to anybody. His *Running Jumping & Standing Still Film* colleague, rotund Australian actor

Leo McKern, was however available for the Sellers-esque challenge of playing an Asian-ish character and escaping with any credibility, as foolish primary antagonist, High Priest Clang, years before John Mortimer's *Rumpole of the Bailey* gave him his defining role.

The phrase 'cultural appropriation' meant nothing at the time besides perhaps Britain's retention of the Elgin Marbles, but if *Help!* has become the poor relation to *AHDN* in the twenty-first century, Behm's use of a nondescript 'Oriental' menace in the plot must be partly to blame. No specific location is given for the death cult (though their nearest airport is Calcutta), but the multi-armed Goddess Kali is a revered Hindu deity, albeit a rather macabre one to Western eyes, and her depiction as the idol of a gang of idiotic religious maniacs played by blacked-up white actors well fits that over-used modern euphemism, 'problematic'. Besides being inspired by Wilkie Collins' *The Moonstone,* Behm may have drawn from a legend in which a band of thieves tried to sacrifice a saintly Brahmin monk to the Goddess, and she repaid them by killing them all and drinking their blood... but that's still no excuse.

As McKern's hapless sidekick, John Bluthal also required a 'gor blimey' Indian persona, as did the film's femme fatale Ahme, played with a gentle charm by regular Cook collaborator Eleanor Bron, so nervous in her first movie role she took some time to overcome an attack of nervous blinking every time Lester called 'Action!' Ahme's goal, to establish a new era for the cult, swapping ritual murder for Peace and Love, went some way to ameliorating the offence, and represents an early emphasis on the ideal of Love as a force for universal good, which would soon become core to The Beatles' philosophy. Whether the inclusion of an Indian restaurant scene in which comedy stalwarts Alfie Bass and Warren Mitchell played blatantly caucasian Brits helped or hindered any accusations of racial insensitivity, it's hard to say. But perhaps if there's one grand consolation to be found in the film's clumsy grappling with Indian culture, it's George Harrison's discovery, on that restaurant set, of the sitar. Coming only a few weeks after the Bahamas' resident Swami Vishnu Devananda had handed

The Beatles a book on yoga, Behm's choice of nationality to demonise would ultimately set George on an all-new path in life, and he would do more to popularise genuine Indian music and philosophy in the West than any other figure in history.

With George honouring his promise to his mum, the remaining cast list heralded the return of Victor Spinetti on good highly-strung form as the 'trite, hackneyed mad scientist' equally intent on getting hold of Ringo's stuck-fast ring, Professor Tiberius Foot, and as Foot's underling Algernon, loveable *TW3* star Roy Kinnear, a roly-poly comedy legend who would go on to be a favourite of Lester's (he tragically died on the set of *The Return of the Musketeers* twenty-three years later in a horse-riding accident which would effectively convince the heartbroken director to retire once and for all). Completing the primary cast as cowardly British Superintendent Gluck was Patrick Cargill, then a comedy bit-part player familiar as Tony Hancock's doctor in *The Blood Donor*, but three years later to hit the big time as the lead in hit sitcom *Father Dear Father*. Back home in Blighty, cameos would be made by other performers claiming their places in the British comedy hall of fame, with Jeremy Lloyd once again as an extra, and Bruce Lacey devoid of lines as The Beatles' devoted Lawnmower.

Oddly, or perhaps a testament to Lester's eye for comic talent, the two old ladies who famously admire our heroes in their first scene (filmed on Ailsa Avenue, with The Beatles apparently living at numbers 5-11) both partnered the aforementioned Warren Mitchell as Alf Garnett in Johnny Speight's smash hit bigot-pillorying sitcom *Till Death Us Do Part*, which began on BBC 1 just a few months later. The second old dear to speak, Dandy Nichols, famously played long-suffering Else Garnett for years, but Gretchen Franklin filled the role in the original pilot, and wasn't to find national fame until being cast as pug-loving Ethel in *EastEnders* in 1985.

THE BEATLES LEAVE THEIR CAR OUTSIDE A TYPICAL LONDON ROW OF TERRACED HOUSES, AND WAVE AT TWO OLD LADIES ON THE OTHER SIDE OF THE STREET.

NEIGHBOUR 1:	Wave.
NEIGHBOUR 2:	Don't like to.
NEIGHBOUR 1:	Go on, wave.
NEIGHBOUR 2:	Shall I? They expect it, don't they?
NEIGHBOUR 1:	Lovely lads and so natural. I mean, adoration hasn't gone to their heads one jot, has it? You know what I mean, success.
NEIGHBOUR 2:	Just so natural and still the same as they was before they was.[102]

To complete the set, Ahme's charlady mother was played by occasional *Till Death* player Patricia Hayes, but the final cameo role of note was from an unexpected performer, Mal Evans being the only person around mad enough to get plastered in fat and play the British swimmer lost on his cross-channel challenge: a cold enough task in its first (which is to say, last) instance, but dicing with death under the Austrian ice. Ringo was also in genuine peril when required to dive from the Professor's yacht, Spinetti recalled, 'They had a bunch of people watching the area for sharks, so Dick Lester said, "Let's do another shot". They dried Ringo off and he was shivering because it was out of season and very cold. We did another take and another, and after the third take, Dick said, "Let's do another." Ringo said "Do we have to?" Dick said, "Why?" Ringo said, "Because I can't swim." Dick went white and said, "Why on earth didn't you tell me?" Ringo said, "Well, I didn't like to."'[103]

Not much fun had been had in the ten days' shooting in the Bahamas, then – Lennon ruffled feathers by criticising the standards in a psychiatric hospital which had doubled for a lock-up, telling the Governor-General, 'We were filming today in what we thought was a deserted army barracks, but it turned out to be a place full of old people and spastics. It was disgusting. So how can you justify all this lavish food?' But Evans' near-hypothermia aside, the icy chill of the Austrian Alps saw the cast and crew thawing out somewhat, Lester joining the band in an impromptu beer cellar jam one night, playing boozy jazz piano with them into the early hours.

Late nights and early mornings played some part in the Beatles' malaise on set, but there has never been much secrecy about the main reason. '*Help!* took longer,' Lester concedes, 'We had more time, and lots more money. But during the filming, The Beatles discovered marijuana. There was lots of smiling... It came at a very, if you like, relaxed time in their lives, when there was a lot of laughter and a lot of merriment, and things didn't seem to matter too much. Certainly, they had a good time, and I hope that was allowed to come out in the film.'[104] 'With *AHDN*, we had a lot of input,' Lennon complained in 1980, 'But with *Help!*, Dick didn't tell us what it was about. I realise, looking back, how advanced it was. It was a precursor for the *Batman* "Pow! Wow!" on TV – that kind of stuff... Maybe that was partly because we hadn't spent a lot of time together since we made *AHDN*, and partly because by then we were smoking marijuana for breakfast during that period. Nobody could communicate with us because it was all glazed eyes and giggling all the time. The best scenes were those when we were sprawling on the floor, breaking up and falling about all over the place, lying on the floor, unable to say a word...'[105] Ringo added, 'Dick knew that very little would get done after lunch. In the afternoon we very seldom got past the first line of the script. We had such hysterics that no one could do anything...'[106] and McCartney (who once recalled running an extra mile in the snow with Ringo for one take just so they could share a J on the return amble) went further when he looked back at those hazy weeks of globetrotting thespianism: 'We would occasionally get stoned on the way to the film set, which was pretty fatal. My main memory is of being in hysterics, because for all of us, one of the great things about early pot was the sheer hysteria, the laughs. Things could appear very very funny, hilariously so. And nobody quite knew why we were laughing, and of course this made it even funnier. It was like kids giggling at the dinner table, it really was... There was a scene where Patrick Cargill, the police inspector, had a gun on us from behind. So we all had our hands up and we were all looking out the window. Then someone would start giggling – "Stop it, stop it," – and after a while you could just see the shoulders heaving, and you could feel people going. It was like all those classic out-takes from Peter Sellers movies, and we were just gone… I don't know how Dick ever put up with us but he somehow had to make a movie under those circumstances.' 'The script was very cleverly written so that there was never a time where any one person had too much to say before someone else said something,' Lester added. 'They were sound bites. One-line gags or a little speech which could be cut away from.'[107] Neil Aspinall was more generous when he insisted, 'One of the things the guys liked about Dick was his innovation, but he also got on well with all four of them, and understood their sense of humour, and his was pretty zany as well. You could always fit little bits and pieces in, you could come up with an idea and he would slot it in to the movie.' And Eleanor Bron, emphasising her naivety back then, paid tribute: 'I think they wanted to act, they wanted to learn something else, and that's one of the things I admired about them.'[108] John, of course, was having none of it, cutting through radio publicity with disdain: 'None of us have ever acted. I think Paul did a play at school once, that's all. He didn't say anything… Whoever cuts it makes it look as though we're nearly acting, but we're not.'[109]

Nevertheless, Lester was very happy with the snowy footage put together in their five days in Austria, and recalled that 'We changed about three shots' – one change being the decoration of unsightly telegraph poles with musical notes, an on-the-spot brainwave – 'other than that, the film just fell into place, it was one of those wonderful sequences where it just cut itself.'[110] Lester and his team were taking the step into colour seriously, drawing aesthetic inspiration from US artist Jasper Johns, and putting every shot through a painstaking process of colour filtering to get the most out of every inch of film. When he wrote an essay for the eventual DVD release forty years later, Martin Scorsese felt that this paid off comedically: 'The colour itself was funny – tamped down, pretty far from the psychedelic palette you'd expect, and it accentuated the comedy… The deadpan tone was pushed much further than in the previous picture… and so was the absurdity, from the proto-Monty Python interpolations ("Part

Three, Later That Evening") to the chattering mechanical teeth used to cut the (indoor) grass... With every frame, the Beatles and Lester seemed to be saying: "Here's the second movie... now it's time for you to do your part: watch and enjoy!" You were let in on the joke, and that made it even funnier.'

TITTER YE NOT

Back home in Blighty for the last stint of filming, with Buckinghamshire pile and Profumo scandal arena Cliveden House standing in for Buckingham Palace, the boys continued to giggle through a plot they never comprehended, and Paul uncharacteristically accentuated the negative: 'We just browsed through it, really, rather than taking it very seriously. We didn't bother learning our lines. I'm sure we were reacting against the lousy script. Basically we lost the plot, but I don't think there was much of a plot there to start with. It was this endless, "The ring must be found! Kali must be appeased!" Maybe that's why we didn't enjoy it. I've always felt we let it down a bit, but we just didn't care...'[111]

There were two huge comedy names signed up for the new film not yet mentioned, due to the fact that their moment of Beatle fame never made it to even the roughest cut of the movie. Early on in the plot, the morning after their first appearance, a sly reference to the Beatles' thespian skills was made by the decision to have them pay a visit to a famed acting coach, at 'The Sam Ahab School of Transcendental Elocution' – the name being 'Bahamas' backwards was a spot of meaningless wordplay, but it was quite an important sequence, establishing the Eastern Thugs' ability to hypnotise everyone with music. Even more importantly, it was intended to be a face-off between The Beatles and one of Britain's most beloved and eccentric comedy heroes. 'One of the people that I'd admired and watched over the years was Frankie Howerd,' Lester said, 'and I thought that he and the boys would get on, and they both liked each other's work...'[112] One of the first sequences to be shot in the UK, the jetlagged boys greeted Frankie – who, like Brambell before him, was a necessarily closeted gay man in a time when it was still illegal, but unlike Brambell, he utilised his unique brand of camp on screen, to great effect. Accompanying them was Wendy Richard, then at the very beginning of a career which would make her a queen of saucy British comedy – particularly as Miss Brahms in *Are You Being Served?* – before joining Gretchen Franklin in *EastEnders*.

Both Beatles movies went through the then typical process of being novelised by budding scribblers, and as the authors were working from early scripts, if the books left behind by John Burke and Al Hine give us anything, it's a tantalising record of what might have been. The novelisation of *Help!* gives glimpses of a few ideas which never made it to screen – the friendly cow hiding behind The Beatles' self-service milk dispenser, the missing part of the final plan which saw George wearing a Ringo mask too, and above all, the business with Sam Ahab. To those familiar with Howerd, his bizarre strangulated vowels can be heard in his every line:

> The Rolls came smoothly to a stop before the acting studio of Sam Ahab, sage and mentor to stars of stage, screen, television and simple hopefulness. There are few actors (if any) so high on the scales of popularity and prestige as not to admit that their art can be sharpened by a brush-up session with Sam Ahab. As for fresh members of the profession, Ahab training is their entree both to casting office and to cocktail party. As much as any one person Sam Ahab had a corner on the development of mimetic talent in the Western world. Naturally, it was to Sam Ahab that the boys turned for training when their sky-rocketing career pushed them from pure musicianship into the dramatic arts.
>
> From the Rolls they mounted the steps of the Ahab studio. The most modest of notices on the door simply proclaimed 'Sam Ahab, Teacher of Dramatic Art.' No more was needed for a name to conjure with on three continents.

Said John to Paul, entering the sacred door: 'I heard you last night doing Shakespeare in the toilet when you thought we were all in our pits.'

'It's no place, is it?' Paul admitted.

'You'll believe me, Sam,' Ringo began a plea as he caught sight of his mentor, a commanding although not tall figure in blue jeans and sweat shirt, standing on the bare stage-like floor of the studio with a handsomely busty young woman costumed as Lady Macbeth. But Sam had already headed directly for John.

'Now, John, Baby,' Sam said, lopping a tutorial arm over John's shoulder.

'I can talk to you, Sam,' Ringo interrupted.

Sam frowned. In his studio he reigned as absolute czar. There was no court of appeal to his decisions. And here was Ringo, a nice enough chap, a Beatle to be sure, but a tyro as an actor, actually *interrupting*.

'Would I be making a tiny ricket if I asked you to lope?' Sam said in a voice of steel.

'Hey, up, Sam!' George tried to put all at their ease. Unsuccessfully...

The discussion, as not infrequently in Beatle colloquies, seemed to skip several frames of reference and break through to the stratosphere.

'I'm here,' Paul said, 'because they expect great things of me in my next film. It has been promised.'

'I know you won't believe me, Sam,' Ringo kept to his plea.

'Do we start right off acting now?' George wondered...

'Acting?' the master lowered his voice but kept its cutting edge. 'In *my* school we don't act. In my school we *transcend*.'

'I'm the only one who's worthy of the medium, y'know,' Paul admitted. 'These others, they're just clowns.'...

'Chat,' Sam said. 'Chat is your God. Will you cease the flaming rabbit... Time enough for chat when you're old,' Sam warmed to a philosophical diversion. 'Like me. Older, and hard pressed.'

'That bird with the lofty carriage,' John said, pointing a discreet finger at the costumed Lady Macbeth whose wriggles were now quite obvious.

'Get away from Lady Macbeth,' Sam said. 'Have you no pity?'

'I was rudely awakened this morning with a fishing rod, Sam,' Ringo managed to start his own weird chronicle.

'...Is she transcending?' John asked, still fixed on the busty actress.

Lady Macbeth was smiling openly now, both smile and decolletage beamed directly at Paul. Sam dashed furiously across the room to stand between them.

'Is she hell as like transcending,' he said. 'She's *acting*. And a right load of old pony it is, too. I've been trying to transcend this one for weeks.'[113]

The sequence at first centred around the boys' progress in elocution, each of them declaiming great Shakespearean speeches with éclat by miming to recordings of Olivier, Gielgud and Burton – all except George, who can only deliver the opening of *Henry V* in his own scouse snarl. Soon after, the religious maniacs attack and try to cut off Ringo's hand, embedding a sacrificial axe in a mirror. Lennon was to remove the axe and proffer it to 'Lady Macbeth', saying, 'Is this a chopper you see before you? Try it on your old man. It's sure to ring a bell.' Sadly, as Lester continues, 'We started to film the sequence, and it was painfully obvious right from the beginning that their two styles of working didn't gel; that Frankie was nervous with them and they were nervous with Frankie. More the former than the latter. I would not say that the Beatles were extraordinarily adept at remembering the lines. There were times when I'd have to say their lines to them, and they'd say them back... and the sequence just painfully didn't fly, didn't come off.' Others on set recalled the volatile Howerd, an obsessive technician, slave to his unique timing, becoming so frustrated with the grinning quartet that he tore into them with a barrage of invective which plunged the entire day's work into gloom, and must have been astonishing to behold – who tells off The Beatles? Needless to say, Sam Ahab hit the cutting room floor, as, sadly, did Wendy Richard's greatest ever cameo, which, with her own brand of caustic sass, she recalled left her 'Absolutely mortified... it was such a cruel thing to do to a young girl.'[114] Howerd's only reported comment on the debacle was to observe of Paul: 'You could be fooled by the fact that he was the big, money-making machine. Underneath all that, he was just a guy. And a very horny one, too.'[115]

The following July, the boys had another negative run-in with a gay comedy hero who one would expect to be mad about the boys. When the 1965 tour reached Rome, Noël Coward attended a show, and recalled his horror in his diary: 'I was truly horrified and shocked by the audience. It was like a mass masturbation orgy... Mob hysteria when commercially promoted, or in whatever way promoted, always sickens me.' Nonetheless, and despite Coward's scorn for the band shown in an earlier *Daily Mail* interview, Epstein was naturally overjoyed to find the theatrical hero keen to have a private audience with his charges. However, exhausted from performing, only McCartney made the effort to struggle down to meet Coward: 'I explained gently but firmly that one did not pay much attention to the statements of newspaper reporters. The poor boy was quite amiable and I sent messages of congratulation to his colleagues, although the message I would have liked to send them was that they were bad-mannered little shits.'[116] Luckily, Paul never held a grudge, and over thirty years later would record an exquisite cover of 'A Room With A View' in tribute to 'The Master'.

Another sequence detailed in the book but nowhere on screen would have shown John's life passing before his very eyes during the last reel's many violent struggles – and required Lennon to dress up as a baby, a schoolboy, and so on, until reaching the ripe age of twenty-five. Without this strange cutaway in the film, there was so little for John to actually do, it's little wonder he said he felt like an extra in his own movie. Producer Shenson admitted, 'The strong supporting cast bothered The Beatles. They felt that they were merely puppets being pulled around on strings and that these very fine actors, like Leo McKern, were actually the stars. I disagreed totally. It was The Beatles who made it work. Their personalities were far stronger than any of the actors.' And director Lester summed them up: 'Ringo, because his was the showy part, he was always the odd one out, so he was given characteristics that were more sympathetic. John I don't think was interested and didn't bother, Paul was too interested and tried too hard, and George was always the one that was forgotten. So he just did it and he got on with it.' But while Ringo was of course the focus of most of the film, fleeing from tigers and murderers and barracudas and more, the Incredible Shrinking Paul had his 'Exciting Adventure' in miniature form (which was at one point to involve a scrap with an actual beetle), and even George was happy to become an action hero for the day, leaping on the back of Prof. Foot's car like Bond in slip-ons to save his buddy. But John, throughout the ridiculous plot, is just… *there*.

As with the previous year's filming, of course, Lennon had his plate piled up elsewhere, working on his second book, *A Spaniard in the Works*. They may have been able to mock up a cover to show him lovingly immersing himself in his own work within the film, but churning out another slim volume of dizzying verbiage took its toll on the author, bang in the middle of what he considered his 'Fat Elvis period', feeling every inch the Nowhere Man. 'Once it became: "We want another book from you, Mr Lennon", I could only loosen up to it with a bottle of Johnnie Walker, and I thought, "If it takes a bottle every night to get me to write…" That's why I didn't write any more.'[117] Despite this creative constipation, Lennon's second book showed signs of evolution, with more committed spoofs of *Snow White*, the news columnist Cassandra, digs at religion and politics, and what he was proud to call his longest piece ever, 'The Singularge Experience of Miss Anne Duffield', a Sherlock Holmes piss-take which stretched to all of five or six pages, all designed, once again, by Robert Freeman (as were the *Help!* credits). Whether the book showed any mellowing of the shock element seen in *IHOW* when it hit the shelves on 24 June can be answered by Ringo's observation, 'John's inscription on my copy when it first came out in 1965 says it all: "To Ringo with love, you dwarf bastard."'[118] Within three months, over 100,000 copies were being pored over worldwide, with those fans not put off by the first plunge into Lennon's psyche returning for the likes of 'Araminta Ditch':

Araminta Ditch was always larfing. She woof larf at these, larf at thas. Always larfing she was. Many body peofle woof look atat her saying, 'Why does that Araminta Ditch keep larfing?' They could never understamp why she was ever larfing about the place. 'I hope she's not at all larfing at me,' some peokle would say, 'I certainly hope that Araminta Ditch is not larfing at me.'

One date Araminta rose up out of her duffle bed, larfing as usual with that insage larf peojle had come to know her form.

'Hee! hee! hee!' She larfed all the way down to breakfart.

'Hee! hee! hee!' She gurgled over the morman papiers.

'Hee! hee! hee!' Continude Araminta on the buzz to wirk.

This pubbled the passages and condoctor equally both. 'Why is that boot larfing all the time?' Inqueered an elderberry passengeorge who trabelled regularge on that roof and had a write to know.

'I bet nobody knows why I am always larfing,' said Araminta to herself privately, to herself. 'They would dearly love to know why I am always larfing like this to myselve privately to myself. I bet some peoble would really like to know.' She was right, off course, lots of peotle would...

A year or more passedover with no changei in
Araminta's strange larfing. 'Hee! hee! hee!' she went
drivan herself and everone around her insane.
THERE SEEMED NO END TO THE PROBLEM.
This went on for eighty years until Araminta died
larfing. This did not help her neighbers much. They
had all died first, – which was one of the many things
that Araminta died larfing off.[119]

The book was only in shops a month when whatever it was
they had spent the spring filming was finally ready for the adoring
film-buffs. For a while the new title '*Eight Arms To Hold You*' had
taken root, suggested by Ringo on beholding the vast Kali statue,
but John and Paul were adamant that they couldn't write a song
called that, and Lester was greatly relieved to find that his original
idea, which had been scuppered by copyright, was still possible
with an added exclamation mark – so *Help!* it was, 'a hundred
minutes of nonsense'.

What a confection Dick and the boys unveiled to the public
on 6 August – technicolor madcap antics with the world's biggest
stars in exotic locations and above all, of course, all those amazing
new songs. Eleanor Bron became an instant '60s icon, two years
before her seminal multi-role appearance in her friends Pete &
Dud's *Bedazzled*, and the careers of everyone else in the cast were
likewise boosted by proximity to the Fab Four. 'STOP
WORRYING! HELP IS ON ITS WAY!' thundered the
commercials, and most reviews offered cautious continuity of
adulation, such as the *Daily Express*: 'Mr Lester's direction is a joy
to watch, and The Beatles are the closest thing to the Marx
Brothers since the Marx Brothers.' However, there is a myth that
The Beatles were critically untouchable until 1967, and even a
periodical as sympathetic as the *NME* sniffed, 'Isn't this sort of
stuff reserved for Saturday morning minors? All right, so it's a
comedy. But John, Paul, George and Ringo have to do their best
with a sequence of thin lines and unfunny quips. There are
moments when John's great natural wit shines through – these
are rare.'[120] In *The Sun*, Ann Pacey echoed the idea that the film

suffocated the stars: 'they are still themselves, but are caught in such a web of wild comedy they seem at times as trapped as four flies waiting for spider Lester to bring them back into the parlour'[121], and no less a critic than Ken Tynan also spied the problem: 'The Beatles themselves are not natural actors, nor are they exuberant extroverts. Their mode is dry and laconic, as befits the flat and sceptical Liverpool accent. Realising this, Lester leaves it to his cameraman David Watkin to create the exuberance, confining the Beatles to deadpan comments and never asking them to react to events with anything approaching emotion. He capitalises on their wary, guarded detachment.'[122]

The Beatles themselves, who naturally only saw the finished film through bloodshot eyes, have never argued against these brickbats. Even shortly after the film's release, George conceded, 'When we first saw the film, we were knocked out, but obviously some people weren't. The whole thing is a fast-moving comic strip, just a string of events.'[123] While John was soon to be quoted saying 'Help! as a film was like "Eight Days A Week" as a record. A lot of people liked the film and a lot of people liked that record. But neither was what we really wanted. They were both a bit manufactured. The film won't harm us, but we weren't in full control.'[124]

Naturally, *Help!* was nothing less than an international sensation and financial smash, beloved by millions, and although there were no Oscar nominations this time (George Martin never even got a look-in for the soundtrack), Dick Lester remained The Beatles' favoured movie mogul, generally attached to any further plans for cinema outings – the next idea, for instance, was to feature the boys as scouse cowboys in Western spoof *A Talent for Loving*, which thankfully fell by the wayside and got made as a sex comedy in 1969. But although he never made another Beatles movie, Lester was able to reflect for the rest of his career, 'I have had the considerable privilege of smelling the sweet air at the core of the universe.'[125] When MTV launched in 1981, they presented the director with a commemorative scroll dubbing him 'The Father of MTV' for his innovative work bringing The Beatles to the screen... but he responded by demanding a blood test.

*

RANDY SCOUSE GITS

There were at least three other apparent reasons for being glad of *Help!* even if some seeds sown by the technicolour caper weren't to bloom until the following year. First of all, Lester's skill in filming musical performance inspired one more step towards pop video culture, as The Beatles realised that a well-made short film would save them making any number of mimed TV appearances. Lester, however, was already at work on *A Funny Thing Happened On The Way To The Forum*, and so super-sub McGrath was the right madman for the job of actually inventing music videos, returning to Twickenham to helm numerous monochrome visual accompaniments to 'Ticket To Ride', 'We Can Work It Out', 'Day Tripper' and others. Sick of miming as they were, The Beatles' new promos openly mocked the practice by having the boys perform the songs in obviously non-live ways, mouthing 'I Feel Fine' in a gym with Ringo pedalling away on the exercise bike and George singing into a punchball, swamping the boys in fake snow for 'Help!' and even just having the band munch bags of chips on film. 'I was given the tracks,' Joe shrugs, 'listened to them, and came up with some ideas, like the gymnasium, and like Dick Lester did in *Help!*, having the Lord Shiva, with The Beatles having eight arms... so I stole a whole load of stuff from Richard.' With 1966's explosion back into colour, McGrath passed the torch onto eager young New York ex-pat Michael Lindsay-Hogg, who was to remain the band's favoured director for most further film promos at Twickenham, such as the tea-drinking equestrian eccentricity of 'Penny Lane', though the remaining Beatle videos always veered more towards the straightforward than the comedic, even given David Frost's cameo on 'Hey Jude'.

The second development which seemed to spin off from the loony antics of *Help!* had actually been in production for much longer by the time it debuted on US TV. Another New Yorker, Al Brodax, producer of cheap but cheerful cartoons starring Popeye and Casper the Friendly Ghost among others, had the initial brainwave a year earlier: 'I was in the animation business, working for King Features, a division of the Hearst organisation. The day after The Beatles appeared on *The Ed Sullivan Show*, I called Brian Epstein and made a terrible deal with him for the rights to animate The Beatles. The budget was $32,000 for the whole half hour, which was ridiculous, and most of it went to Brian. But I thought it was an opening for something new.' King Features was never an animation studio, but worked with creatives around the world to turn their comic properties into cheap and not un-cheerful cartoons similar to the boldly-outlined style already familiar from Hanna-Barbera, though *The Beatles* thankfully stopped short of aping Hanna-Barbera's mad tradition of including a laughter track.

The undeniably poor reputation of *The Beatles* TV show, still barely acknowledged in the band's homeland, has often been blamed on the American producers' inability to fully grasp the Liverpudlian charms of these suddenly highly commercial foreigners, as feared by Lester and Owen a year previously. However, animation was farmed out to teams in Australia, the Netherlands and Canada, plus the UK's TV Cartoons, or TVC, provided a core team of cartoonists (including a young Bob Godfrey, an Australian native who would go on to charm a generation with his work on cartoons like *Roobarb & Custard* and *Henry's Cat*) working from a small Soho studio, while the overall look of the 2D Fab Four was masterminded by a twenty-one-year-old from Bromley, Peter Sander. This was the first time a TV cartoon series had been built around real living people, and the young artist designed a whole alternate version of The Beatles which still has fans to this day. The internal character bible from which he worked ran:

HOW TO ANIMATE THE FAB FOUR:
JOHN, especially when delivering important lines, really looks like the leader. Feet apart, hands on the hips, chin up, looking down his nose... Pulls funny faces especially after giving orders, which he immediately wipes off. He also looks the other way before giving you an order... John never sits, he slouches.

PAUL is the most poised and stylish Beatle. When he talks he uses his hands, with fingers spread to express what he is saying. He always looks straight at whoever he is talking to. He is the one who gets excited when John suggests anything. He doesn't really walk – he skips… When he is making his own suggestions and comments, especially ones suggesting mischief, he covers up by assuming a mock innocent look, eyes wide and head tilted to one side…

GEORGE nearly always gives the impression of frowning. This is because his eyebrows thicken as they reach his nose… George always leans against something. Shoulders hunched, hands in pockets. Legs crossed.

RINGO is the nice gentle Beatle, although he always looks rather sad. Ringo looks a bit disjointed whether walking or standing. Ringo walks in a Groucho Marx pose… When Ringo laughs, having made a funny remark, he squints. His clothes tend to look as though they are a bit too big. Normally, Ringo is always deadpan but should expression be required the main movement is arching the eyebrows.[126]

Each weekly episode boasted two short adventures, each based on a song, plus a 'behind stage' middle section, in which John, Paul or George would lead the kids in two further singalongs, less than impressively assisted by little Ringo as 'prop man', dressing up in quite the wrong theme for the song in question. And of course, commercials galore boosted the 17-minute running time when ABC began the broadcasts, with sponsorship coming from Quaker, Mars, and toymakers AC Gilbert – plus, of course, there was a whole new wave of tie-in merchandise, from soap to candy cigarettes to car mascots.

The Beatles cartoon was anything but sophisticated: it was brash, larky Saturday morning fare for kids to chomp cereal to, with all the daft sound effects and jokes expected of it. Even the

Australian director, Ron Campbell, admitted it was 'A mundane, uninspired, technically deprived and artistically crude Saturday morning children's television series... and it was an enormous hit. A hit like none before it.'[127] Few denied the rough and ready charm of the cartoons, even if the backgrounds were basic and regularly recycled, and often the wrong singer would be shown singing a particular song, and true, the odd Beatle arm could go missing here and there (though the animators always insisted on reshooting sequences with missing heads, no matter what the cost). But then, the twangy new music stings provided by *Sid Caesar's Show of Shows* maestro Bernie Greave allegedly received the Macca thumbs up, and similarly nobody has ever laid much blame on the simple scripts, built around hilariously literal readings of hit songs, and provided by reliable industry bods Dennis Marks, Jack Mendelsohn, Woody Kling and Bruce Howard – the scripters' resumés included *Gilligan's Island* and gags for Milton Berle, Jackie Gleason and Lucille Ball, and the show's eventual 39 episodes aren't without the odd wacky gem.

The heroes were forever fleeing the attentions of crazy fans in bizarre situations the world over, generally kicking off a slight but slapstick plot in which the fourth wall was regularly broken. The series was relentlessly repetitious, with adventures often dropping the boys in a Horror or Western scenario, with numerous songs on repeat, gratingly edited for the singalongs, which were present complete with misheard lyrics and pictures of, say, turtles smoking cigars. But at least the cartoon boys tended to use the right Beatleisms, and even in the very first episode, 'I Want To Hold Your Hand', there are oddly prophetic Beatle elements, including a yellow-ish submarine and a lovelorn octopus who of course finds true love via The Beatles' music:

EXT. SHIP UPPER DECK

JOHN:	Where to now?
PAUL:	How about the lounge? We could be waiters!
JOHN:	Not bad! Hold on. (*Turns to face the viewers*) Hey you, Announcer!
VOICE:	Me?

JOHN:	Yes, you! What part of the boat are you talking about next?
VOICE:	Ah well, I was going to show the people the lounge.
JOHN:	Just as I thought! Well, you go to the lounge, we're staying here. You stop following us and giving away our disguises!

INT. SHIP LOUNGE

VOICE:	Oh, I'm terribly sorry. Now, in the ship's lounge, we find the utmost in luxurious... (*Fades*)

EXT. SHIP UPPER DECK

RINGO:	Has he gone?
JOHN:	I think so. Come on, let's take cover, someone's coming! (*THE BEATLES approach a small submarine.*)
GEORGE:	This looks cosy! (*They enter, PROFESSOR appears from behind the sub*)
PROF:	That's funny, I thought I heard noises. Let me look at the specimen I caught yesterday! (*He approaches a sad-looking OCTOPUS in a shallow pool*) Ah, you are a beauty! But you are so sad! Don't worry. Maybe today we will find your true love! (*He pulls a switch and the submarine is lifted over the side of the ship, and under the waves*)

INT. DIVING BELL

JOHN:	You know what's happened, of course. We're locked inside a diving bell and some silly nit is dropping us into the ocean. (*Pause. Then all react!*)
ALL:	HELP! HELP! LET US OUT OF HERE![128]

Hardly sophisticated British humour, but it made the screen-glued kids chuckle of a Saturday morning.

But the chief reason that the show still languishes, unavailable in any commercial form decades after Apple finally bought up the entire series in the early '90s, is the realisation of the *AHDN* horror of having The Beatles dubbed out of all proportion in order to appease the US market. Brian wasn't usually known for striking US deals guaranteed to enthuse the boys, so it's not too surprising that no Beatle wanted to be particularly involved, the usually gung-ho McCartney being happy to say, 'We all thought the cartoon series was a joke and refused to do the voices for it. But financially it was a good deal and the kids seemed to like it. We weren't really keen on the people from King. They were nice enough but artistically we weren't that impressed.'[129] Al Brodax grouched, 'The thing that attracted them most to the series was all they had to do was sign a piece of paper, and no work was involved. However, Ringo liked animation and he did come to the studio now and then to see what was happening.'[130]

Left so largely to their own devices, the nonsensical fear that a scouse twang would be inaudible outside the UK called for an ultimately catastrophically silly solution, though Brodax stuck to his guns, insisting, 'People understood them! They would never have gotten the ratings they got if we had used Liverpudlian voices.'[131] All male characters were split between two performers, the first being thoroughly English comic actor Lance Percival, a hit in films like *Carry On Cruising* and as improvising balladeer on *TW3*, which even led to his own George Martin-produced cover of classic comedy calypso 'Shame and Scandal In The Family'. Percival provided the more successful voices of Paul and Ringo, who was of course to become the stand-out clown of the show. 'I made the Ringo voice a little more Birmingham, and slower. Ringo probably thought, "what the hell was that?" But it was an accent that could be easily understood in America. I made Paul a lot more up and chirpy because I felt that's the way he was... I've been in movies where the same thing happens. The producers had to sell it to a big market, so the solution was to put in just enough accent to make them sound English. When Paul finally saw the cartoons, he didn't recognise his character's voice. But they all had to understand that King Features wasn't looking for a genuine Liverpudlian accent.'[132] But with all posthumous respect to a true great of cartoon voice acting, veteran of Disney cartoons and *The Rocky & Bullwinkle Show*, the George and especially John voices provided by Paul Frees remain the most problematic spot of unintentional sabotage in the show's creation. The Chicago-born Frees was known as 'The Man of 1,000 Voices', but sadly this didn't extend to any kind of stab at a scouse accent. Harrison ended up with a strange kind of squeaky Irish-cum-Mexican brogue, while Lennon's famous tones were replaced with Frees' stab at a Rex Harrison impersonation. It's true that John could briefly drop into a posh RP voice (as he had when mocking Tory PM-to-be Edward Heath, who had criticised the band's Liverpudlian accents), but the complete misunderstanding of what made John John to this day utterly undoes all the things the animators strove to get right. Certainly, although the cartoon characters were featured in the UK tour programme for 1965, Brian Epstein was appalled by the finished product, and specifically blocked the show from being broadcast on UK TV, lest they all became the wrong kind of laughing stock back home.

Admittedly, there is another reason why the cartoon is so, yes, *problematic* for a 21st century release, and though it's fair to tire of every other comedy creation immediately being traduced for humour 'of its time', even the most casual dip into the series makes it impossible to ignore the staggeringly crass and offensive cultural and racial depictions throughout – certainly, a fresh release could well trigger complaints from those of a Chinese background – and Japanese, Italian, German, Romany, Native American, Hispanic, Indian, British, Extra-Terrestrial… and so on. Some claim that the worst offenders for the racial stereotyping were the Australian animators – but perhaps that observation is in itself a little racist.

The show had gone into production inspired by *AHDN*, but the first batch weren't available for the Beatles to sample until the very day of the *Help!* premiere. 'The Beatles arranged to come for a showing in Soho,' Percival recalled, remembering an afternoon of live action cartoon behaviour, with Paul mimicking Mickey Mouse and John scurrying around under tables on all fours. 'They arrived in a big black limousine, rushed up the stairs and sat down to watch. They were naturally very curious to know who played which voices. Paul in particular was very enthusiastic. I think they really enjoyed it all... Paul was sitting next to me saying, "Is that supposed to be me?" I said, "Don't worry, it's not supposed to be you. It's just supposed to be a funny voice that suits you"... They liked it at first. It was an ego thing, but then they got picky... Ringo was okay with it all, and he said to me, "I see you've made me the dumb-dumb!" I told him no, that's just the way the scripts were written.' 'It was very positive,' insisted Ed Vane of US network ABC TV, 'They were extremely amused by it. Ringo especially. He was chuckling away and making little comments and joshing with the others. The mood when it was all over was one of pleasure and enjoyment on the part of The Beatles.' Certainly the show was a massive hit from the moment it debuted on ABC at 10 A.M. the following 25 September, attracting an audience share of 51.9, but Brodax was to add, 'In the beginning, The Beatles loved the series, as I remember it, because of the high ratings we got. As the years went by, they weren't all that crazy about it because they didn't really like the voices I used.' Repetition soon became tiresome, Vane admitted: 'You can't fool the kids. When they watched "Roll Over Beethoven" the first time, they thought it was hysterical. By the sixth time, it wasn't quite so funny. And that's why the ratings went down.'[133]

From the very start, *The Beatles* cartoon was out of date, due to the band's endless surging forward in every respect, but by the time the third season aired two years later, the use of songs like 'Strawberry Fields' and 'Taxman' seemed more out of place than ever before even with added psychedelic credits, and production was halted forever. The cartoon has diehard fans to this day, was repeated to death for decades after first broadcast, and even briefly washed up on late night UK TV eventually. Tony Barrow buoyantly offered, 'Whilst generally helping to sustain The Beatles' record sales at a healthy level between concert tours (and beyond that short-lived era), the cartoon programmes also preserved in Peter Pan fashion the early carefree and playful "Four Mop Tops" image, which children loved and parents approved of... This crucial aspect of the Al

Brodax venture was not even considered, let alone appreciated, by Brian Epstein, but the rest of us saw it as a significant factor in prolonging the career of The Beatles in the commercially important teenyboppers' sector.'[134] Whether Apple will ever see fit to remaster and release such a cheap and flawed cash-in remains to be seen, but if the views of two Beatles are taken into account, it's still possible – in the late 1970s, Lennon, perhaps surprisingly the most avid collector of Beatle tat, was happy to say, 'You know, when *The Beatles* cartoons come on every Sunday, I still get a kick out of watching them',[135] while the hardest to please of them all, Harrison, perversely insisted, 'I always kind of liked them. They were so bad or silly that they were good, if you know what I mean, and I think the passage of time might make them more fun now.'[136] One notable result of the cartoon's US popularity was the decision to give anarchic *Animaniacs* star Wakko Warner an approximation of Ringo's daft voice, as created by Percival, in tribute.

While keeping their own cartoon at bay, The Beatles also abandoned a separate plan that would have seen them animated by the greatest animation studio in history – Disney's jazz-oriented adaptation of Rudyard Kipling's *Jungle Book* series earmarked a quartet of quirky vultures for a rather shameless shoehorning in of the band, who were designed accordingly with Beatle-ish features, and close harmony outbursts. Ultimately the plans came to nought, jazz-hating Lennon apparently telling the obviously keen Epstein that they should go and hire Elvis instead, but the replacement stabs at scouse accents heard when the film was released in 1967 were at least streets ahead of Paul Frees' voices. When Jon Favreau remade the film in CG, he approached Paul and Ringo once again – to no avail.

The Beatles cartoon may have been the most direct scheme to capitalise on The Beatles' popularity in the world of US TV, but it was not the only one. In the summer of 1965, auditions were held to find 'Folk & Roll Musicians-Singers for acting roles in new TV series. Running Parts for 4 insane boys, age 17-21…' Aspiring young producer Bob Rafelson had apparently thought of a sitcom which centred on a rock and roll band back in 1962, but when the arrival of The Beatles on the silver screen so exemplified what he had in mind, he hooked up with his contemporary Bert Schneider to put the plan into operation at once, and with first choice, New York outfit The Lovin' Spoonful unavailable, the formation of a completely fictional band, The Monkees, was necessary. Where Brodax created a fake Beatles with animation, Rafelson & Schneider used musically-talented actors. Only cute Mancunian Davy Jones (who had appeared as The Artful Dodger in an excerpt from *Oliver!* alongside The Beatles on *The Ed Sullivan Show*) kept any semblance of British inspiration, with Micky Dolenz, Peter Tork and Mike Nesmith having their own distinct styles, but any squinting viewer of the crazy colourful TV show which eventually debuted on NBC in September 1966 would swear that it was a spin-off from *Help!*, with its four young musical pseudo-innocents getting caught up in elaborate scrapes while trying to play 'their' songs. Beatle references abounded in the show too, with Nez shown throwing darts at a picture of the band in the very first episode.

Despite this obvious inspiration (and indeed the oft-trotted-out trivia that The Monkees outsold The Beatles and Stones combined in 1967), there was nothing but sweetness and light between the two bands whenever their paths crossed, with all Monkees in awe of 'the four Kings of EMI' they would eulogise as they began to take glorious control of their own musical output. Lennon took the opportunity to get his own back at his own inane press by dubbing them 'the funniest comedy team since The Marx Brothers', and the boys threw their young pretenders a huge party at the Speakeasy club when they came to Britain in '67, with Nesmith and Dolenz being present for some key *Sgt. Pepper* sessions.

As any Monkees fan will tell you, despite their constrained genesis, the four 'fake' pop stars developed into a fascinatingly proficient combo with fans worldwide. But like their inspiration, their sense of humour remained key – the Dolenz classic referenced above, 'Randy Scouse Git', was not inspired by any Beatle, but by the bigoted bawling of that icon of ironic bigotry, Alf Garnett.

TONIGHT FROM BLACKBURN

1965 rang further bells for the boys with another US tour following their movie release, kicking off with Shea Stadium (where the noise was so loud, John claimed to have sung 'Pissed with gout' instead of 'Twist and Shout') and featuring the famed but less than explosive face-off with a sullen Elvis Presley, who would stun the world when he was posthumously outed as, allegedly, a die-hard, pepperpot-quoting Monty Python fan, prone to calling people 'squire' in Nudge-Nudge tones. George recalled of the crossover evening, 'We were just having fun, we were all in hysterics. We laughed a lot. That's one thing we forgot about for a few years – laughing. When we went through all the lawsuits, it looked as if everything was bleak, but when I think back to before that, I remember we used to laugh all the time. We pulled up at some big gates and someone said, "Oh yeah, we're going to see Elvis", and we all fell out of the car laughing, trying to pretend we weren't silly: just like a Beatles cartoon.'[137] Returning to Blighty to start work on *Rubber Soul*, the band could at least content themselves that they would be spared another panto at the end of the year, just as they turned down any offers to appear before royalty again, MBEs notwithstanding.

The closest thing to festive fooling around came for John and Paul in *The Music of Lennon & McCartney,* a TV special spearheaded by ITV producer Johnny Hamp for Granada, recorded back up north in November for broadcast on 16 December. Admittedly, the composers didn't go out of their way to get laughs, with no scripted gags worth quoting, just the Nerk-Twins-as-was wandering around a cagey set introducing numbers in a lightly whimsical way before a live audience. At least the artists performing their tunes were of a high calibre, naturally including The George Martin Orchestra (paying tribute to Dudley Moore's 'And The Same To You' at the end of the opening 'I Feel Fine' medley), plus Henry Mancini, Lulu, Marianne Faithfull, Esther Phillips, and of course, Cilla, not long before her own joyful guest spot on *Not Only But Also* which presaged her own TV variety

130

show, which would be packed with the best comedians of the decade – and even Ringo.

McCartney admitted, 'We weren't really that keen, but Johnny was very persuasive and a nice bloke, so we were happy to do it for him... It was a great honour that someone as good as Henry would be doing our songs; so, altogether, we couldn't really turn it down.'[138] The only real stab at comedy was provided by one of their greatest heroes, in his first Beatle collaboration. Back in the spring, Peter Sellers had dropped in on the *Help!* set at Twickenham to present Grammy awards to the smirking boys on film, Lennon piping up 'Thank you, Mr Ustinov!' as the gongs were dished out. With Beatles music earning such highfalutin plaudits everywhere, the idea arose to give their lyrics extra cultural weight by having Sellers bark the lyrics of 'A Hard Day's Night' in the unmistakeable guise of Laurence Olivier's Richard III, the hump-backed 'dull Shakespeare' cliché which set the Bard back for decades. The lasting highlight of the programme, this skit was the culmination of a scheme Sellers had been working on in the studio with old mucker George Martin, recording Beatle songs in different spoken styles, which resulted in a single release that December, plus an EP with four differently reimagined lyrics. Besides the Ricardian recitation, 'Help!' was delivered as a soppy sermon, 'Can't Buy Me Love' as a flirtatious dialogue between a cad and what sounded like Sellers' *Ray's a Laugh* character Crystal Jellybottom, and there was a whole array of 'She Loves You' skits, most of which did not surface until years after Sellers' death. The song's conversational lyrics (frustratingly lacking the 'And with a love like that...' pay-off) suggested different scenarios, each with a different stab at a punchline – as interpreted, best of all, by Dr Strangelove himself (to massed fascist cries of 'Ja! Ja! Ja!'), or by cockney geezers ('Why don't you mind your bleedin' business?'), or upper-class twits ('Strange thing is, I'm frightfully keen on her too!'), and finally, the then-certainly-un-releasable pair of Irishmen ('God knows oi love her too, oh God oi love dat girl and oi want to fock her as quick as oi can'). This was Sellers' final recording session for Parlophone, but not the last time he would drop in on his charismatic young friends.

The band may have jettisoned many of their seasonal duties, but the Christmas flexidisc was not just considered a tradition worth keeping, more time than ever was invested in making the fan service a proper laff, with *Rubber Soul* sessions temporarily abandoned to experiment with the sound effects EMI could offer them. The resultant festive message was a pleasingly loose jumble of ad-libbing, essentially mocking their previous well-behaved 'thank you letter' flexis, and bookended by a facetiously droned festive cover of 'Yesterday'. Lennon can be heard protesting against Tony Barrow's attempts to do it the old way, laughing 'I can't read that straight, I mean, if that's what you're waiting for, I can't do it, man, y'know, I don't dig it!' To which Barrow begged, 'Make it stupid, but make it, y'know, good stupid'. There were also paranoid cries of 'copyright!' when John began crooning The Four Tops' 'Same Old Song', but this just hinted at the experiments the boys went through with EMI's royalty-free background recordings that night, playing around with whatever even vaguely seasonal scenario each sound suggested.

Around this time – November 1965 – one of the most celebrated outtake recordings emerged from a day nailing down George's 'Think For Yourself'. The bigger boys' standard casual attitude to Harrison's numbers gave rise to a free-wheeling hysterical vocal rehearsal captured by Martin which was so rich in oddities, it provided both a snatch of harmony for *Yellow Submarine* and the songwriter's laid-back intro '… do what you wanna do', sampled and looped by McCartney for 'Free Now' on the Super Furry Animals collaboration *Liverpool Sound Collage* 35 years later. But it's the infectious giggling and shouted in-jokes which made the outtake so infamous, with John and Paul trading dumb American and Australian accents, slipping into the themes from *Steptoe & Son* or *Stingray* (*'Marina, Aqua Marina, How come you fuck up everything that you do…?'*) or vamping pastiches of their own back catalogue – *'Listen, do you want to hold a penis? Doo-wah-doo…'* George joined in the knowing impersonations of a brash scouse street preacher spouting scripture and crying 'WHY SUCH FURY?! WHAT IS THIS WRATH THAT BEHOLDS YOU? WHY SUCH FERVOUR?!'

– a lost reference which nobody has ever bothered to try and get a living Beatle to explain. The ex-Nerk Twins also developed a mini-psycho-drama of unctuously posh testy theatricals irritated by their failure to get the job done:

JOHN:	I'm so sorry, I feel so stupid, I don't know what to do!
PAUL:	Look, Terrence! If you want to resign from the amateur dramatics, do!
JOHN:	It's not that, I've put a lot of money and thought into the whole thing!
PAUL:	Yeah, but let's face it, you're crap! Aren't you?
JOHN:	Well alright, alright!
PAUL:	I mean, you're only doing walk-ons!
JOHN:	Whose father was it got the hall in the first place?
PAUL:	You're only doing walk-ons, and you keep farting those up!

The festive out-takes often give us The Beatles (reticent Ringo aside) at their free-wheeling funniest: relaxed, making each other laugh, audibly chewing food on mic, and messing about for the craic. Paul was conspicuously the instigator of this experimentation, reacting to sounds of a swirling storm or bubbling water FX as a news anchor, delivering apologies for the heating or the plumbing in the recording studio, before handing over to 'John Lennon: sheep farmer, colour consultant, chain gang foreman, fighter pilot, and well-known table-tennis wicket keeper' – a storming intro which elicited nothing more than a dulcet Wilson-esque 'It's been a long time since I've had a chance to speak to you on this level… and that's about all.' That year, Paul even recorded a faux DJ set and gifted discs to the other three Beatles, entitled 'Unforgettable' – the 1965 equivalent of a mixtape – and even decades later in his *Chaos & Creation In the Back Yard* phase, he gave away a clear adoration of improvising characters over quirky musical backing, playing loops on the Moog and imagining a cockney Lothario seducing a Wendy Richard soundalike, or hitting a lower key to magic up the atmosphere of a German beerhall.

Rights-free effects discs were played in to the studio – a flowing river, a boxing match or a steam train – triggering a stream of consciousness, a kind of spoof news bulletin littered with Harold Wilson impersonations, plus an *Opportunity Knocks* piss-take, as chief mimic McCartney tried to steer everyone towards something suitable for the 1965 flexi – and failed:

FX: SCREAMING BABY

JOHN: This isn't the baby we used in the test, but we got Mrs Williamson to slice up a fresher baby, and here is the baby now in the process of being sliced. There you go.

GEORGE: *(Posh)* As you see, the smaller slices are the only slices that are allowed into the box. Now, all the bigger slices, like the limbs and the head, we keep out, and we use in various other meat products such as PAL, kennel meat and other things like that. But you, the buyers, must realise that only the small parts of this child will end up in your family frozen pack, in your shops from Friday.

PAUL: *(Strident southern reporter)* It's not a pretty sight, I can tell you. It's not a very pretty sight seeing a baby sliced up on a, on a slicing machine. It's not too pretty, folks…

JOHN: Well, I think it's time to put the baby to sleep, eh, Ringo…?

PAUL: *(West country)* Well, down 'ere at the station the constables are just giving me their reports for the evening, and *(Suddenly Transatlantic)* the winner of the personality reports this evening, the best report, neatness taken into account, was PC Lennon! PC Lennon, please come forward and collect your award…

FX: CROWD HUBBUB

JOHN: (*Fey Lancashire*) Thanks very much for the prize, I must say I'm very happy to have it, it's the first time I've won a policeman, and I'm going to look after him as if he was me own... (*Shouts*) Will the next contestant stand up on the winner, please?

GEORGE: (*Lancashire*) I've come along here tonight from Blackburn, and I was there the other night at the labour club, and I saw this fella there juggling...

PAUL: (*Hughie Green*) Isn't that wunnerful, ladies and gentlemen, the labour club? (*Claps*)

GEORGE: And so here he is... here he is...

PAUL: And what is his name?

GEORGE: Yes, well, we've had trouble finding his name due to the fact that he lost his birth certificate when he was born, you see.

PAUL: Well anyway, whoever he may be... (*Loses all energy*) it's knocking again... (*As himself*) If we could just keep going for another couple of hours I'm sure we'll get something.

JOHN: Has anyone mentioned Christmas yet?

PAUL: ...Alright alright, that's enough of that, what are you doing here? Alright, come on! ... What are the three of you doing hanging round here?

FX: CAR BRAKES, SQUEALING, CRASH!

RINGO: Good sound.

PAUL: Is he alright?

JOHN: I think it was just a scratch, sir – just a scratch, sir – I think it was just a scratch, sir – (*Click!*) just a scratch, sir...

ALL: (*In unison*) You-will-notice-that-the-band-is-playing-music-which-is-out-of-copyright-so-that-nobody-has-to-pay-any-royalties!

*

The startlingly black opening of this extract eerily predates the infamous 'Butcher Cover' which got the boys into such hot water a few months later, posed for photographer Robert Whitaker's conceptual piece *A Somnambulent Adventure*. While those record covers shocked everyone and were quickly pasted over with something more benign, the above infanticidal snatch of supposedly private sickness was obviously never intended for public consumption – a potentially Beatlemania-demolishing prospect. Nonetheless, this crossing over the line into Martin's specialist area of audio comedy was to feed back into their core output – the music.

PROSTITUTES AND LESBIANS

The fact that Sellers was able to get laughs from sending up Beatle lyrics shows that hitherto, the musical output which had been sending teens a-swooning throughout Beatlemania had been all-but devoid of levity – they could still gurn and send each other up in between songs, but lyrically 'love' was all they needed. When Lennon appeared on BBC Radio's *World of Books* in June '65, presenter Kenneth Allsop challenged him to start using his eccentric wordplay in his songs, and Bob Dylan similarly wondered at the relatively staid sentiments of most Beatle tracks, given the wild imaginations of the writers. The odd secret smirk at singing 'tit-tit-tit' in the backing for 'Girl' (nothing compared to the all-out scouse masturbation reference in 'Penny Lane', 'four of fish and finger pies'), or perhaps the implied 'prick' in 'She's a big teaser' from 'Drive My Car' was as far as they dared to go. Paul recalled, 'It gave us a laugh. It was to get some light relief in the middle of this real big career that we were forging. If we could put in something that was a little bit subversive then we would. George Martin might say, "Was that 'dit dit' or 'tit tit' you were singing?" "Oh, 'dit dit', George, but it does sound a bit like that, doesn't it?" Then we'd get in the car and break down laughing.'[139] But despite *Rubber Soul* and *Revolver* both having punning names, Beatle single and album tracks alike still overwhelmingly dealt with the usual teen fodder of love and heartache, gag-free. John's summoning up of the autobiographical 'Nowhere Man' was a pointer away from that, and the end of 'Norwegian Wood' could be taken as a very dark joke, but it was *Revolver*, recorded in late spring 1966 before their final US tour, which would signal the real development, a clear gear change in their music's humorous scope. Everybody focuses on John's development as a lyricist, but that is to take for granted the quantum leap showed by Paul in songs like 'Paperback Writer' – he always had a flair for imagining the little lives of the non-famous, but the story of the desperate hack angling for publication seemed to come from nowhere, a spot of first-person character comedy in which the would-be author's lack of self-awareness is summed up by '*It's a thousand pages give or take a few, I'll be writing more in a week or two...*' – a line which an observer of social mores like David Nobbs would have treasured. 'Drive My Car' even ended on a clear punchline.

Everybody knows that 1966 marked the end of the band's touring, finally sick of the screaming, the death threats and all those flying jellybeans, but this final US tour did at least provide one of the funniest comebacks from any Beatle in any press conference, brilliantly delivered by a nonchalant McCartney in San Francisco:

Q: In a recent article, *Time* magazine referred to 'Day Tripper' as being about a prostitute, and 'Norwegian Wood' as being about a lesbian. I just wanted to know what your intent was when you wrote it, and what your feeling is about the *Time* magazine criticism of the music that is being written today?

PAUL: (*Innocently*) We were just trying to write songs about prostitutes and lesbians, that's all. (*Cue hysterics*)

JOHN: Quipped Ringo.

PAUL: Cut!

JOHN: You can't use it on the air, that.

There was one other boon of this US tour – The Beatles' avuncular welcoming in to their sacred circle of one of their biggest fans, the camp (but then still closeted) Merseyside native disc jockey Maurice Cole, AKA Kenny Everett, hailed as a 'genius' by none other than Spike Milligan. Four years into his career at Radio London, Kenny landed the plum job of accompanying The Beatles on the tour, and had a baptism of fire when a screaming crowd surged the caravan with all five men in it, tossing them around like rice in a maraca. Although only a couple of years senior to Everett, the boys took him under their wings; he recalled, 'I would suffer from these Hiroshima-sized attacks of paranoia and just wander into a corner feeling bad for days. Paul McCartney saw all this going on and took pity on me, thank God! He took me into the bathroom of the hotel where we were staying and said, "Why don't you just ask me one question and I'll rabbit on for a bit? Then you'll have enough material for ages."'[140] Kenny's mix of uniquely accomplished radio experimentation, authority-baiting humour and personal cuddliness made him the band's favourite DJ, first port of call for any chat about what the band were up to, and he became particularly close to John, on whom he admitted having a massive crush, to mutual friend Lulu. Ev's first ever acid trip was also administered by John on a rainy Weybridge golf course, apparently inspiring the lyric '*When the sun don't come you get your tan from standing in the English rain*' in 'I Am The Walrus', and Kenny's proximity to the Fab Four was further strengthened when he got his first real boyfriend – Epstein's PA Peter Brown.

It wasn't just the live shows that were being wound down in 1966 – after the previous years' slapstick activities, the year was also notably short on funny TV and radio appearances, with the last Beatles appearance at The Playhouse for *Saturday Club* broadcast on 4 June. McGrath and Lindsay-Hogg's videos frankly saved them the bother of guesting on comedy shows, and they often found themselves featured on TV without their stir anyway – British pig puppets Pinky & Perky had been squeaking popular songs for many years, and didn't just cover The Beatles, they even had their own spoof crow quartet, The Beakles. The wooden swine's American counterparts Alvin & the Chipmunks had already paid homage with a whole album of helium-style covers, and even The Flintstones had donned Beatle wigs for their own inane form of prehistoric rock tribute. The band were all-but unavoidable, so why bother with TV comedy skits? The closest 1966 would come to their usual knockabout activity was Lennon's final appearance on *Not Only But Also* in November, debuting his granny specs to the public by cameoing as the bribe-hungry doorman Dan, guardian of the exclusive lavatory-themed nightclub 'Ad Lav', as investigated by Cook's wooden American documentarian Hiram J Pipesucker in his search for the real 'Swinging London':

JOHN:	Excuse me, sir, are you a member?
PETER:	I'm sorry, I'm not. I'm from American television. I'm doing an interview downstairs.
JOHN:	I'm sorry, sir, you must be a member to get in here.
PETER:	Would it help if I told you that I was the Duke and Duchess of Windsor?
JOHN:	Oh, sorry, sir, I didn't recognise you, madam... Well, actually there is a five pound waiting list.
PETER:	I understand. This is one of the, er, blue ones, isn't it?
JOHN:	Aye. (*Takes money*)
PETER:	Thank you very much indeed. I love your Oxford accent!
JOHN:	Lovely. Follow your nose, sir![141]

The sequence in question closed with a Moore number composed to lightly rib the UK's 'druggy druggy' psychedelic explosion, 'LS Bumble Bee', with a moustachioed Pete and Dud shown recording the number with the most ridiculous 'instruments', from squeezing a stuffed seagull to poking a baby – though the song was largely an excuse to repeat the word 'bum' many times over:

> *There is a little insect not many people see*
> *He's known to all the insects as the LS Bumble Bee*
> *So when you hear him coming just throw away your tea*
> *That psycho-delic humming will mean you'll soon be free!*
> *I can hear the hum of the bubbly L.S. Bum Bum Bum Bumble Bee...*
> *Now it's time to fly out of your mind and into the sky with me...*
> *I fly to the land where my hands can see,*
> *Where my eyes can walk and the mountains talk...*
> *I hear with my knees, run with my nose, smell with my feet,*
> *My mouth is a rose. Ahhh...*[142]

The pastiche was also released as a single on Decca, and despite the clear credit, and Dudley's voice being unmistakeable, some softer-minded Beatles fans over the years have tried to engineer some form of controversy over whether Lennon or any other Beatle had a hand in its writing and recording – which of course, he did not. Nevertheless, in a 1981 letter reproduced on the cover of novelty album *Beatlesongs*, Moore did admit, 'I wrote the music to, in some ways, satirise The Beach Boys rather than The Beatles. But I'm grateful if some small part of the world thinks that it may have been them, rather than us!'

One sequence in *Help!* had shown the heroes fleeing the country in hairy disguise, with Ringo and especially bespectacled John looking uncannily how they would a decade or so later. Otherwise John's round National Health glasses were first seen perched on his nose in character as Musketeer Gripweed in Lester's next film *How I Won The War* – another UA movie, filmed largely in the south-eastern Spanish province of Almeria at the start of autumn. The young generation weren't yet characterised by any fervent anti-war, pro-peace philosophy, but Lester was attracted to the polemic of Patrick Ryan's original novel, and it was right up the street of his favoured screenwriter, military buff Charles Wood, who went right into action as soon as *Help!* was complete, punching up the novel's comedy, and building the plot around the mission to create a cricket pitch in

North Africa. 'I've tried to paint and write, now I'm having a bash at a straight acting role. It's fun. It's hard. It's different... I did it because The Beatles had stopped touring and I didn't know what to do', John said, defining Gripweed, who barely registers in the novel, as 'not particularly nice. He's not *too* horrible, he's just looking after himself all the time. That's the main thing... I'm Crawford's batman. He's Officer Goodbody, and I'm meant to look after him, but I spend most of the time not looking after him and trying to dodge it.'[143] This unexpected voluntary move into character acting was a godsend to Lester and producer Denis O'Dell, who had been busy elsewhere during *Help!* but felt that Lennon's madcap mouthiness would suit the servile sidekick to inept protagonist Lt. Goodbody (played by Michael Crawford seven years before his role as the hapless Frank Spencer in classic sitcom *Some Mothers Do 'Ave 'Em* would earn him an irritating form of comedy immortality). 'I explained to John that the film was essentially an anti-war piece and joked that his character had a wonderful death,' O'Dell wrote. 'John agreed to play the part on the spot, and I came away from NEMS with John Lennon on board and an extra quarter of a million, which wasn't bad for an afternoon's work!'[144]

Many years later John dismissed the film as 'lousy', and directed by a 'zany man in search of power', and Lester's war movie was critically panned when it was released a whole year after production (delayed due to work on subsequent picture, *Petulia*). It's often been implied that the one good thing to come from Lennon's time in Almeria was 'Strawberry Fields Forever', inspired by his villa's resemblance to his Liverpool playground. But though he was lonely enough to encourage visits from Ringo and Neil (who even took a supporting role as an orange soldier), John threw himself into this new venture with surprising verve, liberated by being part of an ensemble, and was said to have turned up on set even when Gripweed wasn't needed. He had complained of being upstaged by McKern and co in the previous film, but perhaps as a result of the lessons he learned from the other actors, particularly Roy Kinnear, Ronald Lacey and the resplendent Michael Hordern, John's performance in *HIWTW*, though undeniably a fluke mis-step in his career, probably constitutes the best sustained comic performance by a Beatle, a revelation, given how little he had to do in the previous film. The Mosleyite fascist Gripweed has few grand speeches, but his constant insincere obsequiousness to Goodbody is so un-Lennon-esque as to be amusing in itself, and John hams it up to just the right degree – even if many of the best lines were given to his co-stars, like Hordern as General Grapple, in the latter sequence where company madman Juniper finally reveals his sanity by absconding with Field Marshall Monty:

GRIPWEED: I liked it better when he was a comedian. He wasn't very funny, but I liked it better. Jokes. Mind you, I'm working class.

GRAPPLE: Ah. (*Puts arms around GRIPWEED*)
            I had a grandfather who was a miner… Until he sold it.[145]

Wood's source material was a far more straightforward satirical narrative, with the shameless Goodbody recounting his exploits to his German captors, but the finished film throws a plethora of eye-opening postmodern techniques into the brew, with each member of Goodbody's platoon addressing the camera, both before and after he leads them to their death – a particularly harrowing spectacle in the case of Lennon. The futility of their sacrifices was hammered home via the shocking inclusion of real footage of murdered conscripts from WWII, a brave move which all but smothered any humour in the proceedings. There was even a jolting sequence which knowingly harked back to *Help!*, cutting to a cinema audience watching the movie – and there's Dandy Nichols and Gretchen Franklin playing the same two old ladies who had so meekly waved at The Beatles.

Defending the film's flop, the director said, 'We thought there were a lot of good things that really came off. A lot of people that we knew felt that it was a good thing to be doing and we were encouraged by that. And there was a lot of hype about it, because of John Lennon. It came at a good time. I remember sitting on our lawn doing the interview with David Frost, and Mick Jagger was there and John was talking about it...' Indeed, nothing hitherto had sparked off quite so much Lennon peace-preaching: 'If they said, fight the war now, my age group would fight the war. Not that they'd want to. There might be a bit more trouble getting them in line because I'd be up there shouting, Don't do it...' 'It had a lot of impact,' Lester continues, 'and then everyone saw it and the response was horrible. Then the National Front threw smoke bombs in the cinema where it was showcasing.'[146] Lennon was never the focus of the film's brickbats, but this was to be the last scripted performance he ever gave – in future, any calls for him to act would be immediately handed over to Starr.

With most of their familiar humorous outlets all but stemmed, perhaps it's little wonder that The Beatles' music began to show more signs of their natural larkiness. The cartoon regurgitated copious maritime plots, enabling the artists to re-use the same ship's deck backgrounds, and whether this inspired McCartney or not (no Liverpudlian could be short of sea-faring inspiration) his dream of a happy life lived with friends in a yellow submarine marked a further step away from the usual love song fare. No sane adult could claim that 'Yellow Submarine' was in itself *funny*, but conceived as a kid's singalong number as it was, the recording was a blast. 'I was laying in bed in the Ashers' garret,' Paul told Barry Miles, 'and there's a nice twilight zone just as you're drifting into sleep and as you wake from it – I always find it quite a comfortable zone. I remember thinking that a children's song would be quite a good idea... I was thinking of it as a song for Ringo, which it eventually turned out to be, so I wrote it as not too rangy in the vocal. I just made up a little tune in my head, then started making a story – sort of an ancient mariner, telling the young kids where he'd lived. It was pretty much my song as I recall.'[147]

Of course, it's the production rather than the lyrics (partially written with Lennon and Donovan) which lifts 'Yellow Submarine' into the realms of audio comedy. Just a few days after the song had been laid down, a merry gathering including Brian Jones and Marianne Faithfull worked together to add a maritime soundscape which would have done The Goons proud. Geoff Emerick unlocked EMI's store of bizarre effects apparatus: 'The cupboard had everything – chains, ships bells, hand bells from the wartime, tap dancing mats, whistles, hooters, wind machines, thunder-storm machines... everything!'[148] Each Beatle got their chance to add to the cacophony, John blowing bubbles in a bucket and throwing in wacky music hall responses with Paul, Ringo standing in the corridor to bellow 'Drop the cable!' and so on, culminating with Mal Evans strapping on a marching drum and leading a spirited march all around the studio. There were to be further marching effects, and an extra injection of Lennon-ese nonsense, in Ringo's intended spoken introduction: '...And we will march till three the day to see them gathered there. From Land O'Groats to John O'Green, with Stepney do we tread, to see us yellow submarine. We love it.' But this of course was dropped before the album's release on 5 August. Martin told the NME, 'It must have been one of the most unusual Beatles recording sessions ever – more like the things I've done with The Goons and Peter Sellers. The boys loved every minute of it... If a comedy idea comes up again then I'm sure they'll try it because they've always had plenty of humour anyway.'[149] Harrison reaffirmed his love of 'novelty' when he said, 'The year that song came out I think it was voted the most popular and the most hated song in Britain. It's one of those songs that the kids all love, the grannies all love, the people who just like The Beatles all love it – and the people who don't like it, hate it. It's one of those songs you can't get out of your head once you hear it. It's a pretty cute song, but it's a children's song, basically.' Starr added, 'That song's given me a career. Everyone can sing that song. Even foetuses know that song.'[150]

Recorded around the same period was the lacerating jolt of 'Taxman', kicking off the first side of Revolver with a cough and a snarled count-in. Despite John being forever rated as the wittiest of all Beatles, this was only the first overtly satirical offering from George, and arguably the first topical comedy song released by a pop band. Lennon's songs could bristle with wit, as could the others', but 'the quiet one' was to be the writer of the band's most amusingly caustic attacks on authority – or at least, the sole instigator, though John was adamant that George had requested his help with the lyrics, which originally contained verses rhyming 'bread' with 'dead', and lacked the pith of '*And my advice for those who die, Declare the pennies on your eyes*', but which Beatle truly came up with the improved verses will remain a mystery. True, to modern ears a millionaire rock star complaining about paying tax should be actively repellent, but by any standards the band's success had set them up for the most punishing tax rates imaginable, in the 90% tax bracket – losing nineteen shillings and sixpence out of every twenty shilling pound earned. With Epstein's Bahamas scheme bungled, even the planet's biggest stars weren't retaining a fraction of the fortune that most of their fans and especially detractors would have assumed. And so they went into action, writing and recording the satirical track in short time, and going so far as to damningly namecheck the prime minister and leader of the opposition, Harold Wilson and Edward Heath, to add extra danger – and date the song forever, always the peril of topicality.

McCartney always underlined the deliberate move towards offering variety with *Revolver*, and this new-found explosion beyond the supposed merseybeat sound they defined, with added measures of Motown and country, was obviously to extend into their next project, which would give the whole band liberating new personas, summoning up a weird world of their own creation. Killing time on a plane with Mal, Paul scribbled down some ideas – 'I started thinking about what would be a really mad name to call a band. At the time there were lots of groups with names like "Laughing Joe and his Medicine Band" or "Colonel Tucker's Medicinal Brew and Compound"'[151] – and a simple pun on their in-flight meal seasoning led to *Sergeant Pepper's Lonely Hearts Club Band*.

These far-out sessions showed The Beatles naturally exploring a new-found freedom, but it's a pleasing coincidence that Parlophone signed up a brand new bunch of loony music-makers in the spring of 1966 who would soon be making good use of Abbey Road's effects cupboards for their debut single, a revival of very silly 1930s novelty number, 'My Brother Makes The

Noises For The Talkies'. The Bonzo Dog Doo-Dah Band were doubtless in the tradition of The Temperance Seven and even more so The Alberts, right down to the use of homemade automata and enormous speech bubbles, but as the anarchic outfit of London Art School eccentrics took brave steps towards professional recording, they were challenging themselves to go far beyond any of their inspirations or competitors.

They had been formed in 1962 as The Bonzo Dog Dada Band, by twinkly saxophonist Rodney Slater, extraordinary ginger geezer and the most ironic of rabble-rousing frontmen, Vivian Stanshall, and a whole crowd of brass-blowing Edwardian-styled misfits, but it wasn't until the addition of musically educated and sensitive-souled nineteen-year-old Neil Innes the next year that the true powerhouse of the outfit was formed. The son of a Scottish warrant officer, Neil spent part of his childhood in West Germany, where piano lessons were soon joined by self-taught guitar mastery, and by the time the Fine Arts fresher walked into Goldsmith's college to be confronted with the Falstaffian Viv replete in fake giant ears, he was ready for any musical challenge.

Sick of being mistaken for imitation jazz throwbacks The New Vaudeville Band, this bunch of anarchic Essex boys (now complemented by fresh blood including louche percussionist 'Legs' Larry Smith) were just about making a living performing to boozy crowds all over the country, but the group decision to turn their tongue-in-cheek approach from scratchy old jazz 78s to any musical genre they felt like lampooning would make the Bonzos the most out-there of all 1960s combos, with the Lennon-McCartney-esque blend of the Stanshall/Innes credit, Viv's mad wordplay and Neil's lush musicality central to their success. On their first day at Abbey Road, Neil nipped out to the gents, and was bedazzled by the arrival of the four-headed monster, silhouetted against the sun, and remembered thinking, 'Oh yes, they record here too, don't they?' As admiring as any great musician would be, Innes was to nip away again to listen in on the band recording George's 'I Want To Tell You', and maybe pick up the odd tip.

The scope of the *Pepper* concept would not be clear for The

Beatles until well into 1967, and in the meantime, of course, recording had to make way at some point for that year's Christmas flexidisc. The previous year's experimentation paid off with the most coherent tangle of Goonish silliness they captured on disc, a conscious attempt to make up for the abandonment of panto, with spoofs of Teutonic jollity and *Winnie The Pooh,* generally inspired by quirky musical loops found on the mellotron:

PAUL: Our story opens in Corsica. On the veranda is a bearded man in glasses conducting a small choir. (*Choral singing*)

RINGO: Meanwhile, high in the Swiss Alps, two elderly Scotchmen munch on a rare cheese.

GEORGE: (*Scots*) Wonderful stuff this, Agnes.

JOHN: (*Also Scots*) Aye, it's wonderful stuff.

PAUL: (*Yodels*)

JOHN: I'm standing in the entrance to the main tent. Immediately behind me, the festivities have already begun.

FX: SOUNDS OF MERRIMENT, FESTIVE MUSIC

JOHN: Tell me, are you enjoying the wine?

PAUL: I am indeed, your Highness. It goes well with me!

JOHN: The King seems to be enjoying himself tonight! ... Is there a doctor round here? Anybody seen one?

FX: NAVAL WHISTLE

GEORGE: At the same time as this, in the captain's mess on board HMS Tremendous, a toast is being proposed.

RINGO: To her Majesty!

ALL: To her Majesty!

FX: SLOWED DOWN LAUGHTER

PAUL: Podgy the bear and Jasper were huddled around the unlit fire in the centre of the room.

GEORGE: (*Squeaky*) There are no more matches left, Podgy!

147

PAUL:	Said Jasper.
JOHN:	(*Deep*) Then buy some, Jasper, old friend!
PAUL:	Said Podgy.
JOHN:	Make a list and afterwards we'll go to the shop and buy matches and candles and buns.
GEORGE:	There's no more paper to write on, Podgy!
JOHN:	No need to worry, Jasper. You keep saying to yourself 'matches' and I'll keep saying 'candles' until we reach the shop. Then we won't need to write it down. We'll remember.
GEORGE:	Who'll remember the buns, Podgy?
JOHN:	We both will, Jasper! Matches!
GEORGE:	Candles! ...
PAUL:	(*Posh*) In the long dark corridors of Felpin Mansions, a door slams.

FX: DOOR SLAM

PAUL:	And the shadowy figure of Count Baldur appears. The Count is the eccentric son of Baron Landsberg, the inventor of the rack. He speaks.
JOHN:	(*German*) Guten Tagen, meine damen und herren! Welcome to Felpin Mansions. Butler'll be showing you to your rooms. Butler?

FX: FOOTSTEPS

RINGO:	Yes, sir?
JOHN:	Show the ladies and gentlemens to their rooms.
RINGO:	Yes, sir. Come this way, please!

FX: MORE FOOTSTEPS[152]

None of these random spots of whimsy led to much in the way of actual jokes, with McCartney bringing the aimless narrative to an illogical conclusion by playing the Baron a thoroughly Goon-inspired piano tune, '*Please Don't Bring Your Banjo Back, I don't know where it's been...*' but then, Epstein's pantomimes were hardly marked by quality gagsmithery, and at least this time they didn't get sidetracked by infanticidal cannibalism.

It's often been remarked that 'the first concept album', *Sgt Pepper*, doesn't quite hold together to merit that title, but with its theatrical intent, it certainly squeezed in more trademark Beatle humour than any previous disc, while playing on the same sense of Edwardian nostalgia which had inspired The Bonzos and their ilk. From the circus barker ethos of 'Being For The Benefit of Mr Kite', capturing all of Lennon's love of the circus sawdust on vinyl, to McCartney's inherited music hall cheek in 'When I'm 64', and the reference to Thora Hird's banal teatime BBC sitcom *Meet The Wife* in 'Good Morning Good Morning', *Sgt Pepper* drips with comedic influences. The album begins with the murmurs of the *Beyond the Fringe* audience, and adds a rare thing for any rock masterpiece – canned laughter. 'We had an audience laughing on the front of *Sgt Pepper,*' McCartney told Miles. 'It had always been one of my favourite moments; I'd listened to radio a lot as a kid, and there had always been a moment in a radio show, say with somebody like Tommy Cooper, where he would walk on stage and he'd say hello, and they'd laugh, and he'd tell a joke, and they'd laugh, and there would always be a moment in these things, because it was live radio, where he wouldn't say anything, and the audience would laugh. And my imagination went wild whenever that happened. I thought, "What is it? Has he dropped his trousers? Did he do a funny look?" I had to know what had made 'em laugh. It fascinated me so much, and I'd always remembered that, so when we did *Pepper* there's one of those laughs for nothing in there, just where Billy Shears is being introduced they all just laugh, and you don't know what the audience has laughed at… We sat through hours of tapes, just giggling, it was just hilarious listening to an audience laugh. It was a great thing to do actually.'[153] The clowning at the top of the LP could have gone further, had Ringo not sworn off delivering the original 'With a Little Help From My Friends' lyric, '*What would you do if I sang out of tune? Would you throw a tomato at me?*'

By this stage, Harrison's ardent passion not just for Indian music, but philosophy and religion, had created a lasting schism in his character – on one hand, George remained the biggest comedy geek in the band, an incurable lover of loony laffs, but for all the Maharishi's incessant giggling, Eastern philosophy didn't seem to sit well alongside this levity, and some would harrumph at the humourlessness of George's conviction that striving for nirvana was the fundamental meaning of life. His own understanding of this dichotomy inspired another memorable rumble of laughter on the album after his 'Within You Without You', as he told Hunter Davies, 'After all that long Indian stuff you want some light relief. It's a release after five minutes of sad music. You haven't got to take it all seriously, you know... That's what people don't understand. Like John's "I Am The Walrus" – "*I am he as you are he as you are me...*" – it's true, but it's still a joke. People looked for all sorts of hidden meanings. It's serious and it's not serious.'[154]

The evocative effects of course were producer Martin's area of expertise, and he recalled, 'Once the boys decided they would not perform any more, they wanted to just work in the studio building up *Sgt Pepper*, it became a bit like working on the Peter Sellers records, because you were building a picture in sound.'[155] When a silent tone audible only to dogs was suggested as 'something silly', he indulgently agreed, saying 'If you want a bit of a joke. I don't think anyone's ever done it, but why not?' McCartney said, 'We thought, "Well, we've got to have a bit that only the dogs can hear. Why just make records for humans?" We put those bits in just for a laugh, really: "Let's have a bit for Martha, Fluffy and Rover."'[156] A sense of humour was even required for session players, with the Beatles insisting on a party atmosphere for the recording of the cataclysmic 'orchestral orgasm' which closed the album – and the odd stuffed shirt balked at the requirement for them to wear party hats and false noses while playing. To cap it all, the album's celebrated eventual cover design by Peter Blake and Jann Haworth cameoed cardboard comedy heroes including Laurel & Hardy, Oscar Wilde, Lewis Carroll, Mae West, Terry Southern, Tommy Handley, Max

Miller, WC Fields and Lenny Bruce, who had died the previous summer.

In the summer of '67, the album was finally ready to share with the fans, and Kenny Everett was overjoyed to be present for the first play, at a private event at Brian Epstein's house, where he also recalled recording a special skit with John and Paul based on 'Lucy In The Sky With Diamonds', which has been lost to us. 'George put it on the gramophone,' Kenny said, 'and we all sat around and this thing started and blew us away, we were completely gone and on another planet. It was a quantum leap, and we thought, music can stop right here, nobody is ever going to produce anything better than this, so all musicians can go back to bed now. It was the best thing we'd ever heard! And George said, "It's quite good, isn't it?"'[157]

PRICK UP YOUR EARS

By this time, the Beatles' usual annual pattern was well and truly disrupted, and Shenson had no luck in finding the right material for their third film for UA. Dick Lester's penchant for Dumas' *Three Musketeers* books made that an irresistible pitch, but it was way off the Beatle path, and even with the offer of casting Brigitte Bardot as Lady de Winter, it was dismissed out of hand, leaving him free to film his own adaptations years later. A project from the mind of Patrick McGoohan was also mooted – George being a particular fan of *The Prisoner*, which had been allowed to use 'All You Need Is Love' in one episode – but, like most movie dreams, it came to nought.

However, a speculative script had been written by British actor-turned-TV-playwright Owen Holder – *Shades of a Personality* – in which the psyche of one man, Stanley Grimshaw, is split into four distinct personalities, culminating in the love interest having to choose between the four. There was talk of Michaelangelo Antonioni helming this experimental picture, but enthusiasm was low. In frustration, Shenson and Epstein reached out to the hottest playwright in Britain at the time – Joe Orton.

34-year-old Orton had been dreaming of literary notoriety for many years before things started to snowball for him in the mid-1960s. Having escaped his provincial background in Leicester for a life of unfettered gay abandon in the capital, Joe lived in a tiny bedsit in Islington with his older partner and self-appointed mentor Kenneth Halliwell, who he'd met at RADA, and the pair of them suffered years of frustration working together and apart on novels and plays designed to horrify the bourgeoisie. Though homosexuality was decriminalised at the end of July this year, Orton shared with Epstein and Brambell a history of risky cottaging, but where Brian's acts had led more than once to shame and pain, Joe took extreme pleasure in the clandestine lifestyle. So keen was he and Kenneth to cause any kind of stir, both ended up doing time in prison for defacing library books, pasting together startling X-rated collages and re-inserting them in books to give old ladies heart attacks. Since leaving prison five years earlier, however, Orton's luck had changed. His funereal farce *Loot* had transferred to Broadway, he won the *Evening Standard* Playwright of the Year award, and soon after came the call from Walter Shenson – the outsider was becoming an insider at last.

Presented with *Shades of a Personality*, Orton only took inspiration from the conclusion, taking it in his own perverse direction: 'Already have the idea that the end should be a church with four bridegrooms and one bride,' he wrote in his diary. 'Lots of opportunities for sexual ambiguities – a woman's bedroom at night, her husband outside and four men inside. I also would like to incorporate a lot of material from the first novel Kenneth and I wrote called *The Silver Bucket*. In it a young girl is expelled from her native village for some unnamed offence. Already see how it could be one boy expelled from some great industrial metropolis by a ceremony of mammoth proportions. Could be funny. As long as I wasn't expected to write a naturalistic script… Basically the Beatles are getting fed up with the Dick Lester type of direction. They want dialogue to speak. Also they are tired of actors like Leon McKern (sic) stealing scenes. Difficult this as I don't think any of the Beatles can act in any accepted sense. As Marilyn Monroe couldn't act.'[158] The truth is that in Orton the Beatles had found their most perfect dialogue provider since Alun Owen – his

152

work was littered with young male iconoclasts of questionable morality who speak in blunt epigrams, the Wildeisms of the 1960s, ideal for the boys to deliver – 'I'm a great success as a lunatic', 'Nobody is provocative at four in the morning', 'You must learn to control your generous impulses', 'We use a variety of tactics: the smear, the lie and, in extreme cases, the truth' and so on. At the same time, given Orton's predilection for sexual obsessions of all kinds, and outrageously dark situations, it's hard to fathom whether Brian knew what he was doing in hiring him. Intriguingly, one thing we learn from Orton's diaries here is that McCartney was already leading the push for a third movie, seen as equal to Epstein, as Shenson told Orton, '"You'll be hearing from Brian Epstein or Paul McCartney, so don't be surprised if a Beatle rings you up." "What an experience", I said. "I shall feel as nervous as I would if St Michael, or God was on the line." "Oh, there's not any need to be worried, Joe", Shenson said. "I can say from my heart that the boys are very respectful of talent. I mean, most respectful of anyone they feel has talent. I can really say that, Joe."'[159] The writer marvelled and sneered in turn upon a visit to Brian's house for dinner, where Paul told him 'The only thing I get from the theatre is a sore arse' – but made an exception for *Loot*. With the deal fixed up, Joe went home to tell Halliwell all about his latest spot of high living, and settled down to work.

A second key source of recycling occurred to him – the grotty and surreal picaresque novel *The Vision of Gombold Proval*, subsequently published as *Head to Toe*, a kind of *Alice* sans charm in which a hapless young man finds himself facing endless unkindness in a series of adventures taking place on a gigantic human body. From this murky plot came a number of threads, including a ditzy but homicidal matriarchal society, the assassination of the female prime minister, and a long painful stretch of imprisonment for the hero. Only with the script all-but finished did Shenson warn Orton that he 'was most concerned to impress me that "the boys" shouldn't be made to do anything in the film that would reflect badly on them. "You see", he said, "the kids will all imitate whatever the boys do." I hadn't the heart to tell him that the boys, in my script, have been caught *in flagrante*, become involved in dubious political activity, dressed as women, committed murder, been put in prison and committed adultery. And the script isn't finished yet.'[160] The four boys were labelled 'McTurk' 1 to 4, a fantastical personality split which the writer employed ad hoc:

THE MAYOR: The townsfolk won't tolerate you any longer, McTurk. Your indiscretions have reached monumental proportions.

McTURK: I'm not responsible for what has happened.

FATHER BRODIE: You deny that you're an evil influence? (*Lifts a folder from his desk*) Who then has committed the crimes listed here?

McTURK BITES HIS LIP. HE LOOKS AROUND THE ROOM.

McTURK: (WITH A SHRUG) Well, it was me, in a manner of speaking, Father. But I'm not one person...

FATHER BRODIE: How many people are you? I like to know of any addition to my flock.

McTURK: I'm four people.

THE MAYOR: (PAUSE) And where are the other three?

McTURK: Here in this room. They're with me all the time.

McTURK 2, 3 AND 4 APPEAR BESIDE HIM.

McTURK 2: It's most inconvenient. And costs a fortune in razor blades.

FATHER BRODIE: You're claiming, in all seriousness, that your escapades haven't been committed by you, but by some kind of triple alter-ego?

CONNIE: Never, in the whole of my life, have

154

	I heard anything so lame and stupid!
FATHER BRODIE:	I shall add insolence to the list of
	misdemeanours for which you're
	to be punished. Sit down.

(McTURK LOWERS HIMSELF INTO A CHAIR.

	Not on that chair. It has a broken
	leg.
McTURK 4:	Have you sent for a doctor?
FATHER BRODIE:	Doctors can do nothing for it. It's
	incurable.
McTURK 3:	What about faith healing?
FATHER BRODIE:	I've no faith in faith healing.

(THE BOYS SIT ON AN OTTOMAN.)[161]

Orton finished the first draft, titled *Up Against It,* so quickly that he requested his agent Peggy Ramsey delay delivery by a few weeks, but then set in what seemed an eternal wait for feedback, causing the writer to curse Epstein as 'An amateur and a fool. He isn't equipped to judge the quality of a script. Probably he will never say "yes", equally hasn't the courage to say "no". A thoroughly weak, flaccid type.' Shenson signalled misgivings that the split personality idea had been dumped, but weeks later came a thump on the doormat: the returned screenplay. 'No explanation why. No criticism of the script. And apparently, Brian Epstein had no comment to make either. Fuck them.'[162] Reflecting on the blasphemies he'd planned for the McTurks, Joe was to admit, 'I can't really blame them, but it would have been marvellous.'

There were to be numerous attempts to 'fix' the troublesome screenplay, writers including Charles Wood and Liverpool poet and Scaffold star Roger McGough doing their best to 'straighten' out Orton's fever dream of a script. The draft as published in 1979 was a reworking by Orton after being bought up by producer Oscar Lewenstein for Woodfall Films with – ironically – a view to Lester directing. 'I don't think he'd put any energy into it', the director told Steven Soderbergh, 'The Beatles had turned it down without even thinking about it. They thought, "Oh, it'd be a good idea, Joe Orton, wow", and then I suspect three of the four didn't read it and it just got abandoned… it was about language. But I thought that maybe there was something in it, that if Orton sat down and really took writing a screenplay seriously, he might be able to pull it off… It was a vaguely musical piece. Just a madness. A sort of *Bed Sitting Room*-style madness of imaginary worlds and landscapes. But it never happened. And certainly one thing was sure with Orton: you couldn't put anybody else to work to try to fix his material.'[163]

The redraft slimmed the four protagonists down to three, the two main parts earmarked for Mick Jagger and young up-and-coming actor Ian McKellen – the only remaining trace of Beatleness was the occasional play on the phrase 'in the town where I was born'. Nonetheless in summary: sharp-tongued ruffian Ian McTurk (generally presumed to be John) and weak, kindly Christopher Low (often spoken of as Ringo's role, though the pretty boy context also suggests Paul) are unfairly exiled from their hometown and embark on a series of satirical face-offs with the most depraved and immoral examples of what passes for humanity in Orton's universe. McTurk forever lusts after the cold-hearted and ambitious Rowena Torrence (who marries cruel millionaire Bernard Coates) while repeatedly breaking the heart of altruistic doormat Patricia Dromgoole. Low is seduced by misandrist police chief Connie Boon, but rejoins McTurk as part of a revolutionary masculinist cell led by rabble-rouser Jack Ramsay (usually presumed to be George) and they drag up to gain access to the Albert Hall, where Prime Minister Lily Corbett is assassinated mid-speech by Jack halfway through crucial announcements about her home furnishings. The plot meanders and constantly repeats, with miraculous survivals and random violence aplenty. Our disparate heroes are imprisoned for years, tunnel out to escape via the sewers and are saved by Coates' yacht, where McTurk again makes a horrifying move on Rowena, and Patricia throws herself into the sea:

101. INT. THE LOUNGE OF THE YACHT. MORNING.
MCTURK, RAMSAY AND LOW. LOW SERVES COFFEE FROM A TRAY.

LOW: (HANDING COFFEE TO RAMSAY) Miss
                Dromgoole was washed overboard last night.
                She left a tin of biscuits in her cabin. Do
                either of you want them?

RAMSAY: How did it happen?

LOW: She was crossing the deck in the dark when
                she mistook the handrail for the companion
                way. The watch heard a cry of 'woman
                overboard' but thought it was a joke.

McTURK: I refused her hand in marriage last night. I
                had to be brutal with her. This persistent
                importuning is most embarrassing.

RAMSAY: She took her life from disappointment. You
                mustn't feel guilty. You did all you could.

McTURK: I've no intention of feeling guilty. I leave that
                to Liberal politicians and clergymen. They
                get paid for it. (HE FITS A CIGARETTE
                INTO A LONGHOLDER) Rowena has
                consented to meet me in her cabin at noon.
                I'm going to give her a good raping. You
                won't either of you disturb me, will you?

HE DRINKS COFFEE. RAMSAY AND LOW LOOK ON
IN DISAPPROVAL.

102. INT. ROWENA'S CABIN.

A LARGE DAYBED WITH CUSHIONS. ROWENA
PACES THE CABIN. SHE TOUCHES HER HAIR WITH
A NERVOUS GESTURE. A KNOCK AT THE DOOR. SHE
CALLS OUT IN A GAY VOICE TO CONCEAL HER
APPREHENSION.

ROWENA: Come in!

McTURK ENTERS

McTURK: (CLOSING THE DOOR BEHIND HIM)
                They're holding a 'silent ten minutes' in
                memory of the woman who washed overboard
                last night. We shan't be interrupted.

HE SEIZES HER IN HIS ARMS. SHE GIVES A LITTLE
SQUEAK OF FRIGHT.

ROWENA: We shouldn't be doing this. Think of my
            husband.

McTURK: I wish you wouldn't keep harping on your
            husband. I took a shower with him yesterday.
            What more do you want?

HE KISSES HER ON THE MOUTH. THEY FALL
AMONG THE CUSHIONS. SHE STRUGGLES. PUSHES
HIM AWAY.

ROWENA: No! Please go away! (SHE BURSTS INTO
            TEARS) I shall ring for the steward.

McTURK: What d'you want the steward for when I'm
            here?

HE TAKES OFF HIS SHIRT. ROWENA GIVES A CRY
OF HORROR.

ROWENA: What are those scars on your back? Are they
            the marks of the lash?

McTURK: No. I've been wearing an overtight string
            vest. (PUTS AN ARM AROUND HER)
            How would you like me? I do a very nice
            semi-nude.

ROWENA STANDS TO HER FEET. HER FACE IS
FLUSHED.

ROWENA: You must go. I can't allow you to behave in
            this terrible way. It's wrong and we should
            be ashamed of ourselves.

McTURK: (STARES AT HER. PUZZLED.) I thought you
            were the most modern woman in the world.

ROWENA: (WITH A TOSS OF HER HAIR) What's
            that got to do with it?

McTURK: Well, I thought modern birds lived for this
            kind of thing.

ROWENA: (GIVES A COLD SMILE. GOES TO
            DOOR.) I'm afraid you're quite wrong.
            Being modern has nothing to do with playing
            nasties. Will you kindly leave my cabin or I
            shall inform my husband of your disgraceful
            conduct?

(MCTURK PICKS UP HIS SHIRT AND, SHAME-FACED,
LEAVES THE CABIN.)[164]

The boys are then left to drift in a lifeboat, washing up in the middle of a full-blown gender war, defecting from one side to another until blown up by a landmine, then blown up further in a series of accident-prone ambulances. Waking up in hospital to find that their actions have resulted in victory for the women, McTurk makes one last unsuccessful advance on Rowena before giving in and proposing to Patricia, who of course never drowned at all. Since PM Boon has made it legal for women to have multiple husbands, Miss Dromgoole decides to wed Ian, Christopher and Jack all at once, with promise of 'a long and happy married life'.

The confusion surrounding *Up Against It* was furthered considerably thirty years later by BBC Radio 3's broadcast of an adaptation in 1997 – a decade after Todd Rundgren wrote the music for a moderately successful operatic stage production. The radio adaptation was a worthy attempt to bring the Beatles movie back to life, allowing many fans to be misled into feeling they 'know' the script, bolstered by the addition of Beatle songs and a stellar cast including Douglas Hodge giving a sterling Lennon impersonation, with Joseph Fiennes and Damon Albarn as Low and Ramsay plus performances from Prunella Scales, Kenneth Cranham, Sylvia Sims and best of all, Leo McKern himself keeping the plot ticking along with a rousing narration, forming a comforting bond with *Help!* However, the script by radio veteran John Fletcher, while using most of the plot, with many of the same sequences in the same order with the same characters, barely uses a quarter of Orton's original dialogue, which was of course the playwright's real strength. On one hand, besides dropping in contemporary references to Channel 5 and New Labour, Fletcher's adaptation rationalises Joe's sprawling plot somewhat, with much of the proceedings powered by Coates' despicable capitalising on the working class boys' ideas, while the matriarchal powers are given more cogent aims. However, at the same time, the writer made full use of the medium of radio to take the story into totally new areas, somehow managing to outdo Joe Orton with its disturbing form of audio psychedelia: Patricia Dromgoole flying through the sky like a 'milky white' goddess, McTurk literally tearing Rowena open to reveal a vast nothingness inside, and oddest of all, the three heroes being formed into one disgusting multi-penised cyborg by Bernard Coates at the end. This horny homunculus then honeymoons with their bride in a huge bed in the middle of the Albert Hall, reaching an 'All You Need Is Love' crescendo with sounds of polyamorous exertion and 'bed springs eternal!', as Low delights that 'Now we know how many holes it takes to fill the Albert Hall'. The radio play is great, twisted fun, good Beatle fan service, but it is significantly Fletcher's work.

Joe Orton just couldn't resist his avowed raison d'etre, to shock and outrage as many people as possible as much as possible – he must have known the above extract would have been impossible for any Beatle to perform, but wrote it anyway. 'The whole script is about schizophrenia', he revealed to himself in his diary during composition, and in some ways the overall arc, turning gender politics into all-out war, could be seen as ahead of its time, while Connie's patronising – or matronising – treatment of pretty little Christopher is a scathing subversion of how attractive women were, and are, treated by chauvinistic men. But the story is so messy and contradictory, it's impossible to glean any meaningful cogent message beyond the writer's cackling desire to offend, and the depiction of the matriarchy as obsessed with dresses and fripperies reeks of lazy misogyny. What seemed inherently amusing to Orton at the time – women having power over weak men – wasn't funny when it formed the basis of *The Two Ronnies* serial 'The Worm That Turned' in 1980, and of course it's endlessly less amusing now. Perhaps the Beatles could have found a way to work with Joe, adding music where necessary, and shaping the general flow of the story into something their fans would not have bridled at in 1968. But we should be glad that they never tried, because what an embarrassment even a watered-down *Up Against It* would have been within The Beatles' oeuvre, utterly indefensible in the 21st century. As it is, it remains a murky, messy riddle which can never be solved, which is probably all for the best.

There's no shortage of intriguing 'out there' films made in the 1960s which don't hold up well today, whose plots are meandering messes filled with sexual and social politics which puts them beyond the pale half a century on – there will be at least a couple more to deal with before this book is through. But of course, the reason *Up Against It* is locked in the amber of 1967, never to become the film it was intended to be, was that the driver who arrived at Orton and Halliwell's bedsit on the morning of 10 August, to take the writer to a meeting with Richard Lester about the script, received no answer to his knock at the bedsit door. And so he peeked through the letter box, only to see a spray of blood – Halliwell had killed his lover with a hammer, and ended his own life with a handful of pills. 'A Day in the Life' was played at Orton's funeral.

How any Beatle reacted to this horrific turn of events has never been recorded, not least because it was less than three weeks before the body of another famous gay superstar of swinging London was discovered early one morning in the middle of the 'Summer of Love', and the news easily erased all thoughts of Orton's murder and the film that never was. Only a month or so earlier their manager had been part of the jolly scene as The Beatles broadcast 'All You Need Is Love' to the world live surrounded by beautiful people, and although suicide seemed unimaginable, the tragic import of Brian Epstein's probably accidental overdose of sleeping pills and death at the age of thirty-two was not lost on John Lennon, who recalled, 'I didn't really have any misconceptions about our ability to do anything other than play music. And I was scared you know, I thought "we've fucking had it now."'[165] As the sad news was delivered to The Beatles in the unlikely surroundings of Bangor, Wales, it was immediately obvious to the world that the boys were truly shocked. And stunned.

– CHAPTER FOUR –
IT'S ALL IN THE MIND

'Reality leaves a lot to the imagination.'

'I used to think anyone doing anything weird was weird. Now I know it's the people that call others weird that are weird.'

'We've been nostalgia since 1967… But now it's funny. It's like being Charlie Chaplin or Laurel & Hardy.'

'The trouble with leaving your feet on the ground is you never get to take your pants off.'

E yebrows may have been raised that, to all intents and purposes, The Beatles' response to being cut adrift without their loving manager was to stage a kooky jolly outing on a brightly coloured bus, setting off on their working holiday only a fortnight after Epstein's passing. But *Magical Mystery Tour* obviously predated Brian's death by some way, its origin paralleling that of *Sgt Pepper*, with Paul and Mal on a plane home – in this case, back from Derek Taylor's house in LA in April 1967, where Macca had happily chewed celery for Brian Wilson's Beach Boys number 'Vegetables'. With sudden inspiration hitting, Paul requested writing paper from the stewardess and began scribbling down loose lyrics of a circus barker once again promising a wonderful time for all, and then on a clean sheet, he drew a circle. He split the circle into four, then eight slices, and began to think of ways to fill them – it was a screenplay, or at least what was considered a viable plan for a feature by this veteran of two films (not including his brass soundtrack co-written with Martin for Liverpudlian author Bill Naughton's 1966 comedy drama *The Family Way*). Amid the failures to find a third movie idea, it was Dick Lester who first proposed that the next logical step would be for the boys to create their own, and here the ever-inventive McCartney took his advice. Brian had been gung-ho for the project, and it would go ahead even without him.

'I'm not sure whose idea *Magical Mystery Tour* was,' Paul nevertheless once had the gall to laugh. 'It could have been mine, but I'm not sure whether I want to take all the blame for it![166]... Even now I'm a bit shy to say I was the director, although it was the fact... I ended up kind of directing it, even though we said "The Beatles" had directed it at the end. Just because I was there most of the time and all the late night chats with the cameramen about what we were going to do tomorrow would tend to be me more than the others.'[167]

As with much of their music at this time, the concept which had occurred to Paul had its roots in nostalgic ideas of the band's Liverpudlian background, but took it to another level. 'It used to just be called a mystery tour, up north', he said. 'When we were kids, you'd get on a bus, and you didn't know where you were going, but nearly always it was Blackpool. From Liverpool, it was inevitably Blackpool and everyone would go, "Ooh, it was Blackpool after all!" Everyone would spend time guessing where they were going, and this was part of the thrill. And we remembered those. So much of the Beatles stuff was a slight switch on a memory; in "Penny Lane", the nurse and the barber and the fireman were just people we saw on a bus route, but this time they'd be with us. So we'd always just heighten the reality to make a little bit of surreality.'[168] By combining this working class tradition with the spirit of US writer and acid evangelist Ken Kesey and his Merry Pranksters' chemical-fuelled bus tours outlined in *The Electric Kool-Aid Acid Test*, McCartney had crafted a vehicle which seemed to sum up The Beatles' humour perfectly – honest northern laffs, blended with mind-warping daftness.

HAVING A LOVELY TIME!

There was one curious souvenir of the band's time in India which never went anywhere, besides sparking a million fanatical imaginations. Denis O'Dell had joined the boys out there, and presented each of them with a different instalment of JRR Tolkien's *The Lord of the Rings* saga, with the clear suggestion that they were the perfect team to bring the fantasy epic to screens – even if they had already had one movie involving a troublesome ring. The Beatles' plans to vanquish Middle-earth have become the stuff of legend, with a popular hunch giving the central role of Frodo to Paul, with Ringo as his companion Sam, John hamming it up as the twisted Gollum and George donning the beard as Gandalf. O'Dell sighed in print, 'I suppose, in retrospect, that not getting to make *The Lord of the Rings* represents the biggest disappointment of my time at Apple. To this day I still think it had great potential'[169], but it's impossible to believe that the scheme could ever have worked, particularly given the fact that there would never have been a moment when all four Beatles were together, unless they took the roles of the four hobbit heroes, and there's little wonder, and eternal gratitude, that the group's chosen director, Stanley Kubrick, turned the idea down without a tremor of hesitation. The whole concept was null and avoid anyway, as Tolkien still had the rights at the time, and made it clear that he would never sanction his work becoming a Beatle vehicle – allegedly, a prejudice enforced by the author's irritation at living next door to a regularly rehearsing rock 'n' roll band. There was a certain irony in the film rights being purchased by United Artists in 1969, but by then of course, there was clearly no chance of another Beatle film of any kind.

Paul had long been passionate about experimenting with the latest film technology at home, akin to Sellers' tinkering which led to *The Running Jumping & Standing Still Film*, but John's final words on what constituted McCartney's directorial debut were unkind, pronouncing *MMT* 'the most expensive home movie ever'. George tried to be positive for the press, assuring them 'We've got to have something good, how we visualise the film. It's got to be at least the difference between the song "Help" and "Sgt Pepper", the movie has got to be that progressed too. It's called a *Magical Mystery Tour...* just a typical coach tour, but anything can happen. You see, that's the difference, because it's magic, then we can do anything. So these parts, these sequences, we just had a few ideas.'[170] Despite John's cynicism, Paul persevered, 'John and I remembered mystery tours, and we always thought this was a fascinating idea: getting on a bus and not knowing where you were going. Rather romantic and slightly surreal! All these old dears with the blue rinses going off to mysterious places. Generally there's a crate of ale in the boot of the coach and you sing lots of songs. It's a charabanc trip. So we took that idea and used it as a basis for a song and the film... *MMT* was the equivalent of a drug trip and we made the film based on that: "That'll be good, a far-out mystery tour. Nobody quite knows where they're going. We can take 'em anywhere we want, man!" Which was the feeling of the period. "They can go in the sky. It can take off!" In fact, in the early script, which was just a few fireside chats more than a script, the bus was going to actually take off and fly up to the magicians in the clouds, which was us all dressed in red magicians' costumes, and we'd mess around in a little laboratory being silly for a while.'[171] As it is, the vague directions scribbled in Paul's magic circle (which included, simply, 'Dreams', 'Busty Hostess, Fat Woman, Small Man, Lads + Lasses', 'LUNCH mangoes tropical (magician)' and of course, 'Hire a coach. Yellow!') were to take them south-west to Cornwall, where George and Paul had hitched as teenagers.

With John so regularly tripped out and his foot off the gas, it was apparent even when Brian was still around that Paul could not help his creativity and energy forcing him into the driving seat, but his enthusiasm about the bus idea received little resistance from the other three – and at last, it was decided, it would be a return to TV comedy, and light (in this case, positively flying) entertainment. 'We wanted to take over the Bruce Forsyth slot,' McCartney told

Miles. 'He was always on: "Hello, everyone, happy Christmas! Had enough Christmas dinner?" We thought we'd had enough of all of that. We wanted to make a change, so we wanted that same big audience slot, which we got. We walked into the jaws of the lion with that, quite naively, quite willingly. It was probably a mistake really in retrospect because those people probably wanted Bruce Forsyth: everybody's had too much turkey and sherry and they're sitting back and they just want, *"Bring me sunshine..."* "Oh, I like that", "Oh, they're funny"... They just want comedy, a few girls kicking their legs up and so on. But because we knew that was the peak time in Britain for people to watch telly, we wanted to have our thing shown then. The kids wanted us, so for the kids it was cool, but it got slated very heavily. It probably would have been wiser, in retrospect, to have it shown late on a Friday night and in colour. We could have aimed it at the Bruce Forsyth thing; if we'd just gone on in our suits and played our songs and had a few guests. But we weren't into anything remotely like that and we'd made this little film of our own.'[172]

'We didn't see any way of making a similar film of four jolly lads nipping around singing catchy little tunes,' George agreed in the *Anthology* series. 'It had to be something that had more meaning.'[173] John's admission at the time that 'We haven't got a script yet, but we've got a bloke going round the lavatories of Britain, cribbing all the notes off the walls'[174] makes it clear that George's search for 'meaning' hadn't yet borne fruit for the project, but ever the egalitarian, Paul insisted that everyone was to have equal input – whether they liked it or not: 'What we would do is, each of us would have talents for impressions, we would do silly little things with each other, we'd use silly voices, and each of us had a talent or a sort of wit which I think was very much part of The Beatles... it was natural that we'd find a vehicle like this to allow us to express that.'[175] Lennon's memory may have been skewed when he told Hunter Davies, 'We knew most of the scenes we wanted to include, but we bent our ideas to fit the people concerned, once we got to know our cast. If somebody wanted to do something we hadn't planned, they went ahead. If it worked, we kept it in.'[176]

Paul had shaken hands with BBC 1 Controller Paul Fox on the plum Boxing Day slot – between *The Petula Clark Show* and a Norman Wisdom film – for which the corporation were willing to pay £9,000, less than a quarter of the eventual budget. Denis O'Dell, back at his wiliest in the producer's chair, was assured that the US college sales alone would fetch millions, but he still voiced concerns about the difficulties the boys would face. Nonetheless, with the theme tune laid down as early as May, they had all summer, minimal *Pepper* release duties aside, to start deciding how to fill up that circle.

One name which went on the list early on was 'Happy Nat the Rubber Man', AKA Geordie music hall veteran Nat Jackley, who had been entertaining folks since the 1920s, and was a childhood favourite of John's. But Paul admitted, 'It did get a bit hairy once or twice. I felt a bit sorry for people like Nat Jackley, whom we'd admired. He was an old music hall comedian who used to do eccentric dancing and funny walks. He was great at all of that, and John and I really loved him. John wanted to do a sequence with him, but he got annoyed because there wasn't enough script.'[177]

A more inclusive role was found for Paul's own casting, Parlophone alumnus Ivor Cutler: 'I knew Ivor, I'd seen him on telly with his very dour Scottish accent, which I like very much, and he used to play this little Indian hand harmonium. He had a song I liked called "I'm Going in a Field", just a lovely little song. I used to want to record that with him. How I got to know him was, I looked him up in the phone book and rang him up one night. I said, "Hello, Mr Cutler. My name's Paul McCartney. I'm one of The Beatles. I'm a great admirer of yours. Would you like to come out to dinner?" "This is very surprising, why are you asking me out?" "Because I like you." "Oh, oh. Oh, very well then. Yes, I wouldn't mind." He's a very precise-spoken Scottish fella, very quiet but real entertaining, real nice bloke. Very sensitive... So in the film he became Buster Bloodvessel and he was very good and very helpful. He made that name up. "Buster, I could be Buster Bloodvessel." "Yes, that's brilliant, got that!" The big fat guy in a band called Bad Manners later used the name.'[178] Cutler himself later admitted, 'John was the one I found easiest to get along with and I suspect it was mutual. Paul was a very intelligent, shrewd man. His mind was really keen, very much a seeker after information, very aware and alive but, and this is not meant as a criticism, with a mind rather like a machine in some ways, busy synthesising and correlating all the time.'[179] So admiring did John become of Ivor's mind, he semi-seriously offered him a job tutoring Julian.

The idea that Buster had a complex which leads him to believe he is the tour courier was developed en route, while the real courier, Jolly Jimmy Johnson, was acrobatic pro Derek Royle (whose lasting comedic legacy became the depiction of troublesome corpse Mr Leeman in *Fawlty Towers*), assisted by 'Busty Hostess' Wendy Winters, played by Miranda Forbes, under the name of Mandy Weet. Ringo recalled poring over copies of theatrical periodical *Spotlight* to cast these necessary roles, but he was sadly to rue one key casting, Jessie Robins as his 'Fat Auntie'. Paul knew from the start to make loveable Ringo the focus of any 'plot', but his improvised bickering with Robins was fuelled by personal discomfort at being twinned with the loud cockney actor, particularly after a day or two on the road, when her personal aura apparently made nasal inhalation an impossibility for him. However, she was to prove a kindred spirit in one way, when filming for a deleted dining scene allowed her to show off impressive drumming skills.

Besides diminutive happy-snapper George Claydon and a few models, the coach load of happy holidaymakers was fleshed out with fans and friends including, of course, Mal and Neil (who was required to capture second unit shots of the bus – and himself – where possible) plus 'Magic Alex' Mardas, Lennon's visionary Greek pal, a TV repairman whose claims to be able to engineer wallpaper speakers, impregnable forcefields and invisibility paint have become a comedy staple of their own to Beatle fans.

Finally, after a few hours' delay to finish the garish decoration, the coach was ready to roll on 11 September, picking up John, George and Ringo on the way down to the first port of call in Devon. This initial sally was the most mysterious to everyone, but it was still quite an impressive feat of organisation during a difficult period, many elements arranged while Epstein was still in charge. Nonetheless, O'Dell regretted, 'Unfortunately my concerns proved well founded. Without adequate preparation the filming inevitably took off in complete chaos. There were all sorts of logistical problems, The Beatles having no idea about the degree of planning necessary to make a successful film.'[180]

Regardless, they started grabbing what footage they could as the coach meandered through Teignmouth, Plymouth (getting stuck on a narrow bridge), Bodmin and so on, until settling in at The Atlantic Hotel in Newquay for three days, and then back to London for the weekend. On this first trip numerous sequences were filmed but never used, including Cutler's 'I'm Going in a Field' (If the BBC had their way his romantic dream with Aunt Jessie would have been wiped too, it was deemed too weird for broadcast), the dining room sequence and of course, Jackley's odd model-chasing episode around the Atlantic pool. 'Paul said, "Well, here's a segment, you write a piece for that"', John complained to Jan Wenner, 'And I thought, "Fucking Ada, I've never made a film. What does he mean write a script?" So I ran off and wrote the dream sequence for the fat woman and the spaghetti and all that.' The weakness of Lennon's 'Happy Nat' sequence was not lost on any of them, McCartney said, 'We thought, ah, Nat Jackley. He's great. He just looks funny. He's got a little Hitler moustache, little cloth cap and he's a beanpole of a man... But John didn't really prepare anything and hadn't thought up much for him to do. Nat just walked from person to person and it wasn't very funny and I think he quite resented it.' Indeed he did, joining in the eventual chorus of disapproval by blasting, 'I thought it was shocking! I couldn't make head nor tail of it. All my comedy stuff – twenty minutes – was cut out.'[181] 'He was never going to understand what we were doing,' Paul continued, 'we were drug-children and he was an old-school music hall, vaudeville performer. Nat did not like how he came out in the film. He was amongst our most vociferous critics when they all came looking for us. And I can't blame him really because it didn't exactly enhance his career.'[182] On the other hand, when *MMT* debuted on DVD, McCartney more bullishly reflected: 'It probably is how most people in the world would know of Nat Jackley now. Those days, it was likely he might have been forgotten, unless you were a student of British radio shows or early television. So in a way it was quite a good thing, and I think Nat's performance is terrific, he's a natural comedian, doing the funny walks and the funny faces, and that was really all we needed.'[183]

Another sequence which only provided vignettes showed the whole retinue piling in to Smedley's chip shop in Taunton – owned by the grandparents of four-year-old 'Little Nicola' Hale, star of one of the most endearing moments in the finished film, the wee tot sitting on John's lap as he presented her with a balloon and recited his own version of 'Two Little Dickybirds'. John and George otherwise sat together mutely like a couple of young toughs with little interest in the proceedings – which indeed they were.

Some ideas had obviously been brewing on the first trip, however, as the following week saw the entourage heading east out of London rather than west, to capture remaining sequences at West Malling RAF base in Kent (now the King's Hill estate). Before that, though, the male contingent repaired to the Raymond Revue Bar on Monday, to shoot a striptease sequence which totally bulldozed any claimed intent to provide festive family entertainment – even with 'censored' signs covering nippleage. Besides the desire for 'a bit of blue' in their feature, though, The Beatles' motives were quite honourable – a few new numbers of their own would be expected, but they decided to share screen time with selected other bands: The Moody Blues and Cream were considered, and Traffic were filmed miming to 'Here We Go Round The Mulberry Bush', but failed to make the final cut. There's some confusion as to how the one band to make it into *MMT* came to be nominated, however – some say The Beatles just wanted a quirky act, and thought of The New Vaudeville Band, but McCartney would have been aware that was a fake outfit, and had apparently seen The Bonzo Dog Doo-Dah Band perform at the Isle of Wight festival, so knew what madness they were all capable of. Other reports say that Mike McGear suggested the Bonzos to his brother, The Scaffold being regular gig-mates with them. Viv Stanshall himself said, 'McCartney came to one of our gigs (I know he was at the Lyceum and the Albert Hall), and I think he persuaded Lennon that it'd be a good idea to put us in that film. And that kind of put the Good Housekeeping seal of approval on us. The thing that pissed me off though was that they never put us on the record... mean buggers.'[184]

One oddity all agree on, however, was that Lennon fought *not* to have the era's greatest musical comedy combo in his film, and Paul won. Whether the presence of a bigger freak than himself in Stanshall was a threat or not, the Bonzos were jubilant when they arrived to back up dancer Jan Carson with their mimed performance of 'Death Cab For Cutie' (a song Harrison suggested as a single, and which inspired the name of a US rock band), with Rodney Slater sporting a t-shirt reading 'LUMP IT, JOHN!'

The Bonzos' new manager, Eleanor Bron's brother Gerry, worked the band to death on tour, so this was an unusual treat for them, not even spoiled by the last minute theft of all their gear on the recording day, and mad inventor Roger Ruskin-Spear recalled, 'Paul seemed to be the one who was trying to get it all together. He seemed to breed off it. The others were just sort of looning around. They said they wanted to be like us – George especially. He envied our way of life. He was caught between wanting to be silly and going off his head on mantras.'[185] 'It was a long day, getting up to mime to the song again and again,' Neil Innes takes up the tale. 'It started at 10 am and there was very little brief of what they wanted us to do. We just mimed to the backing track, which gave us the licence to wear all these silly masks. We offered things up to the camera and they just took 'em. Viv offered up his own strip routine, which he'd got from Lindsay Kemp, pretending to undo his bra, his hands extended out from his body, miming these enormous breasts... Paul was magic man in those days. He put out and he was so generous. Paul was directing the scene. He was in charge. You could tell Paul wanted to keep The Beatles brand going. George was quite involved in our performance and how it should be, but the rest of the band were far less approachable. Ringo wasn't sending out. He was just watching with John, giggling away together. John was scary... I think we related to them because they were mischievous and funny, but we didn't care about show business particularly.'[186] A splendid day was had, Neil added, 'But that was just one day in our lives. We'd do *MMT* and meet The Beatles and then we'd be up north again.'[187] Harrison volunteered to Innes a certain envy of The Bonzos' freedom to get away with murder, Neil said: 'One thing we discovered in The Bonzos, as we met more and more people of their ilk – Eric Clapton once said to us, "I'm really jealous of you guys, you can go on stage and mess around. I've always wanted to go on stage with a parrot on my shoulder." I said, "It's your own fault, you shouldn't be going round with a perm, on a poster saying 'CLAPTON IS GOD'! You're setting yourself up!"'

For all the lack of a script, the *Anthology* book shows a scrap which suggests that the sequence was to have had a comic pay-off:

> *The men have been separated from the women who are having tea on the coach. They are led through a door to a small club by the roadside where music is playing. Inside there is a stage on which a stripper strips alongside a singer. She does her act to the singer, who sings an unsuitable song or tries to tell jokes. The men clap loudly as she finishes her act with a flourish… and the curtain closes… When it opens again the women from the bus are there in her place. They look up to see what the applause is about. The men stop clapping and walk out…*[188]

Sadly, this was the point at which the finished feature simply dropped everything and cut to the final song and dance number, guaranteeing disappointment for anybody who had been following the shenanigans on board with any expectation of closure. Thitherto, a game attempt had been made to string things together from the start via John's sarcastically cuddly narration:

JOHN: (VO) When a man buys a ticket for a Magical Mystery Tour, he knows what to expect. We guarantee him the trip of a lifetime, and that's just what he gets. The incredible Magical Mystery Tour…

Richard B. Starkey and his Aunt Jessica are always arguing about one thing or another... And what with today being Sunday and the weather looking up, you'd think they'd have given it a rest! But no – on and on they go...

Beyond the blue horizon, far above the clouds, in a land that no one knows, live four or five magicians who spend their days casting wonderful spells. Come with me now into that secret place where the eyes of man have never set foot...

Meanwhile, back on the bus, things are happening – and life lobbles on...[189]

For the rest of the week, the cast and crew were resident in Kent, filling up the remaining holes in the circle. Some of the oddest material was amassed here, including the 'Marathon' sporting activities which necessitated the emergency sourcing of a gang of dwarves to strip off and wrestle, plus a gaggle of rowdy vicars and so on, to join the merrymakers in a tug of war and a motor race, for which Ringo got to sit at the wheel and take the bus for a mad thrash around the track: 'It was so great 'cause we could just do anything!' he admits, 'You couldn't do it now – I couldn't jump in that damn bus and drive! It was just so open. I had no great plan, I was just blah-ing away, keep it rolling, y'know. I don't honestly think we were like, "Oh, let's do a Keaton or Charlie Chaplin sort of thing." It's involved in some way, 'cause it's in your psyche. The tent – when we walk in and there's hundreds of us... it's such an old gag, but we'd use it.'[190] Only a small sample of Richie's unpleasant riffing with Jessie made it into the film:

JESSIE: (READING MAGAZINE) Oh, innee lovely, look at him, he's got such pep and life, look, just look at him!
RINGO: Who's that?
JESSIE: It's Ringo, one of The Beatles, he's marvellous!

RINGO:	Oh, those fellas, huh!
JESSIE:	Oh, he's smashing, he plays those drums and he goes out and he earns five bob. Not like you!
RINGO:	Listen, I've heard a few stories about those boys.
JESSIE:	I don't care what you've heard, they're smashers. You shut up. If you learned to play the drums, you could earn an extra five bob.
RINGO:	I'm not doing so bad, am I?
JESSIE:	Doing so bad? You're as skint as armholes every week! What's the matter with you?[191]

Kent also saw the return of an old favourite – Victor Spinetti was too busy to play the courier, but having seen his similar turn in *Oh, What A Lovely War*, Paul added a particularly tangential military enrolment sequence to make sure there was no Beatle film lacking Vic's presence. 'I said, "You know the thing you did in *Lovely War*? That was fantastic, can we have that character, pretty much, and just kind of make it up. I'll be sort of 'Yes, jolly good', and just nod occasionally, and you just take the scene, you know, go!" Because I knew he could do it.'[192] Spinetti's surreal drill sergeant gobbledegook was such a highlight, he reprised the role for Beatlemaniac comedian Paul Merton's sketch show twenty-five years later. The stuffed cow hollered at by Spinetti put in another appearance in the aforementioned memorable dream sequence, inspired by Lennon's own nightmare, which saw him playing 'Pirandello', a greasy waiter apparently modelled on his stepfather, who heaps tons of spaghetti onto Jessie's plate – a scene which proved as disgusting to film as any nightmare could be. George recalled, 'There were always a couple of good songs, and there were a few funny scenes. To me, the scene that stands out is the one of John shovelling the spaghetti onto the fat woman's plate. That was the best bit of the movie for me.'[193]

*

THE JOKER LAUGHS

If anyone on board had misgivings, the one thing which had to be beyond reproach was, of course, the music. 'Blue Jay Way' was partially filmed at Ringo's house in Surrey (the last scraps of footage filmed showed the boys sawing at a white cello and having a kickabout) and 'Fool On The Hill' surreptitiously shot on a day trip to France, but West Malling was to be the location for the whole of 'I Am The Walrus', a song which, it's easy to forget, was entirely written in the spirit of piss-taking, when John learned that Beatle lyrics were being studied at his old school and wanted to give fans a barrage of mental debris to really puzzle over. In some ways it is *MMT*'s most straightforward song visualisation in that it's the only time the band line-up is used, the animal costumes, eggman bald-caps and swaying bobbies amusingly undermining the orthodox set-up. As O'Dell observed, it's easy to be blasé about the sight of a line of policemen holding hands, but over fifty years ago such subversion from the nation's favourite pop band was guaranteed to raise the blood pressures of those who deserved it: 'In a sense, it can be seen as The Beatles' cinematic counter-cultural manifesto,' O'Dell wrote, 'a surreal indictment of the British establishment which, with its cheating vicars, psychotic army drill sergeant and dancing policemen, gently ridicules the pillars of the status quo... It was, in some respects at least, ahead of its time. Its surreal humour certainly predated Monty Python, and its radical style unquestionably influenced modern pop videos and pop musicals such as The Monkees' *Head* and Frank Zappa's *200 Motels*.'[194]

Although 'The Fool On The Hill' is anything but funny, Paul's identification with the figure of The Fool was another cosmic comic reference, no doubt at least partly influenced by the band's numerous ties with Dutch design collective The Fool, who were responsible for the *Sgt Pepper* inner sleeve, the 'I Am The Walrus' costumes, and most strikingly, the elaborate psychedelic mural which briefly adorned the Apple building, until cruelly painted over by the council only months after completion.

With the boys playing alternate universe versions of themselves on the coach, the only chance they got to really show off their wacky skills was as the barmy and fey gang of wizards who preside over the Magical Mystery Tour – Ringo squeaky, Paul red-nosed, John the most egregiously camp, and George quietly fiddling with a telescope, all ensuring the best time for the earthbound travellers. The sketch-like nature of the sequences highlighted more than ever the missed opportunity of not preparing a few solid gags for the film, but if anyone got the laughs, it was probably Mal:

JOHN: (VO) Ooh! Wonder what the magicians
               are cooking up now?
ENTER JOHN IN A BLACK WIZARD COSTUME, WITH
A TEA TRAY.
JOHN: Tea up, fellas!
PAUL: Ooh, goody!
JOHN: Ooh, talk about your magical mysteries,
               I've spent half an hour looking for that sugar,
               I tell ya…
RINGO: Is there one for me?
JOHN: Aye, there's one over here, Richard. Oh, how
               are you, Bonzo? All right? Any news of the
               bus?
PAUL: The bus? It's ten miles north on the
               Dewsbury road. And they're having a lovely
               time!
ALL: They're having a lovely time…!
MAL: Can you tell me what's next on the agenda?
GEORGE: (TO CAMERA) A song! (MAL CROONS
               OPERATIC GIBBERISH)
RINGO: Not you! Them! On the bus![195]

The finale did make some attempt to tie things up by having the whimsical camp magicians show up at the very end, and also had the distinction of being the only spot of choreography performed by the world's greatest rock group in their entire career. 'Paul was mad about Busby Berkeley at the time so we had the whole of the Peggy Spencer Formation Dancing Team,' Alistair

Taylor wrote. 'We invited all the people from miles around and thousands came. The idea was that the four boys appeared for one last time in the Magical Mystery Tour bus with a great crowd following them like the Pied Piper of Hamelin. There were grannies and women and babes in arms and gangs of Teddy Boys, all sorts had arrived. We were just setting up this big finale when suddenly there was a power cut and every light in the place went out. It was Sunday afternoon. We needed another generator and we got one just in time, just as the crowd were losing interest and starting to drift away. We were just ready when suddenly every light went out again. More people left and by the end there were about twenty-five of us trying to make ourselves look like the sort of crowd you usually see at Wembley.'[196]

The greatest challenge of all, however, lay ahead in a small editing studio in Old Compton Street, presided over by editor Roy Benson. Paul had set aside two, maybe three weeks to knock all their footage into shape – but, notwithstanding the outré nature of the entire project, Benson was dismayed to discover that a clapperboard *had* been used, but only as an optional extra for heaps of footage, leaving ten hours of barely identifiable film to lick into shape for TV. Three weeks became ten, with all four Beatles regularly dropping in, often to undo all the work the previous Beatle had demanded from the poor editor.

One relatively easy sequence put together in the edit earned a reprimand from one of the world's greatest directors, when visuals were needed to accompany the instrumental 'Flying', and O'Dell and Benson were tipped off that reels of unused aerial footage from *Dr Strangelove* were sitting in a cupboard available to use, just requiring the odd colour tint to add a psychedelic twist. Stanley Kubrick was not happy when he found out, but at least it meant that some element of indisputably classic comedy did make its way onto the screen.

Incidentally, The Beatles' only instrumental on an official album was eventually given lyrics by one of the most beloved Beatle obsessives who ever lived – Timperley musician Chris Sievey, AKA fantastic George-Formby-inspired papier-mâché-bonced superstar Frank Sidebottom. Among Frank's many Beatle tributes and covers was a masterly stab at lyrics which, once heard, made it difficult to ever hear 'Flying' without Frank's words coming to mind:

> *We are The Beatles, there are four of us,*
> *Direct from Liverpool, we got here on a bus,*
> *John, Paul George and Ringo,*
> *John, Paul George and Ringo, that is us.*
> *George plays electric guitar, Ringo has loads of rings,*
> *John plays another guitar, and Paul McCartney sings,*
> *And then one day they broke up and Paul McCartney formed Wings.*
> *You know he did, he really did.*[197]

Despite the editing nightmares, of course a finished film was ready by Christmas, and of course, it became The Beatles' greatest flop – although, as we've seen, it's a myth that it was their first creation to receive flak from the critics, with *Help!* also divisive. Some fans who had forced their reluctant parents to sit and watch felt humiliated, and the feedback was so damning plans to air the film on US TV foundered. However, the worst criticisms came from the areas you would expect, with right-wing rags like the *Daily Express* hooting on the front page that it was 'blatant rubbish' and 'the bigger they are, the harder they fall' while the *Mail* similarly delighted in the freedom to label it 'Appalling!' and the now defunct *Evening News* sneered, 'There was precious little magic and the only mystery was how the BBC came to buy it.'[198] Of course, broadcasting the feature in monochrome was a massive handicap, and the damage was done before the colour repeat on BBC 2 in the new year – but even at the time, many critics took a more reasonable view, with Keith Dewhurst in *The Guardian* admitting, 'My feelings on finding myself almost alone in praising… *MMT* are amazement, and the sad conviction that as a mass the public is more stupid and ignorant than it is as individuals, and does not like to be told so'[199], while in *The Times*, Henry Raynor offered a lukewarm 'Realities are annihilated by cinematic devices, few of which seem particularly new, and a sort of well-meaning, good-humoured anarchy prevails.'[200] The BBC's own Audience Research Report could not have been more damning: 'They could hardly find a good word to say about the programme, considering it stupid, pretentious rubbish which was, no doubt, intended to be very clever and "way out" but which was, they thought, a complete jumble with neither shape nor meaning, and certainly no entertainment value whatsoever.'[201]

The very next day, two months after John and George had been on David Frost's programme discussing transcendental meditation, Paul paid a visit, going so far as to humiliate himself in front of a vinegar-faced live audience, protesting, 'We tried to present something different for the viewers but, according to the newspapers, it did not come off. We thought we would not underestimate people and would do something new. It is better being controversial than purely boring...'[202] He added to the press with some cheek, 'It wasn't the worst programme over Christmas. I mean, you couldn't call the Queen's Speech a gas either, could you?'[203]

Nearly thirty years later George reasoned, 'They really didn't like the film, but that's understandable because from an artistic point of view it wasn't a brilliantly scripted affair that was executed well. It was like a little home movie. We just had fun. We were supposed to; we were on the bus with crates of beer and an accordionist!'[204] But another two decades on, the sting subsided, Paul's protestations have grown. Calling it 'A dream, a little fantasy', and 'a zany representation of *vivid* minds of the time', he shrugs, 'They were all looking for the plum-pudding special. That's what they were expecting, and they very much didn't get it! This very much wasn't that, loves, we weren't even intending giving you that. We were giving it to the young kids. We figured there would be young kids looking on Boxing Day. Why shouldn't they see something far out? I understand that Steven Spielberg and some of the guys in film school thought it was really cool and it was quite influential on their early stuff. Probably just the fact that it was so free. You get people like that appreciating and analysing it. Just the fact that we had the balls to go out there and had the sheer determination and perseverance to go and make it, I think validates it all now.'[205]

Besides Spielberg, the film received another vote of confidence from Scorsese, the great director admitting its influence on films like *Mean Streets*, and adding, 'This picture probably reflects their state of mind more than anything else they had done at the time. That's the way they perceived the world around them. For me, the freedom of the picture was something that was very very important, the sense of breaking all the form. Obviously some of it I didn't quite understand in terms of the humour, but it's the way it was in those days. I mean, people were trying everything and whether it fully succeeded or not was really beside the point.' And Neil Innes went further: 'I love it! The public reaction was a perfect example of people at their worst. People at their worst throw stones at things they don't understand. As the world gets colder it's one of the fires you'll want to be around…[206] Derek Taylor was very wise. He said, "It was their turn to get knocked." But if they hadn't made *MMT* you wouldn't have *Python* or *The Rutles*. A silly movie with music, that is the root of *The Rutles*.'[207]

'At first people thought we were mad,' McCartney concludes, 'and just thought it was completely indulgent, and I must say I kind of took that onboard and thought, "yeah, it's certainly not untrue," it *was* pretty indulgent. But I enjoyed what we'd done and thought it worked out in a quirky way… it finally found its place. And we had a good time making it anyway.'[208] On the subject of good times, a fancy dress party was held at Lancaster Gate to celebrate the film's completion. Notoriously Beatle-phonic comic icon Kenneth Williams was typically *outraged* to be asked to compère and declined icily, but stars included The Bonzos (Neil on crutches as Tiny Tim, Viv sporting a plastic mac adorned with fried eggs) who jammed with a couple of Beach Boys plus Cilla Black dressed as Charlie Chaplin, while George and Judy Martin lorded over all as Prince Philip and HMQ, Harrison turned up as a medieval minstrel, and Lennon took the easy route, dressing as a Teddy Boy greaser. John got so wasted he waltzed with his famously estranged father Freddie, and then tried to hit on belly-dancer Pattie Boyd, for which Lulu – apparently this social group's regular agony aunt – loudly lectured the greaser in broad Glaswegian while dressed as Shirley Temple, which is arguably a funnier scenario than anything in the actual film.

THE RICH MAN'S UKULELE

Far from being dissuaded from filmmaking by the experience, even before the edit was finished, McCartney was back behind (and in front of) the camera, directing video promos for 'Hello Goodbye' which were entirely tongue-in-cheek. Filmed at the Saville Theatre (still then leased under Epstein's name – it's now the Covent Garden Odeon), the boys switched between *Sgt Pepper* dress and the by-now hugely unsuitable collarless Moptop suits, danced with hula girls, and even added an almost subliminal visual gag, by having Ringo play on both a tiny and a gigantic drum kit, which changed from shot to shot.

As if this wasn't activity enough for the boys, there was of course, once again, the festive flexi to get done for the fans. The 1967 offering was a much tighter retread of the kind of media-spoofing stream-of-consciousness heard in the 1965 outtakes, this time aided by both Mal and George Martin, and broken up by the closest the band ever got to recording their own seasonal single – 'Christmas Time Is Here Again', closing with 'Auld Lang's Syne' and Lennon's mumbled Hogmanay doggerel, which successive brave transcribers have tried to render, with limited success:

When Christmas time is o'er, and your bonnie glay is rue,
I'll be bristlin' to you people, all the best from me to you.
When the beasty dragon mutton, to the heather in the glen,
I'll be struttin' oot in my tetherin', to your arms, once back again.
Och away, ye bonnie...[209]

The disc opened with the group attempting to gain entry to the BBC, and then rapidly took the listener through parodies of talk shows, game shows and drama. The polish heard on this flexi could be attributed to the choice of editor, Kenny Everett, certainly an expert in taking the mick out of the BBC. He even got to give himself the credit 'Kenny Foreverett had a nice time mucking about with the tapes and deserves to be called producer though this is an unpaid position', but subsequently played down the job title: 'I think I was the only DJ that really spent a lot of time in the studio messing around with tapes… one of them said one day, "If we give you some tapes of them messing around, do you think you could edit them so we can release them on a jolly floppy disc?" That was such an honour, I mean it wasn't given to me as an honour, it was just, "Here, can you make something of these?" But I considered it to be a great honour as they could have chosen anybody, and it was fun to do.'[210]

Paul's association with The Bonzo Dog Band did not end with *MMT*, and their madness was to spread. On the very same day *MMT* was broadcast on the BBC, the commercial channel debuted *Do Not Adjust Your Set,* a new comedy sketch show for the children's schedules created by Humphrey Barclay, who drafted in young writer/performers including David Jason, Denise Coffey, Oxford boys Michael Palin and Terry Jones, and recent Cambridge Footlights president, Eric Idle. Accompanying them in every episode were the Bonzos, bringing their mad music to life with props and costumes presented in glorious monochrome. The band's absurdism could not have complemented the daftness of the sketches more perfectly, and in Eric, Neil found an instant friend and creative partner. The quasi-Python forerunner quickly became hugely popular with adults as well as children, and sales of The Bonzos' debut album *Gorilla* were on the up.

Meanwhile, the remainder of the Footlights generation, team Cleese and co, had their own TV vehicle in *At Last The 1948 Show,* but an even bigger following on BBC Radio thanks to *ISIRTA, the* youth comedy hit of the '60s – and one of the things which marked their generation out from previous comedians was the flair for spoofing current trends, and particularly, thanks to Bill Oddie, rock and roll. Nobody before had ever shown any such ability to write catchy pop tunes which were packed with gags, and he had even recorded his own album on Polydor in 1967, *Distinctly Oddie*. Since the early use of Idle's 'I Want To Hold Your Handel', the madness of 'Radio Prune' had cocked the odd snook at The Beatles despite all present being big fans – *Sgt Pepper* was sent up via the much posher song 'Nigel-Carter-Smith's Society Band', and in 1968 the Wonder Team went to town on 'The Magical

Mystery Bore', performing the song 'I Am The Milkman', a carefully crafted parody of Martin-produced psychedelia performed live on stage by Dave Lee and the Boys, and Brooke-Taylor et al's best scouse 'goo-goo-g'joobs'. This ribbing was preceded by a withering sketch about The Beatles' Indian leanings:

HATCH:	Tell us, why did you take up meditation?
CLEESE:	(*Lennonesque*) Well, we'd reached the stage where our preternatural urges were being sublimated by an over-indulgent materialistic ego and in a new spiritual sense, in a pre-occupied cosmic being…
HATCH:	Ah. In other words…?
GARDEN:	We were bored.
HATCH:	And what happened when you landed in New Delhi?
KENDALL:	We went to the house of the great Maharishi Yogi.
HATCH:	And did he take you in?
KENDALL:	Oh yes, completely![211]

Despite the Bonzos' rise, what they sorely lacked was a hit single, and though Stanshall's slice of rock spoofery 'Canyons Of Your Mind' was a strong contender, it was an Innes composition which was a cert for the A-side, 'I'm The Urban Spaceman' being a more melodically silly toe-tapper inspired by the original name for brownfield sites in towns and cities – with a psychedelic seasoning. Simple though the ditty was, the Bonzos were having trouble getting it down on tape effectively, and one evening in the Speakeasy club, in March 1968, Viv was complaining to Paul about the process of recording with manager Gerry Bron at the controls. The Beatle's enthusiastically supportive response supplied Stanshall with the burn of a lifetime when his request for Bron to stand aside elicited a pained 'Who else are you going to get to produce this?' from the manager. McCartney arrived at the Chappell of Bond Street studios like a dose of salts, and revolutionised the band's playing. 'Here's one I wrote last night!'

Neil recalled him announcing, sliding onto the piano stool within moments of entering the studio, and playing a fully-formed 'Hey Jude', before any other Beatle had heard it.

Ruskin-Spear remembered, 'He certainly did have the golden touch alright. I don't know what he did, but suddenly it sounded more like a proper record. He was playing the ukulele…' 'Paul was a genius,' Innes added. 'He made me sing every time we ran through the song and kept trying things until it was rocking. He decided to double-track the drums and then added the "rinky-dinky-dink-dink" burlesque bit on ukulele underneath, which gave it a great groove. Viv wasn't very happy though because McCartney insisted on playing all the ukulele parts himself.'[212] When Bron's wife Lilian dropped in, attracted by the presence of rock royalty, she eyeballed the noble little instrument and sniffed, 'What is that, a poor man's violin?' to which McCartney shot back, 'No, it's a rich man's ukulele!' With his characteristic verve, the secret producer played numerous parts – particularly, of course, bass – before wiping them from the tape for the Bonzos to recreate, and although the band's recordings could arguably be even more experimental than The Beatles' (who never wrote a single song to be played on an artificial leg theremin) it took Paul's star power to silence the obstruction of the studio's staff and really try new things out. Stanshall insisted that the track needed a solo played on the garden hose, which he swung round his head with funnel and trumpet mouthpiece attached – the McCartney solution was simply to place mikes all around the studio to capture the swirl. With the song's final twang on tape (played, naturally, on a clothes shop dummy) Paul made it clear that his role couldn't be hinted at to anybody, and when the nom-de-plume 'Apollo C Vermouth' was suggested, he was very happy to accept the moniker.

Neil laughed, 'After the session Larry wanted badly to be seen next to Paul McCartney and I remember Paul saying, "Cheerio, lads, it was great. Thanks very much." Our manager was saying, "Can we have a meal, Paul?" He said, "No, I've really got to go." There he was, strolling down the road with Larry still walking beside him, not really thinking about anything but trying desperately to be noticed.' The track was finally mixed by regular

Bonzos engineer Gus Dudgeon, who would go on to wave his audio wand over out-of-this-world classics including 'Space Oddity' and 'Rocket Man'.

The *MMT* double EP, released before the Boxing Day debacle, had featured the first official Beatles comic strip, drawn by regular fan club cartoonist Bob Gibson and condensing the TV feature's 'plot' with greater charm than the film itself. But this was of course far from their debut in comic panels, the boys having unwittingly cameoed in numerous teen girl romance rags early on, with *Archie* comics heroines falling for their charms, and in 1965, Marvel's Fantastic Four having an adventure on the way to see the band play in concert – The Thing even sported a Beatle wig. In the same year, Asterix and Obelix's journey to Britain featured a very familiar quartet of British bards making the maidens swoon. DC Comics took longer to follow the trend, and it wasn't until 1970 that Batman and Robin became embroiled in a plot based on the 'Paul Is Dead' hoax, featuring an obvious cipher for the band, dubbed 'The Oliver Twists' (spoiler alert – it turns out that *only* the Paul character is real, with the other three being replacements). Surreal and witty visualisations of the Beatle songbook were also being masterminded by trippy artist Alan Aldridge for the seminal *Illustrated Lyrics* coffee-table books which would be in shops by the end of the decade, and still selling to this day.

But it was a different artist who was to redefine The Beatles' image in 1968, for an almost universally admired work of classic animation, feted as great art and one of the most influential cartoon films of all time, and from the most unlikely of sources – King Features. Of course, Brodax knew the boys had no time for his rough and ready cartoon show, and that it would never be critically acclaimed, as if that was ever a priority for him. But although his original plan was to extend the existing show for cinemas in a promised bid to complete United Artists' pesky three-picture deal, a debt is owed to the producer for recognising, with the help of the ambitious and frustrated artists at Soho's TVC, that his ambition to release a feature-length spin-off required a change, something out of the ordinary. Besides, as he was told, The Beatles' artistic growth and increasing strangeness meant that the wacky innocence which originally inspired the series was patently out of date.

The TVC animators, led by thoroughly anglicised Canadian George Dunning, had been struggling with the band's development for a while, with attempts to make the final season more psychedelic – particularly noticeable in the episode *Strawberry Fields Forever*, which sees the zany funsters getting lost in dreams, their car floating away on balloons at the end as John shrugs, 'It's all in the mind, y'know!' – a quote from Milligan and co-scripter Larry Stephens in *The Goon Show* which was included by a keyed-in writer, eventually becoming George's catchphrase in the finished feature. Singalongs for songs like 'Eleanor Rigby' also seemed to inspire the animators to go beyond their typical broad designs, and experiment with using bleak still photographs to depict Eleanor's sad and lonely world – an idea developed by key animator Charlie Jenkins, whose fingerprints were metaphorically on some of the film's most experimental sequences. None of the kids watching could have guessed that these breaks from their usual sugary fare were clues to what was brewing at TVC through 1967 and '68.

THEY LOOK LIKE DROP-OUTS TO ME

The story of the making of *Yellow Submarine* is an epic mess, plagued with misinformation, bragging lies and poor recall, but then, the production itself was undeniably chaotic – all of which belies the cogent (albeit mind-expanding) artistry of the finished product. It took eleven months of twenty-four-hour work for over two hundred artists, TVC's staff supplemented by art students colouring cels through the night, peppered by regular trips to the local Dog & Duck: a combination of hard work and swinging excess which Dunning estimated resulted in numerous marriages, and at least thirteen children, illegitimate and otherwise. Some of the key players – including the Dog & Duck's landlord – also showed up in the actual film, thanks to Jenkins' use of photography.

The script, performed in turn by the voice cast, is the be-all and end-all for most animated features, from which the vast team of artists worked. But Brodax had as many nightmares getting a screenplay to work for The Beatles as Lester and others in the realm of live action – he claimed that an excellent, long lost treatment by none other than Joseph Heller was legendarily thrown out by Brian because he didn't like the purple folder it came in, which resulted in Epstein's staff having to pull the incensed producer off their yelping employer. Al knew the Beatles saw him as an old hack, but he heard word of a youthful whizzkid playwright, assistant to Stanley Kubrick on *Dr Strangelove,* and invited this Lee Minoff over to Britain as a kind of bridge between himself and the four lads who had never been fans of his style. Once again, McCartney was the only point of contact with the band, his only demand being that the story had to have 'a monster', and before allowing him to return to the US, Al ordered Lee to sketch a new story outline in his hotel room, *2001: A Space Odyssey* inspiring an epic maritime voyage for The Beatles to flow from his pen. Although this was before Orton had any connection to The Beatles, there are some similarities with *Up Against It* – the boys leave their hometown for a mad journey which sees them take on establishment forces, and win the day with a celebration of Love. Minoff's rudimentary plot began with Ringo in grey Liverpool, and featured his friends joining him in the magical titular submersible – which until then hadn't been confirmed as the title, or key song for the project, though some credited Ringo with the brainwave. This yellow submarine was to be helmed by an old salt called Fred, and ultimately bring joy to the world via the powers of music and, yes, Love. Minoff also introduced the character of the 'Nowhere Man' Boob (not yet Jeremy Hillary Boob Phd), as an attack on a comedian whose talents seemed to have no end: 'the director of my play, *Come Live With Me,* Jonathan Miller. The director and doctor who I was very unhappy with. And who I felt was a great intellectualiser whose narcissism bled all over my play and really helped to ruin it when it finally got to Broadway. I really based the Nowhere Man on Miller who could do everything. He was a writer, a doctor, a director, blah blah blah. But I felt he was ultimately full of shit.'[213]

Like many others who had a hand in the stew, Lee Minoff would have to work hard to retain any credit for his input.

Brodax's next favoured writer was Erich Segal, a Yale graduate who overflowed with sparkling bon mots, often given excess credit for what he brought to the story. Minoff wisely observed that 'the film was drawn rather than written', and particularly as the music obviously remained paramount, the staff did already have a few disparate music sequences to work on, but still only the most rudimentary idea of how they actually fitted together – especially since Lennon had allegedly read Minoff's outline and walked out, complaining 'This is just the bloody *Flintstones*!' In the absence of words, Bob Godfrey was sent for, to add further uncredited value: 'George Dunning invited me. I suppose that it had been going about three months, and he said, "Bob, I want you to make the *Yellow Submarine* funny." And I said, "Okay, George, where is the script?" And he said, "There is no script." And I said, "Well, storyboard?" And he said, "There is no storyboard... I want you to tell me jokes. We are going to put jokes in the *Yellow Submarine.*" George hated jokes. He said, "You will kind of be court jesters. You will tell me jokes, and if I like them, I will put them in the film." ... Then just as I was leaving, he said, "Um, have you ever taken LSD?" And I said, "Shit, no, George, I haven't. Why?" He said that the whole thing is just a psychedelic trip. And of course, that was exactly what it was.'[214]

Minoff has been unfairly dismissed over the years, but his earliest outlines did bring us Old Fred and the Boob, a grey drab Liverpool and a magical land, with the general idea that The Beatles would fight monsters with Love. True, his plot was more than somewhat different to the one we know: in the first outline, Old Fred was a tobacconist with a shrewish wife who heaped abuse on him for the maritime yarns he spun while never going anywhere near water, even with a pet seal who followed him around ('Hillary Jeremy Boob' also originated as a seal). After a spot of fooling around on Penny Lane, The Beatles convince Old Fred to travel with them through a number of seas including the Seas of Cinema, Consumer Goods and Solid Ice, in which everyone becomes frozen except George, who meditates on 'something warm, like Miami' to free his pals, while Ringo is nearly eaten by a dinosaur, until it too becomes encased in ice. John is almost lured away by a siren mermaid until netted by the others, only to find that Lovely Rita the Meter Maid is towing away the submarine for 'snorking in a dorking zone' – she only tears up the ticket when Old Fred romances her, to The Beatles' backing. Eventually, via the Sea of Green, they reach the Land of Submarines (analogous to Pepperland), where everything is submarine-shaped, and shells produce the sound of dry land. Finally the boys take the instruments of their Pepper alter-egos and use their music to free the beautiful people of the land from a thoughtless beast called Big Bertha, who uses subs for picking her teeth (or in a later draft, crayons for playing noughts and crosses). Besides Rita's song, 'Getting Better', 'Penny Lane', 'Strawberry Fields' and 'Fixing a Hole' (in the mesmerising Sea of Holes) were to have been on the soundtrack. The script also had a preoccupation with mentioning 'Argentina', which resulted in only one odd reference in the finished film, but some of Minoff's key elements survived, only to be claimed by subsequent writers – he only kept his name on the credits thanks to a hot-shot agent.

This would be perhaps the messiest period, with writers including Tom Stoppard rumoured to be stepping on board while Jack Mendelsohn, a veteran from the cartoon series, fiddled with Minoff's draft as best he could. Having read a news report about Richard Rodgers' hiring of the young writer as a replacement for the late Oscar Hammerstein, Brodax called in Segal – a fellow Brooklyn native, and Harvard Professor of Classics to be, whose career would reach its zenith with the release of all-time soppy novel/movie *Love Story* three years later. Segal claimed that his academic bubble at the time meant that The Beatles were a closed book to him – when Al assured him that *Sgt Pepper* had sold three million records, he replied 'Good for Mrs Pepper, and all the little Peppers!' – although he insisted this ignorance never held him back: 'I wrote an extra verse of "Lucy In The Sky With Diamonds" and I heard the boys who were playing The Beatles record it. Apparently John Lennon came along and said, "I'm not gonna give bloody Erich any royalties. Take it out." My one bit of fame never got past Dean Street!'[215] Segal's arrival in London to try to kick the screenplay into shape resulted in a more cogent script, but what he felt was a 'finished' draft was still lacking Blue Meanies and packed with highfalutin literary allusions and New York Jewish humour, without any Beatle flavour at all.

Animation director Jack Stokes admitted, 'There was a kind of rough-arse script that we tore apart and ripped up. We had to get some kind of storyline, which was a swine to do considering we had about fifteen ruddy songs, none of them having any connection with each other.'[216] Things weren't helped by the tug of war between Brodax and TVC, the former wanting an Americanised film out as soon as possible, and the valiant Brits demanding that whatever they created, it really had to be *good,* and worthy of the Beatle name. This was the state of play when thirty-three-year-old Czech designer Heinz Edelmann was called to Soho to see how he could pull the myriad loose strings together, with a unique multi-layered 2D style in part influenced by the artist having only one eye. 'I was a graphic designer working in Germany known for my poster work. And Charlie Jenkins, the art director in charge of special effects, happened to be familiar with my work and called me. He was the one who got me into all this mess. I wasn't nervous at first because I assumed I was going to learn from the professionals. But when I came to realise that nobody had any experience in feature films, I started getting worried.'[217] Although Edelmann's esoteric take on the four Beatles themselves landed him his key role, it was a baptism of fire, Heinz recalled: 'the first, second and the several versions of the script got weirder and weirder... As production time drew close and the final presentation, I was given the brief to illustrate Davy Jones in "Davy Jones' Locker" together with some mermaids, and this was on a Friday afternoon when everybody else went away for the weekend, which was at that time religiously observed in London. Now I was not very happy with doing a Davy Jones. Also, I've never done a drawing of a mermaid in my life, and I hope to go to my grave without ever doing one. But there was nobody to resign to on a Friday night...' Instead of developing the idea of John being hypnotised by the mermaid, Heinz began drawing monsters, accompanied by his familiar bottle of gin, and the charmingly surreal – and, crucially, intrinsically zany and comic – mad world he brought to life elevated the entire project once and for all, showing the way for everyone on board, and working through the night even when most of the native staff had gone off to the pub. The most important piece of the puzzle came with Edelmann's design for the bad guys, whose destruction of jolly, colourful 'Pepperland' gave the heroes their quest – a legend persists that Heinz based the forces of misery on the KGB, intending them to be 'Red Meanies', but equally they were said to be originally intended as purple monsters. Only an assistant's insistence that blue would look better on screen resulted in the defining hue of the iconic menace – the Blue Meanies were born.

Although this allowed Segal to insert Jewish jokes – 'You don't look Blue-ish to me' – his draft of the screenplay remained un-Beatle-ish, and the voice cast were not comfortable with the lines they were given at first. Naturally, the Beatles themselves wouldn't have deigned to perform their own voices for a cartoon, knowing what they did about the quality of the TV series, but although George happily admitted 'The thing I liked most about the movie was that we didn't really have anything to do with it'[218], subsequently his bandmates made claims to have supported the project and even rued the decision to hire actors. Ringo regularly popped into the studios to complain that his nose wasn't big enough, and John even claimed 'Brodax got half of *Yellow Submarine* out of my mouth! The idea for the Hoover, the machine that sucks people up – all those were my ideas. They used to come to the studio and chat: "Hi, John, old bean. Got any ideas for the film?" And I'd just spout out all this stuff, and they went off and did it… We used to have a laugh putting this, that or the other in, in a light-hearted way.'[219] Paul, perversely, was always the least keen on the film both before and after completion: 'I talked to them about "Yellow Submarine", which they wanted to build the film around. I told them that I had very definite thoughts about this. There is a land of actual submarines – all different coloured and in fact it's a commune. All four of us hoped for something a little bit groovier. Sort of more classic *Pinocchio* or *Snow White*. Right away, they made it clear they weren't keen to do just a straight Disney thing.' Indeed, a sign hung blatantly on the TVC wall, reminding artists that their ethos was 'DISNEY – THE OPPOSITE' – and of course, many of Edelmann's Blue Meanies sported Mickey Mouse ears. 'As much as you can capture people's characters in a cartoon drawing, an animation piece, I think they did pretty well, really,' Paul continued. 'It's like being the straight guy in the group. There's George looking marvellous up on a hill, Ringo's is always a good character. My cartoon character's a bit bland. But then the animators didn't know me, the Pepper side of me. So you become the young executive singing ballads. You get typecast. It's just like being in a soap. They've made their minds up on who you are and you just have to live with it. But never mind, it's only a cartoon.' Harrison, on the other hand, was contented to say, 'When you see my character, it's kind of me, isn't it? That's how I was, that's how I am. In my heart, I still am on a mountain in India somewhere – and that suits me... I suppose it's the voices that make it really funny because it's not our voices. But I think it's fun for the cartoon characters to talk like that...'[220] In *Anthology*, he added, 'I'm not sure why we never did our own voices, but the actors probably did it better because they needed to be more cartoon-like. Our voices were pretty cartoon-like anyway, but the exaggeration that you've got with the actors' voices suits it.'[221]

Sadly, none of the six male performers chosen to perform the ever-changing script (allegedly recorded twice over to cover all the developments since the first effort) are still with us to tell their tale. The cast had varying degrees of comedic heritage, but if there was one banker, it was Lance Percival, this time relieved of Ringo duty to give his best doddery voice for Old Fred, while the one other non-Beatle voice, Dick Emery, had already been the star of his own BBC TV comedy sketch show for a few years, and although barely repeatable today, it would go on to greater success in the 1970s, giving a whole generation of schoolboys a raft of catchphrases to parrot in the playground, especially the motto of saucepot Mandy, which gave his own movie vehicle its name – *Ooh... You Are Awful* ('But I like you!'). Perhaps Emery's greatest qualification for providing the voices of the Boob and the Mayor, however, was his place as an honorary Goon, having stood in for Secombe for one wireless recording, and also popping up in movie spin-off *The Case of the Mukkinese Battle Horn* in 1954. Lance and Dick provided a strong comedy team for the ersatz Fab Four to perform against, with two key players, John Clive and Geoffrey Hughes, hired after their appearance in satirical flop *Smashing Time*, a film by George Melly taking aim at 'Swinging London'. Clive, who was to have a memorable cameo as a car salesman in *The Italian Job* a few years later, tended to be the most up-front of the cast (fittingly for the Lennon role), and as the old canard about American understanding of scouse accents arose once again, the actors risked everything by standing up for their real-life counterparts: 'Al was a caricature American film producer,' Clive said. 'He auditioned all of us but decided he wanted the voices to be more transatlantic. I told him to fuck off. Point blank. I was the spokesman for the four of us and I told him The Beatles were *never* transatlantic: they were from Liverpool and always would remain so.' 'Al was Brooklyn. Very Brooklyn,' Hughes added. 'He wouldn't have understood anything outside of Brooklyn, really.'[222] He originally auditioned for the Harrison role, but portraying McCartney was an unusually glamorous early job for Merseyside native Hughes, who gained fame with nine years in *Coronation Street* as loveable ne'er-do-well Eddie Yeats, and then became a beloved sitcom working class hero as Onslow in *Keeping Up Appearances*, repeating the trick as Twiggy in *The Royle Family*, before his death in 2012. Ringo's voice came courtesy of another Liverpudlian, the multi-talented Paul Angelis, who also lent his tones as the narrator and the arch, screaming Chief Blue Meanie. Angelis' versatility was to come in very handy thanks to the choice of voice for Harrison – he was the one Beatle the crew found impossible to cast, until a chance eavesdrop on a young scouser at the Dog & Duck brought the mysterious Peter Batten on board. The young chancer was having a whale of a time as such a crucial part of the groovy young talent pool, and was in bed with his girlfriend, one of the art student colourists, when the military police broke down the door and arrested him for desertion from the British Army – he then positively disappeared forever, and Angelis had to complete the George dialogue as best he could (and few ever heard the join).

Another key Liverpudlian voice provided the real solution to the problem of Segal's un-Beatle-ish dialogue – Mike McGear's poetic Scaffold bandmate Roger McGough: 'It was an American company working for an American market and they said it needed some Liverpudlian element. The work that I did was script-doctoring in a sense, although "Sea of Monsters" I did completely on my own... When I saw the script, I could see why I'd been brought in. It read as if it was set in the Bronx or something... it wasn't so much that it wasn't funny, but it wasn't Liverpudlian, so I was brought in as a Liverpudlian and as a writer. It's the rhythm: the way they cut together, the flat voice of Ringo, certain words they use, the sing-song elements which I suppose, as a poet, I was able to have.'[223] Quoting specific examples is a minefield of attribution, even all these years later, but McGough's grounded groove can surely be heard in many classic quick-fire exchanges:

PAUL:	Look, it's a school of whales.
RINGO:	They look a little bit old for school.
PAUL:	University then.
RINGO:	University of whales?
JOHN:	They look like drop-outs to me...
RINGO:	Hey, I wonder what'll happen if I pull this lever.
FRED:	Oh, you mustn't do that, now!
RINGO:	Can't help it. I'm a born lever-puller...
JOHN:	Hey, Ringo, I just had the strangest dream.
RINGO:	I warned you not to eat on an empty stomach.[224]

McGough's dialogue also popularised for the first time the familiar scouse patter 'Dey do dough, don't dey dough?' – ultimately to reach its apotheosis when parroted by Harry Enfield's Scousers in his sketch show twenty years later. Despite the crucial sprinkling of Beatle magic from McGough, it was only decades later, as remastered releases of the acknowledged classic arrived with great fanfare, that word of his credit began to trickle out. 'It was made clear from the outset that there was a fee but no credit,' he told *MOJO* magazine. 'It will be nice to have people actually know I was involved, after being kept secret.'[225] Where now any animation is followed by an eternity of credits listing hundreds of talented workers around the world, in 1968 a battle had to be fought against not just King Features' pressure to finish and get the film out, but Brodax's subsequent campaign to limit any share of credit, including a desire to remove any mention of the British studio at all. The lowest point came when rumours of a King Features takeover of TVC towards the end of production resulted in a brief strike, and Dunning reportedly kidnapped reels of the film with all the negatives as a bargaining ploy, hiding them in his garden shack just outside Guildford. Despite this ploy helping to cool off animosity, TVC still teetered on bankruptcy even after the release, and it took a lot of commercials to right the ship – the studio survived to animate for many decades more, being responsible for further celebrated features including all the great Raymond Briggs animations, and a classic rendition of *The Wind In The Willows*. Many team members, including Edelmann (who, after several months of barely sleeping, suffered a breakdown and nearly went blind) were only given subsequent contracts, cutting them out of any fair percentage of the movie's earnings.

These earnings were eventually impressive, particularly given the unprecedented breadth of international merchandising generated by the film, from the beloved Corgi model of the submarine itself to t-shirts, alarm clocks, lollipops, juiceboxes, jigsaw puzzles and numerous books, some adapted from scripts so superseded they bore little resemblance to the film in cinemas. The Gold Key comic book and 'Gift Book' from World

Distributors both reflected the earliest Minoff stories, packed with mermaids, frozen dinosaurs and forgotten seas, while the popular 'full color' novelisation by jobbing writer Max Wilk contained special sections co-written with Segal, including submarine maintenance instructions and tickets to Pepperland's victory concert. 'Although movie merchandising was hardly new in 1968,' O'Dell observed, 'the vast range of related items which the film generated formed an important blueprint for the multi-marketing spin-offs of such '70s productions as *Star Wars,* a tradition that continues to this day.'[226] The wrangles over The Beatles' music ownership kept *Yellow Submarine* off the shelves for the longest time, despite numerous TV broadcasts, but since the first commercial revival and digital remastering in 1999, the merchandising list has bloomed, with everything from action figures, LEGO sets and big-head vinyl dolls to lava lamps, pepper pots, Monopoly boards, socks, cuddly toys, Christmas decorations and so much more, all modelled on Heinz Edelmann's designs.

The cast were also threatened with anonymity, credited only as 'Sgt Pepper's Lonely Hearts Club Band', with the studio concerned that fans would be put off by the absence of the real Beatles, and John Clive once again made a stand: 'From a professional point of view, I think we did a bloody good job, because the fact is the public didn't realise it wasn't the Beatles, and that is what matters. We really captured their wordplay, their humour, the way they related to each other, the way they loved and made fun of each other. It was good. But if you ask me how I felt about it for a very long time, I felt we'd been cheated. It was very early in our careers as actors, and to have created something that is going to stand the test of time, and yet the public will never know, was the ultimate put-down. The actor has a right to a round of applause and to say thank you, and take a bow.'[227]

TVC gained minor revenge for their treatment via the depiction of the Chief Meanie and his yes-man – or rather, no-man – Max, which knowingly poked a tongue out at Al and his faithful sidekick Abe Goodman, who was sent over from the USA to hustle the TVC staff to get everything finished. Nonetheless, Brodax protested: 'I would have liked to have had another year doing it, but that wasn't the deal. It was my job to deliver the film... I'll never do anything as good as *Yellow Submarine* again. A wonderful accident is the best way I can describe it.'[228]

John, Paul, George and Ringo naturally knew nothing of any inter-studio tussles, and when they first saw finished chunks of the cartoon, with Edelmann's eye-arresting visual style, psychedelic effects and the multi-authored, gag-packed and quirkily performed dialogue, they were knocked out. Far from least, the final key ingredient was the sumptuously composed and orchestrated incidental soundtrack from George Martin with a 41-piece orchestra, a musical odyssey which filled half of the movie's soundtrack album and beautifully evidenced Martin's years of funny recording experience, layered as it was with tongue-in-cheek classical leitmotifs, laughing strings and cartoony silliness worthy of Looney Tunes. It was George's idea to add a snatch of Bach's 'Air On A G String' to the monstrous exploding cigar sequence, referencing the popular Hamlet cigar adverts of the time. While Martin slaved away composing new music, the four 'specially recorded' Beatle numbers were generally either written for previous albums and left off, or would easily have sat on their next LP tracklist – music-hall-tinged nursery number 'All Together Now', another slab of simmering Harrison snark, 'Only a Northern Song', plus his jubilant 'It's All Too Much', and John's 'Hey Bulldog', which was cut out of the US film print and unseen for decades, after a separate unit was assembled by King Features to cobble together a new ending behind Dunning's back. But despite their initial scorn for the project, there was no risk in the four trooping along to Twickenham once again, to record a live action sequence which was intended to be as packed with technicolor spectacle as the animation which preceded it, but inevitably, TVC were forced to drop all such plans, to rush the film into theatres. An appearance by the real quartet was, of course, still a huge bonus for the film, the in-person finale popping up after 'It's All Too Much', George's anthem of glorious silliness – '*All the world's a birthday cake, so take a piece, but not too much*':

*

197

PAUL:	Catchy tune, that.
RINGO:	I can't seem to get it out of my head!
GEORGE:	Well, shake it!
RINGO:	That's what we've been doing all night.
GEORGE:	Oh?
PAUL:	Yeah, it was a great party.
GEORGE:	And we brought back lots of lovely souvenirs. Here's the motor. (TWIDDLES TINY MOTOR MECHANISM..)
PAUL:	And I've got a little love! (ANIMATED 'LOVE' GROWS AND SHRINKS IN HIS HAND.)
RINGO:	And I've got a hole in my pocket! (WAVES A FLAT CIRCULAR SHEET OF PLASTIC.)
PAUL:	A hole?
RINGO:	Well, half a hole anyway. I gave the rest to Jeremy.
GEORGE:	What can he do with half a hole?
PAUL:	Fix it to keep his mind from wandering! Ha!
RINGO:	Hey! Look at John, will ya?

(JOHN HAS BEEN GAZING OUTWARDS THROUGH A TELESCOPE THROUGHOUT.)

PAUL:	What's the matter, John love? Blue Meanies?
JOHN:	Newer and bluer meanies have been sighted within the vicinity of this theatre! There's only one way to go out!
GEORGE:	How's that?
JOHN:	Singing![229]

As a reprise of 'All Together Now' closed the film, nobody may have been left rolling in the aisles by this minute or so of Beatle banter, but if nothing else, after all those years of fab fooling for the camera or the crowd, this squib recorded on 25 January 1968 constitutes the very last time that John, Paul, George and Ringo got together on screen just to give their fans a laugh.

With so much going on in the Beatle world in 1968, be it the drama of Apple Corps, the intrigue of India or the arrival on the scene of Yoko and Linda, the film's premiere may not have had quite the bombast of *AHDN* or *Help!* but despite some tabloids continuing their campaign of sniffiness about the Fab Four's alleged dwindling appeal, it received a thawed thumbs up from the less short-sighted reviewers, after the open season of *MMT* ('We're only ever going to be cartoons forever now, because they really put us off, those no-good damned critics', George quipped). *The Daily Mail* was 'punchdrunk from the dazzling imagery'[230] while '*Yellow Submarine* is an exhilarating crash course in today's visual tactics and equipment... it packs more stimulation, sly art references and pure joy into 90 minutes than a mile of op and pop and all the mod cons'[231] was the verdict of *The Observer*'s Nigel Gosling – although *Sight and Sound*'s Gavin Millar missed the point when he complained that 'the children have been left behind.'[232] *Yellow Submarine* was the first animated feature to return to animation's roots, of being for all ages, and with each subsequent generation's celebration of the film, the remaining Beatles have been invited to pass judgement, Paul offering minor qualification in 1999 to his earlier misgivings by admitting, 'I like the main Blue Meanie, he's got a great voice. In fact, I've been doing him at home. His character comes in handy for many situations.' George was the most retrospectively effusive, chipping in agreement: 'I like the Blue Meanies a lot – as opposed to real life where Blue Meanies are pretty grim – in *Yellow Submarine* I think they're really cute. I like their outfits, I like their big boots. And I like the vacuum-cleaning bloke. And the Apple bonkers, because they never say anything. They just go along bonking people. That's quite a good idea really. The more bonking the better... I liked the film, I think it's a classic that works for every generation – every baby three or four years old goes through *Yellow Submarine*... The fact is, with the way the culture and government are now, it's all still happening as it was in *Yellow Submarine*. Except the Blue Meanies have got a bigger stranglehold on the planet now than they even had back in '67. And it looks as though there's no musical group coming along to break the bubble of greyness, because even the music industry has turned grey and is dominated by Blue Meanies.'[233] In the *Anthology*, Ringo added,

'The thing with the film that still blows me away is that in the first year it was out I had all these kids coming up to me saying, "Why did you press the button?" In the film I press a button and get shot out of the submarine – and kids from all over the whole bloody world kept shouting at me as if it was real.'[234] There remains a mystery as to why the Rank organisation failed to properly distribute the film in the UK at the time, but worldwide, the original gross box office was over $8 million and of course, over in the USA the film was a massive hit, with both critics and audiences of all ages, many reviewers claiming it the pinnacle of The Beatles on screen. Renata Adler in the *New York Times* called it 'A family movie in the truest sense – something for the kids… and for parents who can see the best of what being newly young is all about.[235]

Perhaps unsurprisingly, it was Derek Taylor who provided the greatest nostalgic summary of the cartoon's value, telling the artist and devoted detective of *Yellow Submarine*'s history, Dr Robert Hieronimus, 'The input of the Beatles was conceptual and there was this zeitgeist around, which they represented, which was extremely warmly disposed to the human race and to the mode of goodness. And of course, the central song is "All You Need Is Love". The theme, the title song, we know about, and the overall message of that is that "*We all live in a yellow submarine*", and our friends are all aboard, and there's no limit to the number of friends we can have aboard… It's really like a kind of ark, at least that's how I saw it – a yellow submarine is a symbol for some kind of vessel which would take us all to safety, but, be that as it may, the message in that thing is that Good can prevail over Evil, which is quite an old one. And there's enormous hope and reassurance and colour and vitality in the movie… it ends on a very high note. It makes people feel extremely good and full of energy.'[236]

WELCOME TO SLAGGERS…

The Beatles, The White Album, or however you prefer to name the double LP released at the end of 1968, has often been seen as the first great evidence of the painful separation of the four-headed monster into its constituent talents. But there are many ways in which The Beatles' penultimate year showed that the end was drawing near, and as early as February, Ringo was sagging off from a session for 'The Inner Light' by appearing on the second-ever episode of Cilla's self-titled new BBC 1 variety show, sharing the bill with hero Spike Milligan. The other three took a break in the evening to watch Ringo performing live in a number of sketches including an extended ventriloquist dummy routine, with Cilla as the dummy. The show, with theme music by McCartney, was a hit throughout the next decade, a regular spot for the best comedians around, and Ringo was to return twice more, joshing with Basil Brush in Swedish snow while promoting 'It Don't Come Easy' – the only Beatle to back up their old cloak room colleague in this way. But if that wasn't enough, Starr was also about to start filming his own first solo film appearance, in a far less likely vehicle than Lennon's flirtation with acting.

In the mid-1950s iconoclastic American novelist (and Sgt Pepper cut-out-to-be) Terry Southern was living in Europe when he kicked off an epistolary collaboration with compatriot Mason Hoffenberg, which resulted in the picaresque spoof erotica of *Candy*, the tale of a beautiful innocent surrounded by men with only one thing on their minds. They were equally appalled and astonished when the book became a bestseller, and ten years later, the movie adaptation had attracted an unlikely celebrity roster, including Richard Burton and Marlon Brando – and so the addition of a Beatle seemed perfectly natural. Perhaps asking Ringo to lend his dolorous Dingle tones to the role of a Mexican gardener was a stretch, but he travelled to Almeira, just like John before him, and gave it his best shot with a cod semi-Bandito voice, filming the few scenes required, including a memorably mad sex scene on a billiard table – Ringo was never just for the kiddies.

If all that seemed unexpected enough, it was surely nothing compared to the out-of-character decision by George to show up on *The Smothers Brothers Comedy Hour* in November, when over in LA producing tracks for his friend Jackie Lomax. Just as Morecambe & Wise are an all-but closed book to Americans, the careers of Dick and Tommy Smothers never meant a thing to anyone in Britain, except perhaps for hardcore Beatle fans who know about John's run-in with the pair during his 'Lost Weekend' year, 1974, swaying around with the 'Hollywood Vampires' Harry Nilsson, Ringo and co, wearing a Kotex sanitary pad on his head: 'There was this resurrection of the Smothers Brothers going on at a club in LA and Harry and I were drunk. I was drinking Brandy Alexanders for the first time – that was Harry's drink; they taste like milkshakes, and I was knocking them back as if they were – and suddenly I was in the fourth dimension. In the fourth dimension I noticed what I'd always secretly thought, that Dickie Smothers was an asshole even though I always liked Tommy. And so that's what I said, but because I was drunk, I said it out loud. I was a born heckler... On Brandy Alexanders I'm a very loud heckler. So I yelled, "Dickie, you're an asshole!" Tommy tried to cover it up... So then somebody said something to me and I shouted sarcastically, "Don't you know who I am?"' Apparently, his own answer to the ironic question was a roared 'ED SULLIVAN!' as he struggled with staff. 'They were throwing me out. I was messing around, you know. I was hysterically drunk. And of course I was being encouraged by Harry.'[237] Tommy was the one who coolly forgave the legless Lennon, telling the press, 'I understand creative people. They're not doing stuff, they're kind of at loose ends... But they didn't do it mean-spirited. That's why I don't drink or do drugs. I used to! But now I don't heckle anybody... The incident was partly our fault as we had engaged in banter with an already quite drunken John, and the newspaper reports have blown the whole incident out of proportion.'[238] Nilsson was still ruing the debacle in his final interviews, crying, 'Get one Beatle drunk and look what happens!' Back in 1964, the Brooklyn-born Nilsson had attempted to hitch a ride on Beatlemania with flop single 'All For The Beatles', but four years later, thanks to the enthusiasm of Derek Taylor, when asked at the Apple launch press conference in New York who his favourite American artist was, Lennon shot back the simple reply 'Nilsson', and McCartney gave the same reply when asked for their favourite American *group*. As the '70s rolled round, Harry's influence was to grow, and lead to a number of catastrophic creative projects.

LA natives, and only a few years older than The Beatles, the Smothers Brothers began as a folk duo, with comic schtick between (or in the middle of) songs, but once they gained their own variety show in 1967, they moved with the times, and besides being the chosen home for Beatles video debuts stateside, the show began to push the boundaries of what the brothers could get away with, live before the American public – their brand of satire giving early writing work to a young Steve Martin. With the CBS network forever breathing down their necks, even taking the show off-air mid-performance, it was apparently Harrison's own decision to accompany the already-booked Donovan to the studio, and pop up to offer some crucial support:

DICK: Tommy has a special guest and he'd like to introduce him right now.

TOMMY: That's right. I have a Beatle!

DICK: Yeah, but it's not the kind of 'beetle' you would expect it to be.

TOMMY: It's the kind of Beatle that I think you hoped it would be! Ladies and gentlemen, Mr George Harrison!
(*GEORGE enters to an ovation, bows*)

DICK: Beautiful. We thought, Tommy and I both thought that 'Hey Jude' was the best presentation we've ever seen of The Beatles. And we're glad it was on our show.

GEORGE: Yeah. So are we! Have you met my brother Dick? Let me introduce you. This is Tommy, and this is my brother Dick.

TOMMY: (*Shaking hands with DICK*) I've enjoyed your work.

DICK: You look different in person.

GEORGE: It's all the makeup. Too much makeup.

TOMMY: You have something important to say?

GEORGE:	Something very important to say on American television.
TOMMY:	You know, a lot of times we don't have an opportunity to say anything important, *because* it's American television. Every time you try to say something important they, er… (*Mimes cutting throat*)
GEORGE:	Well, whether you can say it or not, keep *trying* to say it!
TOMMY:	That's what's important?
GEORGE:	You got that? Yeah. It's very important… Okay… Cue the clap *now*![239]

George's gesture only went so far, however – the brothers were booted off the network the next year. When Ringo turned up on a programme with the same name in 1975 to perform 'The No No No Song', it was a notably tamer show, though they did send for the comedy police to arrest him.

The 'Hey Jude' promo enjoyed by the brothers had been the last Beatles video recorded at Twickenham, with an invited audience and an intro by David Frost, whose programme was to have the first broadcast of the song – though his presence now seems a non-sequitur, it did allow The Beatles to warm up by vamping a version of Frost's TV theme, composed by George Martin.

While Ringo and George were branching out in their own unexpected ways, Paul was, as ever, immersing himself in every new and hip artistic movement he could, with the brief diversion of recording the theme music for Kenneth Cope-penned, John Junkin-featuring LWT sitcom *Thingumybob* with the Black Dyke Mills Band, which became the first release on Apple. Although that programme never attained classic status, Paul's brother Mike became subsequently responsible for the (trad, arr.) theme tune for a more celebrated sitcom which began the following year. *The Liver Birds*, co-created by Liverpool housewife Carla Lane, boasted a Scaffold theme tune, and gave the world another scouse cliché some have connected to The Beatles – 'Are you dancin'?' 'Are you askin'?' 'I'm askin'!' 'I'm dancin'…!'

Meanwhile, John was being inveigled into another new sphere of comedy – theatre. The process began when award-winning African American playwright Adrienne Kennedy first approached Victor Spinetti in his dressing room, while he was appearing in *The Odd Couple*, with an offer to star in her new theatrical project – a live adaptation of both of John Lennon's twisted books. The author of Beckettian play *Funnyhouse of a Negro* had not arranged any rights for her idea, however, and nobody was better placed to do so than Spinetti – and although Kennedy retained a credit, she soon became somewhat sidelined, as Victor and John put her idea into practice.

Spinetti, who left us in 2012 aged 82, was one of our great theatrical raconteurs, and had the nous to realise, for the rest of his life, that it was The Beatles which people primarily wanted to know about – so perhaps the story is best told by the man himself: 'Adrienne's play had stage directions like, "Christmas Tree turns into a horse and gallops off" and "50 Jewish schoolchildren come out of a grandfather clock." Well, hmm… I said to her, "John's written fantasy but it's all based upon a kind of reality." And, she said, "Ooh would you please come and tell Ken Tynan this?"' Tynan was by then the literary manager of the National Theatre, then housed at the Old Vic, with Sir Laurence Olivier the artistic director, and Victor gamely went along. 'Olivier said, "Oh, very well, my dear baby. You'll have to direct it for us because none of us will understand it." I rang up John Lennon and I said, "John, the National Theatre want to do a play based on your books." He said, "They must be fucking mad. I'll give you the rights, you do it." I said, "No, John, why don't we do it together?" And that was it. When I told Olivier that we now had John's permission to go ahead, he said, "I'd very much like to meet with Johnny Lennon, I've never met him." John and Yoko arrived at the National dressed exactly alike, in white, with their long hair. As they were coming up the steps Olivier said, "Which is which, my dear baby, I can't tell them apart?" Then when they sat down together, Olivier began with, "Now, my dear Johnny…" Lennon said, "I haven't been called Johnny since I was at school!" Olivier didn't hear that shot across the bows. He continued, "My dear Johnny, this play might be turned into a film. As you know nothing about the theatre I must tell you that if that happens the theatre will own 60% OF THE FILM RIGHTS!" Well, John didn't move. All he said was, "Don't you have people that you pay to talk about this kind of thing, who can talk to the people that I pay to talk about this kind of thing?"'

Lennon whisked Spinetti off to Marrakech to work on the script 'somewhere warm', but when they arrived it was snowing and much of the resultant half-hour playlet was put together huddled around a bathroom radiator. 'John was in the lav, and we needed a bit of a Queen's Speech for the play and he wrote it on those bits of cardboard that they pack shirts with, slid it under the door: "My housebound and eyeball take great pressure in denouncing this loyal ship…" A whole piece in two minutes, to the exact rhythms of a Queen's Speech!' Once the project was underway (programmed alongside two other short modern one-act plays in an evening entitled *Three In One*), the artistic director began to flex his muscles: 'Olivier wanted to be in it as well. He said, "It says here that 'Dad' is a cripple. I shall play him in a wheelchair, with hooks!" He was baiting me. He couldn't have been more marvellous after that. That's what he was waiting for. I was in. John Lennon came to the final run-through and by the time it was over he was crying. I said, "Darling, was it that bad?" He said, "No, you bastard, you made me think about all the things I used to think about when I was fifteen." And I thought, that's my review! Whatever happens, that's my review.'[240]

The friends were interviewed for BBC2's arts programme *Release* on 6 June, reminiscing about pre-rock and roll Britain, summed up by Lennon as 'You got yer classic comics, yer *Beano*s, yer school, yer pub, yer TV and yer radio…' 'The play was brought to me to act in, you see,' Spinetti said, 'and when I read it, I began to feel, by reading the poems and the stories, the kind of things that happened to me as a kid, and the kind of things I heard, and thank God, it corresponded with… the kind of things that influenced *him*. The most important line in it really is "the infleances [sic] upon us", the things that makes us what we are, make you what you are now… the things that we half-heard as kids.' The interview also dissected John's playful way with language, and the way the play attacked its targets with humour. 'I feel the same now, really, about organised religion, education and all those things that everybody is still laughing at,' John told interviewer Peter Lewis, 'but I mean, I expressed it that way then. I don't know how I'd express it now, you know. It'd be slightly different really... I am full of compassion really, you can still, sort of, just dislike things. I just hate things less strenuously than I did. I haven't got as big of a chip about it, because maybe I've escaped out of it a bit. I think our society is run by insane people for insane objectives. And I think that's what I sussed when I was sixteen and twelve, way down the line. But I expressed it differently all through my life.' Ultimately, the accidental playwright concluded, 'Universal sorrow just hits you about once a week now – BANG! – but then you might as well get on with it... there are laughs to compensate, because if there weren't, it would be very melancholy.'[241]

The resultant half-hour of theatre was egregiously Beckettian, but when it opened twelve days later, all coverage of the actual production was overshadowed by media obsession with John and Yoko's first public appearance together. Having never been captured on film, the play did provide a lost wonder in the sound-effect-heavy soundtrack, pieced together by John and Victor with George Martin throughout the night at Abbey Road, a recording Spinetti believed to have played a part in the genesis of 'Revolution 9'. The very slight narrative followed the character 'Me', played by Ronald Pickup, and cherry-picked plays and stories from both Lennon books to form a not-too cogent series of establishment takedowns. All of the Beatles attended the first night except Paul, who chose to support Jane Asher – despite this show of support, the couple were on the verge of splitting, and Jane would eventually wed satirical artist Gerald Scarfe, whose twisted papier mâché Beatles caricatures had made the cover of *Time* magazine in 1967.

'Some of the reviews were okay, others less so,' Spinetti concluded, 'It should be part of the history of the National Theatre, but it's been taken out. No one has ever approached me with the idea of putting it on. The day the play opened there was a big rubber elephant at the front door. Around the rubber elephant there was a piece of paper and on it was written, "'I'll never forget Victor Spinetti,' says John Lennon." Well, I mean, that should be on my tombstone.'[242]

An even shorter Lennon sketch was boasted by Tynan's controversial offering the next year, *Oh, Calcutta!* – named after a punning painting by French artist Clovis Trouille ('*O quel cul t'as!*' = 'What an arse you have!'). Despite the involvement of Lennon, Harold Pinter and Samuel Beckett, *Oh, Calcutta!* is mainly remembered for the full cast nudity which was soon all the rage. John's contribution was based on the group masturbation sessions attended by numerous Quarrymen at Nigel Whalley's house in Woolton, where the desperate lads would sit in a circle, get 'em out and call out the names of famous sex sirens of the time like Brigitte Bardot or Diana Dors to aid their mutual fantasies – until John spoilt it all by shouting out 'Winston Churchill!" or 'Fred Emney!' Despite this idea being a firm part of a smash hit show which ran in the West End and Broadway and all around the world for years, somehow the pervy playtimes still made headline news in 2018 when McCartney casually mentioned it to the press.

Although Beckett eventually withdrew his prologue for most productions of *Oh, Calcutta!*, he and John were said to have formed something of a mutual appreciation society, the playwright first inviting the Beatle to tea in 1967, though Lennon regretted that he had little to say on that occasion. Nevertheless, some sneaky fake Beatleologist decided to forge an imaginary interview which belied John's reticence – a Q&A allegedly carried out by the Waiting For Godot writer in New York in the 1970s, a kind of all-too-convincing Vladimir and Estragon patter which has since been debunked:

SAM: Now, John, we've agreed to discuss the major characters or icons in each other's work?
JOHN: We did, yes…
SAM: And we also agreed that I could tell a knock-knock joke… Just one – for only you, me and the tape recorder.

JOHN:	Yes, one, no more. You did promise, Sam.
SAM:	Yes, yes, I did. Only one. I swear!
JOHN:	Can we begin with that, then, and have done with it?
SAM:	The joke? Sure, why not? Here we go. You start it.
JOHN:	Me? Oh, all right... um... Knock knock!
SAM:	Who's there?
JOHN:	What?
SAM:	Who's there?
JOHN:	You can be such a silly fecking twit, Beckett... To most, your most startling imagery was found in the song 'I Am the Walrus'. People have claimed it stood for some sort of universal spirituality which you were attempting to share with the world. I have even seen intralineal 'translations' of this piece arguing such. Can you tell me about
SAM:	the walrus? ... What was the walrus?
JOHN:	A 200-stone sea mammal that lives in the Arctic. Still is, I think.
SAM:	With tusks! Those huge, silly, pointy tusks!
JOHN:	And blubber! Lots of blubber! Rolls and rolls! Practically no legs, you know, so on land, it moves just by heaving its blubber around!
SAM:	Ha ha ha! Ah, wonderful blubber! The sight of it... There can never be enough blubber!
JOHN:	You learn that about life: like the Duchess of Windsor said: 'Your legs can never be too short nor your blubber rolls too wide!'... Oh, brother! Well, let's go!
SAM:	We can't!
JOHN:	Why not?
SAM:	We're um, we're... oh, never mind! I wanted also to ask you about the eggman...
JOHN:	Jerry.
SAM:	What? Who?

Jerry Furman – he was our eggman. Every Saturday Jerry would come around and Mum would give him a bob for a dozen eggs. Once while he was inside the house, I peeked into the back of his van. So many eggs! I'd never seen anything like it! God, I wanted his job... Just one of the many fascinating commodity 'men' I watched when I was small.

SAM: Lord, yes! There was a man for everything, wasn't there?

JOHN: Now that you mention it, Christ! There was a milkman and a breadman, fruitman, garbageman, rag and bone man.

SAM: Neighbourhood life was a daily parade! There was the postman, policeman, fireman, the telephone man, the insurance man, the Fuller Brush man...

JOHN: Right! And always they'd identify themselves as such, like they didn't have a name or something. I mean you'd hear this rap-rap-rap on the door followed by a muffled 'Milkman!' or 'Eggman!' or whatever!

SAM: Thank heavens that all stopped. Can you imagine the cacophony in this age of over-specialised marketing?

JOHN: ...Rap-rap-rap! 'Haemorrhoid Relief-man! Hae-morrhoid-man! Need anythin' up yours today?'

SAM: ...Rap-rap-rap! 'Astronaut! Astronaut!' Rap-rap-rap! 'Paperclip-man!'

SAM: Door to door Einstein: Rap-rap-rap! 'Cosmology-man! Theoretical Physics-man!

JOHN: Fresh-picked photoelectric effects! Nice ripe unified field theories...!'[243]

The boys' extra-curricular antics of course never stopped the flow of tracks which would make up the double album and beyond and although the four distinct voices of the Beatles had never been more apparent, that just meant a greater variety of sound and word than ever – and humour and pastiche remained abundant. For every soulful song of spiritual awakening inspired by their time in India, there seemed to be at least one daft singalong 'novelty' number, be it Paul's flights of fantasy about cowboys or Hollywood sirens, John's satirical attacks on fellow followers of the Maharishi (or even, almost, the Yogi himself), George's ode to Eric Clapton's sweet tooth, or Ringo's first 'solo' composition 'Don't Pass Me By', quirky at best with its loping rhythm and knowingly absurd lyrics: *'I'm sorry that I doubted you, I was so unfair, You were in a car-crash and you lost your hair…'*

When fans placed the first disc of the double album on their record player that November, they found the very first song was a brilliant spoof of The Beatles' closest creative rivals, The Beach Boys, coming from the clearly comic angle of a good old boy in the chilly Soviet Union, but not all Paul's musical pastiches were comedic. It's all too easy to mistake whimsy for comedy, and despite the tongue-in-cheek performances, nobody is claiming that the jollity of 'Ob-La-Di Ob-La-Da' or a throwback number like 'Honey Pie' would have listeners rolling in the aisles. Paul admitted, 'Both John and I had a great love for music hall, what the Americans call vaudeville. I'd heard a lot of that kind of music growing up with *The Billy Cotton Band Show* and all of that on the radio… "Honey Pie" was me writing one of them to an imaginary woman, across the ocean, on the silver screen, who was called Honey Pie. It's another of my fantasy songs. We put a sound on my voice to make it sound like a scratchy old record. So it's not a parody, it's a nod to the vaudeville tradition that I was raised on.'[244] On the other hand, 'Rocky Raccoon' was built around an actual joke, and the composer saw it as 'a Mack Sennett comedy set to music… quirky, very me. I did my tongue-in-cheek parody of a Western and just tried to keep it amusing, really; it's me writing a little one-act play.'[245] Admittedly, some of the outtakes make the song even funnier (*'Rocky said, 'Doc, let's have none of yer cock…'*), but Paul knew what he was doing: 'Rocky Raccoon is some bloke in a raccoon hat, like Davy Crockett. The bit I liked about it was him finding Gideon's Bible and thinking some guy

211

called Gideon must have left it for the next guy. I like the idea of Gideon being a character. You get the meaning and at the same time get in a poke at it. All in good fun.'[246] It certainly was all in good fun, at least until Bob Hope filmed an overly literal cheesy duet of the song with Raquel Welch on his CBS show in 1970 – when it suddenly didn't seem the slightest bit amusing.

John, meanwhile, was disgusted enough by the actions of American visitor to the meditation camp Rik Cooke III (who had reportedly saved his group of elephant-riding adventurers by blowing away an attacking tiger) to immortalise him in 'The Continuing Story of Bungalow Bill' – a children's fantasy number which gave Yoko Ono her first chance to be heard on a Beatles album. Even some songs few would consider humorous had different origins – Lennon labelled 'Happiness Is A Warm Gun' 'a satire of 50's rock and roll', and famously, the first draft of 'Sexy Sadie' was a no-holds-barred spot of cathartic abuse aimed at the questionable spiritual leader: *'Maharishi, you stupid cunt, / You've made a fool of everyone…'* Although the gobbledegook of 'What's The New Mary Jane' was vetoed for release, the Lennon nonsense of old also resurfaced in otherwise haunting songs like 'Cry Baby Cry', and then there's 'Revolution 9', hiding silly stray lines such as *'Then there's this Welsh Rarebit wearing some brown underpants… So, any road, we went to see a dentist instead that gave her a pair of teeth which wasn't any good at all… So I said I'd marry, join the fucking navy and went to sea… In my broken chair, my wings are broken and so is my hair…'* John's best line on the album, however, owes much of its lasting humour from sticking out like a sore thumb on the otherwise perfectly straight 'I'm So Tired' – *'And curse Sir Walter Raleigh, he was such a stupid get!'* This vernacular attack on the Elizabethan tobacco populariser nonetheless fits the mood, by suggesting that Lennon was indeed so tired he couldn't be bothered to think up anything else, and thus the excellent northern English term of abuse 'get', as distinct from the more famous 'git', reached an international audience.

Even when Abbey Road recordings centred on a straightforward love song like 'I Will', the sessions were couched in a spirit of levity and pastiche, perhaps strengthened by the ever-growing freedom they were given in the studio. Outtakes for the song reveal the running in-joke of 'Los Paranoias' – a chintzy Spanish-tinged fantasy cocktail bar outfit, a twist on then-popular Paraguayan combo Trio Los Paraguayos, which in a way mocked McCartney's smooth guitar stylings. The narrative that the four Beatles were growing further apart, though clearly true in a practical sense, didn't seem to mar the usual gag-packed good nature of the band's creative atmosphere when they were playing.

The greatest, most bitingly satirical comic song on the album came, as ever, from George – not the rip-roaring confectionary-based lyrical banality of 'Savoy Truffle', but the all-encompassing attack on corporate greed that was 'Piggies' – a musical tirade which sadly carries even more clout half a century later than it did at the time. As with 'Taxman' (which was actually written around the same time, the 1966 lyrics to 'Piggies' being rediscovered by Harrison at his parents' house), maybe others threw in the odd lyrical suggestion – certainly his mum came up with *'what they need's a damn good whacking!'* – but the social commentary couched in wry, dry wit is 100% George, via an Orwellian inspiration which would have been made more explicit in the final verse, left off *The Beatles*, but reintroduced by Harrison for his 1991 live tour:

Everywhere there's lots of piggies playing piggy pranks.
You can see them on their trotters down at the piggy banks,
Paying piggy thanks – to the Pig Brother!

The sheer weight of puns in the song's lyrics would make it one of the most comedic in the Beatle songbook, even without the added humour of twinning explicitly counter-cultural lyrics with a pretty, nursery-rhyme-tinged baroque arrangement, plus a sarcastic scouse 'One more time' and 'Amen' coda, undercut by John's loops of piggy grunting. Humour was always lingering somewhere around the corner even on Harrison's most spiritual releases throughout his career, and only a couple of years later the generally devout 'Awaiting on You All' on his debut solo album contained the cracking assault on Pope Paul VI '*While the Pope owns fifty-one percent of General Motors, And the stock exchange is the only thing he's qualified to quote us...'* George retained a strain of disdain for organised religion which would have huge comedic consequences a decade later.

Probably The Beatles' most silly song of all, however, 'You Know My Name (Look Up The Number)' did not qualify for inclusion amid the mad excesses of *The White Album*, and was not 'finished' in the studio until April 1969, despite being kicked off by John and Paul in a mood of particular facetiousness in June '67. As ever, Lennon was inspired by whatever floated into his vicinity: 'That was a piece of unfinished music that I turned into a comedy record with Paul. I was waiting for him in his house, and I saw the phone book was on the piano with "You know the name, look up the number!" That was like a logo, and I just changed it. It was going to be a Four Tops kind of song – the chord changes are like that – but it never developed and we made a joke of it. Brian Jones is playing saxophone on it.'[247] Elsewhere dismissed by its instigator as 'a bit camp', he and Macca had nothing to work with lyrically besides the odd diversion from the central 'mantra', such as '*You know my number three and you know my number four*' and of course, the near-namecheck for their movie producer friend in Lennon's greasy nightclub intro, '*Good evening and welcome to Slaggers, featuring Denis O'Bell, come on Ringo, let's hear it for Denis!*' but this just made the track the single greatest display of The Beatles' ability to slip in and out of musical styles, from soulful rock to ska (in a section cut by John for release, and not reinstated until the *Anthology*) to rhumba to swing, plus a Spike Jones/Bonzo-esque section littered with cuckoo noises, and the sound of Mal shovelling grit for no reason whatsoever. Paul has been known to go so far as to call the result 'Probably my favourite Beatles track! It's so insane... I mean, what would you do if a guy like John Lennon turned up at the studio and said, "I've got a new song." I said, "What's the words?" and he replied, "You know my name look up the number". I asked "What's the rest of it?" "No, no other words, those are the words. And I wanna do it like a mantra!" We did it over a period of maybe two or three years... these endless, crazy fun sessions. And eventually we pulled it all together and we just did a skit, Mal and his gravel. I can still see Mal digging the gravel. It was just so hilarious to put that record together. It's not a great melody or anything, it's just unique.'[248]

'We played in all sorts of rhythms and gagged about on top of it,' Lennon added. 'I thought this would make a good Christmas record, because it's a real laugh, or you hate it.'[249] What's oddest of all, given its overtly zany vocals – the closest thing to a *Goons* performance in the Beatle discography – is that they were the last element added to the brew, with each section laboured over in a number of combinations through the summer of 1967, until Lennon and McCartney decided to belatedly finish it off over a year later. Engineer Nick Webb recalled for Lewisohn's *Complete Beatles Recording Sessions* that the ever-more-distant partners clustered around the same microphone, entertaining each other with the maddest sounds they could produce, John audibly corpsing in his Bluebottle-style voice before ending the recording with a barrage of wordless harrumphing speckled with the sound of catarrh, and signing off with a belch.

One of many sources of tension in the group towards the end was Lennon's insistence that the silly song be released as a single, backed by the equally outré 'What's The New Mary Jane?' – which may have been the closest any Beatle lyric came to the perverted grammar of Lennon's books, but if it contained any jokes at all, they were extremely obscure Apple in-jokes, and John subsequently dismissed the track as just 'fooling around'. His plan to release such a bizarre single could just as easily have been cooked up with a view to trashing The Beatles legacy on the way out, akin to the sneering at obsessive fans in 'Glass Onion', on which he 'was having a laugh because there'd been so much gobbledegook about *Pepper* – play it backwards while standing on your head and all that… Some people took it seriously, you know, saying, "What's he trying to do?", but they forget… I've had my tongue in cheek all along… Just because other people see depths of whatever in it, what does it really mean, "I am the eggman"? It could have been the pudding basin for all I cared. It was just tongue in cheek, it's not that serious.'[250] There's such apt cheek to the eventual placing of 'You Know My Name' as the B-side to

'Let It Be' that it's almost a shame the disc was only the band's *penultimate* single release, before 'Long and Winding Road'/ 'For You Blue', rather than their swansong. Nothing says 'Beatles' like a record with one of the greatest universally heart-tugging gospel standards of all time on one side, and a wacky, disjointed novelty song which ends with the passing of gas on the other.

CHARLES HAWTREY AND THE DEAF-AIDS

'Are we supposed to giggle in the solo?' – Lennon's snide quip before one of the endless takes of the aforementioned modern hymn could also be taken as a dig at his erstwhile partner's earnestness, but McCartney's super-fast agreement and on-mike cackle testify to a spot of Beatles blasphemy which has gained considerable weight in recent years – that the 'Get Back' project which resulted in the band's final, controversial album release *Let It Be*, was not entirely the cold, grinding misery that the band always said it was, despite the apparent confirmation provided by Michael Lindsay-Hogg's eventual feature film of the same name – a project which had nothing to do with the UA three-picture deal, already honoured by the live action snippet at the end of *Yellow Submarine*.

There's little room to go too far in disputing this legend of The Beatles' break-up – after all, George did leave for all of forty-eight hours, bringing to an end the chilly fortnight which represented their positively final work at Twickenham Studios. But John had long ago privately announced his own resignation as a Beatle, and even Ringo had walked the previous year, for the Sardinia trip on his very pal Peter Sellers' borrowed yacht which resulted in his finest 'solo' composition (of course finished off with a little help from his friends), 'Octopus' Garden' – another family favourite which is more whimsy than comedy, but given extra oomph via the band's comical performances, and gargled backing vocals.

In June, all four Beatles had been recorded by Kenny Everett for his BBC Radio 1 show, fooling around on different instruments, with McCartney improvising a special jingle, 'Kenny Everett on the Wireless Machine', but the continuing estrangement of the quartet was discernible from the great DJ's 1968 Christmas flexi, which spliced together four separate recordings of Beatles in isolation, each offering only the most basic festive wishes, and George even handing over most of his section to visiting American fruitcake and fellow ukulele lover Tiny Tim, whose falsetto ramblings raised more grins than any Beatle on the disc.

However, even a cursory listen to the hours and hours of audio recordings which resulted from Lindsay-Hogg's extravagant attitude to capturing the group at work show that they were nothing if not typically buoyant in the face of inter-member turmoil and constant surveillance. Recording outtakes always revealed an ever-present jocularity in Beatle sessions. A particularly prized example would be one of Paul's lead-ins to a 'Get Back' take, where George Martin asked, 'What are you calling this, Paul?' and the composer's reply of 'Shit!' earned the dry rejoinder from the unflappable producer, 'Okay – "Shit", take one.' With British stiff-upper-lips and the same flat scouse cynicism in the face of dark times which had always been an essential part of their armoury together and apart, the preserved badinage of the Beatles even in the winter of 1969, in any combination, provided more laughs than the most hepped-up good natured hilarity of their closest rivals:

GEORGE: Maybe we should have a divorce.
PAUL: Well, I said that last week, you know. But it's getting nearer.
JOHN: Who'd have the children?
PAUL: (*Pause*) Dick James.
JOHN: Oh, yeah.

Even in the awkward period after George had packed up and told the others he'd see them 'round the clubs', the remaining crowd whiled away hours not just wildly jamming standards, but making each other laugh. One morning John returned from a particularly tiresome radio interview, and launched right into a piss-take – we can take the regular insertions of (*Laughs*) into the dialogue as read:

*

217

JOHN:	(*Posh*) Now, we were going to discuss, this afternoon, what religion meant to a pop star. And the pop star we've chosen is Ringo McCartney. Tell me, McCartney, does religion mean much to you in this present day, with all the trends and the swinging miniskirts that are about?
PAUL:	*Fuck all!* Fuck all.
JOHN:	Well, I can see that he's been disillusioned by the church in general in his remark of 'Fuck all'.
PAUL:	Yeah well I went to, er, Brighton with the Maharishi. Fuck all it meant to me!
JOHN:	Was it an important step to you?
PAUL:	Nothing, nothing. He didn't groove me.
JOHN:	He didn't groove.
PAUL:	No.
JOHN:	He didn't smoke pot, by any chance?
PAUL:	No.
JOHN:	What about the Reverend Nipples?
PAUL:	Not a chance.
JOHN:	Not a chance... Well, do you like 'X' films?
PAUL:	Yeah. Yeah. Lulu, Barry Ryan, and 'X' films. But Maharishi – no.
JOHN:	That was a pretty concisive opinion of the youth of today. Now we're going on to a rather different group, generation gap, and that's Tumble Starker! Who's sitting here. Now, what do you think about mock-Tudor shithouses in Weybridge and places like that?
RINGO:	(*Also posh*) Well, I don't mind them being in Weybridge. It's just when they try and put them in London, I think they get in the way of all the traffic.
JOHN:	Yes, you're so right. As you said yesterday, 'Neither your arse nor your elbow.'
RINGO:	(*Sagely*) I said that.

JOHN:	I couldn't – I'd never forget it. Well that's all for this evening. (*Hums theme tune*) Hmmhmm... We should hold some sanctions against George. Very tightly.
PAUL:	Wheat. Coal.
JOHN:	Yes. Wheat and coal. Bread loaves. Meat biscuits. Cardboard cut-outs...
PAUL:	Does he make a lot of fun of you, Yoko?
YOKO:	Not enough!
JOHN:	...Well, apart from your part-time work, what are you doing?
PAUL:	Well, I do a lot of dramatic work, in and out of the country.
JOHN:	Presently, I'm working on a Welsh TV series called 'Land for Wecken', in which I appear as a Danish singer of royal blood who turned to folk singing after a disaster in the First World War where the Nazis bombed his house... And he had to move into, er, Norway I think it was. Why, I was born on the train between Ostograd and Fensborough!
PAUL:	Jamaica?
JOHN:	Sometimes.[251]

Spike Milligan had already bagsied 'Across The Universe' for a charity album in aid of the WWF, *No One's Gonna Change Our World*, but otherwise the usual variety and lightness of touch was absent from the eventual *Let It Be* – no Ringo number being a give away. The record was crucially lifted (or, if you're of an anti-Spector bent, deliberately tarnished) by the inclusion of scraps of dialogue from the roof-top concert more amusing than anything in their final festive flexis, including Lennon's random namecheck for the camp *Carry On* star in the intro 'Charles Hawtrey and the Deaf-Aids – Phase one, in which Doris gets her oats!' The plan had been that the 1969 album would be based on a new TV special documenting a momentous return to live performance – be it on a cruise-ship, in a Tunisian amphitheatre, up Everest, in a volcano, or any of the other unlikely arenas which caused so much interminable aggro between all sides of the Beatles camp. But if any of the highfalutin plans had gone ahead, it's improbable that the return to TV would have dished up much in the way of comedy, and so the eventual compromise of a frosty lunchtime on a Savile Row rooftop proved to be more of a laff than any of the complex alternatives. Between songs such as the free-form daftness of 'Dig It', John harked back to their Cavern days by offering joke dedications to 'Daisy, Morris and Tommy', or announcing requests from 'Martin Luther', and the whole band, Billy Preston included, even vamped 'God Save The Queen'. Above all, of course, once the Metropolitan constabulary had plodded along to spoil the fun, this loose swansong allowed for the entire original Beatles discography to end on, what? Peals of laughter, after John's legendary sign-off: 'I'd like to say thank you on behalf of the group and ourselves, and I hope we passed the audition!'[252]

Naturally, the forces of self-mythologising, McCartney and Martin, were victorious in wresting The Beatles' legacy back from this rough-and-ready conclusion thanks to *Abbey Road*, but that last laugh still had the last laugh when *Let It Be* hit the shops in 1970. *Abbey Road* nonetheless regularly had its tongue in its cheek, beyond the charms of 'Octopus' Garden', with the cod Spanish of 'Sun King', 'cake-and-eat-it' and all, joining Lennon nonsense like 'Mean Mr Mustard' and 'Polythene Pam' in adding the crucial spice of silliness to the wistful majesty of both Paul and George's input into the final Beatles LP. 'Maxwell's Silver Hammer' famously bludgeoned the tetchy combo with its composer's dogged insistence on days of retakes which made even Ringo fume to *Rolling Stone*, 'It went on for fucking weeks. I thought it was mad.'[253] Dark and sick the content may be, but it was another spot of McCartney vaudeville: 'It's just a silly story about all these people I'd never met. It's just like writing a play: you don't have to know these people, you just make them up... The song epitomises the downfalls of life. Just when everything is going smoothly – Bang! Bang! – down comes Maxwell's Silver Hammer and ruins everything.'[254]

Very finally, through the sheer accidental serendipity of tape operator John Kurlander ignoring McCartney's order to scrap the recording when 'Her Majesty' was excised from the *Abbey Road* medley, safely preserving it after fourteen seconds of silence, The Beatles' legacy was to end, yet again, on a joke. There's a discernible whiff of George Formby to Paul's throwaway novelty about pining for the monarch, and its questionable level of respect and sheer non-sequitur brusqueness proved irresistible to radical pop merchants Chumbawumba, who covered it in Queen Elizabeth II's Golden Jubilee year, 2002, extending the squib with a bridge and some extra verses:

Her Majesty's a pretty nice girl, but she never does a thing for me.
Her Majesty's a pretty nice girl, but she keeps the worst company.
All her lords and her ladies in waiting all crawling in the dirt like swine.
Her Majesty's a pretty nice girl, but I hope she's the end of the line...
Her Majesty's living in a land of curtsies, a world of blue-ish blood
*   and Nazis, yeah!*
Her Majesty's a pretty nice girl, but I think she ought to call it a day.
Her Majesty's a pretty nice girl, without one good reason to stay.
I'd like to take her for a whiskey or two, but I've got a lot of things to do.
Her Majesty's a throwaway song, just short of a chorus or two, oh yeah...[255]

However, the real punchline of the song wasn't truly reached until later that year, when Sir Paul had the cheek to include it in his setlist for HMQ's Jubilee extravaganza – a liberty the grinning matriarch didn't seem to mind at all.

'Her Majesty' was far from the last song recorded by the band, however – barring overdubs, the final official Beatles recording session was for George's 'I Me Mine' on April Fools' Day 1970, with John's absence inspiring Harrison's snarky intro, shared with the world on the *Anthology* release: 'You all will have read that Dave Dee is no longer with us. But Mickey and Tich and I would just like to carry on the good work that's always gone down in number two...'

There was also the matter of the final Christmas fan club flexidisc to consider, which turned out to be an even paler ghost of

221

what it once had been than the 1968 offering. Once again, poor Kenny had to shuttle between separate Beatles to paste together something suitably seasonal, dubbing festive carols and the like onto brief greetings from them all, and a long walk in the garden with John and Yoko, whose voice was probably the most prevalent on the whole disc – guaranteed to fan the flames of fans' indignation at the Japanese artist who seemed to have stolen away 'their' John.

Ringo, meanwhile, used his moment on the mike to publicise his new film, *The Magic Christian*, which had been filmed in the spring and hit cinemas in early December. A thoroughly unseasonal punchbowl, it was to be Ringo's second Terry Southern adaptation after the relative success of *Candy*, and the tale of its creation was at least as extraordinary and messy as the movie itself. Ten years earlier, Southern's episodic meditation on the nature of human greed, featuring American billionaire Guy Grand and his blithe but misanthropic attempts to reveal the worst natures of those he comes across with a flash of cash, earned notoriety by being temporarily banned, and when a copy fell into the hands of Peter Sellers, he flipped for its outrageous nihilism, buying copies for all his friends, purchasing the movie rights, and bringing Southern in to the creative team for *Dr Strangelove*. Sellers had the constancy of a wave, and although his Hollywood value soared throughout the 1960s, it was a long and winding road to getting the project off the ground, with his old friend and regular sparring partner Joe McGrath at the helm, and the action shifted to the UK, with Sellers in the main role, now 'Sir' Guy Grand. The biggest change from the novella, however, was the attempt to guarantee success by bringing in a Beatle in a newly invented central role – Youngman Grand, a homeless innocent adopted by Sir Guy and slowly inculcated into his bizarre, profligate way of life. The film then followed the book by presenting a series of weird vignettes (albeit almost entirely different vignettes than the source), leading up to the denouement on the cruise liner 'The Magic Christian', and a stomach-churning climax in which passing city types were encouraged to wade into a pool of urine, blood and faeces to collect the hard cash floating in it. The role of Youngman was earmarked for John, but *How I Won The War* had been quite enough for Lennon, who quickly nominated Starr as understudy, and Ringo – particularly with the band's desiccation becoming ever more obvious – found himself genuinely keen to extend his thespian powers. 'I suggested Ringo instead,' Denis O'Dell wrote. 'I argued, first of all, that he was a better actor, and second, he was far more likely to be up for it... The chance to share equal billing with a former Goon and major international star proved irresistible.'[256] Joe McGrath recalled, 'Ringo was friends with Terry, but we had a long talk about it, and we all felt that John had a nasty edge that we rather liked, to go with the nastiness of Guy Grand – "People will do anything for money." We got Ringo in the end, and he plays it as a rather kindly innocent, which is lovely, but John would have played it *along* with Sellers, it would have been more nasty... He was going to do it, but then he couldn't because he was refused entry into America.'

Sellers was known to occasionally drop in on the odd Abbey Road recording session – there's a cringeworthy bootleg of the comedian and McGrath dropping in on the boys and Yoko at Twickenham during *Let It Be,* in which he could only converse by creating a louche junkie character, to fit in with the youngsters:

JOHN: Remember when I gave you that grass in Piccadilly?

PETER: I do, man, it really stoned me out of my mind. It was really Acapulco gold, wasn't it?... I'm not selling any right now, I'm sorry.

JOHN: No, they have now given up, you know, as stated by Hunter Damn-Yer in The Beatles' actual life story.

PETER: Well, I'm sorry about that, fellows... if I'd known I was going to see you I would have had some on me... Because I know how you love it...

PAUL: Can you dig it?

PETER: Oh yes, dig it, dig it.

PAUL: Got it.

JOE:	Do you want to make the scene for the gents' lavatory?
PETER:	That's a groove, as they say. Well, guys, see you.
JOHN:	Bye bye... Just don't leave the needles lying around, you know, we've got a bad reputation now with John getting busted and that. I know what it's like for showbiz people, they're under a great strain and they need a little relaxation.
RINGO:	That's why he's going to bed.
JOHN:	It's a choice between that and exercise, you know, and drugs win hands down.[257]

But Ringo did not find the star easy to work with: 'The amazing thing with Peter was that, though we would work all day and go out and have dinner that night – and we would usually leave him laughing hysterically, because he was hilarious – the next morning we'd say, "Hi, Pete!" and we'd have to start again. There was no continuation. You had to make the friendship start again from nine o'clock every morning. We'd all be laughing at six o'clock at night, but the next morning we'd have to knock the wall down again to say "hello!" Sometimes we'd be asked to leave the set, because Peter Sellers was being Peter Sellers.'[258] O'Dell added, 'Ringo's practical and unassuming personality was an ideal foil for Peter, who could be given to some pretty difficult behaviour at times... Ringo was more famous, but he had an unassuming and equable outlook on life which could not help but have a calming influence on those around him. Even Peter Sellers would have felt ridiculous throwing a tantrum in front of Ringo Starr!'[259]

Besides giving Starr a chance to act alongside beloved comedy greats like Hattie Jacques and John Le Mesurier, plus Spike Milligan as a gutless traffic warden, *The Magic Christian* utilised some of the hottest talent around at the time, with John Cleese and Graham Chapman called upon to add what they could to a screenplay by Southern and McGrath, plus cameoing in different skits within the film. 'Writing for Ringo was lovely,' Cleese told

Marc Maron, 'because he's only got to say, "Good morning", and you're laughing, with that wonderful flat Liverpool accent. He's adorable.'[260] Cleese's highlight scene as an art dealer who emits a muted '*Shit!*' when Grand offers three times the asking price for a Dutch master (before cutting out just the nose) was not made easy for the lanky youth by Sellers' vindictive attacks, critiquing his every move and threatening to fire him on the spot. McGrath recalled, 'You'd have marvellous times, with Milligan, Eric Sykes, Peter, and our wives. At other times, he'd just get up and leave. Or he wouldn't turn up. This is why he identified with Sir Guy Grand... He had this feeling in his mind that he could do all those humiliating, mortifying things to people. He had a cruel streak and enjoyed setting people up, getting them to swim through shit. He was cruel with Cleese. Didn't give an inch with Cleese. In front of the crew and everybody, Sellers said, "Jesus Christ, what ARE you doing?"' Peter Sellers' appalling behaviour on and off-set was already well-known in the business, but the oddity of *The Magic Christian* seemed to make it particularly egregious – he even allegedly tried to walk off the project after the very first take, and Joe only narrowly avoided a sacking. On the other hand, besides Peter teaching the young turk how to upstage anyone by picking your nose in shot, Ringo recalled, 'I had some scenes with Peter which we couldn't do because we were in hysterics. One of us would open his mouth and we'd be gone. We had quite a few days of that.'[261] It was a baptism of fire for Ringo, but although the film was a cataclysmic flop both critically and commercially, Starr's gentle performance was rarely the target of censure, not least with Laurence Harvey stripping as Hamlet, Yul Brynner in drag serenading Roman Polanski, Raquel Welch whipping a platoon of topless female galley slaves, and Christopher Lee in Dracula mode biting Ship's Captain Willard White in the neck – all cameos desperately crowbarred into the screenplay by Southern as the bookings were announced. In time, the film became a jewel within the mini-genre of 'Ludicrously Trippy British Comedies With Embarrassingly Starry Casts Which Make You Wonder How They Ever Got Made' – with, of course, the added appeal of being a semi-Beatles movie, Denis O'Dell's production landing the film a McCartney original, 'Come And Get It', as its theme, slavishly re-recorded by Apple's greatest signing, the ill-fated Welsh combo Badfinger. Some still believe the film also features John and Yoko among the celebrities boarding the titular cruise liner, but these were lookalikes – in an unfortunate mirroring of his quandary throughout the 1970s, John found it impossible to get into the USA thanks to his spurious criminal record on drug charges, and so McGrath and co had to improvise without him.

The Lennon-Onos did show up for the world premiere in December, but nothing could help the film to success, as O'Dell lamented: '*The Magic Christian* performed disastrously at the box office, and I never made a bean out of the film. Why did it fail? I'm not entirely sure… I was naturally disappointed by the film's commercial failure but not devastated. The screenwriter William Goldman once famously said that in the film industry "nobody knows anything". He's right… For the record though, I was pleased with the final cut of the picture and felt it was an entertaining meditation on the nature of human greed, avarice and materialism.'[262]

Ringo valiantly committed to an extensive campaign of publicity, including a *Frost on Sunday* show alongside Sellers and Milligan, plus a solo guest appearance on Dan Rowan and Dick Martin's groovy new smash hit US comedy show *Laugh-In*, which had debuted in 1968 and quickly found a short-lived place in the UK TV schedules. The wacky gag machine featured performers popping out of garish flaps to deliver one-liners, and besides appearing as 'Peter Sellers' impersonation of Ringo Starr' and delivering nonsenses like 'You can be certain that a man with a banana in his ear does not want you to notice his feet', Starr also submitted to a short scripted interview:

DAN:	Ringo, I don't wanna get really personal, but did you honestly pose nude with your wife on an album cover?
RINGO:	No, that was John Lennon.
DAN:	You posed nude with John Lennon?
RINGO:	We're saving that for our next Ed Sullivan show.[263]

226

Reference to *Two Virgins* leads us to one of the oft-forgotten casualties of the tumbling fortunes of Apple and the strong-arm response of Allen Klein after John signed with him in January 1969 – the experimental spoken word label Zapple. Zapple only put out John and Yoko's second avant garde release *Unfinished Music No. 2: Life With the Lions* (named to parody one of the UK's first sitcoms, the radio and TV hit *Life With The Lyons*) and George's *Electronic Sound*, but there were plans to promote some of The Beatles' favourite comedians on the label, including releasing Lenny Bruce's final stand-up set, before Klein pulled the plug. Another deceased artist mooted for the label was Lord Buckley, described by fan George as 'a hip comedian. He was very "up" all the time and he was very important to me during the '60s.' Buckley's monologues, a mix of faux-English-aristocracy and laidback beatnik, earned him a cult following before and after his death in 1960, and George was to pay tribute with his 1976 single 'Crackerbox Palace', named after Buckley's own LA shack. George's other early solo offering *Wonderwall Music* had been the first Apple release, but despite the presence of Irene Handl in the cast, the trippy film it soundtracked was hardly a comedy.

The original cut of the *Let It Be* movie may have been the most mirthless and cold premiere for any Beatles movie when it finally flopped out in May 1970, a month after the typically honest (and typically shrewd) McCartney press release which announced the end of The Beatles; no Beatle turned up to see their dissolution played out on screen in Liverpool, London or America. Despite the reams of witty joshing between the old friends on film, Lindsay-Hogg's cut transmitted every painful moment to the audiences, and though reviews were mixed, UK tabloids kept up their ever-more-pointless assault on the ex-darlings of the swinging '60s – the film would ultimately become the most neglected of all Beatles movies.

Between John's 'audition' crack and 'Her Majesty', then, The Beatles' legacy on disc may have ended with jokes, but as everyone knows, the real story of this period is far less comedic (unless, perhaps, you take the tale of John scrambling over Paul's garden wall to hurl a brick through his window as a kind of naughty homage to his childhood hero, Just William). As Alistair Taylor put it, 'The Beatles took the piss out of the world for eight and a half years. And when it stopped, I think a lot of fun went out of many people's lives.'[264]

When irritated by the incessant cries for the group to reform which would plague the next decade, one ploy attempted by the individual Beatles was to point out that the public now had four times' the music to enjoy. That argument was spurious enough, but the same could never be said of The Beatles' comedy. Although there was much laughter still to come, there would never be anything like the combined wit and whimsy which was generated by the four boys from Liverpool ever again.

Abbey Road Studios – home of music and comedy.

The Beatles fooling around in Sweden, 1963.

The Fab Fools arrive in New York, 1964.

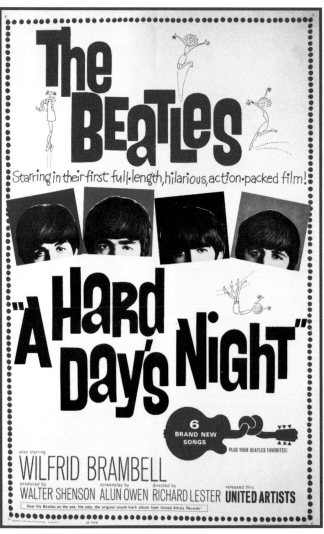

A Hard Day's Night poster, 1964.

Filming A Hard Day's Night, *1964.*

Cartoon Beatles as featured in The Moody Blues tour programme.

Editing Magical Mystery Tour *– slowly – in 1967.*

A small selection of infinite Yellow Submarine *merchandise.*

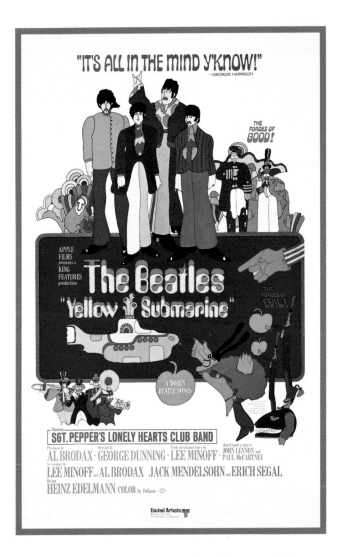

'It s all in the mind' – Yellow Submarine *poster, 1968.*

Olivia Arias, George Harrison, Eric Idle and Terry Gilliam at the premiere of the Monty Python and the Holy Grail *in Hollywood July 1975.*

Neil Innes with The Rutles in 2019 – rocking until the end.

Ron Nasty in happier times with author Jem Roberts.

CHAPTER FIVE

THE $3,000 QUESTION

*'I wouldn't mind dying as the world's clown.
I'm not looking for epitaphs.'*

*'There's nothing like the eureka moment
of knocking off a song that didn't exist before –
I won't compare it to sex, but it lasts longer.'*

*'After all we did for Britain, selling that corduroy
and making it swing, all we got was a bit of tin
on a piece of leather.'*

*'I am a big Beatles fan. And, you know,
unbeknownst to anyone, I used to be one.'*

'I think after The Beatles, Monty Python was my favourite thing,' George said. 'It bridged the years when there was nothing really doing, and they were the only ones who could see that everything was a big joke.'[265] In October 1969, a couple of weeks after John revealed to his colleagues that he was finished with the group, the numerous comic forces that made up Monty Python finally converged on selected regional TV screens on BBC1, in a sketch show which married the sundry madnesses of *Do Not Adjust Your Set* and *At Last The 1948 Show* in a colour medley, their *Flying Circus*. Despite a quiet debut, the chemistry soon proved a fierce hit with millions, and four men in particular.

In Python's own answer to The Beatles' *Anthology,* Michael Palin expressed his astonishment at the calibre of his new fans: 'When we were writing in the late '60s, The Beatles were producing their albums and as far as I was concerned those were the greatest and most exciting examples of pop music around. On the day when we knew an album was coming out we just queued up to get it. The Beatles ruled the world, they were multi-millionaires, we were struggling as comedy writers. Then I heard that during the first series Paul McCartney would stop his music sessions when *Monty Python* was on so that everyone could look at the show, and then they would go back to the recording. That was the first moment I can remember when I thought, "This is extraordinary, The Beatles interested in us?" The other story, which I have no reason to dispute, was that George Harrison says he sent a congratulatory note to the BBC after the first show and it never got through to us, probably the BBC reception didn't know who this Harrison man was, or what the programme was or something. So right from the very start there was this connection between the best band in the world and our little band of comedy thesps. Then gradually one began to hear more and more stories about bands and musicians who loved Python... We were closely intertwined with rock music from very early on. But the fact that the Beatles noticed us was quite something.'[266]

Monty Python's groovy cousins may have gone all-out mop-top in the 1975 special *The Goodies Rule OK* (in which their act 'The Bootles' was shamelessly nicked, songs and all, by four certain roughs from Liverpool), but Python itself rarely trifled with the Beatlesque. The only one of the boys to go so far as to show up in the *Flying Circus* itself was Ringo, ever the most bookable Beatle in the aftermath of the break-up – although his cameo did not crop up until near the end of the third series in 1972. As a guest alongside Lulu on the 'It's' man's own very brief chat show, he never spoke a word, but ended up entangled with Palin's hairy vagrant as the credits rolled. It was three years later that Palin's diaries recorded an odd reason for the first attempted marriage of Britain's greatest musical and comedy groups, on 10th January

1975: 'One of those strange coincidences, today was the day that the Pythons and the Beatles, or perhaps I should say beatles with a small 'b', first came together. It was suggested at a meeting late last year that we should try to put out the *Magical Mystery Tour* as the supporting film to *The Holy Grail*. There was unanimous agreement among the Python group. After several months of checking and cross-checking we finally heard last week that the four Beatles had been consulted and were happy to let the film go out. So today we saw it for the first time since 1967. Unfortunately, it was not an unjustly under-rated work...'[267]

Although all the Beatles dug the programme to some extent, George led the way as a Python fan – Terry Gilliam remembered Harrison describing the rise of the Pythons as a kind of entertainment reincarnation, The Beatles' spirit passing into Monty Python in a kind of 'transference of spiritual essence'. 'Eric is incredible. Michael Palin too. He is very funny. They all are,' he wrote in his extremely expensive memoir *I Me Mine*. 'They filled that empty space for me; after 1969, they really kept me going, you know. What should have happened is that the Bonzos and The Beatles should have turned into one great Rutle band with all the Pythons and had a laugh. Instead, we had to laugh on the other side of our face.'[268]

THE WORLD'S CLOWNS

In December '68 John and Yoko appeared in an attempted BBC special from The Rolling Stones, which involved a little clowning around from Lennon despite his musical input being a live version of 'Yer Blues', and it's possible that the 'Circus' theme put the idea in his head that he and Yoko had a mission to promote peace by lightening hearts. Their highly publicised two-person peace movement was turning John from a supposed satirical firebrand into a target for the harshest lampooning – he knew as much, and did not care. Anyone who had read Yoko's 1964 book *Grapefruit* knew that she was anything but devoid of humour. As gawkers including right-wing US cartoonist Al Capp found different ways to sneer at the fools' 'bed in' tactics, Lennon responded, 'We are not laughing at you any more than you are laughing at us. Our bed-ins were simply our protest against violence. Everyone has their bag and this is ours... A little old lady from Wigan wrote to the *Daily Mirror* asking if they could put Yoko and myself on the front page more often. She said she hadn't laughed so much for ages. That's exactly what we want! I mean, it's a funny old world when two people going to bed on their honeymoon can make the front pages in all the papers for a week... Physically we were exhausted. In fact, we had to go to bed for a week to recover!' Lest the approach seem genuinely flippant, he went on in earnest: 'That's part of our policy, is not to be taken seriously, because I think our opposition, whoever they may be, in all their manifest forms, don't know how to handle humour! We are humorous, we are, what are they, Laurel & Hardy. That's John & Yoko, and we stand a better chance under that guise, because all the serious people, like Martin Luther King, and Kennedy, and Gandhi, got shot.'[269]

From the very start, for all Yoko's comedic reputation as a pretentious artist, humour was essential to the 'johnandyoko' partnership. Ono's attitude to mockery was perfectly illustrated by her reaction to *The Simpsons'* ribbing, which showed her animated avatar ordering (and receiving) 'a single plum, floating in perfume, served in a man's hat' in Moe's Tavern – in 2016, she made sure just such a thing was to be found at her Reykjavik exhibition, and critics could lump it.

When first he sarcastically offered to only pay an imaginary fee for hammering an imaginary nail with an imaginary hammer at her 1966 exhibition, Lennon told the press, 'I took it humorously, which turned out to be fine, but I was sort of reacting like a lot of people react to her humour, which is they get angry at her and say she's got no sense of humour. Actually, she's hysterically funny... Yoko calls her work "concept art". Take the "cept" off and you've got "con art", and you're near the point. We're here to give people laughs as well.'[270] April Fool's Day was a particular trigger for their combined piss-taking of the madness around them, their 1969 Bagism project being presented to the press around that time, as John protested to the massed gawkers,

'If the least we can do is give somebody a laugh, we're willing to be the world's clowns, because we think it's a bit serious at the moment and a bit intellectual. That's the least we can do... hog the headlines and make people laugh. I'd rather see our faces in the paper than another politician smiling at the people and shaking hands.'[271] The following 1 April, the couple announced mutual gender realignments, and three years later the annual pointed 'joke' was the announcement of their conceptual country, 'Nutopia'.

Ono's movie projects were equally knowing in their absurdity, with 1967's *Film No. 4* AKA *'Bottoms'* a perfect example, summarised by Denis O'Dell as 'A short consisting of nude close-ups of men's and women's buttocks. The great and the good, the rich and the poor, the fat and the thin: Yoko's controversial film did not discriminate. I rather admired her cheek.'[272] 'Faces can lie,' she explained, 'backsides can't.' The bodily theme continued in 1971's *Up Your Legs Forever*, featuring 367 pairs of legs, but *Self Portrait* – 42 minutes of John's slow-motion tumescence – was laughed off on the Ono-Lennons' 1971 *Parkinson* appearance: 'That was a joke really,' John protested, 'I made a film called *Self Portrait*, you know, and at that time I was a bit of a prick.'[273]

Another controversial part of early solo Lennon legend has been defended as a joke. The musical sparring between Lennon and McCartney has been debated endless times, and what genuine barbs there were tended to be comedic. McCartney's jibes were the more subtle – the 'fucking beetles' photo on the back of *Ram*, or Linda and he in clownish garb wrapped in a straightjacket-style bag – compared to Lennon's eventual parody of that album's sheep-shearing cover, for which he awkwardly manhandled a pig. But the ice-cold tirade of 'How Do You Sleep?' was of course the epicentre of the feud, and was brainstormed in a hail of laughter, according to eye witness Felix Dennis – future publishing magnate and poet, but then co-editor of counter-cultural magazine *Oz*, whose well-publicised prosecution for 'conspiracy to corrupt public morals' in the mag's 'Kid's Issue' (ironically, given the McCartney connection, featuring a perverted pastiche of Rupert the Bear) would result in a fundraising Lennon single, 'Do The Oz'. As Dennis recalled, contrary to popular belief, 'Yoko wrote many of the lyrics. I watched her racing into the studio to show John, and they'd burst out laughing. The mood there wasn't totally vindictive – they were taking the piss out of the headmaster.' George played slide guitar, but although he did not play on the track, Dennis also recalled the visiting Ringo being the first to stop the mockery and flatly insist, 'That's enough, John.' 'It was a moment's anger,' Lennon asserted, 'but when I sang it wasn't quite as angry, because it was four weeks later. It was like a joke – we didn't take it all that seriously.'[274]

He may have scored a laugh by sending his MBE back 'in protest against Britain's involvement in the Nigeria-Biafra thing, against our support of America in Vietnam, and against Cold Turkey slipping down the charts' ('It was a gag. I'm not too serious a person. People get bored with seriousness. Had I just done it like some silly old colonel, it wouldn't have had that effect.'[275]), but much of Lennon's early solo work, primal scream therapy and all, nonetheless struck many of his fans as an unwelcome diversion from the sardonic wit of his Beatles work. Few of his followers were more adoring than Kenny Everett, but when John guested on his radio show, the host tried to entreat to the old John:

KENNY: You should be the happiest man of the century.

JOHN: Why?

KENNY: I mean, you've been through all that hell and damnation of being dragged up by the heels to the heights of stardom. And now you've sort of secured yourself in your own little studio, in your own huge house, in seventy acres of delightful scenery... So let's have a jolly LP, John!

JOHN: All right then, 'Hahaha...!' (*Singing merrily*) Something like that, you mean?

KENNY: Yeah, that'll do.[276]

With John taking his music so very seriously, it's little wonder that one of the most lacerating Beatle spoofs of all time was released in 1972. The US magazine *National Lampoon* had been launched in 1970, spun-off from the venerable *Harvard Lampoon*, and amid the primary talent on the staff was Tony Hendra, an alumnus of the Python generation of Cambridge Footlighters who had absconded to the USA – and who would find his greatest on-screen fame as the manager of popular heavy metal band Spinal Tap. An audio branch of the National Lampoon project kicked off with the album *Radio Dinner*, produced by Hendra, and he took on the role of Lennon himself for the A side closer 'Magical Misery Tour', in which genuine angry quotes from John were set to a suitably Lennony piano track by Chris Cerf. Where the greatest Beatles spoof would come from a position of pure love, this was a fittingly acidic explosion of bile which has become known by the alternate title 'GENIUS IS PAIN!':

> *I resent performing for you fuckers, tell me, what do you know? A lot of faggot middle-class kids wearing long hair and trendy clothes... I don't owe you fuckers anything, and all I've got to say is FUCK YOOOU! (The sky is blue.)*
>
> *Paul said he hated Yoko! Tell me, why should Yoko have to take that kind of shit from those fucking sons of bitches? George said she gave off evil vibes! I should have beat the fucking shit right out of him, him with his fucking Hari Krishnas...*
>
> *Look, you bastards, I'm a genius! Like Shakespeare and Beethoven and Van Gogh. Don't you DARE criticise my work... I was the Walrus – Paul wasn't the Walrus! I was just saying that to be nice, but I was actually the Walrus...*
>
> *Where are you, Mother? They're trying to crucify me! Genius is pain!!!... YOKO! MOTHER!!!*[277]

In time, the Lennon/McCartney spats lessened along with Klein's influence, and the former was even moved to admit of

Ram, 'The first time I heard it, I thought it was awful, and then the second time, ahem, I fixed the record player a bit, and it sounded better.' In 1973, a press release went out, headed *Newswecanalldowithout*:

> The extreme humility that existed between John and Paul seems to have evaporated. 'They've spoken to each other on the telephone, and in English, that's a change,' said a McCartney associate. 'If only everything were as simple and unaffected as McCartney's new single "My Love," then maybe Dean Martin and Jerry Lewis would be reunited with the Marx Bros., and *Newsweak* could get a job,' said an East African official.
>
> Yours up to the teeth...[278]

Paul himself was intent on forging his new musical machinery with Wings, realising his ambition to get back to live performing, and comedy was low on his list of priorities until he felt he had achieved this ambition – his 1970 purchase of the film rights to his favourite cosy childhood character, Rupert Bear, suggested that entertaining kids like his own was already more important to him. In 1973 he attempted to turn a filmed Wings live concert into family fare with *The Bruce McMouse Show*, in which the titular rodent and his family – wife Yvonne and kids Soily, Swooney and Swat – lived under the stage and complained about the noise. Despite being effectively finished, with voices provided by Deryck Guyler, Pat Coombs and Derek Nimmo, the cartoon never passed the McCartney quality control, and remained under wraps for over twenty-five years. This was quite usual for McCartney at the time – he also paid Isaac Asimov top dollar for a sci-fi movie treatment to feature his new band, which never got any further.

Amid so many half-formed projects, it was a wonder that 1973 also saw the broadcast of a divisive ATV spectacular which raised many a hardcore eyebrow at the time – *James Paul McCartney* being an awkward mix of rock and old-school variety, with the odd shot of northern humour thrown in (Liverpool was explained as being

'Near Wales', members of the public were challenged to sing Beatles numbers, and Paul was shown having a family knees-up in a Liverpool pub). The show naturally did nothing to combat any idea of Paul as the slick showbiz ex-Beatle, but he shrugged, 'I suppose you could say it's fulfilling an old ambition. Right at the start I fancied myself in musical comedy. But that was before The Beatles. But don't get me wrong. I'm no Fred Astaire or Gene Kelly and this doesn't mean the start of something big. I don't want to be an all-rounder. I'm sticking to what I am.' 'I liked parts of Paul's TV special,' John told the press with uncharacteristic civility, 'The bit filmed in Liverpool made me squirm a bit. But Paul's a pro. He always has been.' In fact, he added, 'I'll probably do a TV special, which I've got in my head, if I can find the right frontman.'[279]

The biggest joke indulged in by Wings was probably the cover of Tony Hatch's theme to chintzy UK soap opera *Crossroads* on 1975's *Venus and Mars,* about which Paul admitted, 'It's a bit of a British joke, that. When we were putting on that, I thought, "Well, maybe it's a little bit too British but I'd still like to put it out. I don't care. It doesn't matter if some people don't get it." If you don't get the joke on it, it sounds like a closing theme.'

Lennon's descent into 1970s hedonism on the US west coast has already been touched upon, but of course Ringo was an essential part of that boozy, boorish brotherhood of celeb excess in LA and London, which could be said to have had Harry Nilsson as it nucleus, but stretched out to celebrated alcoholics including Keith Moon, Viv Stanshall, Graham Chapman and others. Once cleaned up, Ringo laughed, 'I remember I did a movie on Harry Nilsson. He had all these players in the band, John Bonham, Keith Moon, Jim Price, and it was costing me just union rate, only about thirty quid a day. But it was costing £1,000 for booze! It was funny. It was fun times, we were just out there playing and making stuff. Someone said, we weren't musicians dabbling in drugs and alcohol, we were junkies dabbling in music.' Besides being the first ex-Beatle to find chart success, Ringo's moviemaking was in overdrive during this period, with 1971 providing a straight role in the Western *Blindman*, and a bit more fun portraying self-defined musical genius Frank Zappa in his Pinewood-produced feature, *200 Motels*. Zappa had long fancied himself superior to the greatest rock band in history, and had hurriedly retooled the 1968 Frank Zappa and the Mothers album *We're Only In It For The Money* to be a pointed parody of *Sgt Pepper* – as if Lennon or McCartney had ever denied commercial impetus for their work, despite still managing to change music in a way Zappa could only envy from afar. John and Yoko showed that there were no hard feelings by popping up to jam at a show in June 1971, Lennon's first greeting to his host being 'You're not as ugly as I thought you'd be'. Despite his highfalutin attitudes, Zappa had at least always made humour a crucial part of his arsenal as a one-man muso explosion, and *200 Motels* was a case in point, albeit Frank himself did not say a word in the film, his part being taken by Starr. Or rather, Ringo played 'Larry the Dwarf', a freak dressed like Zappa who descended on a rope to deliver an eccentric monologue about inserting an Aladdin's lamp up a vagina – basic 'we're being so naughty' profanity being a key feature of the script, somewhat marring the proto-Reeves & Mortimer absurd crassness of the action captured on film (that is to say, videotape, a lo-fi experiment which added to the awkward vibe of a junkie ITV sitcom played before an unamused live audience). Perhaps the most interesting thing about *200 Motels* was that it was originally to feature none other than Wilfrid Brambell as Zappa's bass player, until the aged actor's anxiety forced him to head for the hills at the eleventh hour, causing Zappa to cast literally the next person to walk in the room – Ringo's driver and Apple gofer, Martin Lickert.

Ringo clearly liked to keep busy when he wasn't making albums or co-designing freaky furniture, and the following year came his directorial debut, T-Rex showcase *Born To Boogie,* an hour-long jolly which certainly didn't besmirch the Apple Films roster, nor stretch Starr's skills too far, being mainly concert footage, with a modicum of messing about with a camera crew on Lennon's (and subsequently Starr's) Ascot estate. With Marc Bolan as the Hatter, the latter constituted a couple of Carroll-esque tea party cutaways featuring Geoffrey Bayldon, and Ringo and Marc continually failing to announce to camera 'Some people like to rock, some people like to roll, but movin' and a-groovin's gonna satisfy my soul' without collapsing into a fit of giggles (spoiler: they never achieved it). George Melly wrote for the *Observer,* 'The incidental humour is drawn from the nursery surrealist world of the *Magical Mystery Tour,* but lacks that famous disaster's pretentions. Nuns, one bearded, take tea, a dwarf gnaws ravenously at a car's offside mirror. Simple oral-fixation, but the music goes like the clappers.'[280]

By far the grandest comedic (or at least semi-comedic) Ringo escapade of this time came the following year with Hammer veteran Freddie Francis' comedy horror musical *Son of Dracula,* AKA *Count Downe,* finally released with some difficulty by Apple in 1974. His performance in Ray Conolly's 1973 rock 'n' roll nostalgia film *That'll Be the Day* had given Starr more thespian cachet than ever before, the plot's basis in his own experiences at Butlin's with Rory Storm helping him to a new high of naturalism. But although his arse-flashing filthy-minded Mike provided comic relief for David Essex's intense central performance, it was a short-lived moment of cinematic credibility, and for the sequel *Stardust,* his character was passed on to Adam Faith (with clearly no hard feelings, as they would be voicing mice together a few short years later).

Ringo put a brave face on his next project at first, telling the press, 'I just think that if Dracula were around today he would be into rock... *Son of Dracula* has a great premise, which is that Drac takes the cure and marries the girl. I'm using all the elements: the Wolfman, Frankenstein, Merlin, just the whole gang. It's like a non-musical, non-horror, non-comedy comedy... or it's a horror-horror, musical-musical, comedy-comedy... I think I have had the best lessons by working with the best craftsmen, like Peter Sellers and Richard Burton – people like that. Practical experience is a thousand times better than any class. They all taught me a hell of a lot.'[281]

Despite having drummed on Nilsson's horror-tinged album *Son of Schmilsson,* featuring the singer as a vampire on its cover,

Ringo's decision to marry rock music with horror and a dash of comedy, via a debut screenplay from British actor Jennifer Jayne, had nothing to do with Nilsson until the idea of casting him entered Ringo's head. 'I produced that film and it taught me one thing: never to produce again,' he subsequently admitted. 'It's a headache. I think it's the first musical horror film I know. I don't know any more... I met Harry when I was invited to play a few tracks on his album, then I invited him to work on the movie. When I asked Harry, I had no idea about the cover of his album. I play the part of Merlin. I wanted to work with Harry but Harry's taller than me and Dracula has to be taller so I couldn't have his part. It was very hard becoming a three thousand-year-old man, but I enjoyed doing it. But I don't think it's the best thing I ever did. We asked for a director of horror but I felt it got lost when it got to the rock 'n' roll part and the comedy. He's a famous English horror director. We filmed it all on location in England. It's not the greatest movie in the world but I've seen worse...'[282]

Having been a wizard in *MMT*, in Jayne's eccentric story, Starr took on the mantle of the greatest wizard of all, Merlin, who for some reason (perhaps simply due to costume availability) is in this universe the family advisor to the ancient Dracula line. Nilsson was hero Count Downe, destined to take on the mantle of King of the Underworld after Daddy Dracula's deceasement, but fighting his fate, having fallen in love with a human. With Freddy Jones' Baron Frankenstein pulling him towards his duty, and Dennis Price as Van Helsing, keen to use his expertise to draw Downe's fangs and give him a happy ending in the sunlight, there was no shortage of comic power on set, but little in the script to raise a titter – and even musical numbers involving Klaus Voormann, John Bonham, Leon Russell, ex-child star Peter Frampton and (inevitably) Keith Moon could not bring the cadaverous film to life, no matter how it was edited. The professional actors did their best, but there wasn't really a witty line worth reproducing here – as Merlin, Ringo flits in and out of the action, forever warning of dire consequences for this, that and the other, but there wasn't what you would exactly call characterisation in the performance. By playing such an unusual role in his familiar style, this could be seen as the real start of the cult of Ringo the Actor, the natural clown's genuine thespian yearning let down by a uniform delivery of flat scouse vowels, not without emotional inflection, but ultimately sounding as if he was reading his lines for the very first time.

Starr's decision, however, to hire genuinely funny comedians to entirely dub all the dialogue was an extreme step, even if the existing ADR was atrocious. 'We had the premiere in Atlanta,' he told *Q* magazine, 'it was the first movie since *Gone With the Wind* to open there, and we had 12,000 kids screaming... But we left town the next day, and so did everyone else. In America, the movie only played in towns that had one cinema, because if it had two, no matter what was on down the road, they'd all go there! We went into a studio with Graham Chapman and re-voiced a lot of it, so it makes even less sense now.'[283] As his closeness to Starr at the time would suggest, this was the epicentre of Dr Chapman's hopeless alcoholism, starting every day with a bottle of gin and a splash of tonic to see him through until the pubs opened, and so he needed help – not from any Python pals, but his regular collaborator, equally thirsty Scotsman Bernard McKenna, and the young protégé, an unfeasibly tall and undeniably odd fresh graduate from Cambridge, Douglas Adams.

Adams had numerous obsessions, but his central ambition had always been to be a Beatle – or if, as seemed undeniable, that was an unlikely ambition, at least a member of Monty Python. The latter dream had come close to realisation with bit parts in later episodes of *Flying Circus* and his new role as Chapman's rookie collaborator, and now here was a real-life Beatle to really blow his massive mind. On the other hand, dealing with Graham's boozy excess was a heavy task for the enormous graduate, and Ringo's job seemed to him like a fool's errand: 'It sat on the shelves at Apple for a year or two, gathering dust,' Adams said, 'and they thought, "We'd better do something with it – we need to make it funny!" So they set up in Graham's house one of those big Steenbeck things, gave us the film and said, "Okay, go through the film and write new dialogue for it." We said, "It's not necessary because the movie is not bad, it's actually quite good, and this is the way to really destroy the movie – this is an exercise that can't possibly work." They said, "Well, never mind, here's some money, do it." So we did it, and it didn't work very well, so they said, "Thank you very much", and put it back on the shelves. That's what you get for working with rock stars!'[284] With Chapman attempting his best Ringo voice, the comic trio did their best to dub the renamed *Dracula's Little Boy*, but few living people besides Ringo ever sat through the result – if the comedy dub escaped destruction, either at the time or in the fire which wiped out Ringo's personal archives in 1979, it sits on a shelf in the Apple archives, one of the most valuable comedy oddities imaginable. Starr ultimately felt that Mel Brooks' *Young Frankenstein* had stolen a march on them, by being before its time and generally much better. There were mooted further Nilsson/Starr movies – a take on the old '*The Road To…*' films set in Australia, and an animation to be called *Ringo & Harry's Night Out*, but the former never happened, and the latter remains unfinished.

Ringo wasn't the only Beatle who'd been making use of Apple Films, and in 1974 George was responsible for the film version of *Little Malcolm and His Struggle Against the Eunuchs*, David Halliwell's modest theatre hit starring John Hurt as a proto-*Citizen Smith*-style would-be revolutionary. Years later, George dubbed Apple Films 'the non-happening of the late '60s: "Come all ye faithful and we'll give you all our money." I was a personal friend of John Hurt and I saw him in the play… Apple Films had been set up to make them and I thought, "Let's do this as a movie!" So we did and we had a fantastic cast: John, David Warner and John McEnery. It was so wonderful we didn't even get a distribution deal. It was very depressing. It's difficult enough to get a record distributed, let alone a film…'[285] Despite Harrison's personal stewardship as producer, and providing incidental music, the gloomy comedy suffered as much as many of the aforementioned curious flops – in this case hampered by legal wrangles with Allen Klein – and it took until 1975 for any kind of cinema release, despite being feted at the Berlin Film Festival, thanks to George donating his own personal copy. This was a far from auspicious start to his career as movie producer, but having enjoyed the play, Harrison simply wanted to give

Halliwell a chance to take it further. The first film George saw was *Bambi*, and he claimed a life-long love of the artform: 'I spent most of my schooldays in the cinema. In Liverpool in the late '40s and early '50s there were all these fabulous art deco cinemas with marble floors and goldfish in the foyer and a nice glow with the lights and just to go there was a turn-on.'[286]

At the same time as attempts were being made to salvage Ringo's horror-musical, he and his drinking pals were working together on his fourth album, the sci-fi-flavoured *Goodnight Vienna*, which launched with a cover and publicity campaign based on the 1951 sci-fi classic *The Day The Earth Stood Still*, Ringo's head pasted over that of the alien Klaatu, stood next to the giant robot GORT. Ringo went so far as to stage a UFO flight in downtown LA, filmed for a TV commercial with cheeky voiceover provided by John, and the favour was repaid for *Walls and Bridges*. Saucy TV commercials were *de rigueur* in the US music business, and the previous year, John's *Mind Games* was advertised via Apple promoter Tony King in drag as the Queen, presenting the new record to un-stifled giggles from Lennon, Elton John and others off-camera, like a try-out for *The Kenny Everett Video Show* – outtakes showed John in full 'Lost Weekend' mode waltzing with Her Drag Majesty.

Ringo's sci-fi concept, however, wasn't originally to stop at one commercial, and a script was commissioned to promote his whole solo oeuvre for US TV, a comedy special which saw Starr playing both himself and his intergalactic doppelgänger, 'Rinog Trars'. The mooted special, entitled '*Our Show For Ringo Starr AKA Goodnight Vienna*' was credited to Mrs Nemona Lethbridge and Vera Hunt, but these pseudonyms could not hide the unmistakeable stylings of Graham Chapman and Douglas Adams. Had US network executives appreciated the value of the talent involved in this very silly space comedy, it may have actually been made, but even the draw of a Beatle could not get anyone to bite. The only taster we have of what might have been is the script, eventually published in the 1998 Chapman treasury *OJRIL*, which showed that Ringo was nearly the original model for *Hitchhiker's Guide to the Galaxy* anti-hero Arthur Dent – an innocent abroad, summoned away from Earth in the most unsuspecting way.

Chapman & Adams' Ringo is a lowly office drone with a great line in withering sass, conducting an ongoing feud with the programme's narrator, until the arrival of a gigantic robot from outer space livens things up:

GIRL #3:   Look! (THE WALL BEHIND THEM IS DISINTEGRATING.)

RINGO: What? Oh that. It's just my life becoming more interesting. (GIRL #3 RUNS OFF.) Strange girl.

THROUGH A HOLE WE SEE AN ENORMOUS METALLIC FOOT, WHICH THEN SHRINKS AND WE SEE IT BELONGS TO A SILVER ROBOT, LIKE THE ONE ON THE 'GOODNIGHT VIENNA' COVER. ROBOT WALKS THROUGH THE WALL, ATOMISING THE GIRL #3 AS SHE RUNS OFF.

RINGO: Oh well, I didn't like her anyway. Good afternoon.

ROBOT: Are you Rinog Trars?

RINGO: No, but it's close.

ROBOT: Rinog Trars, I have been sent by our masters in the galaxy of Smegmon to pass on to you the ancestral powers of your race, the Jenkinsons.

RINGO: I think you've got the wrong bloke.

ROBOT: My circuits are infallible, there can be no error.

RINGO: But I'm not Rinog Trars.

ROBOT: Error, impossible, error impossible.

RINGO: My name's Ringo Starr.

ROBOT: That's what I said.

RINGO: No it isn't.

ROBOT: Shut up. It's near enough, I've had a hard day. Come with me...

RINGO: Right. Can I have my powers please?

ROBOT: ...You are now free to travel through time and space at will.

244

CUT TO: RINGO IN ROMAN ARENA WITH LION CHARGING AT HIM. CUT BACK TO: RINGO AND ROBOT IN URINALS.

RINGO: He's right. Anything else?

ROBOT: ...Yes, you can go into nightclubs.

RINGO: Good!

ROBOT: You can write television situation comedy.

RINGO: (DOUBTFULLY) Hmmmmmm...

ROBOT: And you can do quite nice flower arrangements.

RINGO: That'll be useful.

ROBOT: And merely by doing this (HE WAVES A HAND), you can destroy the entire universe.

RINGO: What, just that?

HE STARTS TO WAVE HIS HAND. THE SCREEN SHAKES. WE HEAR A RUMBLE. ROBOT CLAMPS RINGO'S HAND, BUT STILL THE LAVATORY DOORS FALL OFF.[287]

As the story was to unfold, over an hour plus ad breaks and musical numbers, further early jokes and situations familiar to *Hitchhiker* fans would govern Ringo's journey through the stars, culminating with his arrival on the 'B-Ark' – a spaceship filled with idiots in deep sleep, jettisoned from their planet for being the kinds of people the rest of the planet could do without: 'The advertising executives, P.R. men, film producers, deodorant manufacturers, South Africans, The Osmonds, David Frost, politicians, bunny girls... career advisors, telephone sanitisers – that sort of person.' This scenario was originally created by Adams for his favourite non-comedy programme, *Doctor Who,* and would ultimately become a key plot point in *Hitchhiker* in most of its forms on radio, TV and in prose. Where the eventual escapade starring Arthur Dent and Ford Prefect would see the ship crashing into prehistoric Earth, in the Ringo special, the narrator simply talks Ringo out of trouble, the robot runs away with a giant prawn, and Ringo eventually bumps into the real Rinog Trars – to be played by himself in split-screen – and gives him back his special powers before heading home in a UFO just like the one on his album cover… a happy enough ending, until Trars spoils it all by waving his doppelgänger goodbye and destroys the universe.

The humour was undeniably out there, and decidedly British for the intended audience, and many years later, Chapman complained, 'The script was never approved by any networks or by cable TV because I think that they thought it a bit rude and because, quite frankly, I don't think they understood it very much. It would have made a very nice show.'[288] Adams was equally despondent when he added, 'It was eventually not made, partly through Ringo's various difficulties – he lost interest in it – partly because the deal fell through from one angle or another. It could then have gone on further if he'd wanted to deal with the hassles. He didn't.' With both of his chances to work with a Beatle on a project which would actually get made trashed, Adams would soon crumble under the pressure of dealing with Chapman's alcoholism, and not get his career back on track for a few years, when he became script editor for *Doctor Who* at the same time as masterminding the creation of *Hitchhiker* for BBC Radio 4. He remained an obsessive Beatle fan, however – one friend recalled the gigantic fanboy freaking poor George out by tailing him incessantly at one starry party, and once *Hitchhiker* had made him the most successful humorist since Wodehouse, further Fab commissions were to come Douglas' way. He was, however, forced to cut a crucial idea from the original incarnation of *Hitchhiker*: with Earth and all its cultural riches destroyed by the Vogons, the legendary Zaphod Beeblebrox was at first conceived as an intergalactic Beatles bootlegger, taking the greatest music in existence to every corner of the galaxy.

WE'VE ARRIVED! (AND TO PROVE IT WE'RE HERE)

George may have envied Ringo's wordless cameo in the Python TV series, but he had no qualms about taking to the stage in the next best thing. After the group began to dissolve – Cleese of course being the first to grow tired of TV sketches – the individual factions, Beatle-style, began to flex their solo muscles and create their own vehicles. Cleese would beat them all with *Fawlty Towers*, while Palin & Jones mocked Boy's Own adventures with *Ripping*

Yarns, Chapman joined with Adams for the fascinating failure *Out of the Trees*, Gilliam made his first moves towards a movie career – and then there was Idle. Always the outsider in the group, working alone and trying to get his material accepted amid the more powerful partnerships, it's little wonder that George quickly identified with Eric, and the latter's comedic equivalent of *All Things Must Pass*, was *Rutland Weekend Television*. Eric had always been the loudest Beatle fan in the Python team, having voraciously bought all the new LPs on the day of release while at Cambridge, and he recognised the band's comic potential from the start: 'That was the secret to The Beatles, they were funny!' he enthused to Marc Maron. 'When they came to America, everybody knew Ringo's name because he was funny. He had a funny name, a funny nose, a funny haircut, and he was funny. That's what made The Beatles – when they first hit America, all those press conferences, they couldn't just sing, they were hilarious!... George was the naughtiest boy in the room and the most spiritual, he was both.'[289]

The BBC must have popped a cork or two when his new concept was outlined – in 1974, the tiny, largely rural East Midlands county of Rutland was effectively downgraded to only a district of Leicestershire in a shake-up which lasted until 1997. The local TV station would, therefore, be a humble and meagre entertainment service – and so, the budget Idle was given to play with was suitably pathetic, technically a 'presentation budget' rather than a light entertainment one, with only a tiny weather report studio in which to record six sketch half-hours. Luckily he had a talented team around him, including Python irregulars, the versatile Gwen Taylor and imperious Terence Bayler, plus diminutive Henry Woolf, lugubrious David Battley and above all, his maestro, none other than Neil Innes.

The Bonzos had called it a day with relative amiability at the turn of the '70s, burned out from their last tour of America, and Innes had dabbled with fresh projects, including more serious outfit The World, plus a kind of Scaffold/Bonzos supergroup, GRIMMS, and in 1973 his own solo album, *How Sweet To Be An Idiot*. His exploits occasionally called on the talents of young virtuoso guitarist Ollie Halsall and cheeky wee hairy Londoner and itinerant drummer John Halsey, both of whom had been around for years, in early rock and roll and prog rock bands including Timebox and Patto, while Halsey had played on Lou Reed's *Transformer*, besides accompanying Innes in his occasional combo incorporating Patto – Fatso. As a rock wannabe, John also had one memorable celebrity run-in: 'I met Paul McCartney once in a Wimpy Bar in Piccadilly in 1964. I was a teenager then. It was a Sunday night and the bar was packed. Paul walked in and was looking around for somewhere to sit and saw two chairs at our table and came over. We chatted for a while and he said it was nice to meet us and paid for our burgers and shakes. When we left we got as many funny looks as he did!'

The loose collective of GRIMMS didn't just include Mike McGear, but his teenage second cousin, Kate Robbins, daughter of Bett and Mike, many years before *Spitting Image* made best use of her impersonation and chameleonic singing skills, while big brother Ted was embarking on his own comedy career. Family was ever-important to the McCartneys – leaving GRIMMS left McGear suddenly free, and as a single father, in need of an injection of cash. Having signed to Warner Bros, his big brother rallied round with the entire Wings line-up, to help put together the well-loved 1974 album *McGear,* Paul mucking in as performer and producer just as he'd helped Mike's wacky mates with 'Urban Spaceman' – even throwing in a touch of audio silliness in the guise of his *MMT* Major for the scowling scouse track 'Norton'.

Despite Neil's manifold projects, becoming essentially the eighth Python (after, of course, Carol Cleveland) was the unexpected boon to his fresh solo career. Idle's suggestion of his involvement with the *Flying Circus*, as the only survivor from the Bonzos' residency on *DNAYS,* began with the offer of a handy twenty quid as stand-in for usual warm-up Barry Cryer, but he popped up on screen in a couple of latter episodes, most memorably playing his beautiful ballad 'When Does A Dream Begin?' in the silliest circumstances, and was a handy addition to the line-up for live shows at Drury Lane and beyond. Idle may have been his particular sponsor, but the loveable Innes was liked and respected by the whole Python team, and his key role in their first specifically written feature film, *Monty Python and the Holy Grail*, mainly as the Minstrel of Idle's Sir Robin the Not-Quite-So-Brave-As-Sir-Lancelot, but also as soundtrack composer, seemed entirely natural, and wasn't too marred by the replacement of his stirring soundtrack with something off-the-peg which more suited the silly comedy. He was also to be very handy when recording the group's albums, particularly when it came to rock and reggae renditions of historical essays for 'Background To History' on 1973's *Matching Tie and Handkerchief*, providing a number about agrarian reform with more than a hint of 'Hey Jude' about it.

His place as resident maestro for the cash-strapped *RWT*, then, suited Neil perfectly, and every episode was to have one of his esoteric solo numbers as a highlight. The third show, aired in May 1975, featured a very short musical non-sequitur which nonetheless constituted the debut of Innes as Ron Nasty, or rather 'Ron Lennon – songwriter, prophet, babysitter', poised at a white piano, false nose and all, playing an extract of a song then dubbed 'The Children of Rock and Roll', ultimately to find fame as 'Good Times Roll'. Even this was not the first time that Innes had strayed into the area of Beatle pastiche. Besides the '50s lampoon of 'Death Cab For Cutie', the Bonzos' albums presented a huge swathe of mad stylings, from fluty flapper numbers about cartoon characters to the dirtiest rock songs about taking a dump – and amid this ever-changing audio pick 'n' mix, Neil's respectful appreciation of The Beatles' music had already spawned a pointedly Beatle-ish number on The Bonzos' final contractual album, *Let's Make Up and Be Friendly*, 'Fresh Wound', on which Neil piloted a Lennon-esque nasal delivery, and a scouse voice could even be heard in the middle of the fiddly guitar solo, complaining 'Come on, George, snap out of it.'

The 'Ron Lennon' squib was to be the last trace of Beatleness in *RWT*, however, until the question of a Christmas not-very-spectacular was raised at the end of 1975. Ringo may have been the one to cameo in *Flying Circus*, but George was a true devotee: 'I first met Michael Palin and Terry Jones in 1972, I think,' he told *Rolling Stone*. 'I met Eric Idle in 1975, at the California premiere of the *Holy Grail* film. And although that was the first time I'd ever met him, I felt like I'd known them all for years, because I'd watched all the programmes and had had them on videotape. So it only took ten minutes before we were the best of friends.'[290] Despite not being the first Python to befriend the Beatle, Eric claimed an eerie closeness with George from the very start – he even had fuzzy memories of being five years old, playing with a young lad on the appropriately named Red Noses beach in New Brighton, just over the Mersey from Liverpool, and wondering if that had been their first meeting. George in turn, of course, was just as enamoured of the Bonzos, and so *RWT* was a perfect placebo for the end of TV Python for him. Not that Neil was his only Bonzo pal, and drummer Legs Larry Smith had been over the moon to call Harrison a friend – his eccentric pizzazz inspired a track on the 1975 album *Extra Texture*, 'His Name Is Legs': 'It's the craziest song, both lyrically and musically and the story on this one is "Legs". It's actually Legs Larry Smith who was the drummer with The Bonzo Dog Doo-Dah Band, and he's a very nice person who is very eccentric and I'm very partial to Larry. He kept coming and coming and he just amazed me with the things he was saying, "Everything is dinky-doo. Everything that you do. Are you the king of la-de-dah?" He sings the first part of every bridge. I've never seen him since.'[291]

On that night in California, Harrison pigeonholed Idle, sharing a J in the *Holy Grail* projection booth and grilling him about his Python sketches – particularly an Idle item in which Chapman played a cop who brought his own drugs (or rather, his wife's sandwiches, in error) to a bust just in case they never found any on the premises, which George interpreted as a reference to his and John's own suffering at the hands of corrupt DS 'Nobby' Pilcher. The pair spent twenty-four hours intensely getting to know each other, and the friendship deepened when Eric was invited to George's Friar Park mansion – a comical wonderland in itself, created by Victorian eccentric Sir Frank Crisp, and adorned with hidden jokes, such as signs warning visitors, 'DON'T KEEP OFF THE GRASS'.

The friends' first collaboration was a series of radio ads for *Extra Texture*, featuring Idle in Python 'pepperpot' mode, and he received special thanks in the liner notes – alongside Peter Sellers. Harrison soon repaid the favour by producing the single version of Palin/Jones classic 'The Lumberjack Song', released on Chrysalis in November '75 – he had included a version of the song on the interval playlist for his 1974 Dark Horse (or, as he put it, reflecting his famous vocal problems, 'Dark Hoarse') tour. The somewhat obsessive Python fan George often went so far as to check into hotels as 'Jack Lumber', and his Lumberjack credentials were made complete the following spring, when the run of Monty Python shows in New York gave him an opportunity to secretly slip in among his comic heroes on stage, in full Canadian Mountie gear, to perform in the song's roaringly macho transphobic chorus. 'One night he came and asked if he could do "The Lumberjack Song" and we said, "Yeah, of course!" Eric remembered. 'So he came on stage at City Center as a Mountie, and nobody knew it was George. Harry Nilsson found out George had done it and so the next night Harry is going to do it, but Harry's pissed as a fart, and makes a big display: "It's Harry Nilsson!" He's waving and everybody's looking at him and going, "Fuck off, Harry." He's just supposed to be in the chorus. At the end everybody would step back and the curtain would come down, but Harry didn't step back, he stepped forward, the curtain came down, and he fell off the stage into the audience and broke his wrist. Nobody ever recognised it was George, which was really cool and very typically George.' Cleese added, 'I was struck by the extraordinary contrast between George, who did it so beautifully and aesthetically, and Nilsson, who was just a sort of egotistical drunk. It doesn't mean that he wasn't a nice chap but under those circumstances he didn't behave the way he should have done.'[292]

This live cameo, however, was preceded by a far more centre-stage comedy turn from George, when Eric asked for a quid-pro-quo guest star booking for the *RWT* festive special, broadcast on Boxing Day 1975. The ex-Beatle star power was thrown into even greater relief by the humble context of the Rutland studio, and with Idle in his familiar, oleaginous emcee persona, there was much excitement as Harrison strode onto stage to the familiar strains of 'My Sweet Lord', backed by Fatso, only to launch into a very silly number co-written with Idle (though decidedly trad in form), 'The Pirate Song':

> *Oh, I want to be a pirate, a pirate's life for me,*
> *All my friends are pirates, and sail the BBC,*
> *I've got a Jolly Roger, it's black and white and vast,*
> *So get out of your Skull and Crossbones, and I'll run it up your mast!*
> *With a yo-ho-ho, and a ya-ha-ha, and a ye-hee-hee-ho-hum...*[293]

George's book *I Me Mine* suggested the private alternate lyrics *'I want to be a parrot, a carrot's wife for me, / All my friends are parrots and sail the fucking sea, / I've got an oily lodger, he's big and black and vast, So get out of your pyjamas, and I'll shove it up your arse!'* This dose of incongruous jollity – which Olivia Harrison once claimed to be the bravest thing George ever did, even with the clean lyrics – brought 1975 to a triumphantly Fab ending for Eric and Neil, but there was little time lost before the arrival of *RWT* series two, and in fact work had already begun on the show in November – the 24th of that month, in fact, when the crew arrived at Denham Memorial Hall in Buckinghamshire, to film what would be the first relatively canonical Rutles number.

The whole concept began with Innes' innocent creation of an inescapably Beatley tune, and snowballed from there, as he recalled: 'I had the idea of doing it in that black-and-white, semi-documentary style that Dick Lester had used in *A Hard Day's Night,* mainly because it was cheap, which perfectly fitted the idea of *RWT*. The song, "I Must Be in Love", was quite Beatleish and Eric coined the name The Rutles, which I hated. For this clip, it wasn't quite the same group that appeared in the full-length Rutles movie. Instead of Ricky Fataar, we had David Battley as Stig, and John Halsey, who is Barry Wom in the film, was originally called Kevin.' In fact, the 'Kevin' error was not made on the original broadcast, but only appeared in the liner notes for the album *The Rutland Weekend Songbook*, with an Idle-penned *Radio Times* spoof:

5.00 The Rutles in 'Rutles For Sale'

The fab four Rutland lads, Dirk, Kevin, Stig and Nasty, who created 'The Rutland Sound', get together again for tax purposes to sing 'I Must Be In Love (is all you need, apart from the money which can't buy everything.)' (Other Hits include: 'Can't Buy Me Rut', 'My Sweet Rut', and 'A Ticket to Rut'.)
Guitars...ROGER RETTIG and BILLY BREMNER
Bass...BRIAN HODGSON
Piano...NOBBY
Drums...JOHN HALSEY
Director...DICK RUTLAND[294]

The rudimentary lore was also expanded in tie-in *The Rutland Dirty Weekend Book,* with a full-page Rutles ad in a *Rolling Stone* spoof, announcing their new album on the Turnip label, *'Finchley Road',* plus further 'rip-off' merchandise including Rutles gumboots, rattles, split-crotch pantihose, matching bidet and handkerchief, 'little Rutle rude things' and 'real Rutle vasectomies'. 'I hated the name "Rutles",' Innes continued, 'I'm such a pedant, I said, "Well it should have two T's, or they're gonna call it 'Rootles'! Why don't you call it 'Bootles'? At least that's in Liverpool! And it's very close to 'bootleg'." But Eric came up with the names.'

Idle has his own memories of the band's inception: 'In 1975, I was sitting writing and I wrote a joke about the camera pulling away from someone, and leaving them helplessly running after it. I liked the idea very much, and I knew that it was funny. But I wasn't sure what he should be talking about... Neil had a couple of Beatley songs, and there was one on a Bonzo album which was very Beatley. And so I thought that it would be a good idea to combine these two elements, so that the joke would lead into a song, and that's virtually what happened on the show... We shot "A Hard Day's Rut" in black and white, and I played the George character...'[295]

NEIL is in a Moptop wig and dressing gown, moping in the hospital grounds.

ERIC: (*VO*) This man is suffering from love songs. It's incurable, but worth a fortune.

NEIL: *(Sings) I feel good, I feel bad, I feel happy, feel sad, You think I'm in love? (Ahhh) I must be in love!*

CUT TO: Black and white footage, The Rutles in full performance mode, interspersed with archive of teenage girls screaming.

NEIL: *I feel rich, I feel poor, I'm in doubt, I feel sure, you think I'm in love? (Ahhh) I must be in love...*

FADE TO: ERIC in full reporter mode, addressing the camera out on the street.

ERIC: The fabulous Rutles there, in their movie, *A Hard Day's Rut* – directed by Dick Leicester, which is very near Rutland. From these streets very close to The Cavern, Rutland, came the fabulous Rutland sound, created by the Fab Four...

CUT TO: The four Rutles, jump-cutting from one to the other in the same pose, looking pensive by a river, and finally in a group shot.

ERIC: *VO*)... Dirk, Nasty, Stig and Barry, who created a musical legend that will last a lunchtime.

CUT TO: ERIC's piece to camera, as the camera beginning to subtly pull away...

ERIC: They were discovered by their manager, Leggy Mountbatten, in a lunchtime disco very close to these streets. Their first album was made in twenty minutes – the second took even longer. Tonight we examine the legend of The Rutles, we look at their lives, their loves, their music, we examine some of the problems that made them what they are today. (*Running to keep up with camera*) We also ask the question whether these people

254

shouldn't really have been doing something
better for their money. And we shall be
asking some of the people who worked with
them whether they really were the sort of
nice, loveable people that they were made out
to be. Tonight we shall be also speaking to
many of the people who...

The camera has now sped away and turned a corner.[296]

The camera crew are eventually reported to be 'going to the
seaside'. Although the *Running Jumping & Standing Still* techniques
may have been rudimentary even in comparison to the original
film, the ersatz band's grins were real, stepping into such Fab
shoes, Halsey playing a perfect replica of Ringo's kit, with
'Earwig' substituted for 'Ludwig'. Besides the parodic intent, there
was no inherent comedy in the song or its performance, but
whereas ten years earlier comedians putting on Beatle wigs were
ten a penny, by the mid-70s, this was the first time that the Moptop
era could be approached with a new sense of nostalgic irony.

This irony was certainly not lost on the Americans, nor the
cast, crew and crowd enjoying the first flow of success of a new
comedy show broadcasting live from New York City every
Saturday night. Peopled by some of the finest talent out of
Chicago's Second City troupe, with witty Canadians in abundance
all led by one-time *Laugh-In* gag writer Lorne Michaels, *Saturday
Night Live* was then as cool as comedy gets, with the anarchic team
snorting their way through the night to get the show ready for a
gut-churning adrenaline-filled late-night performance, beamed
coast to coast. Python being one of the show's greatest influences,
Eric Idle was soon to become guest of honour among the show's
legendary alumni, 'The Not-Ready-For-Prime-Time Players',
including Bill Murray, Dan Aykroyd, Gilda Radner and John
Belushi.

Towards the end of the first season, Michaels had made a rare
address to camera, to touch on the by then tediously exhausted
issue of a Beatle reunion, particularly the entreaties of US
promoter Sid Bernstein offering endlessly growing financial

incentives to reform the group (or 'twenty million dollars and a killer whale each', as Neil Innes had it), which had inspired McCartney to recite a Mohammed Ali-style rhyme intended to silence gossip: '*The Beatles split in '69, And since then they have been doing fine. And if that question doesn't cease, Ain't no one gonna get no peace. And if they ask it just once more, I think I'll have to bash them on their jaw.*' Perhaps *SNL* were not the first to make a joke out of the four ex-Beatles' constant media onslaught on this issue, but when the bit went out on 24 April 1976, it was surely the first to be seen by John and Paul together:

LORNE: Hi, I'm Lorne Michaels, the producer of *Saturday Night*. Right now, we're being seen by approximately twenty-two million viewers, but please allow me, if I may, to address myself to just four very special people – John, Paul, George, and Ringo – The Beatles. Lately there have been a lot of rumours to the effect that the four of you might be getting back together. That would be great. In my book, The Beatles are the best thing that ever happened to music. It goes even deeper than that – you're not just a musical group, you're a part of us. We grew up with you. It's for this reason that I am inviting you to come on our show. Now, we've heard and read a lot about personality and legal conflicts that might prevent you guys from reuniting. That's something which is none of my business. That's a personal problem. You guys will have to handle that. But it's also been said that no one has yet to come up with enough money to satisfy you. Well, if it's money you want, there's no problem here. The National Broadcasting Company has authorised me to offer you this cheque to be on our show – a certified cheque for $3,000. Here it is right here. A cheque made out to you, The

256

Beatles, for $3,000. All you have to do is sing three Beatles songs: '*She loves you, yeah, yeah, yeah*' – that's $1,000 right there. You know the words, it'll be easy. Like I said, this is made out to The Beatles – you divide it up any way you want. If you want to give less to Ringo, that's up to you – I'd rather not get involved. I'm sincere about this. If this helps you to reach a decision to reunite, it's well worth the investment. You have agents – you know where I can be reached. Just think about it, okay? Thank you.[297]

After half a decade of little love lost between Lennon and McCartney, with John well into his full-time fatherhood phase, the two old friends were just about remembering how to enjoy each other's company with some semblance of their former friendship – at least until John complained about Paul showing up at random with a guitar when he had childcare to see to. John was already in his 'phony retirement period', watching the wheels go round, while Paul's work hadn't been notably humorous of late, besides the whimsy of US Number 1 'Uncle Albert/Admiral Halsey' or the presence of Kenny Lynch and Clement Freud on the cover of *Band On The Run*. Admittedly the following Christmas of 1977 he would have another go at TV sketches, appearing on impressionist Mike Yarwood's festive special on BBC 1, hiding wodges of cash from 'chunky punky' Chancellor of the Exchequer, Denis Healey, and being called 'Mr Jagger'. Both ex-partners remained avid comedy fans, though, so the hottest comedy show on US TV was clearly a must-watch.

This particular Saturday was part of a memorably comradely weekend round John's pad, and Lorne's live invitation to perform for a four-figure sum (split two ways) created what must surely be the single greatest missed opportunity in the history of entertainment. McCartney looked at Lennon, Lennon looked at McCartney and, John recalled, the idea genuinely floated in the air... for a few seconds, at least, to travel the two and a half miles from the Upper West Side to 30 Rock: 'Paul was visiting us at our place in the Dakota with Linda. He and I were watching it and we went, "ha-ha, wouldn't it be funny if we went down and we almost went down to the studio, just as a gag?" We nearly got into the cab, but we were actually too tired.'[298]

For the second season the following fall, Lorne was glad to have booked the most US-centric Python as a guest host, and although Eric took the time to film some special material for the show – working with director Gary Weis on filmed inserts including 'Drag Racing', for which he and Aykroyd had to sprint inLhigh heels – a deal was also struck with the BBC to show a highlight or two from *RWT*, and of course, chief among the video excerpts was the original Rutles skit:

LORNE: Hi, I'm Lorne Michaels. Several months ago I made a bona-fide offer of $3,000 to The Beatles to perform on *Saturday Night*. For months there was no response and then about two weeks ago, I got a long distance phone call from Eric Idle, tonight's host, in London saying that if I would let him come over and host the show, he would bring The Beatles with him. Well, in my excitement, I agreed and foolishly sent him the check for $3,000. You see, he said The Beatles wanted the money in advance so that they could buy some new clothes to wear on the show. Well, when I met Eric at the airport last Monday, I noticed that he was alone. So I said, 'Where are they, I mean The Beatles?' He said, 'Well, their new clothes weren't ready yet, so they were going to catch a later flight.' I still didn't think anything was wrong, until yesterday, when a telegram arrived saying, 'Can't come now – Ringo's pants too long stop. Please send more money for alterations stop. Signed, The Beatles.' When I showed the telegram to Eric, he said he would call London immediately and did, and convinced John, Paul, George and Ringo to send over a film instead. Well, twenty minutes ago, the film arrived from England. I just saw it and it's quite good, only it's not The Beatles, it's The Rutles. Evidently, Eric had a bad phone connection to London and, well, anyway... it's halfway through the show and Eric's already spent the $3,000, so ladies and gentlemen, here are The Rutles...[299]

Idle's further attempt to make up for the Fab Four's absence by ending with a Gumby-esque hollered rendition of 'Here Comes The Sun' was no help, but it seemed nobody much cared – the Prefab Four (a term originally applied to The Monkees) were an instant hit, with fans of the show writing in with further requests to see more. While Eric was still mulling over this sudden surge of interest, George became the first real Beatle to put in an appearance on the show in November, performing a more respectable version of his *Abbey Road* hit alongside Paul Simon, but also seen haggling with Michaels in the opening sequence:

LORNE:	...I mean, how do you think *I* feel? I feel terrible about it!
GEORGE:	You're saying that *now*. I've come all this way. It's $3,000, that was the deal!
LORNE:	I understand. But it was just one of those mix-ups...
GEORGE:	Fine, I'll tell you one thing, you ought to get it straight in the future, you know..?
LORNE:	If you don't go on tonight, it'll break his heart. You see, I thought that you would understand, you know, that it was $3,000 for four people, that it would just be $750 for each of you. I mean, as far as I'm concerned, I mean, you could have the full $3,000. But the network...
GEORGE:	It's pretty chintzy.

LORNE: Well, I'll tell you what. I know there's $250
                available for the opening, for the person who
                says "Live, from New York, it's Saturday
                Night".

GEORGE: (*To camera*) "Live, from New York, it's
                Saturday Night!"[300]

When Idle mentioned the Rutles interest to Harrison, George's years of Beatlesque malaise did not prevent him from being instantly warmly enthusiastic about the idea of fleshing out the alternate group's history, and he even gave his Python pal a rough cut of an official Beatles documentary which Neil Aspinall had been toying with all decade, then pencilled in as *The Long and Winding Road*. Eric had after all been helpful to him with his 1976 album *Thirty Three and a Third*, adding extra vocals to 'This Song', a satirical track commenting on the legal nightmare he had faced unentangling 'My Sweet Lord' from plagiarism prosecution – a problem only solved by buying the rights to The Chiffon's 'He's So Fine'. Neil Innes' own similar battles lay ahead, and he was to comment on the problem of supposed musical appropriation with his own 'Recycled Vinyl Blues', complete with Palin cameo and 'My Sweet Lord' riff outro.

George hired the best session men for his own single: 'I got a friend of mine to put in a bass line so it's got that Tamla sort of sound. I also got Eric Idle, one of the Monty Pythons, to throw in the funny lines, "Could be 'Sugarpie Honeybunch?'" and "Naaooo, sounds more like 'Rescue Me'!"'[301] George hammed it up nicely in the video, playing guitar while handcuffed in the dock, and displayed further wacky comic skills in , 'Crackerbox Palace', an overtly Pythonesque video directed with daft verve by Idle at home in Friar Park (also the location of an Edwardian boating rendition of the oldie 'True Love'). There were more Mad Hatter references, and as George was wheeled in a pram and picked his nose in schoolboy uniform, he joined Neil, Olivia and many other weird pals in the silliest costumes Eric could get hold of: Python pixie hats, pantomime Princess Margaret and all. The video debuted on George's *SNL* episode, perhaps the closest he came to being in an episode of *Monty Python*, and the sheer pleasure can be seen all over his cross-eyed loony face. The song itself was inspired by a different comic hero, George explained, 'I met this guy and the way he was talking, I said to him, "Hey... I don't know if this is an insult or a compliment, but you remind me of Lord Buckley, who is my favourite comedian. But this guy is now dead." Lord Buckley was one of the first very hip comedians. When I said this, this guy nearly fell over, and he said, "Hey, I managed him for eighteen years." He told me that Buckley lived in a little old shack, which he called Crackerbox Palace and I thought, "Wow, Crackerbox Palace." It just sounded so good and I wrote it on my Gitane cigarette packet... It could be the place where you live but I turned it more into the world, the physical world.'[302]

The knowledge that Idle's piss-taking would be central to the 'spoof Beatles' scheme was a huge plus for Harrison, after years of seeing the boys depicted on stage, and almost screen, in a number of productions which had certainly not gained the Harrison seal of approval. First, and most critically acclaimed at the time, was *John, Paul, George, Ringo... and Bert*, the first big professional show written by Liverpudlian playwright Willy Russell, for Liverpool's Everyman Theatre. A rough reconstruction of The Beatles story as it was understood at the time (i.e. inaccurately) with all the damaging clichés about McCartney being the soppy sop to Lennon's sharp wit and so on, the story was further fictionalised by the presence of the character of ex-Quarryman Bert as narrator. The raw talent involved was off the scale, with the title roles taken by Bernard Hill, Trevor Eve, Philip Joseph, Antony Sher... and George Costigan, plus renditions of Beatle classics performed by Barbara Dickson, and it was named Musical of the Year for 1974. However, a movie adaptation was blocked by Paul, who was especially annoyed by the idea that it was he who broke up the band, whereas the premiere seats earmarked for George and Derek Taylor did not remain filled for long, and Harrison's moody exit hit the headlines. An American production turning Beatle songs into a jukebox musical earned even less approval all round, despite Lennon attending early rehearsals for the Robert Stigwood-backed *Sgt Pepper's Lonely Hearts Club Band On The Road*, a painful confection dreamt up by Stigwood and rock journalist Henry Edwards with Broadway bods Tom O'Horgan and Robin Wagner telling the threadbare story of soppy Billy Shears, his plunge into the seedy world of rock music, and his (briefly) tragic love for the equally soppy Strawberry Fields. Again, George's was the most dissenting voice: 'We didn't have any control! I mean, there's been a lot of Beatles things, you know, like *John, Paul, Bert, Ringo, Ted ... and Ringo*, and *Sgt Pepper*, and all kinds of things like that, because the Fab Four were split and all over the world, then it was pretty easy to go and do things like that. All they needed was the songs, and ATV Music owned most of the songs, so it was pretty easy to do that. But, I don't really think they're supposed to do that and, in fact, we've just got together a group of people to go and sue them all!'[303] The most successful production, *Beatlemania!*, made no effort to add anything to the legend at all, and was essentially the beginning of the Bootleg tribute band industry.

Harrison's patronage, therefore, was to be a crucial fillip for the Rutles film – whoever got to make it. Lorne called Eric and was stunned to hear that he was thinking of celebrating the mythical career of Dirk, Stig, Nasty and Barry on their original channel, BBC 2, but it only took the briefest chat with the head honchos at NBC for Michaels to secure a higher budget than the BBC could ever fetch, which would still allow the production to go ahead in the UK, with Weis partnering Idle on the directing side, filming everything he could with 16mm camera on his shoulder as the creator got on with the madness in shot. NBC offered even more money if the film could be broadcast in prime time, but Eric refused to put any fetters on his capacity for filth – although the film was eventually deemed suitable for an earlier broadcast anyway. Eric was invited to talk over ideas with Lorne in the West Indies that Christmas, and Neil Innes was suddenly faced with the challenge of a lifetime: writing a whole album's worth of Beatles parodies as affectionate and catchy as 'I Must Be

In Love': 'The audience got in on the joke and wrote in by the bag load: "The Rutles, yeah, bring 'em back! Long live The Rutles!" before we knew it, things got even sillier. Lorne Michaels asked NBC if he could have the money to make a full-length film about The Rutles, and they said, "Yeah, go for it". I never set out to become a parodist…'[304]

IN THE BACK OF MY MIND…

The key boon received by Idle when wintering at Heron Bay was the friendship of Ricky Fataar: a South-African-born drummer of Malaysian descent who had been touring with The Beach Boys for much of the decade, and the two of them jammed happily on the beach sipping rum punch as Eric turned over his film idea in his head. Returning from the warmth of the West Indies, he then let all that musing spill out onto the page, spending the freezing early months of 1977 writing *The Rutles: All You Need Is Cash* in icy New York, in Dan Aykroyd's Bowery apartment, kept toasty by the heat from the sauna below. This was a halcyon period for Idle, freshly in love with his second-wife-to-be Tania, and besides poring over every single scrap of archive Beatles ephemera he could find, the script simply flowed from his typewriter. *The Long and Winding Road*, destined never to be seen by the public as no two Beatles could agree on anything in it, was such an inspiration that Eric admitted that *All You Need Is Cash* was essentially a parody of a completely unseen movie, particularly thanks to sequences such as an interview with Queenie Epstein which provided perfect research material and impersonation inspiration when recreated by *RWT* regular and Idle's go-to funny woman, Gwen Taylor, the mother of Rutles manager Leggy Mountbatten being a suitably genteel lady, with a fixation on the tightness of the Prefab Four's trousers. Idle called Taylor 'the best comedy actress I ever worked with, she could do anything'[305] and her versatility was underlined by doubling up as the mock Yoko, Hitler's bastard daughter Chastity, though she and Neil and Eric all found it hard to avoid corpsing when improvising in the bath, swapping the infamous bed-in for soggy 'shower power' – 'We're getting wet. In a shower. Because, basically, we talked it over, Chastity and myself, and we came to the conclusion that civilisation is nothing more than an effective sewage system. And so by the use of plumbing we hope to demonstrate this to the world.'[306] Comic improvisation wasn't necessarily Neil's forté, but as Ron Nasty, he could run with any idea with both the sincerity and silliness required, Nasty's desire to own a 'squadron of tanks' being just one example. Taylor would become a sitcom stalwart in the UK, but her work with Idle would never be bettered.

While the story of The Rutles was taking shape in New York, Neil Innes sat at home and tried to get his talent around the task of producing at least sixteen original tracks 'by next Thursday lunchtime', each not just bursting with the utmost Beatle musicality, but in Innes' own weird way, inherently funny. This latter demand was not so essential, but it was still a tall order. 'I made a conscious decision not to listen to any of the records. I did everything from memory of how it ought to sound,' he recalled. 'The psychedelic lyrics were easy; you just rhymed anything with anything else. But the earlier songs were difficult to get right, because one of The Beatles' trademarks is that the tunes and the words were always just a little bit unpredictable, so I was constantly throwing out tunes because they were too ordinary… It was obviously going to follow a chronological path. I tried to remember where I was when these signpost Beatle songs came out – the early period teenage love songs were the hardest to replicate, trying to remember the first time you put your hand in a girl's bra – "Hold My Hand" was my version of "I Want to Hold Your Hand", but I was writing from my experience. Certain songs, like "Ouch!" and "Piggy in the Middle", developed from titles suggested by Eric. I thought some of the unused song titles he came up with were the funniest, like "Your Mother Should Go" and "WC Fields Forever". Quite honestly, when we got up to the psychedelic stuff, it was easy because the possibilities were endless. I loved the primary school morality we slipped into "Cheese & Onions"… it had a message! I didn't want to trivialise the oeuvre, though, I wanted it to be fun but it had to be good music, so we used some top musicians.'[307]

Given Harrison's predilection for Indian culture, Idle had the brainwave of making his character seemingly sub-continental, and although hiring Fataar for his Malaysian appearance may be somewhere in the region of culturally dodgy, it did mean that Ricky could double as both performer and musician – although primarily a drummer, he was also a professional guitarist, which left Innes' friend and *RWT* irregular John Halsey as the perfect drummer, a diminutive clown who could out-Ringo Ringo, as long as he could blanket his North London brogue with the necessary scouse twang. Casting the mild melody-maker Innes, patently the McCartney of the Bonzos, as the Lennon figure may have seemed unusual, but as the musical leader of the project, he was prepared to take on the challenge, though he protested, 'The names were all Eric's thing. I never thought I'd end up playing Lennon, I'm far too agreeable to play him. The story I heard was somebody spotted John in the street in New York and said, "Hey John, what do you think of The Rutles?" and he replied by singing "Cheese & Onions".'[308]

Despite being the most musical Python, Eric was never part of this merry band, not least due to a sudden attack of appendicitis which kept him in hospital at a crucial juncture – he had to be sent home from the first group meeting, and so an ersatz McCartney had to be found. Innes found his ideal Paul in Ollie Halsall, a true master of lead guitar with the perfect singing register to ape McCartney, who had a similarly mixed and unfeted career in rock to his regular bandmate Halsey, and Fataar. 'The whole Rutles group could play,' Innes went on. 'Ollie Halsall, who did a lot on the songs but is only in the film as Leppo, the fifth Rutle, was an incredibly underrated guitarist and singer, as was John... The best thing I did was to insist that we all rehearsed together, playing live several times before filming started, so we became a proper band. Ollie did most of the Paul-type singing and Eric had to mime his vocals. He never quite forgave me for that.' Halsall's further participation only amounted to a tiny photographic cameo as the faux Stuart Sutcliffe, and after he died all too soon in 1992, his old friend

Halsey eulogised, 'Ollie may not have been the best guitarist in the world, but he was certainly among the top two.' He was no actor, however, and though there was a search for someone to play Dirk McQuickly, in the end Eric, having always played well against Neil, and being especially svelte after a long period in hospital, took on the second role with undisguised glee.

Even before the spoof band could get together to jam, Idle was seeding Rutlemania in the American consciousness, inviting Neil to join him as a guest act for his second stint as *SNL* presenter in April 1977. He made the episode a 'Save Great Britain' telethon, and boasted that one of the country's greatest stars was happy to come out of retirement to lend support – cut to Neil as Ron Nasty, chewing gum at a white piano in long wig and specs, debuting his 'A Day In The Life'-a-like epic, 'Cheese & Onions', in a performance so uncanny, the recording ended up on a whole host of Beatle bootleg albums, and is claimed as a genuine Lennon composition to this day by some of the most burned-out Beatle conspiracy theorists out there. 'Within two hours of the Rutles album being released, there were rumours about The Beatles really being on it,' Idle laughed. '"Cheese & Onions" appeared on a bootleg album claiming that it was a John Lennon demo. But it's obviously taped from that show. Mind you, I don't suppose even John could tell the difference at times. Neil has a great John Lennon-sounding voice.'[309] Innes' other input was a jolly performance of the song 'Shangri-La', which at this stage was still decades from being folded back into Rutle lore. Back home, Innes spread the seeds further by playing 'Cheese & Onions' in a John Peel radio session.

Having pulled off these teasing appearances, Neil joined his fellow faux Fab Fools, taking up residence in a house in Hendon, where for several weeks incorporating Wimbledon fortnight he, Ollie, Ricky and John were to rehearse the entire Comedy Beatles oeuvre, joined by Andy Brown on bass. 'Getting all of us together like that was a smart move,' he recalled. 'The Beatles were a really tight band and so were we when we came out of there after a fortnight. A few of the early period songs on the album were recorded live in the studio... George wasn't pleased with the guitar

266

solo in "Love Life", which Ollie did. He said, "He's taking the piss, isn't he?" "Yes, well, a bit..."[310] With the music at their fingertips and irregular Python maestro John Altman on hand to orchestrate the more ambitious spoofs, the fake Fab Four decamped to the same Bond Street studio where Apollo C Vermouth had produced 'Urban Spaceman', where ten days of incredible virtuosity saw them getting the entire soundtrack down on tape, from the Cavern-esque energy of Nazi love number 'Goose-Step Mama' to the epic majesty of 'Let's Be Natural', taking in the bright suburban nostalgia of 'Doubleback Alley', the heart-pumping romantic balladry of 'With A Girl Like You' and the freaky playfulness of 'Piggy In The Middle'. Early playbacks creased a few brows, and it wasn't until the idea arose to doubly compress the 24-track recording to get a 4-track feel that the right Beatlesque sound was nailed down – this crafty decision being taken by the producer Steve James, son of *Carry On* legend Sid, and therefore no stranger to the laughter industry. But then, Innes admitted, 'If anything wasn't quite right, we said, "It doesn't matter, it's The Rutles. Who are The Beatles? They don't exist!" You know, we sort of played that game.'

Innes' main part of the bargain was honoured, and never had a jobbing tunesmith done a better month's work. Idle had to agree: 'The Rutles was a magic project; some things are like that and this was definitely one. Everyone enjoyed working on it, everyone from make-up to wardrobe. Even the minicab drivers would come and watch the rushes. It was great working with Neil Innes, whom I always thought was absolutely wonderful, so it was good being his pal, and conspiring together. Neil wrote all the songs and had perfect freedom in them. I would just comment on what I thought was needed. Obviously, I preferred some to others, and would put them in or feature them more strongly. Then again, he can write to order. I remember calling him up from the US from my hospital bed and saying we needed a sitar, George-type number to cover a short piece of film, and he called me back in a couple of days with it already recorded. Neil really has an incredible ear, a great gift for melody.'[311]

By the time Eric was back in Blighty, he and Gary Weis had

already kicked off filming with an afternoon in New York chatting to Mick Jagger and Lorne's neighbour Paul Simon about the competition which never existed. Once the concept was understood by Mick, he gave more away about his true feelings towards his key rivals than ever before. Weis recalled, 'We used up a lot of favours. Paul Simon, for example, is a friend of Lorne Michaels. He even lives in the same building in New York, so it was a simple matter to go and film him, and Mick Jagger had connections with Eric. The great thing about Mick is that he was simply recalling the real story of what happened between The Beatles and The Rolling Stones and substituting the Rutles' names at appropriate moments. Mind you, it took him quite a few takes to get them all right.'[312]

These were the only famous talking heads in the film, but it allowed Eric to get into character as the hapless globetrotting mockumentary presenter – eventually christened Melvin Hall – whose losing race with the film crew would be repeated in many humiliating ways from the Mersey to the Mississippi, and the ball was at least rolling, ready for the trickier filming in London and Liverpool. Production Manager Roger Simons' assistant director credits included cult rock flick *Slade In Flames*, and eventually the painful 1981 biopic *Birth of the Beatles*, and he remembers the Rutles' headaches: 'We started shooting in the summer and it was fraught with problems. We had a very small budget, under £100,000, I think, a crew of about thirty-five, and we had only four weeks in total to shoot it. To make matters worse, a lot of the actors were taking part purely as favours to Eric, so we had to fit our shooting schedule around when they happened to be available.' On the other hand, he adds, they did have a guardian angel on the shoot: 'George Harrison was involved almost from the beginning. He was around quite a lot, even when he didn't need to be there. We were sitting around in Eric's kitchen one day, planning a sequence that really ripped into the mythology and George looked up and said, "We were The Beatles, you know!" Then he shook his head and said, "Ah, never mind." I think he was the only one of The Beatles who could see the irony of it all.'[313]

A decent spoof is nothing without verisimilitude, and with an iconic story like The Beatles', an extraordinary effort had to be made to make The Rutles match up to the originals. Eric's initial treatment was pasted with research points, and a dedicated team somehow managed to rise to the occasion for every individual sequence, and on a tight budget (albeit not a *RWT* one). Among the crew's numerous Beatle links, Art Director Peta Button was the wife of Joe McGrath, and she blanches to this day at the memory of how hard everyone was working behind the scenes. 'We had loads and loads of Beatle magazines, so you knew exactly what you were trying to recreate. Then you had the problem of sourcing the different guitars!' Harrison was often on hand for an unrivalled fact check, but she recalls him complaining, 'Oh for Christ's sake, Peta, I don't remember a thing about Shea Stadium, never mind what bloody guitar I was playing!' In the circumstances, it's churlish to moan about the odd slip, such as the live sequence in which Stig is shown playing completely different instruments from one shot to the next. On the other hand, great care *was* taken – the first full sequence to be shot was actually the last scrap of Rutles performance, on the roof of the Rutle Corps offices, for which Eric had grown a full beard – but a lens cap failure made half the footage unusable, so a chunk of budget had to be found to return to the same location for a reshoot later on, false beard and all.

Liverpool was the first chief location for a dizzying marathon of Beatlesque sequences, with the beach at Southport standing in for the Bahamas filming a very cheap rendition of 'Ouch!' complete with cardboard palm trees, but it was a warm day, and the fake boys had a far better time than the originals did filming *Help!* in the genuine, windy locale. Button recalls a great boozy time being had by all in The Beatles' home city, and notes a theory about the 'Ouch!' rushes which persists to this day: 'Rumour had it that late one night the clapper loader was so completely out of his head that he dug holes in the sand and buried two or three cans of film, which have never been found, somewhere on the cast iron shore!'

David Battley, having been a prototype Rutle, would be the only *RWT* regular absent from the film, with Terence Bayler playing Epstein equivalent Leggy with characteristic weirdness, and Henry Woolf continuing the Rutland tradition of making the familiar more parochial and grotty by turning the Maharishi into 'Surrey mystic' and dirty old man Arthur Sultan. Among the guest stars joining in the semi-improvisatory shoot up north were Bianca Jagger, whose long-suffering Linda Eastman-a-like, Martini, gave Idle his first on-screen kiss. 'Bianca was absolutely brilliant,' Innes said. 'She supplied her own dress, a beautiful antique lace thing made in 1849, and at one point Eric accidentally trod on it. She said, "Mind my 1849 dress", and Eric shot back, "Is that all it cost?"' Their scenes, filmed at Roger McGough's house (shortly after he filmed his extensive contribution: 'Oh, yes, yes.'), have often been seen as some of the harshest satire in the film, McQuickly's sheer wetness and inept composition was guaranteed to pierce McCartney's generally rhino-thick hide, and Innes concurred, 'I think Eric went over the top a bit, he didn't do it as affectionately as the rest of us. And I don't think Paul has any issues with the rest of us, I mean, he did me a great favour in producing "Urban Spaceman" and I have no intention of undermining or taking the Mickey out of him – I admire the man. But Eric is more of a stiletto man when it comes to lampooning.'[314]

In a sea of world-beating cameos, however, the biscuit was thoroughly taken in Liverpool, when the downfall of Apple was roundly mocked by Michael Palin sending up his friend Derek Taylor with maximum loucheness, and occasional Rolling Stone Ronnie Wood played a Hell's Angel in reference to the famously catastrophic Apple Christmas party where John and Yoko's turns as Father Christmas were undermined by vicious gatecrashers – a bash attended in real life by Innes and his own little boy Miles, who cameoed in the film's end credits alongside little brother Luke and wee Carey Idle as baby Rutles. Interviewing both guest stars was a silver-haired moustachioed news reporter who constituted the one single comedy character ever portrayed by George Harrison. So impressively did he disappear into the role that many there on that day have since dined out on the story of the one cheeky school kid (or American tourist, depending on the teller) who dared to push the bewigged George aside to gaspingly enquire whether Eric and Neil were 'real Beatles?!' Harrison was absolutely in his element.

The real Derek Taylor had in some ways pre-empted The Rutles by writing an un-produced screenplay at the height of Beatlemania about a fictional northern pop group called 'The Myce', and he would ultimately be as good a friend to The Rutles as Harrison, arranging the album's deal with Arista records (with dense collage artwork created by Eric and Basil Pao, who would go on to design Python albums and books and most of Palin's travel tie-ins), and even masterminding a publicity splurge which included sending out postcards bearing scraps of genuine Rutles trousers. Like George, he was all for a timely piss-take which 'sent up, not without love and understanding and style... the notion of a marvellous existentialist Beatles.'[315] The completed album came with extended interview transcriptions from Jagger and Simon, and even a few lyrics which never made it onto vinyl, excised from 'Piggy In The Middle':

Civilising jungle bunnies, guinea pigs including me and you,
Talk about a knock-kneed frog, second cousin to a nun living in the zoo...

AND THEN THERE WAS TEA

The frenetic five weeks of production pushed on to London, and included an astonishing facsimile of The Beatles' Boxing Day debacle, 'Tragical History Tour', incorporating a silly 'Piggy In the Middle' performance which involved a stunning flyover from a glider, hired from a nearby flying school by Weis with so little warning to everyone else that the dancing policemen, whose helmets were nearly knocked off, were close to falling off their wall in shock. In Idle's Rutland universe, of course, The Beatles' experimentation with acid was replaced with nothing more potent than a nice cup of tea – even if pedants may have complained that this caused continuity problems, given the earlier Maysles-esque sequence of the boys enjoying a cuppa.

The other crucial London-based element came from the brief

snippet of The Rutles' animated caper *Yellow Submarine Sandwich*, a brilliant encapsulation of everything achieved by TVC a decade earlier. Idle approached the original animators to provide a pastiche of their opus, and the cartoon excerpt was eventually provided by young artists George Parker and Tony White, AKA Little Big Films – who, like so many others, had done their bit for the film ten years before. The spoof cartoon was allowed to stray into more risqué areas than its source material, with enormous bosomy statues being attacked by the Flying – not Glove, but False Teeth, and Blue Meanie-alikes banging gavels in legal dress, almost daring the rightsholders to sue.

The Rutle circus moved on to New York, one of the production's strengths being the combination of talent not only from Python and *RWT*, but the new generation of *SNL* who had been inspired by Python in the first place. The production brought in friends from the whole expanse of Idle's career, making it surely the only film to boast both Barry Cryer and Bill Murray in the same cast – but hopefully not the last. Besides *SNL* newbie Murray, who improvised reams of over-enthusiastic nonsense as DJ 'Bill Murray the K', Gilda Radner's scene as an all-too-knowledgeable voxpop was a stand-out, and Bill's fellow Ghostbuster-in-waiting Dan Aykroyd had his own sequence as expectorating idiot Brian Thigh, the man who turned The Rutles down. The first US cut of the finished film featured an alternate take, to avoid the all-too-dangerous punchline for a prime-time audience, 'What's it like to be such an asshole?' – apparently suicide was less offensive:

MELVIN:	So you turned down all those millions of dollars' worth of sales, you turned down all those thousands upon thousands of singles, all those gold disks?
THIGH:	(COUGHS) Yeah, that's right.
MELVIN:	What's it like to be such a jerk?
THIGH:	What?!
MELVIN:	Does it bother you, being such a nerd?
THIGH:	Come on, come on, you can't call me that.

MELVIN:	Does it concern you that people say that you're a twat?
THIGH:	Hey, now c'mon!
MELVIN:	A pillock, a berk, a man who has the brains of a duck, the business sense of a cretin and the ideas of an idiot of three? (BRIAN GETS UP AND WALKS OUT OF SHOT.) Does it concern you that you have no business sense whatsoever? (TO CAMERA) Brian Thigh, the man who... (OFF: GUNSHOT, THUD!)... who turned down The Rutles.[316]

The commercial-break-free UK cut, which has gone on to be almost the default version, runs roughly ten minutes longer, adding details like the reference to Yoko's *Bottoms*, which provided an excuse for a snatch of Bernard Bresslaw's 1958 spoof hit 'You Need Feet' – however, a reference to the Prefab Four touching down in 'Wales' was swapped out for 'Cleveland' for the eventual commercial release.

For the not easily pleased Idle, the production went off like a dream: 'The filming of *All You Need Is Cash* was great fun. It's very interesting dressing up and pretending to be other people. Especially if you've seen the other people go through their lives. You get a strange perspective. It's almost more interesting when you know that they were real people, rather than when you just make up some crazy character. So, yes, it was interesting being dressed in that gear and swanning up to Buckingham Palace and watching the tourists having heart attacks like they were time-tripping. We were actually mobbed on the Mersey ferry... It was interesting to find out just how unpleasant it is having people scratching and chasing you. But basically the weather was lovely, and we got to film in the north of England, which is much more friendly than the south, and everyone was very happy. It was just one of those projects.'[317] The five weeks were up all too soon for Idle and co, though he and Weis ventured one final addition invented during the editing stage: *SNL* wild man John Belushi's sequence as Allen Klein-alike Ron Decline, complete with flunkies

Al Franken and Tom Davis, which hit on one of the film's many completely accidental truths, showing that parody can leap right to the root of reality without even trying – Klein was confused as to how Idle knew he prepared for business meetings by talking into a mirror. Weis was painstaking in the edit, treating film in the lab to match the original shots as perfectly as possible, and eventually the last drop of budget was used up by arranging for a gigantic screen in Times Square to flash up 'THE RUTLES ARE COMING!' just as the first ever viewing for the NBC bigwigs came to a close.

The film's BBC 2 debut at Easter was such a hit that it was repeated for an even bigger BBC 1 audience shortly after, but the US premiere fared less well – Eric reserves particular ire for legendary hatchet man Frank Rich, who missed the point and tore the show apart before it had even aired. It ended up buried in the ratings, scheduled up against an apparently unmissable episode of *Charlie's Angels* – but as Neil says, 'I think to this day it's the lowest rated programme ever on prime time, but who remembers that week's episode of *Charlie's Angels*? People who saw *The Rutles* went "What's this?"' 'In Europe, the show was a terrific success'. Eric concurs, 'Thirty-five countries bought it, and many repeated it at once, including England. In the United States, if twenty-five million people watch the show then it's considered a failure. It seems to me that the failure lies with American TV thinking, because twenty-five million is a hell of an audience, larger than most films ever get until they are shown on TV… I'm glad to have gone from a small cupboard on BBC 2 to the vastness of American TV without having to alter more than one "asshole".'[318]

It was undeniably an incredible achievement, *All You Need Is Cash* – there was obviously nothing new about comedy mocking the documentary genre, but as the first ever feature-length mockumentary, everything from *Spinal Tap, Zelig* and *Bad News* onwards would owe it a huge debt. For all the slightly niggling holes some could pick about anachronistic technology, false beards, or tea consumption, Eric's original film has remained a classic adored every bit as much as any of the full-team Monty Python movies.

Critics wisely tended to belie the film's poor reception in the US, with Ray Herbeck Jr of *Billboard* enthusing, 'There is no mindless "Beatlemania" copying, but brilliant Beatle-like creativity, though distilled through a glass mirthfully... Searching for meaning in the Beatles mythology is, as the original foursome has claimed all along, madness – and worthy of a good laugh.'[319] But of course nobody's opinions ever mattered more than those of the Pre-Prefab Four themselves. Though much of the feedback was hearsay, Neil recalls, 'The official thing I heard was that John was fascinated by *The Rutles* and kept watching it... Ringo liked the happy bit but not the sad bit.' One of Idle's greatest challenges was how to deal with the true story's numerous tragedies, but apparently even softening Epstein's death to 'accepted a teaching post in Australia' could not entirely eradicate the sadness for Starr. 'It was too close. That was the big thing about The Rutles, the real story was too sad to tell... it was a way of telling the story without downing the audience, skipping over the sad bits. So I think Ringo was too much reminded of the real break-up.'[320] When asked his own opinion of The Rutles, John allegedly was wont to grin and break into his own rendition of 'Cheese & Onions', which made his position clear. John and Yoko were always said to be Rutles fans, but infamously, the coolest reaction came from Paul, who was publicising the new Wings album *London Town* when The Rutles were first foisted upon the world, and the incessant questions about the send-up managed to get up even the master PR man's nose, resulting in a repeated 'No comment' any time the subject arose. Idle recalled running into Paul and Linda a few months later, and learning that Linda had loved every minute, but she volunteered that the couple were still 'not sure whether we were talking to' their satirical tormentor – at least until Paul learned that Eric had spent part of his childhood in Wallasey, which made him practically scouse, and therefore forgiven. Innes also took his chance when meeting Paul at a subsequent Harrison party: 'I did take him to one side and said, "Look, old bean, I'm really sorry about The Rutles." He said, "Oh no, I know it's affectionate."'[321] This has always been the most essential point about The Rutles in all its forms – the sheer affection with which is was crafted, by genuine fans of the Fab Four, and how could it be otherwise, The Beatles having always shown a razor-sharp humour, fully aware of their own propensity for being sent up? Any harsher satire would have fallen by the wayside. Certainly, John and Yoko apparently never had any reservations about the programme, which Idle has asserted is a particularly strong testament to Ono's sense of humour, as she was depicted as Hitler's bastard lovechild. As Innes said, 'they all agreed to release the Shea Stadium footage and other things and said "good luck to you", because I think they all wanted the record put straight a little bit, even if it was slightly cock-eyed. Really, The Beatles were very good about it. They allowed us to use lots of their old footage and intercut it with newly filmed Rutles sequences to give it more authenticity.'[322]

Of course, this was particularly true of George, whose opinion was never in doubt. In fact, as the years went by, he would refer to The Beatles and The Rutles positively interchangeably, telling *Rolling Stone* 'I loved The Rutles because in the end "The Beatles" for the Beatles is just tiresome; it needs to be deflated a bit, and I loved the idea of The Rutles taking that burden off us in a way. Everything can be seen as comedy, and the Fab Four are no exception to that. And there were so many good jokes in it! Belushi as Ron Decline: "You ask me where the money is. I don't know where the money is, but if you want money I'll give it to you... You know I was never any good at maths." It was just like Klein! Even Allen Klein himself thought it was just like him. I think he liked it. One thing you can say about Klein is that he's got his good side, too. Even though we've sued each other for years I still like the man.'[323] In his memoir, he went further: 'The Rutles told the story so much better than the usual boring documentary. Try and see that film. That is a recommendation rather like saying: "Don't bother me – see my lawyer. He will explain everything." That was an escape valve: being in The Rutles...The great escape. No time to lose. It is all so silly anyway, all the way through.'[324]

'The Rutles were so important to my career,' he always insisted, with only slightly tongue-in-cheek reference to the claims of Blind Lemon Pye. 'Everything I ever knew and wrote was due to The

Rutles. Really, The Rutles sort of liberated me from The Beatles in a way. It was the only thing I saw of those Beatles television shows they made. It was actually the best, funniest and most scathing. But at the same time, it was done with the most love. But the sad thing about it is that the songs, which were so nice and such great parodies, written by Neil Innes, also got ripped off by Sir Lew Greed, because he couldn't afford to sue him back.'[325] Poor Neil was to fall foul of a legal trap from which Harrison of course still bore the bruises, and from the very start, despite Innes' honest claims never to have worked directly from Beatles music, his Fab friend signalled caution, apparently reacting to the first playback with the odd sung snatch of 'Instant Karma' or similar, despite his love for the songs. 'I remember sitting in a viewing theatre with George,' Neil said, 'and we were looking at the footage of "With a Girl Like You". He leaned back and said, "That one's close!" I said, "I know it's close, but it's not the same song." And George said, "Well you can always take your guitar to court and explain it."'[326] Lennon loved the Rutles album so much he refused to return his advance copy, but warned Innes that one track in particular was likely to cause trouble – while most Rutles songs are either Innes originals in the style of The Beatles, or at the most, carefully interlaced spoofs of multiple songs in one, the final song, 'Get Up And Go' suggested Neil's memory of 'Get Back' was all too keen, without even the vaguest fiddling with the notes of the riff or the galloping rhythm, and was left off the LP.

Had it not been for this one musical faux pas, maybe Innes' celebratory lampooning would have avoided censure, but sadly, with The Beatles catalogue owned by Grade's ATV, the affable tunesmith faced a fight which makes him wince to this day. 'They'd commissioned a musicologist report which said that "Hold My Hand" was like "Back In the USSR" and most amusingly, "Twist and Shout", which The Beatles didn't write! So my publishers hired their own musicologist who went through the report line by line saying "See that melody... now see this melody. No case to answer." Our legal people started having fun with their absurd nit-picking, saying things like, "I suggest the words 'Oh yeah' and 'All right' are already in the public domain." But then it got more like the real world because my publishers didn't want to go to court. When I asked why not they said, "Of course we'll win, Neil, but we might not get costs." Then they made me pay the $5,500 bill for the musicologist!'[327] Eric's heart, naturally, bled for his old friend: 'It's a shame that ATV music in America took fifty percent of all the copyright of all Neil's Rutles songs because some of them bear no relationship to Beatles songs, and are just good songs in their own right. Also it would have been stupid writing tunes that didn't sound somewhat like the Beatles originals, because that was the whole point. So I always thought they were very greedy in their demands, and showed no kindness or understanding or tolerance and I hope that one day their factory burns down, and they all have upset stomachs on their holidays and their children are unpleasant to them. I'm sure the Fab Four don't know they own half of The Rutles' music, and I'm damned sure they won't see any money from it. It's just the usual corporate greed, or corporate Grade, as it's known in England. So The Rutles songs are officially by "Lennon-McCartney-Innes" and "Harrison-Innes". I told Neil he should put out an album of these songs called *The Best of Lennon/McCartney-Innes* just to teach ATV a lesson. It wouldn't matter so much if Neil was extremely rich, but he lives off what he writes, unlike ATV, which lives off what other people write.'[328]

Innes was to go on to create his own hauntingly entertaining musical comedy programme, *The Innes Book of Records,* before devoting a decade or more to children's television, but the experience of having his greatest musical feat turned against him was to leave its mark. 'They were willing to give me copyright and 10% royalties,' he once sighed. 'I said, "I'll go to jail, but I will not sign that." In the end, they got copyright and my royalty share was increased to 50%, but I never really got it. It stinks. I don't want to allow myself to get dragged down by the music business, but I've not had the best experiences!'[329] Given licence to vent, the generally gentle-souled Innes added, with a well-worn long-suffering twinkle, 'Also, there's a clause in there saying that if anyone ever does those songs, I am not to be publicly credited with writing them. So I've sent messages back to Paul, saying, "How do you feel about that? Somebody does 'Cheese & Onions' and they're going to say you and John wrote it!" You cannot invent this stuff. I look around at the Earth today and wonder, "How did Kafka know...?"'[330]

This sour note aside, The Rutles songbook would become the most lasting element of the fake band's cult, inspiring an entire covers album, 1990's *Rutles Highway Revisited,* packed with renditions from the most left-field artists including Shonen Knife and outsider hero Daniel Johnston. Long before that, an official fan club briefly flourished, with fanzines boasting genuine interviews with Eric and Neil, but also acres of fan-fiction Rutleania. There was also a strange coda from Eric and Ricky, who released a novelty single in 1979 under the names of 'Dirk and Stig', without the slightest relevance to The Rutles. Admittedly, Eric's George Formby-esque flip-side 'Mister Sheene', in tribute to the motorcycling legend Barry rather than the drummer Barry, was fun, an allusion to George's great obsession with motorsport, but the A-side was a completely gag-free swampy version of the traditional Scouting dirge 'Ging Gang Goolie'. Before the single disappeared with little trace, a fake *Daily Mail* front page was released, annoucing: 'RUTLES SPLIT SENSATION! The world has been rocked recently with the announcement that The Rutles have disbanded. The Pre-Fab Four – as they came to be known – rose from obscurity to become the world's most famous group. Now that they have split, Dirk and Stig have already begun a solo project which promises to overshadow anything The Rutles ever accomplished.'

The Rutles legend would certainly not end there, however, despite Idle's statement at the time, 'The Rutles made the '60s what they are today. Finished.'

VERY NAUGHTY BOYS

SNL would not let the Beatle reunion issue rest even post-Rutles, and in July Dan Aykroyd played Jimmy Carter mediating a reunion pact between Belushi's Lennon and Murray's

McCartney, which required both Yoko and Linda to swear never to sing on any new Beatles recording. *All You Need Is Cash* was by no means the Beatles spoof to end Beatle spoofs; there was something cynical in the air post-punk, a tangible feel that the time had come to look back at the greatest rock band of all time from a new angle. As early as October '77 National Lampoon had published a 'Beatles special' magazine packed with unfettered puerile barbs, fake album covers for the band's unreleased Jewish and Russian discs ('Rabbi Saul' and 'The Little Red Album'), ads for Magic Alex's penis enlarger, and what pertained to be a transcript of an exclusive interview, complete with an astonishingly dire attempt at phonetically capturing the boys' accents – 'Ere, luv, drink soom uv this!' – which barely got a syllable right, and that was before you had to tackle the lazy misogynistic attitude to Yoko, the frat-boy vibe summed up by the heading 'BEAT THE MEATLES'. No wonder The Rutles was to blow these stabs at satirical swipes out of the water – Eric, Neil and co had perfect ears for Beatle talk and song, and nobody else could get near. Scouse wit has always been a particular stumbling block for American comics, the recreated accent often coming out somewhere between Irish and Goofy.

Another tone-hearing-impaired laugh at the Fabs was written in 1977, and despite its obscurity, the book has managed to retain a small coterie of die-hard admirers – Mark Shipper's *Paperback Writer* being considered a lost classic for any rock and roll library by many amused musos. Fully subtitled '*The Life and Times of the Beatles, the Spurious Chronicle of Their Rise to Stardom, Their Triumphs and Disasters, Plus the Amazing Story of Their Ultimate Reunion*', the novel was essentially a rock journalist's half-remembered fantasy of The Way The Beatles Weren't, which twisted and turned into complete fiction halfway through, by showing the world just how crummy a Beatles reunion could be. A self-confessed burned-out music hack, Shipper presented his story as the result of a boozy interview with Ringo from which all the notes had been lost, and so he cobbled together the story as best he could, presented with regular snarky footnotes and lashings of contemporary facsimiles of adverts and articles which seemed somehow to back up the nonsensical narrative.

In this weird and waspish version of The Beatles legend, Paul was a teenybopper star before John lured him into the band, Brian Epstein was a plumber who struck it lucky, George was always a Bible-thumping drag, Ringo was obsessed with billiards, *AHDN* was a Bergman-esque piece of cinema set entirely in a silent library, John and Yoko formed a group with Sonny and Cher called 'The Plastic Bono Band', and Linda threatened to leave Wings when Steely Dan begged her to become their lead singer. Realising their solo careers were failures, these fictional Fabs were shown calling a truce to announce their late-'70s reunion LP, *Get Back*, and accompanying live tour:

> "We have to," Lennon said. "If we're a group, we have to perform. That's how we fell apart before."
>
> Ringo shivered. "My memory of our tours is of one long nightmare."
>
> "Out of shape, Ringo?" George chided him.
>
> "I'm in better shape than I ever was, but that's because I've had thirteen years to recover from our *last* tour."
>
> "What's Jimmy Nicol doing these days?" Lennon asked nobody in particular.
>
> "I hear Pete Best might be available," McCartney announced.
>
> Ringo waved his white napkin over the table in a gesture of surrender.
>
> "Have you two got any tunes?" Harrison asked John and Paul.
>
> "Fresh out," Lennon answered.
>
> "What about you, Paul?"
>
> "Same here, but I'm not worried. The old Lennon-McCartney team was never songless for long, were we?"
>
> "Well, I'm dry myself at the moment," Harrison confessed, "but I should have a couple of things

ready by the time we record."

"Isn't anybody going to ask me?" Ringo asked with a hurt voice.

"Okay, Ringo," George said with great resignation. He knew what was coming. "Do you have any songs ready for the new album?"

"Me? Since when am I supposed to write songs? I'm just the drummer in this group."

The midget brought more Coors to the table. Ringo held him there while he inquired if the others wanted anything else. "More pizza, Paul? George? John? Kotex for you, perhaps?"

John laughed, then pushed the slice of pizza he was holding into Ringo's face. Thirty minutes of hysteria ensued, then it was back to business.[331]

Like *The Rutles*, the book in some ways came from a loving position, its approach requiring a good knowledge of the real story before it could be trashed – but unlike *The Rutles*, its attacks could be lacerating, particularly in the depiction of the washed-up desperate has-beens who end up supporting Peter Frampton and The Sex Pistols on tour when their reunion album turns out to be unlistenable tripe filled with tracks like George's 'Disco Jesus' and John's interminable love song inspired by US sitcom *Gilligan's Island*. The book provides its own over-written rock journalism critique of the disastrous disc:

The Beatles are back. And I think we all wish they'd stayed away. To comprehend the magnitude of the tragedy that is *Get Back*, we must first sound the depths of the depression and disillusion establishing the ambiance of the late '70s... It is difficult to imagine what possessed the once insightful Lennon & McCartney (this is the team that wrote 'Mean Mr Mustard', damn it!) to focus on such a woefully inane main mass entertainment shuck as *Gilligan's Island* as a wellspring of hope, particularly when most informed observers would agree that an infinitely more suitable source follows immediately afterward in most major metropolitan television markets. I speak, of course, of *Leave it to Beaver...*

Better they allowed us to cherish our reminiscences of the glorious Fab Four of yore than tarnished them with such a hopeless sham. A final love letter to The Beatles: Get back where you belong – to our hopes and dreams, and our *memories.* May they rest in pieces.[332]

The book was all-but swept away into the furthest corners of cult fandom by the success of The Rutles, and of course in the meantime, far from getting back together, the four ex-Beatles continued to make their noises, with even Lennon eventually feeling ready to get back into the business. While others were mocking his greatest achievements, Ringo was finally seeing through one of his TV schemes, and just over a month after *All You Need Is Cash* debuted on NBC, Starr's own TV movie, designed to promote his new album *Bad Boy,* was broadcast on the channel. The creatively titled *Ringo* took one element from Chapman & Adams' script – Ringo's doppelgänger – and spun it out into a Hollywood retelling of *The Prince & The Pauper*, with lowly geek Ognir Rrats scratching a living selling maps to the Hollywood stars' homes until a run-in with jaded rock star Ringo, who just happens to have the exact same beard and mullet combo. The resulting musical sees the pair failing to settle into each others' personas while running into the likes of *The Honeymooners'* Art Carney as Ognir's abusive father, Carrie Fisher (gearing up for the infamous *Star Wars Holiday Special*) as Ognir's jailbait girlfriend, awkwardly serenaded with 'You're Sixteen' by the 38-year-old, and Vincent Price as a sinister hypnotist, rounding the hour off with a jam featuring the legendary Dr John. Best of all, however, was a poodle-haired George popping by to assist his old colleague as Narrator, and slipping in a fresh Rutle reference only appreciated by the initiated:

V/O:	We now join the George Harrison press conference already in progress.
GEORGE:	That's a good question, er, I think it was the trousers. But let's stay with the purpose of this press conference, which is to clean up some of the rumours surrounding Ringo and his concert which will be broadcast by satellite later this evening.
Q:	Mr Harrison, is it true that Ringo can no longer play the drums?
GEORGE:	Well, as far as I know...
Q:	Is it true that he's singing stranger than usual?
GEORGE:	I was worried about that myself until last night when I received a collect-call from Ringo.
Q:	Are you sure it was Ringo?
GEORGE:	Sure, yeah, he always calls collect.
Q:	Where was he calling from?
GEORGE:	He didn't say, he couldn't talk, he was being chased by the police.
Q:	By the police?
GEORGE:	Well, a fireman wouldn't chase you would he? Unless of course you're on fire.
Q:	What has happened to him?
GEORGE:	Let me start Ringo's story at the beginning. It seems two babies were born, the very same moment, the very same second, in the very same country – England. Remarkably both children, though born to different parents, looked exactly alike. One of the infants was taken to America, the other became quite well-known in certain circles. But fame and fortune did little to make him happy...[333]

The story continues with a moping Starr surrounded by starlets, to the tune of Lennon's already tongue-in-cheek boast-set-to-music, 'I'm The Greatest', and ends with George shrugging

284

'What do you want from me? I'm a musician, not Mark Twain!' In between, Ringo made a stab at creating a Woody Allen-esque character for Ognir, but moody outtakes suggest a less than jolly shoot for the star, and the resultant special stuck out like an excruciatingly sore thumb in the disco era, garnering one of the lowest and least appreciative TV ratings of the week. *Ringo* may only have been rookie work from writers Neal Israel and Pat Proft, who went on to co-create *Police Academy* and, in Proft's case, contribute to classics like the *Naked Gun* series, but the drubbing it received seems harsh a few generations later, with its failure to capture the zeitgeist giving the show an oddly timeless quality – plus the garish hornpipe to George Martin's orchestral take on 'Yellow Submarine' is good enough value on its own, putting *Ringo* at least on par with *James Paul McCartney* in the 'fascinating solo Beatles TV special' stakes. Both deserve restored releases, if only their stars could bear the reminders.

Besides, Ringo appeared in a far bigger turkey in the same year, Mae West's seedy swansong *Sextette*, which gave him a cameo among a stable of hot actors drawn into the veteran sex siren's web of barely-double-entendres, switching the age discrepancy with Fisher and extending it – which turned out to be something cinema audiences weren't prepared to stomach. 'I thought it would be fantastic to play with Mae, just to see what the legend was really like,' he told reporters, 'but on the first day of shooting I got really uptight. I felt completely left out of things. But by the end of the second day's filming, I would have stayed on as long as she wanted me. She's old enough to be my grandmother, so it's sort of embarrassing to say, but she's bloody attractive. And Mae's no Garbo. Mae doesn't want to be left alone...'[334] Ringo held his own in West's weird orbit, popping up amid the stiltedly hammered-home innuendo to play one of Mae's many ex-husbands, passionate German Director Laslo, and with Tony Curtis, Timothy Dalton, George Hamilton, Alice Cooper and, yes, Keith Moon also on the star's 'to do' list (not to mention Dom DeLuise performing a raunchy reading of 'Honey Pie'), he was at least in very good company as the movie sank beneath the waves of innuendo.

There was something of a glut of doomed and daft Beatlesque

cinema offerings in 1978, as the rock opera *Sgt Pepper's Lonely Hearts Club Band On the Road* dropped the last three words for a movie adaptation embarrassed by a predictably golden cast. A couple of years previously, Tony Palmer's oddball documentary *All This And World War II* married WWII footage with covers of Beatle songs, and three were provided by one of the hottest bands of the decade, Lancashire brothers and Kings of Disco, The Bee Gees. Chief Bee Gee Barry Gibb would go on to write the title song for the movie musical *Grease*, co-produced by Stigwood, but both would be left with egg on their faces for putting their names on the feature-length Beatle romp, despite Gibb's hubristic claim on release, 'There is no such thing as The Beatles now. They don't exist as a band and never performed *Sgt Pepper* live in any case. When ours comes out, it will be, in effect, as if theirs never existed.'[335] He and his brothers played back-up band to Peter Frampton's bimbo Billy Shears and semi-official Beatle blessing came from the presence of Billy Preston as the golden spirit of Sgt Pepper himself, and particularly George Martin on soundtrack duties, working again with Geoff Emerick, plus Peter Brown somewhere in the sea of producers. 'The great excitement for us has been re-recording The Beatles' songs with George Martin,' Gibb told reporters in more humble style. 'The fact that we've been doing Beatles harmonies since we were kids helped. It was easy for us to become a foursome with Peter Frampton... more than anything we'd like the boys, The Beatles, to like it.' Frampton added, 'I see Billy Shears as Mr Clean, the naive virginal farmer's son who has a magical grandfather and becomes a big star. In a lot of ways, the character and I are very similar, though I'm not as goody-goody as Billy. It's a send-up of me, the whole rock business and the idea that money is the essence of life.'[336]

The showiest parts went to great comedians doing their best with very little indeed – crumbly George Burns as half-hearted narrator Mr Kite (the only part with new dialogue), Steve Martin on maximum wacky setting as Maxwell Edison, and Frankie Howerd finally getting his Beatle gig as the despicable Mean Mr Mustard, though he later said of the film, 'It was like *Saturday Night Fever*, but without the fever.' With musical cameos from Alice

Cooper, Aerosmith, Earth Wind & Fire and even Dame Edna Everage in the closing ensemble, the combination of star power and the greatest music should have guaranteed some degree of success, but very few critics lost time in rolling up their sleeves and unleashing their most select vitriol for the queasy confection, palpably a gaudy, mawkish mess, when it hit silver screens that summer. Janet Maslin went to town in the *New York Times,* calling it 'the ultimate multimedia mishmash, so diversified that it doesn't fully exist in any one medium at all. This isn't a movie, it's a business deal set to music... The musical numbers are strung together so mindlessly that the movie has the feel of an interminable variety show. Characters are named, invented or introduced to one another simply to provide excuses for the various songs... The movie may have been conceived in a spirit of merriment, but watching it feels like playing shuffleboard at the absolute insistence of a bossy shipboard social director. When whimsy gets to be this overbearing, it simply isn't whimsy any more.'[337] As George observed of the creative team, 'They didn't *need* to do that. It's just like The Beatles trying to do The Rolling Stones. The Stones can do it better.'[338] McCartney tried for a relative note of positivity, shrugging, 'I've heard George Burns sing "Fixing A Hole", which sounds interesting and The Bee Gees do a few, Frampton does a couple. Geoff Emerick was working on it and he likes it. He says it's great... The film doesn't worry me. They're plugging my songs,'[339] but that was as close as Gibb could claim to any official approval.

Stigwood at least avoided being sued by the boys, a measure deemed necessary against the hit *Beatlemania* tour, and Paul commented, 'I think it's a bit weird when somebody is going around impersonating you while you're still alive. At least you feel that somehow they should have asked us, or you should have a say in it. But then again, I've been coping with weirdness for years.' But the increasingly irascible Harrison was steaming: 'It became a free-for-all! People were just thinking that The Beatles were like popular domain, like Mozart or something and that's what has been happening to us. With *Beatlemania*, we had to sue them and the funny thing is that we were going to settle with them out of court for a million dollars and they refused or they had an insurance company who refused to pay the million dollars. So it went to court and the judge awarded us $11 million! We settled with them for some figure below that. We did that to say, "Look, you can't just go round pilfering The Beatles' material... it makes me feel like I'm dead, if you want to know.'[340]

Despite these offences, lasting comedy greatness was to come that year from a different Beatleish direction. 1978 may have been the zenith of Harrison's comedy performing career, but it was soon overshadowed by his next step into movie production, no longer on behalf of Apple Films, but off his own back. The story of *Monty Python's Life of Brian* has of course been told and retold beyond banality by now, from Eric Idle's breezy announcement of 'Jesus Christ – Lust For Glory' to Palin and Cleese's endlessly replayed face-off with a Bishop and priggish Malcolm Muggeridge on BBC TV, but the kernel of the infamous epic tale has always been the divine intervention of George, when all seemed lost for his favourite comedy troupe.

The group's first creation for the cinema, *Holy Grail*, had only reached screens via the financial support of rockers including Led Zeppelin and Pink Floyd, but as the follow up was readied, sets secured in Tunisia, flights booked, the deal completed with Lord 'Bernie' Delfont at EMI (brother of ATV boss and Beatles catalogue owner Lew Grade) seemed to guarantee a smoother production – until he actually read the script, and pulled the plug in a fit of cowardice at the film's stance on organised religion. Only then did Eric dare to wonder whether their illustrious fan might be interested in purchasing what he eventually called 'the most expensive cinema ticket in history'. Not knowing what a big change in career this would become, George told *Rolling Stone,* 'As I'm a Monty Python fan, I wanted to see the movie – I like to go and have a laugh too – and a friend suggested that I try and raise the money. So we just got a loan from a bank. It's a risk, I suppose... I did it because I wanted to see the film. I couldn't stand the idea of it never being made.'[341]

George's business manager was Denis O'Brien, a seemingly sedate, besuited American legal expert who had entered The

Beatle's sphere via mutual friend Peter Sellers, and O'Brien's calculations, comprising the remortgaging of Friar Park, told him that they could indeed bankroll *Life of Brian*. Director Terry Jones admitted of the risk, 'No wonder they were nervous. I'm just glad I didn't know it at the time, I thought, "Oh what are they worrying about? They've got endless pots of money!"' And so Harrison was back in the producing game, but this time, the move necessitated the creation of a new company. Inspiration having struck after the purchase of some 'British Handmade Paper' from a mill near Wookey Hole, he was convinced to drop the 'British', and so HandMade Films, the name before some of the greatest and direst British films of the following decade or two, was born. 'I was friends with Michael Palin and I was very excited when EMI took on *Life of Brian*,' he said. 'I had followed it all the way and I had heard all the gags. In 1978, when Lord Delfont stopped the film, I asked Denis if there was any way I could help out the Python team myself. I thought he had forgotten about it, but a day or two later, he came back to me and said, "I've found a way to make it. We'll be the producers." I had watched that Mel Brooks film *The Producers* hundreds of times, Peter Sellers introduced it to me, and it was a hilarious idea.'[342]

Of course, the Pythons weren't about to let their saviour go without a very special set visit, and so for one final time, George was to get his millisecond of non-fame as part of a Python production. In breathless fan mode, he recalled, 'I went out to Tunisia... the place where they shoot all these Biblical kind of films. I believe they had just shot a Fellini film there. So I was meant to be leaving one night and I got shoved into wardrobe and make-up and before I knew it, I was dressed up as an Arab. There's a scene where Brian comes out in the morning and he's surrounded by people saying, "Put your hand on this, Brian!" and "I'm afflicted by a bald spot!" And John Cleese is saying, "Will all those afflicted by the Devil form a group on the left and all those with gifts form a group on the right." And as he's going through the crowd, he says, "Oh, Brian, I'd like you to meet Mr Papadopolos who's going to loan us the Mount for Monday afternoon." You have to stop-frame the film to see this was me.

We ended up investing five or six million pounds in Brian. We made a bit of money on it, which we then put into the next one. Terry Gilliam had this idea scribbled on a piece of paper, and it was *Time Bandits*...'[343] The few frames of Beatle cameo went by so quickly, Palin was called in to dub over his best nasal scouse 'Hello' to alert cinema-goers to who the smiling figure in the red robe was. Palin recalled, 'He was given the little-sought-after role of 314th Jewish Man in Kitchen during the scene in which Brian returns home and finds a huge Messiah-expectant crowd lying in wait for him. For George, the shock of finding himself in a crowd mobbing someone else was too much and he took early retirement and went back to his previous career as a musician.'[344]

The experience wasn't entirely joyful though, as Gilliam added, 'When we did *Life of Brian*, there was one meeting that George came to. We'd done the first or second cut of the film and we'd looked at it. It's funny, it's like if you're a fan of The Beatles you want to feel that The Beatles all worked wonderfully well together, an ideal working relationship, and George came to this meeting of us talking about what to do with the film and I could just see his eyes getting wider and his disappointment getting greater because none of us seemed to agree on anything and it was not clear at all how we were going to salvage this fucking mess. And I think it was the last time he ever came to a meeting... he just didn't want to see this side of Python.'[345]

That aside, the great scouse hope of British cinema concluded, 'I don't profess to know anything about the business, except that it's very confusing. Denis is the one with no hair on his head. As for the Pythons, let's face it, there are certain things in life which make life worth living and one of those things is Python, especially for someone like me. When you've gone through so much in life, and you're supposed to decide on what is real and what isn't, you watch the television and you see all this madness going on and everyone is being serious and accepting it, and you're ready to bang your head against the wall in despair, then someone says, "And now for something completely different..." That saves the day. Laughter is a great release.'[346]

*

UNIVERSAL SORROW JUST HITS YOU

With the huge success of *Brian* enticing the fat wallets of Universal Pictures for the follow-up, George would not work with the Monty Python team again, besides HandMade's involvement with their live film made at the Hollywood Bowl (for which he declined an invitation to rejoin the Mounties) but individually his friendship with the members would hold strong – unlike O'Brien's, once Idle had dared to warn Harrison that his partner was not to be trusted. Denis, utterly failing to grasp the nature of Monty Python, had foolishly threatened Eric with removal from the group, and as a result, found himself quickly fired as their business manager. 'We never had a contract with Python to say that you must stick with us forever and ever,' George said. 'If I can help someone like Gilliam, with his eccentricities which border on genius, I will, subject to Denis putting it on a realistic basis so that we don't go bankrupt within six months.'[347] Projects continued to be sniffed out for HandMade, with legendary rock percussionist Ray Cooper drafted in as creative director, basically George's artistic canary, testing the value of every screenplay received. Becoming a father to Dhani would further diminish any interest he had in business, whereas the birth of Paul's only son James in the same year would trigger an outpouring of further family friendly McCartney projects in the ensuing decade.

Before that, though, he would unwittingly help provoke his old partner back into creativity, according to John, largely via the success of his 1980 hit 'Coming Up'. Wings had never floated Lennon's boat, even when the depleted line-up's release of 'London Town' saw Paul reunite with their old very pal Victor Spinetti, who showed up in the video in full clown makeup. The celebratedly silly video for 'Coming Up' showed Macca donning disguises not just as a Moptop Beatle, but a whole host of music stars, from Sparks' Ron Mael to Frank Zappa, and debuted on *The Kenny Everett Video Show* in the UK, but whether the video's subsequent airing on *SNL* (with Billy Crystal surprising a sleeping Paul and Linda in London by singing them a Beatles medley lullaby) had anything to do with it, regular viewer Lennon declared himself stung into activity at last by the number's brassy energy. In 1975, his final live performance had been a contractual obligation at a tribute to the song-robbing Lew Grade – fittingly presented by old tour pal Dave Allen. But now, it was time to come back on his own terms.

It's long been known that Lennon wasn't quite so entirely overtaken by fatherhood and housework that he abandoned creativity altogether (especially given the employment of staff and a nanny), and he was to admit to *Rolling Stone* that the writing bug had bitten him, inspiring 'about two hundred pages of mad stuff' which was stolen from the Dakota, not recovered until 1982, and eventually gifted to publishers by Yoko four years later under the name of *Skywriting By Word of Mouth*.

Admittedly, the collection would make even *A Spaniard In The Works* seem cogent, being in the main composed of stream-of-consciousness faux autobiography, packed with a horny bawdiness less prevalent in the Beatle-era books, but with fewer cartoons and poems squeezed in:

> 'Welcome to Chapter Sixteen, by the order of St. Thomas,' said my genial host. 'You couldn't have come at a more inconvenient time!' He smiled between bites of a French widow by Duchamp. I smiled back, declining his offer of abundance...
>
> I felt his hot pants over my shoulder. I turned to find him disrobing in a disarming fashion. 'Talk about meat shortage!' I thought. 'This is a chilly dog!' He performed cunnilingus on my boots and begged to be relieved of duty. I patted him on the head and gave him something to chew on: "Food for thought," I murmured, coming to a halt in his mouth.
>
> I quickly left the perpetrator and ran down the street, a feeling of Virgin Mary engulfing me. This was not the first man I had made love to, but it was the first with tits. I put it down to experience, and checked into the local fleapit.
>
> 'Any bags, sir?' inquired the receptionist with an air of finality.

'No, thanks, I have my own,' I replied in kind. I ran into my room and collapsed, sobbing, onto the double entendre. The hours passed slowly as I played with myself in the mirror, trying desperately not to think about him, her, it, shit! Room service!

I placed my cock in the bedside drawer and answered the door; no one was there... Was I going sane? Had my family been rigid enough? Am I my brother's keeper? What kind of zoo is this? Am I just a tool of the bourgeoisie? Or am I just a prick?

These questions and more raced through my head like *The Sonny and Cher Show*. My neurosis was growing fast. I had it trimmed to a point at the back. The relief was as immense as the bill.

I crept into the dining room to see if she was still sleeping. She was, her face smiling at me from a plate of community vegetables...

I pictured myself on a boat on a river with tangerine trees and nervous dysplasia. This was to be the final chapter in my life savings.[348]

Nonetheless, the one-liners, when they do crop up, are sharper than anything in the earlier works: 'Insomnia was cured by putting people to sleep'; 'The benefit of knee-jerk intellectualism is, it keeps you fit'; 'They looked at him with that look they reserved for outpatients'; 'Their property was divided equally between the deaf, dumb and blind "to ensure no fighting"'; 'I had suicidal tendencies, but luckily had them removed at age thirteen. I never knew my parents; I could never get an interview with them. I went to finishing school in Paris but never finished'; 'I was beside myself with joy. That made two of us'; 'She was a mine of information, all of it completely useless'; and queerest of all: 'When you're dead, anything's funny.'

Even more remarkably, one of John's very last compositions, when he should have been working on a planned sentimental musical about his love for Yoko, was the most egregiously comedic song he ever wrote. The famous Lennon ability to skewer and lacerate those he disdained was activated by Bob Dylan's overt championing of Christian conversion in his 1979 track 'Gotta Serve Somebody', as performed on *SNL*, and although the initial reaction as John watched was 'he wants to be a waiter now?' he was careful to explain in interviews that he respected Dylan's faith, but objected to any religion involving proselytising. In private, however, he vamped and revamped away at his ragged, angry musical riposte, an extraordinary snarling scouse rejoinder which never officially saw the light of day until nearly twenty years later, entitled 'Serve Yourself':

You say you found Jesus? Christ! He's the only one?
You say you've found Buddha sittin' on his ass in the sun?
You say you found Mohammed kneelin' on a bloody carpet facin' to the East?
You say you found Krishna with a bald head dancin' in the street?
Well there's somethin' missing in this God Almighty stew, and it's your mother!
Don't forget your mother, la!
You got to Serve Yourself! Nobody gonna do for you...
Well you may believe in devils and you may believe in laws, but Christ, you're gonna have to serve yourself and that's all there is to it.
So get right back here, it's in the bloody fridge!
God, when I was a kid, didn't have stuff like this, TV fuckin' dinners and all that crap. You fuckin' kids are all the fuckin' same. Want a fuckin' car now! Lucky to have a pair of shoes...
Well, you may believe in Jesus, and you may believe in Marx, and you may believe in Marks & Spencer's. and you may believe in bloody Woolworths,
But there's something missing in this whole bloody stew – and it's your mother!
Your poor bloody mother! She what bore you in the back bedroom, full of piss and shit and fuckin' midwives. God, you can't forget that all too quick, you know. You should have been in the bloody War, la, and you'da known all about it...

For a man who had worked so hard to become a US citizen, that working class Liverpudlian piss and vinegar – reminiscent of Paul O'Grady's acid-tongued alter-ego Lily Savage – came easily and potently to John at 40, and the voluble gleeful snickering left at the end of the take included on his eventual 1998 *Anthology*, recorded in Bermuda to amuse 'Mother' Yoko, showed that he was loving every minute.

He seemed equally gleeful about his more commercial offering, *Double Fantasy*, released in a fifty-fifty deal with Yoko the following year, and the flurry of publicity which accompanied its release late that autumn spoke of a more mature Lennon less prone to lashing out in print and just happy to look to the future. As Andy Peebles discovered during his two-hour chat for BBC Radio 1 on 6 December, John was also still every bit the comedy fanboy, enthusing about the current UK hit *Fawlty Towers* (which McCartney also adored, booking Andrew Sachs to serve at an MPL Christmas party in character as Manuel). John sounded somewhat homesick, but was still able to make the DJ fall about when the subject of Blighty came up, with effusive blasts of pompous poshness and broad cockney accents:

ANDY:	You're wasted, Mr Lennon, you're wasted.
JOHN:	I love *Fawlty Towers*; I'd like to be in *that*, you know? Part of me would sooner have been a comedian, I just don't have the guts to stand up and do it, but I'd love to be in Monty Python, you know, rather than The Beatles, in a way! Or The Goons, you know?
YOKO:	That's the thing that saved us, the fact that he's funny, and he says I'm funny, so…
JOHN:	Most peculiar…
YOKO:	…Both make each other laugh, in a way.
JOHN:	*Fawlty Towers* is the greatest show I've seen in *years*. They have it over here now, God it's *great*. I mean, what a guy, he's great! I saw

<table>
<tr><td>ANDY:</td><td>him explaining how he only gets half an hour to produce it once a week, but what a masterpiece, what a beautiful thing.</td></tr>
<tr><td>ANDY:</td><td>We now have a new one called *Not the Nine O'Clock News*, which runs on a Monday night while the News is running on BBC 1…</td></tr>
<tr><td>JOHN:</td><td>Oh, great, well it'll come here, Public TV here buys them all, you see, we get all the *Masterpiece* series stuff … I see the English countryside, and it saves getting on the plane, there it is, all green and wet, and it looks beautiful…[350]</td></tr>
</table>

Forty-eight hours later, he was dead. *Not the Nine O'Clock News*, the first British sketch show to shrug off the cataclysmic influence of Monty Python, was already at the end of its third series, and for the last episode the following week, the writers struggled to think of anything amusing to say about the story which dominated every news bulletin, as head gag-writer Richard Curtis recalled, 'As members of this generation we sort of couldn't do our job that week, and it ended up that we just didn't have enough material to fill the half hour, because no one was in a mood where they could rise to the humorous occasion. So we stopped the show three minutes early, and just had black credits.'[351] For the first and final time in its anarchic history, the programme closed with a note of unfunny sincerity, as 'In My Life' played over the stark closing titles.

On the other hand, by the time this tribute aired, somebody somewhere may already have come up with the gag the *Not* team had missed, and which would eventually become a staple of many sick joke-swapping gatherings:

Q: What would it take to reunite The Beatles?
A: Three bullets.

John would surely have laughed.

– CHAPTER SIX –
ALTOGETHER NOW

'Why does the chicken cross himself, I wonder?'

'My grandkids always beat me at Rock Band. *And I say, "Listen, you may beat me at* Rock Band, *but I made the original records, so shut up!"'*

'There will never be a Beatles reunion as long as John Lennon remains dead… How many Beatles does it take to change a lightbulb? Four!'

'People on the outside perceive Paul as thinking he's the only one left. Actually, it's me. I am the last remaining Beatle.'

The 1980s was an extraordinary period for British comedy in particular, but fatherhood and the scrabble to remain relevant in the music world meant that it didn't heavily impinge on the surviving Beatles' careers throughout the fecund era. McCartney's life-long love of the *Daily Express'* blandly friendly adventurer Rupert Bear of course gave us *Rupert and the Frog Song*, Paul's long-wished-for sumptuous animation, brought to reality by quirky animator Geoff Dunbar, promising a dose of Disney-esque magic which McCartney had missed from the *Yellow Submarine* trip (although the title of his abandoned 1987 album *Return to Pepperland* showed that he had more than made peace with the 1968 masterpiece). It was a long and winding road to the Rupert cartoon's completion, and at one point some of the era's greatest comic minds were brought in to work on a full feature, with Douglas Adams, *Not* producer John Lloyd and Python Terry Jones all briefly beguiled by the Beatle into fiddling with concepts which could have sparked a bigger success, but all to no avail.

Despite lacking any of this top-drawer comedy influence, Dunbar's frog-packed 13-minute short won a BAFTA and became the biggest selling video of 1985. Above all, of course, the project gave us 'The Frog Song', AKA 'We All Stand Together', which if nothing else gives all Beatle fans the ultimate litmus test, in that only the most snotty miserablists like to crow about the song's tweeness, Exhibit A in the case for Saint John over Paul Salieri, rather than the truly stirring, life-affirming musical triumph that it is, certainly for a song performed by amphibians. Swapping rock glory for children's entertainment did, however, give many comedians simple tools to mock Macca for years to come – not least Harry Enfield, whose 'Fab FM' dinosaur DJ Dave Nice banned 'The Frog Song' from his playlist, disgusted by the repeated utterances of 'bum bum bum'.

The combination of talents who stuck a finger into the *Rupert* pie showed that Paul was keeping a finger on the button of UK comedy, as the old guard begrudgingly budged up to make room for a new generation of anarchic clowns. George too never let a comedy trend escape him – Ben Elton and Rik Mayall were huge Beatlemaniacs, having managed to wangle the use of two Beatle songs for the first broadcast of *The Young Ones,* and when they went to see Carl Perkins at the Hard Rock Café a decade later, Harrison sought the pair out to let them know the admiration was mutual, allegedly enthusing, 'Thanks for keeping us all amused during the '80s!'

PICTURE YOURSELF AS A TRAIN IN A STATION...

George had no intention of turning kiddy entertainer, but went so far as to write the foreword to a 1990 book about mute ursine puppet Sooty, a favourite of little Dhani's: 'Sooty symbolises the speed at which I wish the world was still turning. Harry Corbett created him in a time when life was less complicated, less competitive and certainly, in media terms, much less violent... (he) kept the routine simple and, with a very intriguing northern cunning (in the best sense of the word) engaged our attention with a basic music-hall routine with himself as the straight man and the naughty Sooty (and sidekick Sweep) as the mischief makers. Let's face it, it's pretty corny stuff. Yet Sooty is a subtle character who, if you missed him in your childhood, you may discover as an adult with your own child, as I did with my son Dhani.'[352]

For all that Paul's Rupert devotion earned him endless stick for the unforgivable crime of family-friendly knitted-jumper-wearing cosiness (a prosecution which had probably begun even before he covered 'Mary Had A Little Lamb'), in mitigation for the defence, few bring up his championing of a far more subversive children's book, *Fungus the Bogeyman*, Raymond Briggs' filthy comic masterpiece which nearly translated to the screen at the start of the 1980s, with music supplied by McCartney: 'The story is a bit strange, and the basic idea is that the bogeymen are people who make bumps in the night. They live beneath the ground and come out at night and frighten people and they like everything that is opposite to what we like. If we like warm dry clothes, they like wet slimy ones. And they've got all sorts of crazy books in their library, like "Lady Chatterley's Bogey". It's just a great book, but it's crazy and it just tickled my fancy when I got it.' The only remnant of the mooted project was the *McCartney II* track 'Bogey Music': 'I had that book in the studio one day and opened it to a page where the young people in Bogeyland rebel against the old people who hate music. They all start to get dressed in warm clean clothes and actually take baths, which is unheard of, and get into rock 'n' roll. So I just took that page, looked at it a bit, and just thought, "Well, it looks like a bit of rock 'n' roll." So I made up the track and called it "Bogey Music". It's a crazy fantasy, really, but that's what I was thinking of when I did it.'[353]

It's little wonder that this was the era when this generation had children on their mind, it was the epicentre of parental life for many of them, and Neil Innes himself spent years delighting generations with shows like *Puddle Lane, The Raggy Dolls* and *East of the Moon*, based on Terry Jones' fairy tales. Ringo was not exempt from this joyous infantilism, though the decade began with the mixed blessing of his 1981 silent (well, grunt-packed) comedy *Caveman* – 'mixed' in that the film did very little business and received lukewarm critical attention (the aforementioned Janet Maslin admitted it was 'dopey, but also lots of fun'[354]), but at the same time, he met Amazonian star Barbara Bach.

Although his prehistoric character's actual love interest was the more obviously wholesome Shelley Long, Ringo found lasting matrimonial happiness behind the scenes with the Bond girl. 'Maybe *Caveman* is the dawn of a new era for me,' he suggested at the time. 'I have already lined up my next film, a modern comedy in which I play a way-out psychiatrist. But my big ambition is to play a real, sadistic villain. Acting is going to be my main career priority from now on, although I do want to make one rock 'n' roll album a year. Once a rock 'n' roller always a rock 'n' roller!'[355] He and Barbara also had comic cameos in the 1983 US TV movie *Princess Daisy*, but otherwise his acting career was pointing in a different direction.

Having already dubbed over Dustin Hoffman's narration for a VHS re-release of Harry Nilsson's musical cartoon *The Point,* Ringo's own defining children's entertainment gig was just around the corner – his flat but friendly narration debuted on the CITV semi-animated classic *Thomas and Friends* in 1984. A few years earlier in '77 Ringo essayed the title role in the weird family entertainment *Scouse the Mouse*, a planned TV cartoon created by horror legend Donald Pleasance, but a strike prevented the animation being completed. All that emerged was an obscure soundtrack album to a proto-*American Tail*, with Starr as the Liverpudlian vermin hero who emigrates to the USA, joined by Barbara Dickson and, of course, Adam Faith. It's possible that this odd release caught the attention of TV producer Britt Allcroft, who had a passion for the train stories written by the Rev. Wilbert Awdry, and when she bought the rights to transfer them to screen, the perfect cosy voice to bring them to life turned out to be Starr's gentle Liverpool lilt. Although he first announced himself stunned at the suggestion, complaining that what kids wanted was 'dinosaurs with handguns', Ringo never treated his association with Thomas wholly flippantly, taking on the magical role of Mr Conductor in the American spin-off, *Shining Time Station*: 'Mr C, the conductor, is a magic man. I appear in gold dust, like *Star Trek*'s "Beam me, up, Scotty" all over again... *Shining Time Station* is meant to be a children's series, but it's going to become a big hit with mums and dads, too. It's got that magical quality, which appeals to the kid in all of us. I've always got on with kids. John had the intellectuals; Paul had the teenies and George the mystics. I always got the mothers and babies.'[356] In a pleasing callback to *Yellow Submarine,* Starr's narration on the UK series was eventually all-but seamlessly taken over by fellow Liverpudlian Michael Angelis – brother of Paul.

Even when the men themselves weren't immersed in some kind of kiddy fare, many kid's shows were packed with Beatle references without their stir, just as Pinky and Perky had jumped on the bandwagon at the height of Beatlemania. The wacky hippy sensibilities of The Muppets made their classic TV show's many Beatle allusions seem anything but out of place, stretching right back to the end of the '60s, when *Sesame Street* began something of an obsession with Ringo's underwater opus for Jim Henson and his team. An octopus popped up spewing weak puns about his garden in a 1970 *Ed Sullivan Show* special for which Henson also sketched out an unused design for puppet Beatles who could perform their latest hit for them, but instead he performed the song himself as Kermit in *The Muppet Show,* serenading a mermaid Miss Piggy. 'Octopus' Garden' was far from the only Beatles song to be subjected to Statler and Waldorf – the fact that the Muppet Theatre's resident bass player was called Sgt Floyd Pepper shows the Muppets' debt to The Beatles. *Sesame Street* also had its own regular Moptop Beetle puppets, expertly inserting educational messages into classic songs like 'Letter B' and 'Hey Food' – joined, naturally, by the Cookie Monster.

The numerous family-friendly pursuits fuelled a fair few comedic attacks on the ex-Beatles, and lampoons continued to proliferate, the post-Lennon security of The Beatles as a cornerstone of British culture making it a natural target for tomatoes from many quarters. The über-Beatles fan Douglas Adams may have rued the failure of the Rupert project to give him a solid collaboration with his hero McCartney, and in fact his strongest Macca connection came via his childhood friend, to whom he once gave rudimentary piano lessons, who eventually became McCartney's right-hand keyboardist for most of his career – Paul 'Wix' Wickens. Douglas may have felt glad to have been asked for his help at all, given the playful jabs at Paul he worked into 1982 *Hitchhiker's Guide* instalment *Life, The Universe and Everything*. In the novel, the murderous alien Krikkit race are shown to have long lived in idyllic ignorance of the rest of the universe, as the Guide recorded: 'Night had now fallen on ancient Krikkit... a small group of people were walking home across the hill towards the town singing a song about how terribly nice everything was... Arthur could almost imagine Paul McCartney sitting with his feet up by the fire one evening, humming it to Linda and wondering what to buy with the proceeds, and thinking probably Essex.'[357] Only on discovery that the universe teems with life does the species become genocidal. When rock-star audio visionary Dirk Maggs adapted the novel to radio after Adams' death, he did not have to look far for a musician to bring this pretty McCartney-esque music to life, with the resultant treacly pastiche co-created by Macca insider 'Wix' and cast member Phil Pope, eventually becoming a highlight on the live *Hitchhiker's Guide* tour: '*Our lovely world's so lovely, see how the flowers grow / It's such a shame my dog died, he loved those flowers so!*'[358] Pope admits, 'Douglas laid the blueprint out in the book, it just sort of came from that – thinking what a McCartney song by the Krikkits might have sounded like, trying to get his rocky voice, reflecting the tricks of how he would change chords and find a particular twist. It's amazing how many different tunes you can get out of fairly straightforward chord sequences. The genius of McCartney is to come up with something which is deceptively simple, something that feels like you've always known it...'

In addition to being a scene-stealing sitcom cameo legend in shows like *Blackadder* and *Only Fools & Horses*, Pope is one of

Britain's foremost comedy composers and pop pastiche artistes, with McCartney-aping a life-long speciality. His musical input was key for Central TV's great 1980s satirical institution *Spitting Image*, which didn't let Kate Robbins' place in the voice cast for the grotesque rubbery puppets prevent merciless attacks on Paul and Linda in the early days, as Pope recalls, '*Spitting Image* was *Grand Guignol,* Punch & Judy stuff so you could go a bit further – chop people's heads off and have them grow back in the next scene. It was interesting performing with Kate, because she would have a twinkle in her eye, saying "Our Paul will be all right." He had a good enough sense of humour that he could laugh it off.' The writers took their cue from *The Rutles* by showing a tiny sad-eyed Paul plinky-plonking away at the piano crooning whatever candyfloss melodies came to mind. Linda's musicality was often more cruelly targeted, even before the infamous 'isolated vocal track' of Linda backing Paul for 'Hey Jude' at Knebworth in 1990 was leaked, while Ringo was less prevalently sent up – although his puppet was almost indistinguishable from Yasser Arafat's.

But Pope's history of Macca mockery goes back even further than *Spitting Image*, thanks to his membership of the Oxford Review team of 1978 who went on to create hit Radio 4 comedy *Radio Active*, the spoof output of a fictional radio network where all the music was recreated by Pope, often with lyrical fuel from fellow Oxonian and Fab Four worshipper Richard Curtis. The stand-out spoof may have been Bee Gee piss-take The Hee Bee Gee Bees, but both the show and the album *439 Golden Greats – Never Mind The Originals* also featured 'Paul McCarthrob and Wangs' performing 'Simple Song'. Curtis' spoof lyrics tended to be quite poisonous, no matter how much of a fanboy he was, and 'Simple Song' made effectively the same 'soppy' swipe as The Rutles and *Spitting Image*, taking inspiration from the infamous lyrical stumble/non-stumble in 'Live and Let Die':

> *Now we come to the second verse in which I'm singing in now,*
> *I wonder what I should say in it – oh well, it's over anyhow.*
> *And so instead I'll… Sing a song, a simple song, as simple as they come,*
> *Taking care not to offend the record-buying mums,*

By avoiding words like – bums…
And I have got my wife here with me,
She may be playing in a different key,
But I love her and she loves me, because you see,
To be in love as lovers is so lovely…[359]

'I'd grown up with The Beatles as a small boy,' Pope says, usefully clarifying, 'I didn't live with them or anything like that – but they were always on in our house; my mother was the one who got me listening to the musicianship of The Beatles. So in a way it was second nature… 'Simple Song' was more Wings than Beatles.' For many *Radio Active* pastiches, he adds, 'I think the basic approach was "This is what we sound like and we make lots of money!" What I used to try and do was to write a song as if it had been written by them, arrogant and presumptuous though it sounds, to inhabit the brain of the songwriter, write a melody they may possibly write, etc. Even though the words may have sounded a bit attacking, I think there were degrees of attack – some we took the mickey out of, we really felt they should be brought down a peg or two, but with Paul… we thought maybe he had gone a bit soft, but it *was* a tribute. Everyone knew and loved The Beatles so much – the soundtrack to life. We're all fans first… We were told he had responded by saying "I'm just a simple bloke, with a farm for each foot." But I think that was probably made up by our publicity people.'

Radio Active was also responsible for one of the most notorious Beatle 'jokes' of all time, as highlighted by radio archivist Tim Worthington after years of misinformation which gave rise to a poisonous gag misattribution. For decades, a supposed John Lennon quip insisting of Ringo 'The best drummer in the world? He wasn't even the best drummer in The Beatles!' took on a life of its own, unthinkingly regurgitated by lazy journalists and self-appointed wits the world over, until frustrated drumming experts who knew the scale of Starr's unique skill demanded solid proof that John ever flamed his old friend in such a way. Credit was initially taken by brummie comedy legend Jasper Carrott, with a similar line used in his 1983 show *Carrott's Lib* – at that time considered to be penned by Rob Grant & Doug Naylor, head writers at *Spitting Image,* who were known to drop Ringo disses into their work (*Red Dwarf*'s computer Holly once explained that in a parallel universe 'Ringo might have been a really good drummer'). However, the line has been traced back no further than a sketch in the second series of *Radio Active* in October 1981, penned by series scribes Angus Deayton and the late great Geoffrey Perkins, and performed by Deayton with Michael Fenton-Stevens as a rock promoter with the unfortunate 'Showbiz Jew' accent which was seemingly not yet beyond the pale:

MIKE: Just one thing you need for the LP – Ringo Starr.

ANGUS: Ringo Starr?!

MIKE: Alright, maybe Ringo Starr wasn't the best drummer in the world. Alright, maybe he wasn't the best drummer in The Beatles, but he's a known![360]

Innes and Pope were far from the only comedy maestros to get stuck into the Beatle sound, and Phil's *Spitting Image* cohort Peter Brewis provided *Sgt Pepper* spoofs for two different double acts – Hale & Pace's generic psychedelia send-up 'Life Is So Strange', and a whole host of uncanny Lennon recreations for *Alas Smith & Jones,* in an extended sketch following a nostalgic 'Head To Head' session from Mel and Griff, spoofing the prevalent 'twenty years ago today' documentaries of the time. Lennon's many inspirations from newsprint suggested forgotten songs inspired by the worst of tabloid rags, and the idea that 'Lucy in the Sky with Diamonds' hid the druggy initials 'LSD' was refuted by backroom boy Smith because it actually signified 'L.I.T.S.W.D.', and that folk may be thinking of another forgotten track of the period, rendered gloriously believable by Brewis:

Desperate Remedies, Useless Gun Ships,
Drowned Rats, U-boats, German Spies,
Don't Relax Until Grandma's Sober,
Damsons Ripen Under Gooseberry Skies![361]

Double acts have been often drawn to the Fab oeuvre – French & Saunders formed Lananeeneenoonoo (essentially Bananarama's Rutles) to record 'Help!' for Comic Relief in 1989, while Bob Odenkirk & David Cross formed their own Rutles for one *Mr Show* sketch: The Fad 3, a very photogenic group who never actually played any music, and split after 'Neville' claimed to have been photographed more than Jesus. Around this time, Mick & Keith's corner shop on *Stella Street* saw a dream-like Fab Fool takeover courtesy of Phil Cornwell and the much-missed John Sessions, and his close friend Stephen Fry joined colleague Hugh Laurie performing 'Hey Jude' in very squeaky and very low voices on their own sketch show (for reasons which neither colleague could imagine when asked decades later). Matt Lucas & David Walliams' silly 1999 series of shorts *Rock Profile* devoted a whole episode to The Beatles, with presenter Jamie Theakston encountering a haunted, brainless Ringo possessed by the spirit of Thomas and (perhaps inevitably given Lucas' penchant for Indian accents) a George who sounded like Peter Sellers at his most ethnically insensitive. He also interrupted a scally Paul, tucking into a big plate of sausage, bacon and eggs:

JAMIE: Paul, your latest album, *Flaming Pie*...

PAUL: Oh, I am sick of talking about flaming *Flaming Pie*! All anyone ever wants to ask me about is my solo career! 'Were you on LSD when you recorded 'Spies Like Us'? What's the hidden message at the end of 'Simply Having A Wonderful Christmas Time'?' You know something? Thirty years ago, I was in a band called The Beatles, we made some crackin' stuff! No one ever mentions that!

JAMIE: Really? Well I mean if you're happy, I'd love to talk about The Beatles!

PAUL: Ah, you're just saying that... Yes, I know 'The Frog Chorus' redefined music, but I did make

	a record called *The White Album,* you know!
JAMIE:	I know, I'm a huge fan! To be honest, I didn't really like your solo stuff.
PAUL:	No, me neither, it's rubbish! It's very mediocre...
JAMIE:	If you're happy to talk about The Beatles, then maybe we can talk a little about your relationship with John Lennon?
PAUL:	You know the saddest thing? No one ever mentions him. [362]

I DEMAND TO HAVE SOME BOOZE!

'Everything that drove George fused into HandMade Films,' Michael Palin once paid tribute, 'it thrived as a pretty complete reflection of George's personality – a generous, engaged, committed and occasionally quite silly man... George believed in creativity.... and this respect for the artist underpinned much of the success of HandMade Films.'[363] Nonetheless, in his casual role as HandMade movie mogul, statistically Harrison was having as many outright disasters as successes.

There were tussles with Gilliam to get semi-Pythonesque metaphysical romp *Time Bandits* out, Terry G being unable to function without studio friction, but it turned out to be a classic, complete with end credits theme by Harrison, 'Dream Away' – a lyric which Gilliam took as a direct message, given his reputation for clarity of vision and refusal to compromise with producers, which producer George complained put him in mind of Lennon – '*Lucky you got so far / All you owe is apologies...*' 'What I discovered after the event was that that song is George's notes to me about my attitude on the film,' Gilliam laughed. 'On the lyric, there's something about "apologies". He felt I owed Denis and him some apologies because I was so unbending in the way I approached things. It's really funny because I enjoyed listening to the song but at the time I had no idea it was George writing his notes to me.'[364] Palin's quirky and earnest Edwardian period piece *The Missionary* was less of a hit, and indeed less of a comedy, though his lead role in Alan Bennett's wartime pig-murdering farce *A Private*

Function in 1984 was a return to form, Harrison's relationship with the elder comic Bennett proving far more respectful. For every major hit like *The Long Good Friday* (which George hated) and *Mona Lisa*, there were all-time comedy turkeys like *Bullshot* and 1985's painful *Water*, both of which belied the involvement of the finest talents, including sitcom legends Dick Clement & Ian La Frenais, Billy Connolly, Leonard Rossiter and Michael Caine – plus cameos from George and Ringo, jamming on stage in the final act – none of whom could prevent *Water* flushing down in history as the rankest kind of cinematic effluent.

George could sometimes be called upon to put in the odd cameo for HandMade – a cleaner in *Checking Out*, and a night club singer in *Shanghai Surprise*, the 1986 Madonna/Sean Penn period screwball caper which made *Water* seem like an acclaimed labour of love, causing the irascible producer far more trouble than it was worth: 'It was like "Springtime for Hitler" in *The Producers*. We got the wrong actors, the wrong producer, the wrong director. Where did we go right? It wasn't easy, but I was determined not to let it get me depressed.'

Thankfully, Ray Cooper came up trumps with a script by one frustrated thespian which resulted in the company's biggest non-Python comedy hit the following year – certainly, after its cinematic failure gave way to unimaginable cult popularity on video. Bruce Robinson lightly fictionalised the hedonistic excesses of his thespian clique in the late 1960s and gave the world perhaps the most quoted British movie of all time – the gross, lyrical masterpiece *Withnail and I*. It seemed at first like a typically doomed grotty British comedy, but Harrison fixed it for the film to have the rare distinction (*Ferris Bueller's Day Off* aside) of a genuine Beatle song on the soundtrack – a very brief snippet of his own 'While My Guitar Gently Weeps' – and he even made a low-key set visit with Ringo in tow, giving green young actors, fellow scouser Paul McGann and Richard E Grant, the shakes. Ringo commented that the greasy den they were filming in reminded him of The Cavern. Here it was that iconic stoner Danny would slur his generation-damning speech: 'I recommend you smoke some more grass... That is an unfortunate political decision. Reflecting these times… Politics, man. If you're hanging onto a rising balloon, you're presented with a difficult decision – let go before it's too late or hang on and keep getting higher, posing the question: how long can you keep a grip on the rope? They're selling hippie wigs in Woolworths, man. The greatest decade in the history of mankind is over.'[365]

'George has been the surprise I think,' Paul told one interviewer, 'because when we did the movies, probably the one least interested was George. He'd turn up, he'd play and didn't want to know. He was serious, he didn't like the movies. He thought it was a bit stupid, you know, all the acting… "I just want to play my guitar!" But he's turned out to be the most successful.'[366] Despite this unusual blast of praise for his younger comrade, McCartney may not have received the mogul's viewpoint happily when Harrison was called upon to confer faint praise on his old bandmate's own meat-free turkey in 1984, *Give My Regards To Broad Street*: 'Over the last few years, I've been telling him what I think, you know, exactly every time I've felt, you know, something like *Broad Street* I thought was a big mistake. Not making the film, because I quite enjoyed it myself, but the idea of trying to write and do everything yourself.'[367]

Paul's first attempt at long-form authorship was an account of his porridge in Japan, written for his children, but this experience now inspired a new writing challenge. One rainy morning in a London traffic jam, Paul put pen to paper with his first filmic intentions since the *Magical Mystery Tour* circle. A couple of years earlier, his company MPL had produced a short to promote Ringo's latest album *Stop and Smell the Roses* called *The Cooler*, directed by Lol Creme, with the main man starring as a mistreated prisoner seeking escapism via song. Paul and Linda joined Ringo and Barbara in the cast, which may have been the springboard for the semi-Beatles movie reunion McCartney had in mind. Ringo agreed to play himself in Paul's mooted film as long as he could deliver the line 'Have we got any agents, or are we practicing to be Canadians?', with his other half on hand as a lovestruck journalist, but that was as far as the Beatle casting went. 'Because Ringo's in it and I'm in it, it implies that maybe George ought to have been in it, too,' Paul admitted when the result hit cinemas. 'The truth is, he's not a ham. I don't think he's got any ambitions in front of the camera. He was the least keen to be acting in *A Hard Day's Night* and *Help*... Ringo and I are like hams; we like to gag it up for the cameras.'[368] There would have been the added Beatle flourish of Dick Lester behind the camera, but he passed in favour of ad director Peter Webb, only making it up to Paul by helming 1991 concert film *Get Back* – his last directing credit.

It would perhaps be unfair to loiter too long on the subject of the auteur McCartney's quixotic cinematic misstep because, despite his quick wit and life-long penchant for a good laff, *Broad Street* could not really be called a comedy; it's a musical where the music arises solely from the reality of the hero's life as a rock star, but very little between the songs has any substance, let alone comic value – characters say things like 'How are you?' and others reply, 'Fine thanks, can't complain,' and any quirkiness comes from the odd subtle glance at the oddities of showbiz. No one sensible would ever deny the power of McCartney's music, particularly as the film featured his greatest compositions, revisited in the recording studio with Martin and Emerick both at the controls, but for the meat of the movie – which centred around the mysterious disappearance of a dodgy MPL employee, Harry, who seems to have absconded with the tapes for the latest McCartney album – Macca was to set his jaw against an unprecedented bevy of brickbats. 'There's a side of me, a little conscience, saying "Come on, you're just posing, you just wanna be well thought of." It's that kind of Liverpool thing, saying, "You big poser!" you know? So I've got to be really sure in my own mind that I'm not posing. I don't want to do something just because it's poncy... I'm rather nervous that most of the people that are going to have a critical opinion on it are writers. That's a bit intimidating. For what the film is, and it ain't Shakespeare, being a gentle, light-hearted English picture, I believe we accomplished that. So I'm proud of it to that extent... Don't go in there expecting some kind of huge sci-fi blockbuster or something with incredibly deep meaning. Just go for a pleasant evening out, and I hope you come out of it with a warm glow.'[369]

For years, McCartney had tried to get a sci-fi blockbuster off the ground featuring Wings, with Gene Roddenberry along for much of the ride, but his sole solo film could not have been further from a space epic.

'I'm putting my whole reputation on the line,' the star admitted, adding that it all began innocently enough: 'I was sitting in a traffic jam, bored, and I had been trying to get together a film of some kind. At first, it was going to be based on *Tug of War*, an anti-war film. We were working with Tom Stoppard, who's a great writer, but it wasn't happening. I think if it's someone else's idea, it's not as easy as if it's your own… it was all falling down, and I was stuck in this traffic jam, so I said, "I'll write something then!" I wrote it first as an account… in the same way, really, that *A Hard Day's Night* was just these four guys going round from song to song and being chased by a lot of fans, which was a kinda parody of what was really happening to us. Well, this is a sort of parody of me now. I wanted to do a movie because it was the only thing that I hadn't done in my life… When we began filming, I put up the first bit of money. I thought just over a million dollars would see us through but in the third week alone, we had spent nearly all that and I was ordering new cheque books.'[370]

The plot, such as it was, was criticised both for its dumb simplicity and impenetrable complexity, which is quite an achievement, with an extended Victorian dream sequence receiving particular pulled faces from critics and audiences. After ninety-plus minutes of musical numbers and scenes of extremely mild peril, it could be claimed that Paul's best joke came last – when he makes it to Broad Street London Underground station (which closed two years later, presumably incidentally) and finds Harry stuck in a shed he mistook for the gents' toilet. That this solution to the mystery was then immediately undercut by the greatest of all writer's sins, the reveal that everything since the first scene had been *all a dream*, could also be claimed as a deliberate joke on McCartney's part, but if so, not even the most star-struck critic gave him any benefit of the doubt about it. It was down to the *NY Times* Janet Maslin once again to try to put a positive spin on things, going against the grain by writing 'Director Peter Webb has no comparable flair to Richard Lester, who brought such exuberance to The Beatles' films... *Broad Street* is a home movie on an amazing scale. But it has enough good musical sequences to please Mr McCartney's many fans. It also shows the singer in a relaxed, unselfconscious mood that goes a long way toward making the film appealing.'[371]

The film's cold reception was a huge knock for the ever-resilient McCartney, and not even the exciting release of a computer game sequel for the ZX Spectrum could soften the blow, nor a resultant bizarre offer from *Dallas* for the Beatle to join the regular cast as a bespoke character. Regardless, as he told presenter Melvyn Bragg on the accompanying *South Bank Show* special, 'I quite liked the experience, and the disadvantages were outweighed by the advantages, so I would take on another one. I'd probably try not to write it next time, or not be nearly as heavily involved. Probably if you asked me I'd rather have a little character role, rather than the sort of leading man. I'd probably rather just get made up as some 103-year-old fella who sits in the corner going "Wahey!" – that's what I really fancy, something that I've never done. I don't even know if I could do it, but I like having a go at these things.'[372]

The cast wasn't heavy on comedy talent, though Ralph Richardson did his best in a twinkly later sequence where he seemed to be playing the spirit of McCartney's late father Jim. Paul was wise to bring into the cast one of the UK's hottest and most versatile comedy talents, Tracey Ullman, on the brink of moving from fresh fame in shows like *Three of a Kind* and *Girls on Top* to her own huge US success – however, her character Sandra was required to do nothing but cry and spout banalities. While admitting this, life-long Macca devotee Ullman was far too bowled over by his attentions to hint at any misgivings, protesting, 'Paul was lovely. It was so exciting, I went hot and cold all over. It wasn't too long before the ice was broken and we were running round taking the mickey out of him and his Liverpool accent. But we were friends, really... The plot for *Broad Street* is incredibly complicated. All I know is that I get in and out of vans a lot and I never stop crying from the start of the movie till the end of it, and I look absolutely dreadful, as usual. I play this bird who can't stop crying. It's not a big part or anything. I enjoyed doing it and I got to know Paul and Linda quite well. Paul's excellent in it. He's a really good actor actually.' He was certainly good enough to cameo in her new pop video, a cover of Kirsty McColl's 'They Don't Know', as her dream boyfriend, but both were easily at their funniest off duty, interviewed by suave anchor Michael Aspel for his ITV chat show *Aspel & Company,* which clearly had a guest booker second-to-none. Though still somewhat defensive, Paul's guest spot alongside her saw him flowing with anecdotes and scouse charm, the developing chat show persona of good old two-thumbs-aloft chummy McCartney – as well as performing a Buddy Holly song in the style of trade unionist Arthur Scargill, for no apparent reason.

A few years later an even bigger coup was pulled off by Aspel when he played host to both George and Ringo – the latter clearly in the epicentre of his destructive addiction pile-up, loving every minute, shortly before his joint clean-up time with Bach in 1988. This was also a particularly litigious period, with McCartney snubbing The Beatles' entry into the Rock & Roll Hall Of Fame, and writs about percentages flying left, right and centre. Ringo twirled onto the set with a huge grin, chain-smoking, playing up to the crowd while his old friend chuckled away next to him, and he made even himself snigger with quips like 'I never go to bed. I am an insomniac, mainly. When I'm not an insomniac, I sleep.' He crowed about the pleasure of doing *Thomas the Tank Engine* and flicked the backward Vs for a change as he chortled about George's most recent legal case against him:

ASPEL:	You lived in each others' pockets, didn't you? It was like being a family.
RINGO:	Oh, he's always lived in mine. (*George looks askance*)
ASPEL:	You have family rows?
RINGO:	We do, we have terrible rows.
ASPEL:	What was the main cause of your squabbles

	in the early days?
RINGO:	(*Long pause*) I'll leave that one to you, George.
GEORGE:	I don't remember any squabbles!
RINGO:	You don't remember anything, do you?
GEORGE:	No, instant amnesia!
ASPEL:	What about now? What makes you cross with each other now?
RINGO:	Well the last time we were cross was when George was suing me.
GEORGE:	That was the last time Paul was cross!
RINGO:	Oh, he's still cross... What's nice though is, he (*George*) calls me up, and says, 'I'm going to sue you.' I said, 'Now George...' He said, 'No, I'm going to sue you, I don't like what you've done' – because he wrote this song and I had it mixed by somebody else... so in the end, I said, 'Well, sue me if you want, but I'll always love you.'[373]

Even when the subject of Lennon's death was brought up, Starr collapsed with comic anguish, complaining, 'You've certainly brought the party down, Michael!' Harrison reverted to his stock reaction when the topic arose – quoting The Rutles, with the subject-closing insincerity of mouthing 'Shocked and stunned...'

The two had recently worked together on the last hit album of Harrison's lifetime, *Cloud Nine*. Where 1981's 'All Those Years Ago' had featured all three surviving Beatles on the recording, the video for 'When We Was Fab' replaced Paul with a stranger in a walrus costume, but otherwise revelled in tongue-in-cheek Fab-referencing, directed by Godley & Creme and packed with Ringo mugging. The album's stand-out hit cover 'Got My Mind Set On You' also had a video which reunited George with a familiar director: 'My humour is such that I have to be able to have something funny happening around me so I can be deadpan, as I'm not really into acting. That works very well for me. The director was Gary Weis, who incidentally directed *The Rutles*, so

314

he's a very funny fellow himself. He thought of having a simple setting like a room and making it move so I could just play it straight and everything else would be the joke.'[374] Weis recalled that George wasn't too pleased to see his stand-in performing backflips, as he was worried people would think he was really able to do them.

It was this period of solo success which led to George's last great larky hurrah. The need to record an extra track for the last single off the album while in LA saw the star reaching out to his good mate, brummie ELO maestro Jeff Lynne, who was in the middle of producing a new line of hits for Roy Orbison, and they decamped to Bob Dylan's home studio to knock something together, having stopped off at Tom Petty's place to pick up George's guitar. The original planned supergroup name of 'Trembling Wilburys' would have been funnier (and avoided US spelling), but the brief moment of group greatness the gang experienced, albeit marred by the sudden loss of The Big O, suggested that Harrison had picked up plenty of tips from Dirk, Stig, Nasty and Barry. The Traveling Wilburys was a spoof band in a similar vein to George's idols The Rutles, each member forging a fake persona as part of the Wilbury family. The name evolved from Harrison & Lynne's catchphrase that they 'will bury' certain sounds in a song mix, and was headed by Nelson (George), with Otis (Jeff), Lefty (Roy), Charlie T Jr (Tom) and Lucky (Bob). For the second outing, not terribly meaningful name changes to Spike, Clayton, Muddy and Boo were brought in – albeit, George's new name was clearly an allusion to his old pal Milligan, who was also by this time a close neighbour to Paul in his rural corner of Rye.

Spike maintained unique friendships with his two famous fans, and a queerly affecting letter of complaint sent from Spike to George was uncovered, eventually performed by Irish actor Andrew Scott as part of charity theatrical event *Letters Of Note*:

> You once said to me – the world is full of arseholes, and I'm not one of them. I have a love for certain people and I have one for you, but by sheer lack of

contact it's running out. I phone you frequently and never get a reply. This is what you do, it's very simple; you stand in front of a telephone and you insert your fingers in the holes and carry out a series of numbers which have been given to you. Of course, if you are rich you have buttons, which Irishmen usually sew on their coats. Of course, if you are extremely rich you don't have to get in touch with anybody, and that's what I am worried about.

The funeral takes place at Golders Green Crematorium, no flowers please, just money. You will recognise me, I am the dead one.

Love, light and peace, Spike Milligan.

PS Thank you for sending the letter about the Fender Guitar, believe it or not, I'm now playing the guitar, and the silly bastards who insure it want living proof that it was a George Harrison guitar, and I said to them, it was a George Harrison guitar, but it is now mine.'[375]

Furthering the comedy connections, each Wilbury album (the second, of course, being Volume 3) boasted liner notes by Michael Palin and Eric Idle, as naughty academics:

The original Wilburys were a stationary people who, realising that their civilisation could not stand still forever, began to go for short walks – not the 'traveling', as we now know it, but certainly as far as the corner and back. They must have taken to motion, in much the same way as penguins were at that time taking to ledges, for the next we hear of them they were going out for the day (often taking lunch or a picnic). Later, we don't as yet know how much later, some intrepid Wilburys began to go away for the weekend, leaving late Friday and coming back Sunday. It was they who evolved simple rhythmic forms to describe their adventures…

As the Wilburys began to go further in their search for musical inspiration they found themselves the object of interest among many less developed species – nightclub owners, tour operators and recording executives. To the Wilburys, who had only just learnt to cope with wives, roadies and drummers, it was a blow from which many of them never recovered.

A tiny handful survived – the last of the traveling Wilburys – and the songs gathered here represent the popular laments, the epic heroic tales, which characterise the apotheosis of the elusive Wilbury sound. The message of the music travels, as indeed they traveled and as I myself must now travel for further treatment. Good listening, good night and let thy Wilbury be done...

Hugh Jampton, E.F. Norti-Bitz reader in applied jacket, University of Krakatoa (East of Java)[376]

The etymological origins of the Traveling Wilburys have aroused something of a controversy amongst academic circles. Did they, as Professor 'Bobby' Sinfield believes, originate from the various Wilbury fairs which travelled Europe in medieval times, titillating the populace with contemporary ballads, or were they rather derived from 'Ye Traveling Wilburys', who were popular locksmiths during the Crusades and used to pick or unlock the jammed chastity belts (rather like today's emergency plumbers)?

Dr Arthur Noseputty of Cambridge believes they were closely related to the Dingleberries, which is not a group but a disease. I think this can be discounted, not only because of his silly name but also from his habit of impersonating Ethel Merman during lectures...

One thing, however, remains certain. The

circumambulatory peregrinations of these itinerant mundivagant peripatetic nomads has already disgorged one collection of popular lyrical cantata, which happily encapsulated their dithyrambic antiphonic contrapuntal threnodies as a satisfactory auricular experience for the hedonistic gratification of the hoi-polloi on a popular epigraphically inscribed gramophonic recording. Now here's another one.

Professor "Tiny" Hampton is currently leading the search for intelligent life amongst rock journalism at the University of Please Yourself, California.[377]

Everyone in the band was crazy about Monty Python, and allegedly Orbison, like Presley, could reel off whole episodes of *Flying Circus* by heart. Maybe Dylan was seen as the least amusing of the bunch, but Harrison was happy to refute this: 'A lot of people take Bob seriously, but if you know Dylan, he's such a joker really. He just sat down and we said, "Okay, what are we gonna do?" And Bob says, "Let's do one like Prince!" and he just started banging away: "*I love your sexy body…!*"[378] The daft video for dance pastiche 'Wilbury Twist' ('*Lift your other foot up and fall on your ass / Get back up and put your teeth in a glass*') gave one last chance for Eric to pop up in one of George's music videos, accompanied by John Candy, and directed by Clement & La Frenais, putting *Water* well under the bridge.

Paul and Ringo may never have been invited to become Wilburys, but the former did have one foray into comedy during this period – cameoing on BBC 1's zeitgeisty scouse sitcom *Bread* in October 1988. There was something of a cult for Liverpool drama and comedy in the '80s, perhaps encouraged by the gritty/chirpy drama of Alan Bleasdale and Willy Russell and the soap opera *Brookside,* and 1986 saw the launch of a BBC 2 sitcom about happy scallies entitled *Help,* complete with relevant Beatle theme – which was not true of Laurence Marks & Maurice Gran's 1992 sitcom *Get Back*, even though every episode was named after a Lennon/McCartney song, and packed with references, from

Loretta and Martin Sweet to Bungalow Bill. Although *Help* lasted for two series, the sparky scouse comedy soon vanished into obscurity compared to Lane's similarly themed BBC 1 equivalent. Post-*Liver Birds*, Carla Lane's TV CV had grown, and many would see her serial about quirky benefit-grubbing Dingle family the Boswells as her most important and popular work – though many scousers equally despised the family show for its damning representation of their city as the home of untrustworthy unemployed opportunists, the kind who gave rise to Harry Enfield's troublesome permed criminals 'The Scousers', and a million punch-down jokes about cars up on bricks.

A strong bond had been formed between Carla and Linda, who met at a party hosted by Chrissy Hynde, and all three were quickly united in their furious passion for animal rights. The gang's radical activism was of course shared by Paul, since that fateful springtime Sunday dinner of roast lamb which coincided with the sight of the little woolly critters gambolling around the McCartney farmstead, whereupon the life-long carnivore (who had once assured many a teen mag his favourite food was 'beef and chips') made meat avoidance a key part of the McCartney brand – Linda and Paul also co-wrote music for Lane's animal rights protest poems, *The White Coated Man* and *Cow*, which a decade later ended up on Linda's *Wide Prairie*. Carla convinced Linda to make an appearance in the fourth series of her hit show in '88, popping round for a rather credulity-stretching cup of tea with Boswell matriarch Nellie, who throughout their typically earnest, lyrically Liverpudlian natter never cottons on about her visitor's husband's identity ('Your husband got a job has he?' 'Yeah, at the moment, so far.' 'Not made redundant like my Adrian?'), until the mystery man arrives to pick her up at the end, to the astonishment of Joey and Billy Boswell. Paul told the writer 'You write it, I'll read it, and I might do it, our Carla', and proved as good as his word – if you can count driving up for the single line, 'Did you bring me a cake?' Completing the circle, McCartney was at the time collaborating with Carl Davis, the husband of Nellie Boswell actress Jean Boht, on the *Liverpool Oratorio* alluded to at the very start of this book. They would eventually collaborate again on a song for the touching Raymond Briggs animation *Ethel & Ernest*, thirty-six years after the sound of *Bogey Music*.

This was all irrelevant to George, who had promised to tune in on the Sunday night to watch his old pal's slice of *Bread*, but got the time wrong and accidentally watched banal yachting soap *Howard's Way* instead: 'I'd never seen the show before, and I just couldn't figure out how Paul was going to fit in with all these posh people on boats.'[379]

This pastel-tinted era bristled with further minor comedy connections – in 1985 Paul released the theme song to John Landis' comedy *Spies Like Us,* starring Dan Aykroyd and Chevy Chase, who fell over each other to goof around with the Beatle in the music video. He also extended his association with the new breed of UK comedians by popping up in the second cinematic offering from The Comic Strip – 1987's dark state-of-the-nation flop *Eat the Rich*. He didn't join Lemmy on the soundtrack, but randomly cameoed as a guest at Home Secretary Nosher Powell's banquet, being dragged out during a food fight, protesting 'I'm with the group!'

Ringo added to this story's regular preoccupation with Lewis Carroll by essaying a wacky Mock Turtle alongside Sid Caesar's Gryphon in an embarrassingly star-studded 1985 TV special, which saw him sing and dance the number 'Nonsense' in some very iffy tights. In the same year, he remained a fixture on the celeb scene, popping up in *An Audience with Billy Connolly*, and *Dame Edna's Hollywood* a few years later in his now familiar guise of dark glasses, earring, beard and double-take-worthy haircut, just as Paul settled into his given publicity circuit persona of waggled double thumbs up and chirpy cheekiness, gleefully embarrassing his son James on Saturday morning kids' TV and so on. George, as far as possible, just kept out of such arenas. Then in 1986 came a most unexpected comedy collaboration for charity – anti-heroin charity double album *It's a Live-In World* featured straight songs from both Paul and Ringo, but the latter also joined his previous satirical attackers, birthday-brother Bill Oddie and John Cleese, contributing nonsense to the track 'Naughty Atom Bomb', a very silly number about nuclear war which ended with the cry '*One thing's for sure, we're the first country to get a coyote into orbit!*'

Two years later, he may also have joined Connolly, Idle, Dudley Moore and Julie Andrews in the ignominy of starring in insipid or ill-fated US sitcom vehicles. His mooted comedy, *The Flip Side*, co-starring and produced by *Miami Vice*'s Don Johnson and written by *Caveman* director Carl Gottlieb, would have stretched him to the right degree by casting him as an ageing pop star forced to quit the concert circuit to care for his orphaned children after the death of his first wife.

Ringo's last notable comedy cameo of the 1980s owed a huge amount to the mockumentary stylings of *The Rutles*, like *Spinal Tap* before it. In 1987 HBO aired *The Return of Bruno* – a Bruce Willis vanity project which nonetheless showed that the suddenly hot star knew the value of mixing music with comedy. It was a fake TV special celebrating the career of Willis' alter-ego Bruno Radolini, who, like The Rutles, was claimed to have started half the revolutions in rock and roll history, many of them in distinctly Beatlesque style. With names like Elton John, Brian Wilson and The Bee Gees only the choicest in a whole cast of legends sending themselves up, Ringo provided the all-important Beatle element, explaining 'Bruno introduced me to George one night at the Cavern Club. And that's how it all started, you know? I was derelict on the street and he brought me into this club, introduced me to George, and, well – the rest is history!'[380]

Post-National Lampoon at least, American humour always seemed to treat the three remaining Beatles with far more awed respect than their UK equivalents, and the Beatlemaniacs behind the most successful cartoon of all time were positively orgasmic to complete the set of possible Fab cameos within the first few years of its relentless marathon run. *The Simpsons*, having grown out of a strand in the hit US show from Paul's pal Tracey Ullman, has thrown in far more Beatle references than we can cram in here, but getting the men themselves to lend their voices to their guest appearances was the pinnacle of the ambitions of Matt Groening and co. 'It was so nice meeting Homer in real life', Ringo said of his starring role in the 1991 episode *A Brush With*

Greatness, in which Marge was revealed to be a life-long Ringo fan, bowled over to finally receive a diligent reply to her teenage fan letter from the great man decades later. George followed with a brief but crucial walk-on part in the entirely Beatles-inspired 1993 show *Homer's Barbershop Quartet* – a retelling of The Beatles story in which titular band The B-Sharps' hit song 'Baby On Board' gives them a music career closely copying that of the Fab Four, right down to Yoko cameo and the rooftop swansong which Harrison assured everyone had 'been done!' Paul and Linda joined the club in 1995, groovily advocating the vegetarian life while visiting their old friend Apu, in *Lisa The Vegetarian*. Writer/producer Jeff Martin enthused on the *Something About The Beatles* podcast in 2017 about what a blast Ringo and George were in the studio, while he travelled personally to Rye to record the McCartneys at home: '*The Simpsons*, especially when I was running it… was incredibly influenced by Python, and English comedy in general – which means it was incredibly influenced by The Beatles, and The Goons. The Beatles are so intertwined with comedy – one of the main things that Beatle recordings are is pure joy. There is such joy in virtually everything they produced… almost everything they do is on the edge of laughter. You hear that on the outtakes, how close they are to being funny, and thinking it's hilarious – even their serious songs, the minute they have a moment they start making fun of their own songs… That is a real power, it's a very zen state of mind, to know that everything is just a laugh.'[381]

NIAGA ECIN TUO DENRUT

The Traveling Wilbury legend did not last long, but it was a glorious refresher for George before the serious business of the '90s came around – the creation of the *Anthology*. Or, as he himself reflected, in a mellowed, reflective vein, music didn't have to be that serious: 'You have to do a lot of promotion work. I'm on my own, whereas in the past I had three other smart-arses with me all cracking jokes… I miss that side of it. We used to have good fun at press conferences. They used to be great because there would always be someone with a wisecrack. I do miss that side of the Fab Four, I admit. Now, people seem to give me respect, which is quite nice.' His old school pal Paul concurred around this time, telling press 'I pick up papers now and it's like everyone's thinking very deeply about music. We weren't. We were just having fun and I don't see music as that serious.'[382]

Harrison's thaw when it came to the Fab Four could also have been influenced by the bitter end of the glorious HandMade Films period of his life. The comedy masterpieces which bore the HandMade stamp may have ultimately been few (though *Nuns on the Run* remains undervalued), but the discovery of Denis O'Brien's many nefarious activities as his right-hand businessman, which led to the company's meltdown, was a huge blow, as Idle recalled: 'I know that George never forgave Denis. He hated him with an intensity that was quite rare for George. He felt bitter, betrayed, angry and let down. In fact, he wrote a song called "Lying O'Brien" which he played me. It took him a long time to get over all that… Then he lost half a lung to cancer, and then half a lung to some fucking loony stabbing him… I'm sorry it worked out the way it did for George. One always hoped that Denis was on the level; you hope they're right. It turned out that he wasn't… He worked on absolute trust, George, he always told the truth, he never lied, even when it was painful. So the idea that somebody would not be telling the truth to him didn't actually enter his head. He was susceptible.'[383] Having celebrated ten tumultuous years, Harrison finally admitted at a HandMade party, 'I hate fucking films anyway', and the company was sold off.

The idea of providing incidental music for the ten-part TV special *Anthology*, vastly extended from the *Long and Winding Road* project which had been cribbed by *All You Need Is Cash*, soon gave way to the concept of building up some of Lennon's piano demos, and when 'Free As A Bird' debuted to a breathless public at the end of 1995, it followed the unspoken pattern of The Beatles' output, by ending on a laff – a music-hall-echoing sample of George Formby-esque banjolele from Harrison, accompanied by John's backward delivery of the Lancashire lad's catchphrase,

'Turned out nice again!' The track was produced by Wilbury Jeff, George Martin having announced his hearing no longer up to the job – though prior to his belated knighthood, Sir George was to sign off an unassailable career with one last album of Beatle songs, 1998's *In My Life*, almost defiantly emphasising his comedy credentials, with whacked-out covers of 'I Am The Walrus', Come Together' and 'Mr Kite' from Jim Carrey, Robin Williams and Billy Connolly, plus a giggly 'A Hard Day's Night' from Goldie Hawn.

The whole *Anthology* project was awash with instances of Fab humour hitherto unknown to the audience – madcap outtakes; corpsing vocal tracks as John and Paul chuckled through 'And Your Bird Can Sing'; John's undercutting intro to 'Let It Be' – 'Are we supposed to giggle in the solo?' – answered in the affirmative by Paul's laugh; the Morecambe & Wise appearance complete with 'Moonlight Bay' and more, providing a timely reminder that the world's greatest group were all about the laffs, after a decade and a half of mournful struggle to adapt to a Lennonless world. It was a joyous rebirth, marking a new era for Beatle worship, but of course a show like *Spitting Image* in its late period remained firmly on the cynical bench, with a quickie featuring the closest they had to a George puppet as well as a new, bigger Paul:

THE BEATLES are seated around an ouija board.

GEORGE: Speak to us! Speak to us through the board, y'know, tell us what to do, John! Show us the way!

RINGO: (*Grabs the glass*) Hey – drum solo! He says drum solo!

GEORGE: (*Grabs glass back*) Sitar break here.

RINGO: (*Grabs glass back again*) More drumming! Loads more drums!

GEORGE: Gerroff! (*Glass starts to move animatedly*)

PAUL: Hey, lads! It really is movin'! Erm – Leave-my-music-alone!-I'm-spinning-in-my-grave!-You-money-grabbing-bastards!'

RINGO:	Hang on, that doesn't even rhyme!
PAUL:	Hey, John, can you hear me? That doesn't rhyme! We're counting on you, John!
RINGO:	Hey, Lennon's lost it![384]

In the epicentre of the Britpop explosion, *Anthology* gave the world The Beatles afresh, and the final sight of 'The Threetles' together at Paul's home studio at Hog Mill, sitting on the lawn drinking tea, getting into comical clashes over their differing memories ('I say it was Candlestick Park...!') and jamming ukes is as perfect a final image for The Beatles story as could be desired. Long after George's loss, in the 21st century, the humble ukulele has come in for endless vicious campaigns of hatred from sniffy muso critics, not helped by its over-use by endless braindead advertising executives, giving rise to a hipsterish reputation for musical tweeness which has robbed the four-stringed musician's friend of much of its egalitarian charm. But George was *never* without a uke or two wherever he went – its compact simplicity making it the easiest possible way to make music, and in some ways its innocent stripped-down tinkling the best test of any song's strength. His final posthumous album *Brainwashed* was awash with the sound of ukuleles, and as the sentimental George Formby Society honorary member said in a hand-written note in 1999: 'Everybody should have and play a uke – it's so simple to carry with you and it is one instrument you can't play and not laugh! It's so sweet and also very old – some are made of wood, some are made of armadillos. I love them – the more the merrier. Everyone I know who is into the ukulele is "crackers". So get yourself a few and enjoy yourselves!'[385] *Brainwashed* did not empty Harrison's bottom drawer, either – one of his final compositions was a freaky little ode to his other favourite band, the Bonzos – themselves no strangers to the uke – three years after Vivian Stanshall left this world in a tragic blaze of fire. His 1998 demo 'Do The Bonzo', sadly, was recorded for a tribute album which has not yet seen the light of day.

As Idle hinted, George's final years of pain and suffering did not dim his inextinguishable humour, to the last. When he and

Olivia were attacked in their home at the turn of the millennium, despite the traumatic drama of the altercation, the ambulance staff were already being entertained before they had even wheeled their desperately wounded patient out of Friar Park – he insisted on his stretcher being halted so he could ask a 'shocked and stunned' new member of his staff how she felt the job was going, and reflected that his mentally ill attacker 'wasn't auditioning to be in the Traveling Wilburys'! He probably wouldn't even have minded the eventual *Family Guy* aside where Peter Griffin claimed to be the oblivious security guard that night ('Quiet down up there, ya wacky Beatle!'). Of course, the harrowing experience did George no favours, given the struggles he already faced with throat cancer, but as it became clear that his days were numbered, unquestionably aided by his strong faith, Harrison's desire to lighten the mood did not waver. When he requested that fish and chips be put in his IV drip, medical staff dismissed it as delusional, but Dhani responded 'It's called humour' – and even as his dearest friend Ringo had to tear himself from his bedside to fly to be with his daughter Lee, who was undergoing surgery for a brain tumour, George's last words to him were an insouciant 'Do you want me to come with you?' 'He loved comedians,' Eric concluded, 'poor, sick, sad, deranged lovable puppies that we are, because they, like him, had the ability to say the wrong thing at the right time, which is what we call humour.'[386]

The 2002 Albert Hall tribute, a year after Harrison's entry into another phase of life, of course burned with catharsis for all, and it would have been unthinkable to stint on the comedy content. Olivia requested the surviving Pythons to perform a rendition of 'Piggies', but this proved a tall order for the not-wholly-musical gang, and so a reprise of their bums-out barbershop number 'Sit On My Face' filled the void, plus of course a 'Lumberjack' reprise respectfully crashed by Tom Hanks, after which the Mounties saluted their lost brother. Idle recalled the experience as being a raw one, floods of tears hidden away in the toilets, but there was a pleasing poetry to his being comforted on the evening 'like a big brother' by his satirical counterpart, Paul McCartney hugging Dirk McQuickly, with all remnants of wounds from satirical barbs long forgotten.

Neil saw so many of his friends go before him, he paid tribute in his heartbreaking song 'Friends At The End Of The Line', and The Rutles even added George's classic requiem 'All Things Must Pass' to their final set-lists. 'Probably one of the most special evenings of my life was participating with other Pythons in *The Concert for George*, he reflected, 'though the last thing I felt we ought to be doing there was turning round and baring our bums – which was the climax, so to speak, of the Pythons' appearance. But George would have hooted about it. He was a very special man. To have known him was a privilege and to be friends with him was even more so. That evening was a very, very moving experience but it was good to remember how acute George's sense of humour and irony was. He wasn't some mystical, misty-headed person; he was very, very sharp and hugely witty. Wonderful fun! He could brighten any room.'[387]

Paul played big brother at the Albert Hall, but after all, he's had a long life of dealing with senseless bereavement. George's tribute came only three years after he had managed to get through the tribute concert in the same venue for the lovely Linda – an emotional evening given its own crucial lighter shade via the hosting of Eddie Izzard. In 2012, Izzard – already practically an honorary Python by this point – had the honour of introducing McCartney at an LA tribute show for the charity MusiCares, retelling their Person Of The Year's biography in his own semi-imitable way:

> Paul McCartney was born in June the something, 1962, in the city of Liverpool in the country of Ireland... Paul's father was Jacques Cousteau, the famous fisherman, who changed the family name to McCartney after his boat hit a cart. Everyone made jokes and the name stuck...
>
> By 1962, Winston Churchill was running a pub in Hamburg, Germany – which as you probably all know, is only five miles from Liverpool, a city in Russia. The Beatles at this point were a seven man group, John Lennon on guitar, George Harrison on

lead guitar, Stu Sutcliffe on bass, Pete Best on drums, Muhammad Ali on flute and Charles de Gaulle on xylophone... Eventually John Lennon, son of the same Lennon that had led the Russian revolution in 1917, got pissed off with Charles de Gaulle, who played an indifferent xylophone anyway, always faced the back and could only make a plinky, plinky, plinky noise with his instrument. So just like that, in 1962, Charles de Gaulle was out of The Beatles and Paul was in – initially on the xylophone, which he had to play upside down as he was left-handed...

Events were moving so fast now that biographies had become hard to follow... On 7 February 1962 The Beatles finally landed in America and the reaction was huge. They went on The Ed Sullivan Show and were watched by seven trillion people, way more than the population of the world. When people said how can this be, they discovered that people from other planets were watching as well...

Wings had had many hits and had played many huge stadiums, but the battle of the bands with 'Beaks' had made Paul McCartney stop and think: What was it all about? How could bands like 'Beaks' do so well? How come he now spoke German? And also – who the bloody hell was writing this biography? This wasn't his life. Some bastard was just going on and on, writing for some Grammy programme, while large men were pushing pianos around a stage. This guy's making up rubbish, right there in the middle of a show celebrating the life of Paul McCartney. And the trouble is, this gig is happening in America and people could well believe this shit and write it in history books: How Paul McCartney played the xylophone upside down 'cos he was left-handed and how Muhammad Ali played flute with The Beatles and how every single thing happened in bloody 1962!

...So, what have we learned here about Paul McCartney? Well, not much from all the crap that I just said. But then again, these tribute events can just end up being a long line of people, making loquacious salutations that hang briefly in the air before they slide forgotten, into the landfill of speeches past. I prefer to remember that someone once wrote – 'What we do in life, echoes in eternity.' For Paul McCartney words are not needed, the music speaks for itself.[388]

George's magical Albert Hall tribute was undeniably an emotional maelstrom for his many friends, but the fraught chemistry may have been further complicated by one particular reunion – Ron Nasty and Dirk McQuickly being forced together several years after the latter had blurred fiction and fact in the most unfortunate way, by taking legal action against his former fellow Rutle over what we'll call 'The *Rutles Archaeology* Saga' – Nasty Vs McQuickly.

UNFINISHED SOUP LIKE CHEESE & ONIONS

As time goes by, a cultural cornerstone as central and rich as The Beatles' music begins to be replicated within the warp and weft of our world's connected cultural DNA, to the point that it becomes impossible to track every single Beatle joke, allusion, tribute, meme, trope and reference across the planet's light entertainment output in a book any smaller than Kent. The Bootleg Beatles had been spreading ersatz joy with live spectaculars for over a decade by the time the Britpop renaissance arrived: entertainment trailblazers who practically invented the entire universe of tribute bands. Whole subsets of Fab fandom had long proliferated by the *Anthology* era, giving rise to esoteric albums from *Beatlesongs* to the *Exotic Beatles* series, packed with novelty songs, mind-popping foreign covers, freaky samples and even William Shatner performances to test those at the further reach of fanaticism – many such quirky tracks have already been mentioned throughout this history. The numbersome happy tribes of Beatledom eventually began to have mass celebrations, festivals and conventions, in Liverpool and around the world, all dedicated to the four boys who shook the world, and exploring every anal avenue of their influence, and eternal merchandising possibilities.

One such of these was, and is, Beatlefest – an American festival given the go ahead by Lennon in 1974 with the assurance, 'I'm all for it! I'm a Beatles fan too!' Although lacking the authenticity of Liverpool's Mathew Street festival, Beatlefest's extraordinary success has led to over forty-five years of events all over the USA – the 1994 Beatlefests in New York, Chicago and LA begin the *Archaeology* saga. Regular co-host of the US events, English-born producer Martin Lewis, was a one-time Derek Taylor protégé with fingers in a whole host of Beatley and comedic pies, and had known Neil since both worked on the first ever Amnesty fundraiser which gave rise to *The Secret Policeman's Ball*. Lewis felt it a coup to get Innes over to reminisce about his many Fab credentials, but the real revelation for crowds was Neil's willingness to get up and perform a few old Rutles numbers for the first time in public. These impromptu performances went so well, in September, he was invited back to the Lewis-curated 25th anniversary fest *Monty Python Lust For Glory* to headline a special Rutles event at LA's famous Troubador club, spoofing ageing rock bands who tour with only one living member by staging *Ron Nasty & The NEW Rutles*, with original orchestrator John Altman arranging for dinner-jacketed classical musicians to provide stirring backing. The event sold out so quickly a second was hastily added, with uber-fans like Jeff Lynne and Harry Shearer, and even Julian Lennon, all roaring their approval. For Neil, who had ploughed his own kiddy furrow in the two decades since The Rutles' invention, it was a heart-warming revelation, the *LA Times* heralding the comeback as 'Beatles music from a parallel universe!'

Shortly after, Lewis began work with Taylor on *The Beatles at the BBC* while Derek was drumming up PR for the *Anthology*, and both agreed that a new Rutles piss-take would be a very timely accompaniment to the new releases from Apple. Neil had enjoyed performing the songs after so long, but was extremely unsure whether a second album was what he wanted to do next – particularly as his faux McCartney, Ollie Halsall, had died three years earlier in Spain, at the age of only 43, after a life of addiction problems. The loss of such a key voice, particularly given the coincidence that two or three unreleased rough recordings still existed in the archives from the 1977 recording period, did add extra layers of uncanny parallels with the real non-Pre-Fab Three, and yet still Innes wavered. It was one thing to show Nasty rolling off down the hill in his wheelchair, but now his real-life counterpart had so tragically 'accepted a teaching post in Australia', how could his alter ego stage a comeback? With no ersatz Paul in the studio or on film, it was like the wrong band member had gone too soon. This was only explained during publicity by the excuse that 'Sir Dirk McQuickly' – the "Knight In White Satin" – is no longer with us. He's gone into comedy.'

Eventually, the ultimate decision had to come from The Rutles' biggest fan – George Harrison. He and Neil had maintained their friendship stretching back to the '60s – on one occasion, Eric and Neil had been hanging out at Friar Park with both George and Ringo, who serenaded their satirisers with a rendition of 'Ouch!', and Idle pointed out that together they made one full quartet, and should go on tour as 'The Brutals'. Having no film deadline to prick the sides of his intent, while mulling over Lewis' suggestion, Neil had begun folding some recent – and not so recent – compositions back into potential Rutle lore, numbers which he had performed elsewhere without the weight of Rutledom, such as 'Joe Public', 'Questionnaire' and 'Eine Kleine Middle Klasse Musik', socially interested toe-tappers which Innes considered 'more of an homage' than the straight-up spoofs of the first LP. After three or four numbers, the grinning Harrison gave up trying to work out which Beatle song was being sent up and stopped him, saying, 'Hang on, these are *your* songs, don't be shy!' 'I wasn't too convinced about doing another Rutles thing,' Neil confirmed, 'but a lot of Beatle fans were, and I went to see George, and said "What do you think?" And he's got this dark sense of humour, he immediately said, "Oh yeah? Well, which one of you's going to be shot?" I said, "Precisely, George, where's the fun?" But he said, "No, you should do it, because it's all part of the soup."'

Enthused by the brainwave that any new Rutles release had to be called *Archaeology*, Neil assented to Martin Lewis' entreaty and left him to fix all the deals and release details, attracting great interest from Virgin and making Lorne Michaels' day by guaranteeing a huge upswing of interest in the original Rutles film, marketed by his company Broadway Video. Everyone seemed pumped for the Rutle renaissance as Neil went back into the studio with Halsey (coaxed out from behind the bar at his pub in Cambridgeshire), Fataar (on tour with Bonnie Raitt) and John Altman, to see what could be done with the '77 recordings, and work together on new ones. Neil had been sure to contact his old mucker Eric about the proceedings first and foremost, inviting him to be involved in any way he fancied, despite not being on the original album. Idle, however, firmly declined the invitation, as he had declined to turn up to any of the LA shows despite living very nearby. Neil was hurt, but carried on regardless. The album was all-but complete when word came through that the whole enterprise was being shaken. As Innes diplomatically euphemised the situation, 'Eric got very "proprietorial" (Lorne Michaels' word) about The Rutles and *Archaeology*. He told his lawyer to tell Virgin USA that they didn't have permission to use The Rutles' name. In fact, Lorne owns the name, and his company Broadway Video had been very enthusiastic about the project. However, when Eric kicked up a fuss, Lorne decided to follow his "code" (which he explained to me over the phone) and go along with whoever had first brought him the project.' As a result, Virgin got cold feet and all sorts of big plans to throw metaphorical tomatoes at the official Beatles *Anthology* went by the wayside, including the reveal of a huge *Anthology*-pastiching billboard in Times Square, right along the poster for the real thing. It was also made clear that Idle's likeness would not be allowed anywhere near any *Archaeology* material, and so a carefully masterminded spoof of the Beatle CD packages had to be dropped, in favour of an almost 'plain packaging' solution, closest to the *Past Masters* discs. Every CD would have to carry a clear credit: 'The Rutles were conceived and created by Eric Idle.' The bottom line from the band, however, was 'This album is dedicated to John, Paul, George & Ringo with love from Neil, Ricky, John & Ollie.'

Despite all the drama, Innes was happy to say, 'That album was much, much better than the first. Its songwriting is more of an homage to the Beatles – this great, tight, little rock and roll band. I think it's the music business' best kept secret!' This time, 'the quiet one' Fataar got to sing two songs and Halsey gave us more of his ersatz Ringo on 'Easy Listening', 'The Knicker Elastic King' and 'Rendezvous', which followed 'Major Happy's Up-And-Coming Once Upon A Good Time Band' to deliberately resemble 'With A Little Help'. The specially written song 'Don't Know Why' consciously paralleled 'Free As A Bird', Ron Nasty 'reforming with himself' on a recording supposedly discovered in an East-end garage, and was originally written in 1996 as a very gently ribbing end credit sequence for *Rory Bremner: Who Else?* on Channel 4. Stand-out singalong 'Shangri La' – a song old enough to have been performed on the same *SNL* episode as 'Cheese & Onions', now fully bent back into official Rutle lore as the album's sole single – allowed Neil a rare moment of jubilation by opening with a riff referencing both his trademark ballad 'How Sweet To Be An Idiot' and 'Whatever' by Britpop stars Oasis, a song which so closely echoed the first line of Innes' own that for the first time in his life, he got to win a plagiarism case, re-crediting their song 'Gallagher/Innes'. Half-finished tracks like the 'Back In the USSR'-esque 'We've Arrived (And To Prove It We're Here)' gave just the right element of archival verisimilitude, closing with a spot of scatology with an intoned 'Number two, number two...'

Then there was the literally unfinished recording 'Unfinished Words', on which the three surviving Rutles lent their talents to the existing track featuring Halsall, bringing a new level of genuine emotion to the Rutles oeuvre. Among the track's many hidden gags, Innes included nods to Lewis' own attempt to out-hoax the 'Paul Is Dead' freaks in 1971, as a young rock journalist, when he invented supposed unreleased Beatle songs entitled 'Colliding Circles',

'Deckchair', 'Pink Litmus Paper Shirt' and 'Left Is Right (And Right Is Wrong)', the latter two turning up in 'Unfinished Words' (while the other titles were recorded as Beatlesque offerings by American outsider artist R Stevie Moore). The song's biggest Beatle parallel, however, may be 'How Do You Sleep?' – hearing by now of Idle rumblings abroad, Ron Nasty added a dourly delivered spoken section to the instrumental: '*I can't pretend to be someone who pretends to be someone else. / Or so my pretend friend tells me*…[389]

The album was stuffed full of more Beatle references than ever before, with the later Japanese version of the CD taking the joke further, 'Baby S'il Vous Plait' badly translating 'Baby Let Me Be' into French to ape 'Sie Liebt Dich', and no doubt delighting George by referencing his favourite instrument in 'My Little Ukulele', while a budget release ten years later added Cole Porter's 'Under My Skin' performed as a boozy Hamburg-style run-through. Perhaps the central *Archaeology* song, however, was the 'When I'm 64'-esque closer 'Back In '64', which also made good use of the four-stringed weapon of hipster doom for one of Innes' most wistful lyrics, which seemed to underline the essential strength of The Rutles' music – a deep love for the era and the four friends who inspired a generation:

> *Many years from now, when your grandchildren climb up on your knee,*
> *You may be quite astonished to see how many channels they can change on TV.*
> *When some old film in black and white comes on and there you are up on the screen,*
> *Or is it someone just like someone you've been?*
> *Looking not a day over nineteen.*
> *'Granddad,' the little ones are asking you,*
> *'Why do you look so sad?'*
> *So you tell them all about the fun you had…*
> *Back in '64, before you were born,*
> *People had no time for pouring scorn (Or scoring porn),*
> *On dreams of love and peace,*
> *No one was obese, only tight trousers were worn…*[390]

Archaeology launched with a pop in October 1996, entirely accidentally on the same day as the third and final *Anthology* release, and Neil gamely did his best to prod it along the publicity circuit, as Ron and himself. Nasty told *The Austin Chronicle*: 'You can't turn your back on the world, because when you do, you look ahead and there's still just as much world ahead of you...' But out of character, Neil did mention his regret that Eric was not on board for the reunion, after so much water 'has passed under the bridge, gone out to sea, turned into a cloud, come back and rained on many a parade.'[391]

All three Rutles were in joshing form, in and out of character, when they met Richard Porter for an article in fanzine *Off The Beatle Track*: 'I asked them whether they had something to say to Brian Thigh, the guy that turned down the Rutles. "Yeah, thanks for the pizza – keep the change", said Nasty. "Don't forget to set your runner bean flowers in cold weather", said Barry. I then asked about what they'd been doing since The Rutles. Barry said, "I had a hairdressing Empire, the Hackney Empire. However, after a berserk lady customer ran amok with hot curling tongs and I suffered a terrible injury, I sold the empire." Stig said (*sic*), "I've been with lots of airlines since Air India..." Nasty is no longer with Chastity but they became firm friends after she gave up the Nazi stuff...' Neil then steered the chat back to reality: 'We really missed Ollie Halsall who sang on the first one, but we've got him on the archive tracks. We've done the best we can singing wise between us but he had the best singing voice of all of us. Though it's widely tipped that Barry Wom is going to be made male vocalist of 1997.' 'I've been nominated for a Granny!' Barry interrupted... When asked about the possibility of live performances Neil replied, 'It depends on how the LP goes – but we could certainly do the songs live.' 'It's been twenty years since the last LP,' added John, 'If we wait any longer we'll be making dead appearances! Here they are – The Rutles, dead on stage!'

The conversation turned to the video for 'Shangri La', Innes admitting, 'It's a bit of a mess but hopefully there's something there in the edit. Lots of people said they'd like to be in the video and we thought it would be nice to have some lookalikes too. We had Columbo, Madonna, Whoopie Goldberg, Rod Stewart, Pat Boone...' and John interrupted, 'No he was real!'[392] Although packed with lookalikes, the *Our World*-alike video for 'Shangri La' also attracted an eclectic bunch of real stars to the New York studio for a daft singalong with the 'Lah-de-doo-dahs': Peter Gabriel, Graham Nash, Cyndi Lauper, Gloria Gaynor, Slash, Ben E King, Nancy Sinatra, Eartha Kitt, Bill Maher, Janeane Garofalo and more. The Rutles even performed on the roof of the city's Hard Rock Café one lunchtime in October, Neil resplendent in a white Rutle wig to cover his famously shiny bonce. Only after Nasty, Stig and Barry had taken their bows did the silver hammer from Idle's lawyers come crashing down, and Innes dejectedly accepted every demand, despite the hobbling effect on the release.

Archaeology was well received by the fans for its skilful stretching of the Rutle universe, but it was a muted return, and led to bad feeling which it would be convenient to ignore in the name of peace and love, were the tensions not so very public. Caught between Nasty and Dirk was their ailing old friend George, who could not believe that two jokers and old friends could so entirely lose their senses of humour, given all the years of 'Sue Me Sue You Blues' The Beatles had gone through. On one of the rare occasions he managed to get the pair together, he protested, 'You're supposed to be sending us up! You're not supposed to be emulating us!'

But for all the almost amusing parallels to be drawn with John and Paul's feuding, there are a couple of points to be made about Eric and Neil's issues, which weren't alleviated by Innes' woes over royalties from the hit *Holy Grail* musical *Spamalot,* which need not detain us here. Firstly, any fan who laments a fall-out between two former collaborators should ask themselves, how many well-matured folk still hang out with the pals and co-workers they were close to in their twenties? A select few. And the more you examine the personalities of Ron and Dirk, the more surprising it becomes that they ever came together at all. Art School charmer Neil Innes spent over fifty years forging what he always insisted was an accidental showbiz career, seemingly bumbling along and 'really expressing himself' – or as Eric put it in a painfully exposing exposé in the *Chicago Tribune* in 2005, 'Neil is a clever and gifted singer and songwriter who's determined to be a failure, and his determination succeeds.' Innes could only have raised Idle hackles higher by shrugging, 'I look at it all with some kind of amusement because I'm not showbizzy and I think probably Eric is, and if people want to be possessive and don't want to share their toys in the sandpit, I couldn't care less.'[393] The wonderful heights of Innes' career, however, do suggest that the ever-modest maestro was happy to have his cake and eat it – it's useful to take to the stage protesting 'If you don't rehearse, nothing can go wrong' – but nobody tours the world to delighted crowds entirely by accident. Then there's former Footlights President Eric Idle, who has brought millions of fans hours of the greatest joy and hilarity in the last century of world humour, but there's an equal cake-having-and-eating element to the comic exaggeration of what we could call his pragmatic attitude to show business – or to put it Eric's own way, he's 'the sixth nicest of the six Pythons', the star of the 'Greedy Bastard Tour' who mocked Palin's trademark 'niceness' by maybe not even half-joking, 'Many fine people have lived richly fulfilling lives without having to worry about being nice. In fact many great artists weren't very nice at all.'[394] But while freely admitting all this, Idle still lives to make us laugh, and nobody can deny that almost everything we know about The Rutles universe flowed from his mind – except for the music, which has perhaps turned out to have the most lasting power, even without the comic context. But, as George said, it's all part of the soup.

The former muckers thankfully had their ups as well as downs, with gusts of autumnal creativity inescapably bringing them together at times, typically in front of fan convention crowds. Eric was pointedly absent from the 1997 Rutlefest in LA – a fun-packed weekend of film viewings, puppets shows, and tribute acts like Rutland, joined by original Quarrymen member Len Garry, and musicians like Denny Laine (performing tracks from McQuickly's album *Flaming Punk*), and acres of merchandising... followed once again by the surviving Rutles. The event was enthusiastically put together by Lewis, but it's unsurprising that Idle felt that his ball was palpably being played with. Having witnessed the warm responses triggered by The Rutles canon around the world, nobody could blame Innes for the inkling that further shows could be a public and a personal blessing – particularly after the *Archaeology* debacle left him in a position precarious enough to necessitate selling his family home. And so a touring band was formed despite Fataar's disinclination to rock up in the provinces, with Halsey tempted out from behind the bar and extra backing from hard-playing pals like Rutlin' Ken Thornton, Mickey Simmonds, Mark Griffiths and Dave Catlin-Birch (himself the original Bootleg Paul). Nasty developed a new taste for the touring life in the new millennium: besides his solo oeuvre, the 2006 Bonzos reunion featuring Stephen Fry, Ade Edmondson and others in the place of the irreplaceable Stanshall gave Neil a three-pronged fan-pleasing schedule for years to come – Bonzos, Rutles and solo, with Rutles shows in pride of place.

Eric did, however, merrily join Ricky, Neil and Gary Weis in 2001 for an LA Director's Guild Q&A, where he announced a project to redraw the Rutles lines, as it were: a new piece of 'rutlementary' entertainment, *Can't Buy Me Lunch* – not, he stressed, a sequel, but a 'remake supplement'. The new film ultimately proved hard to find a home for, and has still had no official UK release, but it was an updated voxpop package presented by the sadder, not much wiser Melvin Hall. Where *All You Need Is Cash* was based on the unseen *Long and Winding Road* project, this follow-up was inspired by the now forgotten ABC TV special *Beatlemania*, and robbed of this context, it was essentially a talking head package backed up with fresh links and every extant scrap of footage unused in the first film, some even synced up to *Archaeology* tracks, bringing the two sides of The Rutles briefly back together again. Idle insisted to everyone he was a 'one-man band' on the project – Weis never even knew about it until Eric mentioned it at the 2001 event – and although that does tend to show, and it was a missed opportunity to expand on what Dirk, Stig, Nasty and Barry had been up to in the previous three decades, the special did throw a few revelations into the soup, introducing Catherine O'Hara as German photographer Astro Glide (originator of the tight trousers) and bringing lost concepts like Nasty and Chastity's 'Shower Power' into focus, along with an added suggestion that 'curry' may have made a better LSD euphemism than 'tea'. Plus, besides Eric's dragging up as British Ambassador's wife Lady Beth Mouse-Peddler, it brought some very big names into the Rutles fold, including Idle mates Tom Hanks, Carrie Fisher, James Taylor, Graham Nash again, Ricky's pal Bonnie Raitt, Salman Rushdie, Garry Shandling, Mike Nicholls, Steve Martin, a very angry Billy Connolly ('Change the world? The Rutles never changed their socks!') plus Robin Williams as German rockologist/sexologist Hans Hänkie. All of the above were easily upstaged by renowned comedy geek David Bowie, whose iron-faced Streeb-Greebling-style swerves of fancy spilled over into the DVD extras:

DAVID: Really, I guess the crowning glory to their 'career'... I suppose you have to call it that, a 'career', don't you? – is this piece of marketing extravagance... (HOLDS UP VINYL COVER OF 'THE RUTLES 1' WITH THE STICKER '27 NUMBER 1 SINGLES ON 1 CD'.) *The Rutles Number One*. Inevitable. Especially in these days of rock being a career choice and all that, you know, which it's become, really, for most folk, I think. This kind of selling out is expected. All the old favourites, stick 'em all together, sell more albums than any other album's ever sold. You see, it's just not about that! It's not About Number Ones! Or Number Twos, or Number Threes!

MELVIN: Number Fours?

DAVID: It's about Number Fours. Which, of course, is my next album... The most extraordinary thing about Barry, that I'll never forget, is that he would talk with me, or rather, Barry would talk *at* me for hours. I never understood a word he said. It was ages before I realised in fact that he was using words! It was just this long drone, which, like sausage meat, was cut off every few… with an intake of breath. (MAKES GUTTURAL BARRY NOISES.) I thought he was still on the curry.[395]

If anything, the 2002 follow-up extended the narrator's backstory more than the Pre-Fab Four's: an identically-raincoated presenter dogged Hall throughout his links – a nod to Monty Python's 'Competing Documentaries' sketch, with Palin and Cleese violently snatching the mike from each other. The tiresome interloper ultimately revealed himself to be Hall's bastard son in an emotional conclusion: a great honour for *SNL*'s hot new star Jimmy Fallon, who would go on to bag every possible Beatles fan's perk as presenter of his own *Tonight Show,* busking with Paul and backing Ringo's rendition of *Yellow Submarine* on dinky classroom instruments, as well as playing John in his own skit to mark the 50th anniversary of the *Ed Sullivan Show* debut: 'We're the Beatles! Don't forget to like us on Facebook! And you can follow us on Twitter at @TheBeatlesUK! We're also on Instagram, that was just The_Beatles1. Check it out to see some exclusive backstage pics and some Throwback Thursdays…!'[396]

When the *Chicago Tribune* came calling a few years later, Idle described the special as 'a labour of love. It made me laugh. It was an exploration to see what I could come up with.' But even then, as Neil and John and friends continued to take 'Cheese & Onions' to the masses, he added, 'Neil seemed to forget that it was a joke. The Rutles is a parody of something that exists. You're constrained by what's happened. He seemed to have missed that point slightly.' But the point Eric seemed to have missed back then was that The Rutles universe, once released upon a planet of Fabs fans, was always going to have a life of its own. Like *ISIHAC*'s timeless pastime 'Mornington Crescent', the sheer glee of keeping the big joke going without letting on about something as dull as reality was always one of the greatest appeals of The Rutles in all forms; the universes of The Rutles and The Beatles have long since crossed over and back again – they were almost synonymous for Harrison. Fans have only (non-canonically) added to the lore over the years, going right back to the original fan club, with a whole Wiki-ful of entirely made-up Rutles facts, and online virtual shelves of Rutles albums that never were, a kind of musical fan fiction pieced together from old tracks by The Bonzos, Python, Innes, Halsall, Fataar, Halsey and others within the micro-genre of Beatley pastiches, from a reconstructed *Shabby Road* to Stig O'Hara solo smash *All Things Fall Down.* The Rutles belong to everyone – no matter how lawyers might decide whose bank accounts get trickled into.

The warmly-welcomed success of the Rutles tours did show Eric that there was a real appetite out there for Rutles fun, and he and Lorne Michaels decided to wrest the initiative back in March 2008 by staging *Rutlemania!* at Hollywood's Mods & Rockers Film Festival (admittedly a Lewis brainchild), with another short run shortly after in New York. This 'semi spectacular', marking the non-band's 30th anniversary, featured Beatles tribute act The Fab Four as The Rutles, both performing the hits and, as with the *Beatlemania* show, recreating key moments from what Bowie deemed their 'career', such as the time Dirk met a pissed Nasty, and helped him to get up. It was a raving success with the fans, but best of all was the accompanying Q&A which saw all four 'real' Rutles appearing in public together for the first time in... forever, as they realised when they took to the stage. Or as Idle put it, 'It's the first time that people have reunited before they united.' Everyone was on best bad behaviour as the old stories flowed – John plugged his Cambridge pub to an LA audience, Ricky said several words, and Neil and Eric grinned through it all, typically Buddha-like Neil in full 'Ego Warrior' mode semi-quoting Palin by insisting 'I think it's great, because you can't keep bickering about who killed who...' When asked to name a favourite Rutle song, Idle even ventured, 'I'm very fond of the songs on *Archaeology* – it was very interesting, very nice music, and Neil had continued along the path of inhabiting Nasty's skin, and his songwriting ability, so I like "Don't Know Why", one of my favourites, it's a beautiful song.'[397]

Besides a further Albert Hall crossover the next year, when Monty Python's 40th was marked by Idle's *Not The Messiah* oratorio, and Innes popped up as a Mexican, Dirk and Nasty shirked retirement in their own ways, leaving it to the Pre-Fab fans to make up their own stuff. 'Ron Nasty's Last Song' did follow in 2009, 'Imitation Song' recorded with Mickey Simmonds and launched on Innes' own website as an intended final word on the Rutles canon, 'Imagine' very much in mind:

Imitation song, Imitation tune, Imitation words,
Empty speech balloons…
Copycat ideas, Virtuality, Imitation games,
For you and me.
Poppycock-eyed world, We are family,
I'll make believe in you,
You make believe in me…[398]

While *Rutlemania* only ran briefly, however, The Rutles live show continued to tour for twenty years after the loss of The Rutles' greatest fan, Nasty, Barry and the other guys bringing those heady days of '64 to venues nationwide, leaving every provincial dance hall a happier place. Prior to the 2019 tour, Barry Wom even staged his own latest gamble on chart success, the grumpy ballad 'Enough!', backed by Wom Direction, and Liverpudlian 'Bonzo Dog Junior' Mike Livesley. Halsey was on a stick throughout the tour, but never missed a beat, with the beaming boss Neil out in front, head-duck firmly in place, and for many punters, all gleefully sharing the same big joke, it almost felt like the closest they would ever get to going out for the night, and seeing The Beatles play – or at least, two men who met some Beatles. After all those years of rights wrangling, Innes even found himself in a position to put out two limited edition albums: *The Rutles – Live + Raw* and *The Wheat Album*, a collection of *Archaeology* rehearsals, plus 'Imitation Song'.

The pleasure of enjoying cultural greatness at one comical remove was something Neil was always hugely keen to foster, and celebrate: 'I'd love the word "Rutle" to be a verb, because everybody's at it. To Rutle: "To copy or emulate someone you admire, especially in the music business." We are the apes who play with fire and aping is copying, that's what humans do. Rutle-ing is part of our DNA. The Beatles rutled Eddie Cochran, Duke Ellington, Gene Vincent and Elvis, and Mozart rutled whoever he heard playing the harpsichord. He thought, "I'm having some of that!" You do it because it excites you... We all rutle each other. We rutle our parents or our favourite uncles. And we've just got to learn to rutle only the good stuff and not the crap... Everybody is impressed by something, to be a musician. This is human. If you broaden it outside of music, rutling is also going on between children and their parents. Copying is aping and we are, let's face it, apes, and we're good at copying. So I'd like to spread the word that "rutling" is a verb, and because of that, The Rutles are the biggest band in the world.'

'And in the end', as Eric had it, 'the lunch you take is equal to the lunch you bake.'

GATHER ROUND ALL YOU CLOWNS

Each time Paul and Ringo have taken to the stage together since George's move into the next realm, the world has shaken a little with pleasure – the two survivors, the Butlin's-trained 'hams' who were always most comfortable before audiences, able to gee them up and make 'em laugh.

Both have *SNL* on their resumés, naturally, Paul debuting on the show in 1980 when John was still around to watch him, and returning numerous times over the years with albums to push, popping up in sketches with everyone from Chris Farley to Billy Crystal to Steve Martin and Martin Short (for whom he deigned to ineptly play the triangle in a Holiday Special), plus giving his best Camilla Parker Bowles impersonation for Weekend Update, and starring in the show's 40th anniversary bash. Ringo actually hosted the show in a 1984 episode which opened with the indignity of the host dressed up in Moptop gear, being auctioned off as a piece of '60s memorabilia at a bargain price. Both have also been lampooned more than once throughout the show's many years of Beatle-teasing which even included Malcolm McDowell as a wet-blanket cake-baking Lennon as far back as 1980 (surely also watched by John himself) while Bill Murray and particularly Dana Carvey have given their best McCartneys, as has guest host Alan Cumming, in a sketch dubiously entitled 'Fried Chicken Fields Forever'.

Again, the beknighted pair's readiness to have a laugh as their careers have mellowed provided a barrage of comedy oddity, from Ringo's joining of The Monkees for Pizza Hut, to his starring role as mad mathematician Fibonacci Sequins in a *Powerpuff Girls* special, incorporating an in-person cameo performing cute track 'I Wish I Was A Powerpuff Girl' – less incongruous when you realise the cartoon had already included a Beatle-themed episode, *Meet The Beat Alls*. Kid's TV continues to love referencing The Beatles – in 2016 Netflix launched its own CG series for pre-schoolers, *Beat Bugs,* which tells its own stories via the complete Lennon/McCartney/Harrison/Starr songbook, starting Fab fans early. Though not a regular in animation, Paul made a notable appearance as himself bursting out of a cake in another Netflix show, nihilistic cartoon *Bojack Horseman,* and made a return to his own animation with 1997's conservation-minded caper *Tropic Island Hum,* starring Wirral the Squirrel. He told the *Liverpool Echo,* 'In animation it's good to have a bit of a childlike quality about yourself and I certainly have, it's just something that's in me. I'm still fascinated by things that fascinated me as a kid – the passion for adventure, humour or romance. Sometimes people grow out of them, or they sort of force themselves out of them, but I've been lucky – because I've been involved in music I've not had to lose those qualities.'[399] This was most poignantly shown when Sir Paul finally achieved his life-long ambition in 2012, guest-starring in the sadly very last ever issue of *The Dandy,* 75 years after its launch, getting his fingers crushed by Desperate Dan. Grandfatherhood also inspired him, like so many stars, to turn to children's books, with a revival of Wirral's antics in 2006's *High In The Clouds* joined in 2019 by picture book *Hey Grandude!,* about a magical OAP able to whisk his grandkids anywhere in the world with a spin of a compass – both tales sprinkled with copious scouse twinkle.

Another eerie realisation of McCartney's ambitions came when he finally got to nab the precise daft movie cameo he suggested for himself after the release of *Broad Street*, and in a Disney movie, no less. For 2017's *Pirates of the Caribbean: Dead Men Tell No Tales,* he took a hint from George by playing pirate, cameoing as Uncle Jack, joker brother to Captain Jack Sparrow's ne'er-do-well father, Keith Richards. He revelled in donning dreads and a gigantic beard, discovered mouldering in his cell playing cards and singing that old Liverpool air, 'Maggie Mae' as his nephew is dragged by, sentenced to hang:

JACK:	Uncle Jack!
UNCLE JACK:	Jacky boy! How's it going?
JACK:	Can't complain really. You?
UNCLE JACK:	I've been waiting all morning in here for a beating. But the service is terrible.
JACK:	Shameful.
UNCLE JACK:	The oceans have turned to blood, better to stay on dry land where it's safe.
JACK:	I'm about to be executed on dry land.
UNCLE JACK:	Good point. Did I ever tell you the one about the skeleton?
JACK:	Yes you have, many times.
UNCLE JACK:	A skeleton goes into a bar, orders a beer and a mop! (PAUSE. DISTANT ISOLATED LAUGHTER.)
JACK:	Funny as ever!
GUARD:	Come on, let's go. (BEGINS TO DRAG JACK OFF)
UNCLE JACK:	Oh, if they disembowel you, ask for Victor, he's got the softest hands! Mention my name, they won't cut yer feet off![400]

Paul enthused on set, 'I've known Johnny a while, you know, I've always admired him as Jack Sparrow, and he said, "I'd love you to be in the next one." I said, "What, me? A pirate?" He said, "Yeah, you could do it, we'd have a lot of fun!" So he wrote me in, and I'm loving it! He's done me a lot of favours in the past, he's been in some of my music videos, so this is a way of repaying him. My character is Jack's uncle, who he was named after. And I'm an old pirate awaiting execution, just like he is – it runs in the family, I'm afraid to say. I started telling him about my Liverpool relatives, and I centred on this Uncle Jack of mine, and he said, "Well yeah, channel Uncle Jack!" So I told him a few stories, he always used to tell jokes, Jack was the family joke teller... I'm very impressed.'[401]

McCartney and Depp have a mutual friend in British comedy's most chameleonic geezer, Paul Whitehouse, and as a fan of *The Fast Show*, Macca collaborated with his namesake in 1999 on the video for *Run Devil Run* single 'Brown-Eyed Handsome Man'. The high-octane Buddy Holly cover soundtracked line-dancing from a whole host of minority groups led by Macca with Whitehouse and Charlie Higson's break-out characters, Ted & Ralph, the humble groundskeeper and his silently adoring aristocratic master, who were also seen scratching at the decks – a sight which Higson admits, 'Must have left many people around the world bemused. It was fun though.'

How McCartney felt about Whitehouse ultimately repaying this invitation to dance along by depicting a gang of soppy geriatric Beatles we don't know. The third series of his sketch show with Enfield, *Ruddy Hell! It's Harry & Paul*, featured The Silver Beatles – denizens of a bizarre alternate universe in which society is stuck in the age of deference, the boys never having touched drugs, Indian mysticism or anything at all controversial, but all reaching their autumn years as the same old loveable Moptops seen in *AHDN*, still chain-smoking but now chased by 'lovely wobbly randy old ladies'. Their modern melodies, including the theme tune explaining the set-up, were created, naturally, by Phil Pope: '*Yeah yeah, we're The Beatles, still having fun! / We never took no drugs, not even one! / We're still together, fifty years on – ooh!*'

'It was very strange,' Phil laughs, 'I'd been doing the music for *Harry & Paul* for a long time, as I did for *The Fast Show*, and this seemed a bit of a challenge, really. Harry said, "We want it to be pre-*Rubber Soul*, the innocent early Beatles, the four whacky, scally Beatles, not the ones who were experimenting with drugs and that sort of thing." The music had to reflect that, and Harry came down quite heavily on one song, which I said sounded like something Paul or John would write, but he insisted it sounded post-*Revolver*, he felt it sounded of a particular period, so I had to go away and re-write it, I had to do what the man in charge wanted! Again, it was quite simple, but it was still interesting music – there was one song, "Hello, Good Morning, Evening, Afternoon", a very silly idea, but it gave me a chance to do something with that sort of moving bass like "Can't Buy Me Love". I really enjoyed that, and did all the singing on it, though Lewis Macleod is a great impersonator. It was fun.'

Whitehouse at least avoided playing Paul himself, providing George to Harry's John, with impressionist Lewis Macleod as Paul and as Ringo, 'The Actor' Kevin Eldon. An occasional bandmate of Innes in charity outfit The Spammed, you would be hard put to find a bigger Beatles fan in the comedy universe than Eldon – even Liverpudlian musical comedian Mitch Benn, who formed an entire Edinburgh show and Radio 4 programme around his claim that *Mitch Benn Is The 37ᵗʰ Beatle*. Although the turn may have been that bit funnier when the great man was still with us, Kevin found he was able to deliver an uncanny impersonation of Sir George Martin at his most breezily expository, reeling off hours of studio secrets in his affable burr, even when, as in Linehan & Mathews' sketch show *Big Train*, he is being kidnapped by terrorists. In his own cartoonish sketch series *It's Kevin*, Hitler was shown discussing the crazy days of the Third Reich in exactly the same urbane tones, and the impersonation proved so irresistible that there was a reprise for *Harry & Paul*, Eldon doubling up in a studio scene to play both Starr and a no-nonsense Martin, ticking off Lennon for his skew-whiff tie, and daring to mention 'making love' in a song. Eldon wrote apologetically to Sir George about his impersonation, and only after his death was assured by Giles Martin that his dad had loved it.

Eldon's closest competitor for the title of biggest Beatlemaniac comedian may be Peter Scrafinowicz – a deeply vocally adept pastiche artiste, and Liverpool born and bred. His criminally undervalued *Peter Serafinowicz Show,* broadcast on BBC 2 in 2007,

347

made regular characters of the Fab Four, largely through the frame of 'Ringo Remembers', in which the laconic drummer gave his own 'ber-looody' side of the Beatles story. Serafinowicz played all four Beatles in the show and even earlier, in an online 'O! News' sketch about the 'Apple Vs Apple' furore, showing that John Lennon invented the iPod in 1969, but called it The BeatleBox – basically a fridge filled with vinyl. Then there were the *Let It Be* outtakes in which the band was so 'uptight' they couldn't move their bowels, even when they took to the roof of Apple to perform the song 'Go For A Poo' – only McCartney being relaxed enough to defeat constipation. All Serafinowicz's rutling needs were taken care of with impressive satirical verisimilitude by bombastic clown and recording artist Matt Berry, as were further numbers like Paul's festive tune 'Sexual Christmas Time' (so licentious that Ringo had no regrets about reporting his old friend and sending him to prison for indecency), John's big-headed first draft of 'Imagine', and Ringo's bid to write the Bond song for *Goldfinger* (which he only managed to finish seven years after the film's release). Working on a shoestring, the creative team's obsessive level of detail, from film grain to fake moustaches, added to the titular star's ability to mimic all four boys' speaking and singing voices, making for some of the most accomplished Beatle spoofs ever broadcast, even if it was all ultimately in service to a song about taking a dump. Serafinowicz has lent his Beatle voices to most of the media he's dipped into, as well as recording twisted covers like the minor-key dirge 'Bad Night Moonlight', similarly unhinged 'I'll Kill', and 'Blackbird' update 'Head Lice' – not to mention the 15-minute opus that was his 'A Full Day in the Life', with McCartney's section extended a further twelve minutes to take the tawdry protagonist right up to bedtime. His own BBC 6 Music show boasted an audio extract from the band's forgotten Columbo-style TV pilot:

RINGO: Hello, Beatle fans, it's time for 'Ringo Remembers'! Well, it was 1974, and the four of us hadn't seen each other for ages. Then NBC television rang us up and asked us if we'd like to be in a new TV show! Well, we all said

348

yes, on one condition: that we could all be detectives.

<u>GRAMS: 'HEY BULLDOG'-STYLE THEME.</u>

Got a crime, but you're outta time? And you can't reach Mr Policeman on the line? You'd better call The Beatles Murder Mystery Squad!

PAUL: So, what have we got here, lads?

JOHN: The victim's mid-thirties, female, caucasian, looks pretty well off to me.

PAUL: Estimated time of death?

RINGO: I'm on it!

GEORGE: There's no sign of any sexual motive.

PAUL: Thanks, George. Hey, wait a second!

JOHN: What is it, Paul?

PAUL: Isn't this Lady Ashcroft?

JOHN: What, you mean that wealthy heiress who disappeared on the cruise ship?

BACON: Yes, that's exactly who she is, The Beatles!

RINGO: Evening, Captain Bacon.

BACON: …And we're taking over this investigation now.

PAUL: Sorry, Captain, but if you take a look at this document signed by the Attorney General, you'll see that we have full jurisdiction!

BACON: Well, I guess this means we'd better start working together, The Beatles.

KID: Captain, The Beatles, you gotta come, it's Daddy, I think he's dead!

<u>GRAMS: MUSIC SWELLS</u>

RINGO: Poor old fella, looks like he could be just asleep.

JOHN: Yeah, if it wasn't for that hammer sticking out of his skull.

KID: Daddy's been depressed for some while, I think he must have committed suicide.

PAUL: I don't think so. And by the looks of him, he definitely knew his killer.

GEORGE: There's no sign of any sexual motive.

PAUL: Thanks, George. Hey lads, pick up your
               instruments, I think I feel a song coming on...
GRAMS: DUB OF THE BEATLES COVER OF 'ANNA'
JOHN: *(Sings) The person you are looking for, is standing*
               by the door, it was him...[402]

So famed was Serafinowicz's aptitude for summoning up the
Fab Four, he was a shoo-in for the voice/mo-cap cast announced
for Robert Zemeckis' CG *Yellow Submarine* reboot in 2010,
rumoured to be the new animated Paul. Utilising the latest
animation technology to stage a feast of eye candy returning us
to Pepperland in a sequel, maybe even using some of the concepts
which never made it to screen in 1968 and providing a fresh filmic
answer to Cirque du Soleil's hit international spectacular *Love*,
could be a project worth egging on. But as a stated remake, many
fans breathed a sigh of relief when the whole production foundered
a few years after teasing announcements: the original *Yellow
Submarine* is an undisputed animation masterpiece with zero need
for remaking.

It would have been far from the only cinematic oddity to play
fast and loose with the Beatle universe, however. Besides the steady
flow of biopics on TV and in cinema, ranging from the gloss of
Nowhere Boy to Christopher Eccleston's storming performance
opposite Andrew Scott's McCartney in *Lennon: Naked,* we've had
a further jukebox musical, *Across the Universe*. Masterminded by
those likely lads Clement & La Frenais alongside director Julie
Taymor, the soulful hotchpotch had a limited release in 2007 to
mixed reviews no better than the *Sgt Pepper* film, despite Eddie
Izzard's enthusiastic turn as Mr Kite. Tampering with real Beatle
history also took off with the 2013 TV play *Snodgrass*, based on a
novella by sci-fi writer Ian R Macleod. The Sky Arts short benefitted
from Ian Hart's admired depictions of a younger Lennon in *Backbeat*
and *The Hours and the Times* to imagine how a washed up fifty-year-
old John, who missed the toppermost of the poppermost entirely,
may have turned out (the answer: surly). It was adapted by comedy
writer David Quantick, who also explored the entire *White Album*
in his 2002 book *Revolution*.

Another alternate Fab Four provided a highpoint in 2007's US comedy *Walk Hard*: a biopic-blasting spoof of Johnny Cash flick *Walk the Line*. The fictional career of John C Reilly's melodramatic junkie heartthrob Dewey Cox was wide-ranging in its rock biopic targets, and in 1967 the washed-up Cox headed out to India to learn Transcendental Meditation techniques from the Maharishi, but was instantly turned on to acid by the most appallingly accented (and uncredited) Fab Four on film: Paul Rudd's John, Jack Black's Paul, Justin Long's George, and Jason Schwartzman's Ringo. The acid triggered a groovy animated *Yellow Submarine* spoof which quickly turned into a bad trip for Dewey. Far from loving and peaceful, this violent quartet couldn't stop scrapping, underlining the incongruous casting when Lennon snarled that McCartney was a 'fat cunt', provoking the tubby Paul to dispense with peace and love entirely and start a brawl. Despite his awful McCartney, Jack Black's comedy metal outfit Tenacious D once paid tribute to the real Beatles with a blistering acoustic rendition of the *Abbey Road* medley which has to be heard to be believed.

The biggest blockbuster wallow in the Beatles universe came in 2019 with Richard Curtis' *Yesterday*. As we've seen, sci-fi has toyed with the Beatlesque – even *Doctor Who*, besides featuring a snippet of the band playing 'Ticket To Ride' on the TARDIS Time-Space visualiser back in 1965, built an entire audio episode around the Doctor finding himself in a Beatle-less universe, in fifth Doctor adventure *Fanfare For The Common Men*. *Yesterday* takes a similar line, as with *Snodgrass*, of a world which never learned that All You Need Is Love back in the '60s. The rough story outline actually originated with Mackenzie Crook, the creator of pastoral sitcom *Detectorists* who had lent his hangdog comic presence to the video for McCartney's 'Dance Tonight'. This early treatment, known as *Cover Version*, was taken on by TV writer Jack Barth and subsequently rewritten from scratch by rom-com and sitcom legend Curtis, ultimately becoming the story of hapless and desperate musician Jack Malik (Himesh Patel) who crashes his bike one dark and stormy night and awakes to a world entirely ignorant of The Beatles canon, subsequently daring to claim their songs as his own, to internationally ecstatic acclaim.

Being fully supported by Apple (McCartney suggested the alternative title *Scrambled Eggs*), *Yesterday* had so many hallmarks of an official Beatle production, some firmly expected the two living Beatles to at least cameo. A sequence with the hero faced with his plagiarism by the host of *The Late Late Show* on CBS, Essex foghorn James Corden, teased an intervention by Ringo and a bare-footed Paul... but of course, it turned out to be 'all a dream'.

There wouldn't have been too much astonishment at the septuagenarian Twotles showing up in person, as both have shown they're happy to work with the latest comedy stars: nostalgia-addicted stand-up Peter Kay's 2008 talent show spoof *Britain's Got the Pop Factor... (And Possibly a New Celebrity Jesus Christ Soapstar Superstar Strictly on Ice)* featured Paul mentoring Kay's trans hero Geraldine McQueen on her performance of 'The Frog Song', while Ringo reprised his Thomas for Kay's Children In Need kid's TV hero singalong ('Hey Jude' included) the following year. Besides, national treasure Curtis' Beatle credentials are considerable. A life-long Beatle-lover, aged seven, little Richard watched the boys waving from the balcony of a Stockholm hotel, his third movie *Notting Hill* was inspired by a recurring childhood dream of revealing The Beatles from a cupboard for his sister's birthday present, and *Love Actually* turned 'All You Need Is Love' into as-good-as a traditional wedding hymn.

Skipping over the empty talk of a Fab-flavoured 1960's incarnation of Blackadder (who was allegedly to have managed a beat group featuring drummer 'Bald Rick'), Comic Relief, the fun fundraiser co-founded by Curtis, has featured Paul and Ringo in person – again, with Corden, who completed the hat trick in 2018 by nabbing McCartney for a jocular *Carpool Karaoke* around old Liverpool haunts while on the *Egypt Station* publicity trail. For Comic Relief's Red Nose Day in 2010, Corden was in full hooligan mode as *Gavin & Stacey*'s loud-mouthed plumber Smithy, charged with employing his wideboy skills to decide which celebrity from a bickering panel (including Gordon Brown, Dermot O'Leary, Roger Lloyd-Pack, Rupert Grint and more) should fly to Africa to present a special report. Having tearfully put himself forward for the task, backed by Justin Bieber on piano, a familiar voice was to burst Smithy's bubble:

PAUL: Biggest load of rubbish I've heard.

SMITHY: What?!

PAUL: You can't go!

SMITHY: Why? Because I'm not famous?

PAUL: No, because you're a bloater. People don't like tubbies in Africa. You know the argument, if they were eating less food themselves, no one would be starving.

DERMOT: That's a fair point.

ROGER: Hear hear!

RUPERT: I hate tubbies.

PAUL: I've kept quiet, I've heard what people have had to say, but you all know that the only person around this table who can go is me. I was in the biggest rock and roll band in the history of music.

SMITHY: That's a bit disrespectful in front of JLS.

PAUL: I've had a longer career than all of you put together, my music has touched millions of people around the world, and I am the last remaining Beatle.

RINGO: What about me?!

PAUL: I'm one of the last remaining Beatles.

RINGO: My God.[403]

With no cameos from the veteran rockers, the closest *Yesterday* came was to echo *Snodgrass* – director Danny Boyle's go-to actor Robert Carlyle making an uncredited appearance as a digitally manipulated (though still somewhat diminutive) OAP Lennon, in this universe a retired sailor tracked down by Malik living quietly in Ireland, ready to distribute wisdom to the guilt-riddled superstar in his darkest hour. In this fantasy, the senseless murder which threw Curtis and co on *Not*, defined by the writer as 'a tear in the universe', never happened. 'It was the scene that had the most meaning, and was in some ways the pivotal scene of the film,' he told *Empire*, but though the John sequence split audiences, there were originally to be three further Beatles appearances: 'When he first goes to Liverpool, I'd written a long scene where he just goes to a pub and he bumps into George and Ringo. It was, I hope, a sweet scene, and they were just two delightful, oldish men who'd once been in a band together. They bought him a couple of drinks, and it was all very sweet because they were clearly music enthusiasts who had never got any further. Happy people who loved music, like so many of us do, and formed a band or been in a pub band... At the very end Jack was going to move to the Isle of Wight, to a cottage, and you were going to hear outside his window someone saying, "Vera, Chuck, Dave!" There were going to be three dogs, and Paul was going to be walking them.'[404]

That just such a 'what if' living Lennon was also the focus of acclaimed 2015 novel *Beatlebone* by Kevin Barry shows that there was little unique about *Yesterday* except perhaps the scope of its devotion to the Fab Four. It undeniably took only the tiniest tug of one thread for the whole implausible concept to evaporate in a cloud of mild pedantry (how could Oasis exist in a world with no Beatles?), but there were comic highlights courtesy of Meera Syal and Sanjeev Bhaskar as Jack's parents, plus *SNL* graduate Kate McKinnon as an amoral manager, and the film's open-hearted, light-headed love-letter to The Beatles' music made it a box office smash, only failing to warm the cockles of the most passionate Ed-Sheeran-phobe. Curtis told *Time* magazine on release: 'I've always felt that what I was trying to do as a writer was to feel like The Beatles in trying to bring people joy. Even when you're dealing with serious things, try and do it in a way which had a joyful context. I wanted to write films that had the same effect on people as listening to a moderately good Beatles song'.[405]

As we near the 60th anniversary of Beatlemania, the Beatles brand has been broadened by further films, books, and even the hit rhythm-action videogame *The Beatles Rock Band,* and after Ron Howard's 2016 tour documentary *Eight Days A Week,* Peter Jackson is adding to the extended canon of official Beatle movies with a reworked 50th anniversary reconstruction of *Let It Be* designed to renovate the problematic documentary, returning the original light which accompanied the shade of the band's break up. It's certain to be far from the final release from Apple, even after that dreaded day when we do become unfortunate enough to find ourselves living in a Beatle-less word, for real.

Until that sad time, as further films, spoofs and re-packagings emerge, it would seem wise to stand up now and warn against losing sight of The Beatles' real X factor – that Liverpool *humour* with which practically everything they ever did was awash, that four-headed Fab Fools charm which marked them out as a totally unique monster in global culture, and which kept those four boys sane amid the whirlwind of Beatlemania. Some will, and do, take The Beatles far too seriously, just as many disdain 'comedy songs', when at its best, the hybrid artform of music with built-in laughter represents the very apex of entertainment: comedy and melody entwined.

It's unthinkable that The Beatles' legacy can ever be untangled from the tendrils of comedy history, when their idea of 'a good laff' is all part of what makes the band lighten hearts and gladden lives to this day. As Lennon observed, the world is a better place 'when we smile. If I smile at you, you're liable to smile back. If I don't, you're liable not to, or if I'm aggressive with you. And what we're trying to do is to smile to the world, you know, and hope that maybe they'll smile back. And then we'll all get laughing!'[406] – or to put it another way, 'Turned out nice again!'

How will it be when it's your turn to go?
Will you find a few famous last words to say?
Or will you simply fall asleep knowing that nothing in the universe
    ever really goes away?
Oh my, nobody wants to die, but it can hit you right between the eyes,
When you're talking about Friends at the End of the Line...[407]

There were times when John's comic avatar Neil Innes expressed a little discomfort at not being appreciated for his less humorous songwriting, but spreading happiness was always the fundamental purpose of his life and work, too – never mindlessly, and usually mind-expandingly. As he told the fans on the release of his troubled and unexpected swansong *Nearly Really* in September 2019, 'All I wanted was to share my songs – not spread gloom and disappointment.'[408] It's true that towards the end, the great man's patience was agonisingly tested by the UK's many political calamities, his Twitter stream awash with rage at the iniquities of Brexit Britain. But when a punter came to see him really express himself, whether solo or in ersatz Bonzo or Rutles company, he left them feeling better for the warming embrace of his daft and/or deep music.

Thousands of fans counted themselves lucky for the personal connection Neil allowed them to feel they had with him, each devotee glorying in the illusion of exclusivity as he kindly gave them his precious time – and backstage at one date on the final Rutles live tour of 2019, he was happy to plunge into the Rutles story yet again: '…Clearly it was getting silly, and something sillier had to be done! The Rutles came about because it was *time*. The Beatles broke up, and broke millions of hearts, and people were depressed! And it seemed a funny way of doing something about it, to ease some of the pain, because real life happens and things can't work at that level of pressure for too long. The timing was right, and it took no imagination at all – after Lorne had shown that clip of The Rutles, the mailbags were just bulging… it was a labour of love, and everybody involved in it knew what to do.' Talk of the need for a fresh history of The Beatles as a comedy phenomenon had the great man fully charged up: 'Include me, I'll do anything I can – The Beatles *were* funny! And you won't be wasting my time, because I am a Beatles fan. The songs were great, and they were really funny… A lot of people think of George as this terribly spiritual person, but he had a wickedly dark sense of humour. Always carried a spare uke!' We jammed a little on 'My Little Ukulele', deepest thanks were given for Neil's kindness, and a promise to pick up the conversation at a later date presaged a reluctant goodbye.

He was such a solid, cheery, beery, active, 'hail, well met' fellow, as irrepressibly alive in mind as in body, nobody dreamed that such a promise wouldn't be fulfilled. Two days before the start of the 2020s, Neil Innes collapsed en route to his home in France, entirely out of the blue – painlessly, suddenly, leaving all of us who love him, Rutles, Bonzos and Beatles fans the planet over, truly shocked, and stunned. Nobody wanted or expected the final punchline to the big joke to come so soon, but perhaps it settles once and for all who truly kept the Pre Fab-Four flame burning. With Nasty finally accepting a teaching post in Australia, The Rutles story, like The Beatles story, is complete – in anything but tribute form. And so, dear friends, we just have to carry on.

In Neil's memory, the joy of rutling will continue for as long as the conceptual combo's inspiration is celebrated, as long as artists continue to inspire each other, and as long as bubbles need to be burst with affectionate mockery. The Rutles were borne of a loving desire to prevent us all drowning in excess seriousness, and there will never be a time that becomes unnecessary. As Neil observed, with that broad, gnomic smile: 'FAB FOOLS: We're all one, y'know?'

THE END

APPENDICES

THE BEATLES ON SCREEN

Around The Beatles (ITV/Rediffusion, Rec 28 Apr, TX 6 May 1964)
Hour-long music show featuring PJ Proby, Cilla Black, Millie, Long John Baldry and Sounds Incorporated, topped by The Beatles performing an extract from Shakespeare's *A Midsummer Night's Dream* with Trevor Peacock and Andre Tayir. Produced by Jack Good.

A Hard Day's Night (United Artists, released 6 Jul 1964)
A typical day or two in the company of Britain's biggest band, as they try to record a TV appearance amid a host of brickbats, pretentious creatives and Paul's 'mixer' grandfather. *Featuring Wilfrid Brambell, Norman Rossington, John Junkin, Victor Spinetti, Anna Quayle, Deryck Guyler and Richard Vernon. Written by Alun Owen, directed by Dick Lester, produced by Walter Shenson.*
50th Anniversary Restoration Blu-Ray: Second Sight 2014

Help! (United Artists, released 29 Jul 1965)
Ringo accidentally accepts the sacrificial ring of a homicidal Eastern cult who worship the Goddess Khaili, and with the help of his friends, has to escape his fate, and the attentions of a mad scientist avowed to steal the ring for his own nefarious ends. The adventure takes them from the Alps to the Bahamas, with danger never far behind. *Featuring Eleanor Bron, Leo McKern, Victor Spinetti, Roy Kinnear and Patrick Cargill. Written by Marc Behm and Charles Wood, directed by Dick Lester, produced by Walter Shenson.*
Blu-Ray: Universal 2013

*

The Beatles (ABC TV, TX 25 Sep 1965-21 Oct 1967)
Featuring Paul Frees, Lance Percival Julie Bennett and Carol Corbett.
Written by Dennis Marks, Jack Mendelsohn, Heywood King and Bruce
Howard, produced by Al Brodax.
Season 1 (1965) 1. *A Hard Day's Night / I Want To Hold Your Hand*: The
boys meet a monster in a Transylvanian castle. / An underwater
expedition to help an Octopus in love. **2.** *Do You Want To Know A Secret
/ If I Fell*: In Dublin, the Beatles attract a female leprechaun. / John's
brain is desired by Dr Dora Florahyde, for her own monster's use. **3.**
Please Mr Postman / Devil In Her Heart: The boys are out of money after
Ringo spends everything on fifteen rings / A Transylvanian witch wants
Ringo for a husband. **4.** *Not A Second Time / Slow Down*: The Beatles
avoid screaming girls and snapping crocodiles on an African safari. /
It's gold-rush fever for the band at Ringo Ravine. **5.** *Baby's In Black /
Misery*: Paul is kidnapped by Professor Psycho as a suitor for a
vampiress. / A vampire hunts down the boys as they visit a wax
museum. **6.** *You've Really Got A Hold On Me / Chains*: The boys get a
flat tyre in Africa, and turn to a witch doctor for help. / Ringo dreams
himself as The Bounty's Captain Bligh. **7.** *I'll Get You / Honey Don't*:
Alan Watermain encourages the Beatles to hunt a lion in Africa. /
Ringo is inveigled into riding a wild bull. **8.** *Anytime At All / Twist And
Shout*: On tour in France, the boys imagine themselves as Musketeeers.
/ The Beatles help inspire a young artist on a gallery visit. **9.** *Little Child
/ I'll Be Back*: A young Native American shows that girls are as good
as boys by tracking The Beatles. / The boys foil a robbery – the golden
guitar presented to them by the Mayor of Texas! **10.** *Long Tall Sally /
I'll Cry Instead*: The Beatles stay at a castle for the night, and Ringo and
John don suits of armour for a scrap. / George contracts 'autographitis'
of the hand in Japan, and attempts a karate cure. **11.** *I'll Follow The Sun
/ When I Get Home*: A notorious highwayman helps the boys when their
car breaks down. / In Notre Dame, the band meets Quasimodo. **12.**
Everybody's Trying To be My Baby / I Should Have Known Better: Back in
Japan, the Beatles are mistaken for ancient ancestors. / The band play
the Coliseum in Rome. **13.** *I'm A Loser / I Wanna Be Your Man*: Ringo's
time as a Hollywood stuntman lands him in hospital. / Back in Rome,
the boys buy a statue of the Goddess of Music. **14.** *Don't Bother Me /
No Reply*: Spies try to steal The Beatles' songbook. / A jewel thief called
Anyface disguises himself as Paul: which is the real one? **15.** *I'm Happy
Just To Dance With You / Mr Moonlight*: Paul wins a dancing bear called

Bonnie in a Roman festival. / Prof Ludwig von Brilliant teaches the boys about eclipses. **16.** *Can't Buy Me Love / It Won't Be Long*: John unwittingly agrees to marry the daughter of a Native American Chieftain. / George shrinks when swimming in a magical Japanese pond and is mistaken for a doll. **17.** *Anna / I Don't Want To Spoil The Party*: Paul is lured into the Japanese ghost ship 'Anna'. / John wants to go to a museum, the others sneak off for fun in New York. **18.** *Matchbox / Thank You Girl*: John encourages the others to stay in a state-of-the-art caravan. / When Brian tells them they're too fat, the boys are locked away, but sneak out to a French bakery. **19.** *From Me To You / Boys*: George takes part in a surfing duel in Hawaii. / The Beatles get mixed up with the Mr Hollywood contest. **20.** *Dizzy Miss Lizzy / I Saw Her Standing There*: George partners with a girl called Lizzy in a boat race. / John is challenged to a duel by a jealous lover in Madrid. **21.** *What You're Doing / Money*: Ringo is pursued by a gypsy girl on a fishing trip. / Ringo is followed when John puts him in charge of the group's cash. **22.** *Komm Gib Mir Deine Hand / She Loves You*: The band climbs a mountain in the Swiss Alps. / The Beatles try to save a girl imprisoned on a ship, until her boyfriend gets the wrong idea. **23.** *Bad Boy / Tell Me Why*: The band tries to comfort a runaway boy who wants to become a Beatle. / Ringo enters a donkey in a Spanish race. **24.** *I Feel Fine / Hold Me Tight*: Actor Dick Dashing puts Paul through his paces as a Hollywood actor. / George and Ringo visit the Statue of Liberty, where they believe a mad bomber will strike. **25.** *Please Please Me / There's A Place*: Ringo turns matador in Madrid, but it's okay: the bull is just John and Paul. / John helps Mr Marvelous, a trained ape, to escape his showbiz prison. **26.** *Roll Over Beethoven / Rock And Roll Music*: An elephant called Beethoven takes a shine to Paul. / The band are hired as a string quartet at a Duke's palace. **Season 2 (1966) 27.** *Eight Days A Week / I'm Looking Through You*: Paul stands in for actor and great kisser, Lips Lovelace. / A ghost steals Ringo's body in an Egyptian pyramid. **28.** *Help! / We Can Work It Out*: Paul pursues art thief Jacques Le Zipper up the Eiffel Tower. / Superstitious George meets con man 'The Lucky Wizard'. **29.** *I'm Down / Run For Your Life*: Ringo accidentally upsets a vat of wine on a distillery tour. / Ringo dreams of the days of Louis XVI on a trip to Versailles. **30.** *Drive My Car / Tell Me What You See:* The Beatles aid a couple to win an old jalopy race. / The Man of a Thousand Faces encourages the boys to try some new personas. **31.** *I Call Your Name / The Word*: Ringo's frog Bartholomew is offered a movie deal, but where is he? / When they view the unveiled faces of an Egyptian harem, the boys are doomed unless they can recall the password, 'Love'. **32.** *All My Loving / Day Tripper*: The band learn how to charm an Indian tiger. / An alien beauty tries to kidnap the band. **33.** *Nowhere Man / Paperback Writer:* The boys interrupt the peace of a cave-dwelling hermit. / John, Paul and George dream up unlikely stories of how they met Ringo. **Season 3 (1967) 34.** *Penny Lane / Strawberry Fields:* The boys plan to foil a bank raid to out-do heartthrob James Blonde. / The band cheer up a group of orphans with their music. **35.** *And Your Bird Can Sing / Got To Get You Into My Life:* The band are tracking a rare bird: the green double-breasted tropical worsted! / In India, the boys learn the ability to separate their souls from their bodies. **36.** *Good Day Sunshine / Ticket To Ride:* The Beatles' music turns a rainy day at Carney Island into sunshine. / Ringo's hobby of 'collecting birds' has to be stopped when it's revealed he means 'girls'. **37.** *Taxman / Eleanor Rigby:* Knocked out en route to the bank, the boys dream of Robin Hood. / The band sings a song to educate rude kids who insist old lady Eleanor is a witch. **38.** *Tomorrow Never Knows / I've Just Seen A Face:* The boys fall down a well and find themselves in a strange new land. / Ringo is sent to a haunted house to get his singing voice 'scared' back into him. **39.** *Wait / I'm Only Sleeping:* The Beatles help the Prince of Krapotkin to save his girlfriend from the villainous Prime Minister. / John dreams of life in Arthurian times, singing to a sleepy dragon.

The Music Of Lennon & McCartney (Granada, Rec 2 Nov, TX 16 Dec 1965)

Showcase of Beatle songs presented by John & Paul and featuring Cilla Black, Marianne Faithfull, Peter & Gordon, Esther Phillips, Peter Sellers, Billy J Kramer, Lulu, Henry Mancini and The George Martin Orchestra. *Produced by Johnnie Hamp.*

Magical Mystery Tour (BBC 2, TX 26 Dec 1967)

Richie Starkey and his fat Auntie Jessie are among the strange characters enjoying an increasingly bizarre surprise charabanc trip down to the West Country. Featuring Jessie Robins, Ivor Cutler, Derek Royle, Victor Spinetti, Miranda Forbes and The Bonzo Dog Doo-Dah Band. *Written and directed by The Beatles, produced by Gavrik Losey and Denis O'Dell.*
Blu-Ray: Apple 2012

Yellow Submarine (United Artists, released 17 Jul 1968)

Four Liverpool lads embark on a mission in a flying submarine to save the colourful world of Pepperland from the villainous, fun-spoiling Blue Meanies, aided by Captain Fred and the Nowhere Man, Jeremy Hillary

Boob Phd. *Featuring John Clive, Geoffrey Hughes, Peter Batten, Paul Angelis, Dick Emery and Lance Percival. Written by Lee Minoff, Jack Mendelsohn, Erich Segal and Roger McGough, directed by George Dunning, produced by Al Brodax.* **Blu-Ray: EMI 2012**

Let It Be (United Artists, released 14 May 1970)
Documentary covering the supposed creation of a Beatles TV special. *Directed by Michael Lindsay-Hogg, produced by Neil Aspinall. Re-edited and re-mastered as Get Back, for Apple Corps/Wingnut/Disney by Peter Jackson, 2021.*

Eight Days A Week (StudioCanal/PolyGram, released 15 Sep 2016)
The Beatles' touring documentary, directed by Ron Howard.
Blu-Ray: Noble Entertainment 2016

THE COMPLEAT RUTLES

Rutland Weekend Television (BBC 2) S1 E3 (TX 26 May 1975) 'Ron Lennon' pops up to sing a snatch of 'Good Times Roll'. **S2 E1 (TX 12 Nov 1976)** The first mention of the Pre-Fab Four, and the debut of 'I Must Be In Love'.
The Rutland Weekend Songbook (BBC Records 1976) 'I Must Be In Love' / 'The Children of Rock and Roll'.
The Rutles: All You Need Is Cash (NBC TX 22 Mar / BBC 2 TX 27 Mar 1978) The full story of the Pre-Fab Four, Dirk, Stig, Nasty and Barry, presented by Melvin Hall.
    Featuring Eric Idle, Neil Innes, Ricky Fataar, John Halsey, Gwen Taylor, Terence Bayler, Henry Woolf, Michael Palin, Barry Cryer, Roger McGough, Frank Williams, Bill Murray, Gilda Radner, Dan Aykroyd, John Belushi, Ronnie Wood, George Harrison, Bianca Jagger, Mick Jagger and Paul Simon. *Written by Eric Idle, with music by Neil Innes, Directed by Gary Weis and Eric Idle, Produced by Lorne Michaels, Gary Weis and Craig Kellem.*
The Rutles (Warner Bros 1978) Soundtrack album, all songs by Lennon/McCartney/Innes. Recorded by Neil Innes, Ollie Halsall, Ricky Fataar and John Halsey, orchestrated by John Altman, produced by Steve James.
SINGLES: 'I Must Be In Love' & 'Cheese & Onions' /'With A Girl Like You'; 'Let's Be Natural'/'Piggy In the Middle'; 'I Must Be In Love'/ 'Doubleback Alley'

DIRK & STIG: 'Ging Gang Goolie'/'Mr. Sheene' (EMI 1978)

The Rutles 12" EP (Warner Bros 1978)

The Rutles Archaeology (EMI/Virgin 1996) Non-soundtrack album, all songs by Innes. Recorded by Neil Innes, Ricky Fataar and John Halsey with archive material featuring Ollie Halsall, with Mickey Simmonds, Malcolm Foster, Dougie Boyle and Bernie Holland, orchestrated by John Altman, mixed by Steve James, produced by Neil Innes.

The Rutles 2: Can't Buy Me Lunch (Warner Bros DVD 2002) Eric Idle's follow-up mockumentary, featuring Catherine O'Hara, Robin Williams, Steve Martin, Jimmy Fallon, Carrie Fisher, Billy Connolly, David Bowie, Garry Shandling, Tom Hanks, Salman Rushdie and many more. Directed by Eric Idle, Produced by Eric Idle and Lorne Michaels.

The Rutles Live + Raw (East Central One, 2014) Live CD available online.

The Wheat Album (Neil Innes Music Ltd. 2018) CD of live and rare tracks available at live gigs.

The Rutles were conceived and created by Eric Idle.

BIBLIOGRAPHY

Adams, Douglas, *Life, the Universe and Everything,* Pan 1981; *Austin Chronicle,* November 1996; Axelrod, Mitchell, *Beatletoons,* Wynn Publishing 1999; Badman, Keith, *The Beatles: The Dream Is Over,* Omnibus Press 2001; Badman, Keith, *The Beatles After The Break Up 1970-2000,* Omnibus Press 2000; Barrow, Tony, *PS I Love You,* Mirror Books 1982; *The Beatles Anthology,* Cassell & Co. 2000; *Billboard,* June 1999; Bramwell, Tony, *Magical Mystery Tours,* Robson Books 2003; Burke, John, *A Hard Day's Night,* Pan 1964; Chapman, Graham, *OJRIL,* 1998; *Graham Crackers,* 1997; Davies, Hunter, *The Beatles,* Heinemann 2002; Davies, Hunter (Ed), *John Lennon Letters, The,* W&N 2012; Doggett, Peter; *You Never Give Me Your Money: The Beatles After the Breakup,* 2011; Forsyth, Bruce, *Strictly Bruce,* Transworld 2015; Giuliano, Geoffrey, *Lost Lennon Interviews,* Omnibus Press 1998; *Glass Onion: The Beatles In Their Own Words,* 1999; *The Hapless Dilettante,* 1970s; Harrison, George, with Derek Taylor, *I Me Mine,* W&N 2002; Harry, Bill, *The Beatles Volume 4: Beatlemania: An Illustrated Filmography,* Virgin Books, 1984; Hieronymus, Robert Richard, *Inside The Yellow Submarine,* KP Books 2003; Hine, Al, *Help!,* Mayflower 1965; Hogg, James & Sellers, Robert, *Hello, Darlings!,* Transworld 2013; Idle, Eric, *Always Look on the Bright Side of Life,* Orion 2018; *Kettering magazine; Liverpool Echo* May 2013; Lahr, John, *The Joe Orton Diaries,*

2013; Lane, Carla, *Someday I'll Find Me,* Anova 2006; Lennon, Cynthia, *John,* Hodder & Stoughton 2005; Lennon, John, *In His Own Write & A Spaniard In The Works,* Jonathan Cape/Pimlico 1997; *The Lennon Play: In His Own Write* (With Adrienne Kennedy and Victor Spinetti), Simon & Schuster 1968; *Skywriting By Word Of Mouth* (with Yoko Ono), Pan Books 1986; Lewis, Roger, *The Life and Death of Peter Sellers,* Arrow, 1995; Lewisohn, Mark, *All These Years Vol 1: Tune In,* Little Brown 2013; Lewisohn, Mark, *The Complete Beatles Recording Sessions,* Bounty Books 1988; *The Daily Mail,* 1968; Martin, George with Jeremy Hornsby, *All You Need Is Ears,* St. Martin's Press 1979; *Melody Maker* 1964; Miles, Barry, *Paul McCartney: Many Years From Now,* Secker & Warburg, 1997; *Daily Mirror,* 1963; *MOJO magazine,* October 1999, Winter 2000, July 2001, Beatlemania/Psychedelia special editions; Morgan, David (ed), *Monty Python Speaks!* 1999; *NME Originals: The Beatles* 2002 *The Beatles Solo* 2005; *New York Times* 1972, 1978, 1984; Norman, Phil, *John Lennon: The Life,* HarperCollins 2008; *New York Times* 1984; Norman, Phil, *Paul McCartney: The Biography,* W&N 2016; *The Wit of The Beatles,* Michael O'Mara Books 2005; O'Dell, Denis with Neaverson, Bob, *At The Apple's Core,* Peter Owen Books 2002; *The Observer,* 1968; Ono, Yoko: *Grapefruit,* Simon & Schuster 2000; Orton, Joe, *Head To Toe,* Methuen 2001; *Up Against It,* Grove 1979; Owen, Alun, *Three TV Plays,* Jonathan Cape 1961; Palin, Michael, *The Python Years,* 2006; Payn, Graham, Morley, Sheridan, *The Noël Coward Diaries,* 2000; *Playboy magazine,* 1965, 1980; *The Pythons On The Pythons,* Orion 2003; *Q magazine* 1998; Randall, Lucien and Welch, Chris, *Ginger Geezer,* 4th Estate 2001; Reiter, Roland, *The Beatles On Film,* Transaction Publishers 2008; *Rolling Stone magazine,* 1979; Ryan, Patrick, *How I Won The War,* Corgi 1967; Sellers, Robert, *Very Naughty Boys: The Amazing True Story of Handmade Films,* Titan 2013; Sheff, David, *The Last Interview,* Pan Books 2001; *Shindig magazine,* 2000; Shipper, Mark, *Paperback Writer,* Ace Books 1980; *Sight and Sound,* 1968; Soderbergh, Steven, *Getting Away With It,* Faber 1998; Sounes, Howard, *FAB: An Intimate Life of Paul McCartney,* HarperCollins 2010; Southern, Terry, *The Magic Christian,* Penguin 1969; Spinetti, Victor, *Up Front,* Portico 2006; Starr, Ringo, *Postcards From The Boys,* Cassell 2005; Taylor, Alistair, *A Secret History,* John Blake 2001; Taylor, Derek, *As Time Goes By,* Faber 1973, 2018; Tibballs, Geoff, *The Secret Life of Sooty,* Interpret Publishing 1990; *Time Out; Uncut magazine,* October 2015; Wenner, Jan, *Lennon Remembers,* 1971; White, Charles , *The Life and Times of Little Richard,* 1994; Wilk, Max, *Yellow Submarine,* Signet 1968.

SELECTED AUDIO & VIDEOGRAPHY & LINKS

439 Golden Greats – Never Mind The Originals 1981; *Alas Smith & Jones,* BBC 1987; *Arena: Magical Mystery Tour Revisited,* BBC 1 2012; *Arena: Produced by George Martin,* BBC 1 2011; *Aspel & Co,* ITV 1988; *BBC Radio 2 Beatles Pop-Up Station* Summer 2019; *The Beatles Anthology,* Apple 1995; *Big Night Out,* ABC 1964; *Big Train,* BBC 2 1998; *Book Week,* BBC Radio 1964; *Bread,* BBC 1 1988; *Comic Relief Red Nose Day 2010; Desert Island Discs,* BBC Radio 4 1980; *Kenny Everett's Monte Carlo Radio Show* 1971; *The Frost Programme,* ITV 1967; *Great Lives: Victor Spinetti,* BBC 1 Wales 2011; *Harry & Paul,* BBC 2 2010; *The Hitchhiker's Guide to the Galaxy: Tertiary Phase,* BBC Radio 4 2006; *ISIRTA,* BBC Radio 2; *Inner-View,* KMET Radio, Ringo Starr Interview with Elliot Mintz, 1976; *Late Scene Extra,* Granada 1963; *The Magic Christian* 1969; *Monty Python's Flying Circus,* BBC 1969-74; *The Morecambe & Wise Show,* ATV 1964; *National Lampoon's Radio Dinner,* MCA 1972; *Not Only… But Also,* BBC 2 1964, 66; *Parkinson,* BBC 1 1971; *Release,* BBC 2 1968; *Pirates of the Caribbean: Dean Men Tell No Tales,* Disney/Jerry Bruckheimer 2017; *The Return of Bruno,* HBO 1987; *Rowan & Martin's Laugh-In,* NBC 1970; *Rutland Weekend Television Christmas Special,* BBC 2 1975; *The Rutland Weekend Television Songbook,* BBC Records 1976; *The South Bank Show: McCartney's Broad Street,* ITV 1984; *Radio Active: What's News?,* BBC Radio 4 6 October 1981; *Ringo,* NBC 1978; *Rock Profile,* UK Play 1999; *Rule of Three Podcast; Saturday Night Live,* NBC 1976; *The Peter Serafinowicz Show,* BBC 6Music 2010; *The Smothers Brothers Comedy Hour,* CBS 1968; *Something About The Beatles; Songs for Swingin' Sellers,* Parlophone 1959; *Spitting Image,* Central TV 1994; *Tomorrow with Tom Snyder,* NBC 1982; *The Tonight Show with Jimmy Fallon,* NBC 2014; *Up Against It,* BBC Radio 3 1997; *WTF With Marc Maron:* Eric Idle & John Cleese; *Withnail & I,* HandMade Films 1987; *Yesterday,* Working Title 2019

The Beatles Official: thebeatles.com; The Beatles Bible: beatlesbible.com; Candy Jar Books: candy-jar.co.uk; Eric Idle: ericidle.com; I Am The Eggpod: iamtheeggpod.com; Jem Roberts: jemroberts.com; Neil Innes: neilinnes.media; Rule of Three Podcast: ruleofthreepod.com; The Rutles Official: therutles.com; The Rutles Unofficial: therutles.org; A History of The Rutles: rutlemania.org; Something About The Beatles: somethingaboutthebeatles.com; Some Of The Corpses Are Amusing: sotcaa.org

While every effort has been made to contact copyright holders, the author and publisher would be grateful for information about any material where they have been unable to trace the source, and would be glad to make amendments in further editions.

REFERENCES

1   *As Time Goes By,* Taylor, Derek, 1973
2   *John Lennon: The Life,* Norman, Philip, 2008
3   *George Formby: The Emperor of Lancashire,* BBC Radio 2 1991
4   *The Beatles,* Davies, Hunter, 1969
5   *The Beatles Anthology,* Cassell & Co., 2000
6   *All You Need Is Ears,* Martin, George, 1979
7   *Anthology*
8   *New York Times,* Lennon, John, 1972
9   *AYNIE*
10   *All These Years Vol 1: Tune In*, Lewisohn, Mark, 2013
11   *AYNIE*
12   *Getting Away With It,* Soderbergh, Steven, 1998
13   *AYNIE*
14   *MYFN*
15   *The Beatles*
16   *MYFN*
17   *The Beatles*
18   *New York Times*
19   *Mersey Beat* magazine
20   *Anthology*
21   *John Lennon Letters,* Davies, Hunter (ed), 2012
22   *Desert Island Discs,* BBC Radio 4 1980
23   *MYFN*
24   *Anthology*
25   *The Beatles*
26   *The Beatles*
27   *Anthology*
28   *Lennon Remembers*
29   *Glass Onion: The Beatles In Their Own Words,* Giuliano, Geoffrey, 1999

30   *Anthology*
31   *MOJO*
32   *Beatles, The*, Davies, Hunter, Heinemann 2002
33   *Songs for Swinging Sellers*, 1959
34   *Anthology*
35   *The Last Interview (Playboy)*, Sheff, David, 2001
36   *John Lennon Letters*
37   *John Lennon Letters*
38   *The Life and Death of Peter Sellers*, Lewis, Roger, 1995
39   *ATY Vol 1*
40   *Anthology*
41   *Arena: Produced By George Martin*, BBC Four 2011
42   Selina Scott interview, 1988
43   Radio Doncaster, 1963
44   *Beatles For Sale* liner notes, 1964
45   *Life and Times of Little Richard, The*, White, Charles, 1994
46   *John Lennon: The Life*
47   *The Beatles: Off The Record*, Badman, Keith, 2000
48   *The Beatles at the BBC*
49   *The Beatles*
50   *A Hard Day's Night* DVD, 2002
51   *Anthology*
52   *Anthology*
53   *Late Scene Extra*, Granada 1963
54   *The Morecambe & Wise Show*, ATV 1964
55   *MOJO Beatlemania Special Edition*, 2002
56   *Anthology*
57   *Magical Mystery Tours*, Bramwell, Tony, 2003
58   *PS I Love You*, Barrow, Tony, 1982
59   *NME* 1963
60   *MYFN*
61   *Strictly Bruce*, Forsyth, Bruce, 2015
62   *The Beatles*
63   *Big Night Out*, ABC 1964
64   *Beatles On Film, The*, Reiter, Roland, 2008.
65   *AHDN* DVD, 2002
66   *GAWI*
67   *Three TV Plays*, Owen, Alun, 1961
68   *Beatlemania: An Illustrated Filmography*, Harry, Bill, 1984
69   *AHDN* DVD
70   *MOJO Beatlemania SE*
71   *Many Years From Now*
72   *Beatlemania*
73   *AHDN* DVD
74   *Uncut*, October 2015
75   *MOJO Beatlemania SE*
76   *AHDN* DVD

77   *AHDN* DVD
78   *AHDN* DVD
79   *AHDN* novelisation, Burke, John Pan 1964
80   *The Beatles*
81   *Anthology*
82   *In His Own Write / A Spaniard In The Works,* Lennon, John, 1997
83   *Melody Maker,* 1964
84   *Release,* BBC 2 1968
85   *NME* 1964
86   *IHOW / ASITW*
87   *IHOW / ASITW*
88   *World of Books,* BBC Home Service
89   *IHOW*
90   *AHDN* DVD
91   *Uncut*
92   *Anthology*
93   *Around the Beatles,* Rediffusion 1964
94   Unidentified US Radio interview 1964
95   *IHOW*
96   *NME Originals*
97   *NME Originals*
98   *Many Years From Now*
99   *GAWI*
100 *GAWI*
101 *Help!* DVD, 2005
102 *Help!* DVD
103 *MOJO Psychedelic SE,* 2002
104 *Help!* DVD
105 *The Last Interview*
106 *Anthology*
107 *MYFN*
108 *Help!* DVD
109 Unidentified 1964 interview
110 *AHDN* DVD
111 *MYFN*
112 *Help!* DVD
113 *Help!,* Hine, Al, 1965
114 *Help!* DVD
115 *Daily Mail,* 2006
116 *Noël Coward Diaries, The,* Payn, Graham, Morley, Sheridan 2000
117 *Anthology*
118 *ASITW*
119 *IHOW / ASITW*
120 *NME*
121 *The Sun*
122 *Beatlemania*
123 *MOJO*

124   *MOJO*
125   *Help!* DVD
126   *Beatletoons,* Axelrod, Mitchell 1999
127   *Beatletoons*
128   *The Beatles,* ABC TV 1965
129   *MYFN*
130   *Beatletoons*
131   *Beatletoons*
132   *Beatletoons*
133   *Beatletoons*
134   *The Beatles on Film*
135   *NME Originals: The Beatles Solo* 2005
136   *Billboard,* June 1999
137   *Anthology*
138   *MYFN*
139   *MYFN*
140   *Hello, Darlings!* Hogg, James & Sellers, Robert 2013
141   *NOBA* 1966
142   *NOBA* 1966
143   *Assignment: Hollywood,* Robbins, Fred US radio interview 1966
144   *At The Apple's Core,* O'Dell, Denis with Neaverson, Bob 2002
145   *How I Won The War* DVD, 2019
146   *GAWI*
147   *MYFN*
148   *Complete Beatles Recording Sessions,* Lewisohn, Mark, 1988
149   *NME* 1966
150   *MOJO*
151   *Anthology*
152   *The Beatles Christmas Flexidisc 1967*
153   *MYFN*
154   *The Beatles*
155   *Arena*
156   *Anthology*
157   *Hello Darlings*
158   *Orton Diaries, The,* Lahr, John (ed) 2013
159   *Orton Diaries*
160   *Orton Diaries*
161   *Up Against It* first draft, courtesy of the University of Leicester Joe
      Orton collection
162   *Orton Diaries*
163   *GAWI*
164   *Head to Toe and Up Against It,* Orton, Joe, 1998
165   *Rolling Stone*
166   *Anthology*
167   *MYFN*
168   *MYFN*
169   *ATAC*

170   *Scene & Heard,* 1967
171   *MYFN*
172   *MYFN*
173   *Anthology*
174   *Anthology*
175   *Magical Mystery Tour* DVD 2012
176   *The Beatles*
177   *Anthology*
178   *MYFN*
179   MOJO
180   *ATAC*
181   *MOJO*
182   *MYFN*
183   *Magical Mystery Tour* DVD, 2012
184   *Ginger Geezer,* Randall, Lucien and Welch, Chris 2001
185   *MOJO*
186   *MOJO*
187   *Ginger Geezer*
188   *Anthology*
189   *MMT* DVD,
190   *MMT* DVD
191   *MMT* DVD
192   *MYFN*
193   *Anthology*
194   *ATAC*
195   *MMT* DVD
196   *A Secret History,* Taylor, Alistair 2001
197   © The Chris Sievey Estate
198   *The Evening News,* 1967
199   *The Guardian,* 1967
200   *The Times,* 1967
201   *The Beatles* 2018 Special Edition
202   *The Frost Programme,* ITV 1967
203   *Anthology*
204   *Anthology*
205   *MYFN*
206   *Arena: Magical Mystery Tour Revisited* 2012
207   *MOJO*
208   *MMT* DVD
209   The Beatles 'Free As A Bird' single 1995
210   *Hello Darlings*
211   *I'm Sorry, I'll Read That Again* S5E1, BBC Radio 1968
212   *Shindig* magazine, 2000
213   *Inside the Yellow Submarine,* Hieronimus, Robert 2003
214   *ITYS*
215   *MOJO*
216   *MOJO*

217   *MOJO*
218   *MOJO*
219   *Anthology*
220   *MOJO*
221   *Anthology*
222   *MOJO*
223   *MOJO*
224   *Yellow Submarine* DVD, 2012
225   *MOJO*
226   *ATAC*
227   *Inside the Yellow Submarine*
228   *MOJO*
229   *Yellow Submarine* DVD
230   *The Daily Mail* 1968
231   *The Observer,* 1968
232   *Sight and Sound,* 1968
233   *MOJO*
234   *Anthology*
235   *The New York Times,* 1968
236   *Inside the Yellow Submarine*
237   *Playboy*
238   Unidentified publication, Bill DeYoung, 1974
239   *The Smothers Brothers Comedy Hour,* 15 November 1968
240   *MOJO*
241   *Release,* BBC2, 1968
242   *MOJO*
243   *The Hapless Dilettante,* 1970s
244   *MYFN*
245   *The Beatles* SE
246   *MYFN*
247   *The Last Interview*
248   *Complete Beatles Recording Sessions,* Lewisohn, Mark 1988
249   *Lost Lennon Interviews*
250   *Lost Lennon Interviews*
251   *Get Back* outtake, 1969
252   *Let It Be* 1970
253   *Rolling Stone* 2008
254   *Anthology*
255   © Lennon/McCartney/Chumbawumba?
256   *ATAC*
257   *Get Back* outtake, 1969
258   *Anthology*
259   *ATAC*
260   WTF with Marc Maron podcast, 2018
261   *Anthology*
262   *ATAC*
263   *Rowan & Martin's Laugh-In* NBC 27/01/70

264 *A Secret History*

265 *Rolling Stone* 1979

266 *Pythons On The Pythons*, 2003

267 *Python Years, The,* Palin, Michael 2006

268 *I Me Mine* 2002

269 Acorn For Peace Conference London 69

270 *The Last Interview*

271 Bagism press Conference, Vienna 1969

272 ATAC

273 *Parkinson* BBC TV 1971

274 *MOJO*

275 *Lost Lennon Interviews*

276 *Kenny Everett's Monte Carlo Radio Show,* 1971

277 *National Lampoon's Radio Dinner,* 1972

278 *John Lennon Letters, The* 2012

279 *The Beatles After The Break Up 1970-2000*, Badman, Keith 2000

280 *The Observer,* 1974

281 TBATB

282 TBATB

283 *Q magazine,* 1998

284 *Monty Python Speaks!* Morgan, David (ed) 1999

285 *TDIO*

286 *Time Out*

287 *OJRIL*, Chapman, Graham, 1998

288 *Graham Crackers,* Chapman, Graham, 1997

289 *WTF with Marc Maron* podcast, 2018

290 *Rolling Stone,* 1979

291 *I Me Mine*

292 *POTP*

293 *Rutland Weekend Television Christmas Special*, BBC2 1975

294 *The Rutland Weekend Television Songbook,* BBC Records 1976

295 *The Dream Is Over*, Badman, Keith 2001

296 *Rutland Weekend Television S2E1*, BBC2 1976

297 *Saturday Night Live,* NBC 1976

298 *Playboy* 1980

299 *SNL* NBC 1976

300 *SNL* NBC 1976

301 *TDIO*

302 *TDIO*

303 *TBATB*

304 *Shindig*

305 *The Rutles: All You Need Is Cash* DVD Commentary, 2008

306 *The Rutles: All You Need Is Cash* DVD

307 *Shindig*

308 *Shindig*

309 *TDIO*

310 *Shindig*

[311] *TDIO*

[312] *TDIO*

[313] *TDIO*

[314] *Shindig*

[315] *I Me Mine*

[316] *The Rutles: All You Need Is Cash* (US edition) NBC 1978

[317] *TDIO*

[318] *TDIO*

[319] *Billboard*, April 1978

[320] *TDIO*

[321] *FAB: An Intimate Life of Paul McCartney*, Sounes, Howard. 2010

[322] *TDIO*

[323] *Rolling Stone*

[324] *I Me Mine*

[325] *TDIO*

[326] *Shindig*

[327] *Shindig*

[328] *TDIO*

[329] *Shindig*

[330] Britclip YouTube channel

[331] *Paperback Writer*, Shipper, Mark 1977

[332] *PW*

[333] *Ringo*, NBC 1978

[334] *TDIO*

[335] *You Never Give Me Your Money: The Beatles After the Breakup*, Doggett, Peter 2011

[336] *TDIO*

[337] *New York Times*, 1978

[338] *Rolling Stone*

[339] *TDIO*

[340] *TDIO*

[341] *Rolling Stone*

[342] *TDIO*

[343] *TDIO*

[344] *Very Naughty Boys: The Amazing True Story of HandMade Films*, Sellers, Robert, 2013

[345] *VNB*

[346] *The Life of Python*, Perry, George, 1999

[347] *TDIO*

[348] *Skywriting by Word of Mouth*, Lennon, John, Pan 1986

[349] 'Serve Yourself', *John Lennon Anthology* 1998

[350] Radio 1 interview with Andy Peebles, 1980

[351] *Dermot O'Leary Meets Richard Curtis*, BBC Radio 2 Beatles Pop-Up, October 2019

[352] *Secret Life of Sooty, The* 1990

[353] *TDIO*

[354] *New York Times*, 1981

355 *TDIO*

356 *TDIO*

357 *Life, the Universe and Everything*, Adams, Douglas 1981

358 *Hitchhiker's Guide to the Galaxy: Tertiary Phase, The* BBC Radio 4 2006

359 *439 Golden Greats – Never Mind The Originals* 1981

360 *Radio Active: What's News?* BBC Radio 4 6 October 1981

361 *Alas Smith & Jones*, S4E5 BBC November 1987

362 *Rock Profile*, UK Play 1999

363 *Very Naughty Boys*

364 *Very Naughty Boys*

365 *Withnail & I*, 1987

366 *Rapido*, Channel 4 1987

367 Toronto Press Conference, 1988

368 *GMRTBS* press conference, 1984

369 *GMRTBS* press conference, 1984

370 *TDIO*

371 *NY Times* 1984

372 *The South Bank Show*, 1984

373 *Aspel & Co*, ITV 1988

374 Toronto Press Conference 1988

375 The Spike Milligan estate

376 *Traveling Wilburys Vol 1* 1988

377 *Traveling Wilburys Vol 3* 1990

378 Toronto Press Conference

379 *After the Break-Up*

380 *Return of Bruno, The* HBO 1987

381 *Something About The Beatles* 2017

382 *Glass Onion*

383 *Very Naughty Boys*

384 *Spitting Image* Central TV 1994

385 The George Harrison estate32

386 *Always Look On The Bright Side Of Life,* Idle, Eric 2018

387 Penny Black Music interview, 2015

388 Eddie Izzard speech at MusiCares Person Of The Year Award event, LA 2012

389 The Rutles *Archaeology* EMI/Virgin 1996

390 The Rutles *Archaeology* EMI/Virgin 1996

391 *Austin Chronicle,* November 1996

392 *Off The Beatle Track,* Porter, Richard, 1996

393 *Chicago Tribune,* May 2005

394 Idle, Eric, award acceptance at LA Phil, unknown year

395 *The Rutles 2: Can't Buy Me Lunch* DVD Warner Bros 2002

396 *The Tonight Show with Jimmy Fallon,* NBC 2014

397 *Rutlemania* Q&A, Los Angeles 2008

398 © neilinnes.media 2009

399 *Liverpool Echo* May 2013

400 *Pirates of the Caribbean: Dead Men Tell No Tales,* Disney/Jerry Bruckheimer 2017

401 *POTC* press pack, Disney/Jerry Bruckheimer 2017

402 *The Peter Serafinowicz Show*, BBC 6Music 2010

403 *Comic Relief Red Nose Day 2010*

404 *Empire,* 2019

405 *Time* 2019

406 Toronto bed-in, 1969

407 Neil Innes, 'Friends At The End', *Works In Progress,* 2015

408 *Nearly Really* update, neilinnes.media

INDEX

277, 313–14, 336; on Beatles tributes 261, 262, 287–8; reunion on Harrison's albums 314; thaw on Fab Four 322–3

BIOGRAPHY/LIFE: early life 7–9; marriages 89, 180, 252, 326; fatherhood 291; Friar Park mansion 250–1, 260, 289, 326, 331; health 323, 325–6; death of 325, 326; *The Concert for George* 326–7, 329

CHARACTER AND INTERESTS: drug use 250; Indian culture 106–7, 150, 192, 265; motorsport 279; religion and spirituality 214, 247; sitar 106; ukulele 325, 334, 356

COMEDY/HUMOUR: and Bonzos 250, 325; Eldon on xii; Elton and Mayall on 298; on humour 57, 322–3; humour of 21, 32, 46, 103, 144–5, 150, 211, 213–14, 247, 290, 314, 325–7, 356; as Jack Lumber 251; *Life of Brian* 288–91; 'The Lumberjack Song' 251; and Monty Python 229–31, 246–7, 249–51, 260, 288–91; on problematic humour 25; quotes 1, 58, 102, 162, 229, 297; The Rutles 260, 262, 265–71, 276–8, 283, 314–15, 331–2, 336–7, 341; and Sellers 288, 289

PORTRAYALS OF: *The Beatles* cartoon 122, 124, 126, 128; *Harry & Paul* 347; *John, Paul, George, Ringo… and Bert* play 261, 262; *Rock Profile* 306; Serafinowicz 349–50; *Sgt Pepper's Lonely Hearts Club Band On The Road* musical 262; in Shipper's *Paperback Writer* 281–2; *The Simpsons* 322; *Spitting Image* 324; *Walk Hard* 351; *Yesterday* film plan 354

RELATIONSHIPS: and Adams 246; and Bennett 308; and Donegan 9; on Dylan 318; and Gilliam 307; and Idle 247, 250–1, 260–1, 288, 291, 336; and Innes 250, 275, 277, 327, 331–2, 336, 356; Lester on 79, 116; Milligan letter 315–16; Pattie Boyd (first wife) 89, 180; Olivia Harrison (second wife) 252, 326

works

ALBUMS: *Abbey Road* 220; *All Things Must Pass* 213–14, 247; *Anthology* 322; *Brainwashed* 325; *Cloud Nine* 314; *Dark Horse* tour 251; *Electric Sound* 227; *Extra Texture* 250, 251; *Sgt Pepper's Lonely Hearts Club Band* 150, 151; *Thirty Three and a Third* 260; *Wonderwall Music* 227

FILMS: on acting 314; on Apple Films 242; *Checking Out* 308; on cinema 40, 243, 309, 323; HandMade Films 289, 307, 323; *A Hard Day's Night* 71, 76, 78–81, 89, 101; *Help!* 101, 102, 105–7, 112–14, 116, 118, 119; *Little Malcolm and His Struggle Against the Eunuchs* 242; *The Lord of the Rings* plan 164; *Magical Mystery Tour* 165, 166, 168, 170–2, 174, 176, 179, 180; *Monty Python's Life of Brian* 288–91; *Ringo* 283–4; *The Rutles: All You Need Is Cash* 270–1; on *Sgt Pepper's Lonely Hearts Club Band* 287; *Shanghai Surprise* 308; *Time Bandits* 307; *Up Against It* (Orton film script) 156; *Water* 308; *Withnail and I* set visit

Hoffman, Dustin 300
Holder, Owen, *Shades of a Personality* 151
Holly, Buddy 313, 346
Hollywood Bowl 67
The Holy Grail (Monty Python film) 231, 249, 250, 288, 336
Hope, Bob 212
Hordern, Michael 141, 142
'Hound Dog' 13
The Hours and the Times 350
Howard, Bruce 123
Howard, Ron, *Eight Days A Week* film 355
Howerd, Frankie 111–12, 114, 115, 286
How I Won The War 140–3, 222–3
Hughes, Geoffrey 193
humour: Beatles band rapport 20, 34, 44, 57, 322–4; Beatles legacy vi–ix, x–xv, 355–6; Beatles songs 136, 143–4, 150, 211, 213; black humour 20–1, 25, 220; comedy songs 144, 355; craic/crack 2; Eldon on x–xv; Harrison on 57, 290, 322–3; Idle on 326; Innes on 356; Lancashire 3; Lennon on 5, 355; Liverpool xi, 2, 4, 28–9, 57, 76, 355; musicality of comedy xi, xii; problematic humour 3, 19–21, 25–6, 38, 87–90, 106–7, 126, 296, 306; race-based humour 3, 19, 88–9, 106–7, 126; satire boom 42, 98; sick humour 20–1, 220, 296; surreal humour 4–6, 10–11, 39, 77, 105, 153, 163–5, 174–5, 185, 191, 239; wartime entertainment 4
Humphries, Barry 98
Hunt, Vera 243; *see also* Adams, Douglas
Hurt, John 242
Hynde, Chrissie 319

The Idiot Weekly Price 2d 14, 72
Idle, Eric: as Beatles fan 247; Cambridge Footlights 43, 51,

337; 'Dirk and Stig' 279, 363; *Do Not Adjust Your Set* 182; and Harrison 231, 247, 250–2, 260–1, 288, 291, 323, 325, 326, 331; on humour 326; and Innes 182, 247–9, 267, 270, 278, 332, 334–8, 340–1; 'I Want To Hold Your Handel' 51, 182; legal battles 278, 332, 336, 337; and McCartney 275; Monty Python 250, 288, 291, 336, 337, 342; *Not The Messiah* oratorio 342; and Palin 337; 'The Pirate Song' 252; *Rutland Weekend Television* 247, 251–2; The Rutles 252–4, 258–60, 262–75, 276, 279–80, 329, 331–41, 343; *The Rutles: All You Need Is Cash* 272–5; *The Rutles 2: Can't Buy Me Lunch* 338–40; *Saturday Night Live* 255, 258–9; *Spamalot* (musical) 336; and The Traveling Wilburys 316–18; US sitcom 321
Idle, Tania 263
Ifield, Frank 24
Illustrated Lyrics books 185
I Me Mine (Harrison memoir) 8, 231, 252, 276
I'm Sorry, I Haven't a Clue (*ISIHAC*) 12, 340
I'm Sorry I'll Read That Again (*ISIRTA*) 50, 182
Indian culture 31, 106–7, 150, 164, 183, 192, 199, 211, 265
The Indra, Hamburg 27
In His Own Write (Lennon) 83–9, 97–8, 117
Innes, Neil: and The Beatles 249, 256, 275–6, 305, 356; The Bonzo Dog Doo-Dah Band 146, 171–2, 182–4, 247, 249, 265, 338, 356; children's shows 299–300, 330; early life 146; Eldon on xiv–xv; GRIMMS 247; and Harrison 277, 327, 331–2, 356; on humour 356; and Idle 182, 247–9, 267, 270, 278, 332, 334–8, 340–1;

dress/disguise 17, 29; on his reputation 52–3; 'Lost Weekend' period 202, 243; on religion 22, 294

COMEDY/HUMOUR: audio comedy recording 23–4; as comedy fan 257, 295; early influences 5–6; Eldon on xii; and The Goons 5, 9–10, 16, 19, 46, 295; and Innes 277; Lennon's humour 5–6, 16–21, 25–6, 29, 32, 46, 87–90, 144, 207, 211, 231–4, 295, 324, 355; on Monty Python 295; print humour 18–20; problematic humour 19–21, 25–7, 87–90; quotes 1, 58, 102, 162, 229, 297

PORTRAYALS OF: *Alas Smith & Jones* 305; *The Beatles* cartoon 121–4, 126, 128; Fallon 340; *Harry & Paul* 347; Ian Hart 350; *John, Paul, George, Ringo... and Bert* play 261; *Lennon: Naked* 350; *National Lampoon* 235; *Private Eye* 99; *Radio Active* 'best drummer in The Beatles' quip 304; *Rock Profile* 307; The Rutles 249, 265, 275–9; *Saturday Night Live* 344; Serafinowicz 348, 349–50; *Sgt Pepper's Lonely Hearts Club Band On The Road* musical 261; in Shipper's *Paperback Writer* 281–2; *Spitting Image* 324–5; *Walk Hard* 351; *Yesterday* film 353–4

RELATIONSHIPS: and Beckett 208–10; and Cook 98–9; and Cutler 167–8; on Epstein's death 161; and Everett 138, 234; and Harris 48; Lester on 80, 116; and Little Richard 47–8; Mike McCartney on 29; on The Monkees 129; and Nilsson 39, 202; and Olivier 205–6; and Sellers 223, 224; and Smothers Brothers 202; and Spinetti 207–8; and Zappa 238; Cynthia Lennon (first wife) 28, 99; Yoko Ono (second wife) 205, 207, 232, 293

works

ALBUMS: *Abbey Road* 220; *Double Fantasy* 295; *Mind Games* 243; *Sgt Pepper's Lonely Hearts Club Band* 149, 151; *Two Virgins* 226, 227; *Unfinished Music No. 2: Life With the Lions* 227; *Walls and Bridges* 243

FILMS: on acting 141, 201; on cinema 40; *A Hard Day's Night* 70–2, 76–80, 83, 89, 90, 109; *Help!* 105, 108–10, 113–16, 118, 119, 140; *How I Won The War* 140–3, 222–3; *Jungle Book* 128; *The Lord of the Rings* plan 164; *Magical Mystery Tour* 165–76, 180; *The Magic Christian* role 222–3, 226; *Self Portrait* 233; solo films 201; *Up Against It* (Orton film script) 156, 159; *Walk Hard* 351; *Yellow Submarine* 188, 189, 189, 191, 193, 194, 197, 198

RADIO: Peebles interview 295–6; *World of Books* 136

SONGS: Christmas flexidisc 65, 132, 134–5, 147–8, 181, 222; 'Cold Turkey' 234; 'The Continuing Story of Bungalow Bill' 212; 'Cry Baby Cry' 212; 'Do The Oz' 234; 'Free As A Bird' 323; 'Get Back' 216; 'Happiness Is A Warm Gun' 212; 'Hey Bulldog' 197; 'How Do You Sleep?' 233–4, 334; 'I Am the Walrus' 150, 175, 209, 215;

film 222, 223, 224, 225, 226; and Peta Button 269

McKellen, Ian 156

McKenna, Bernard 241; *The Odd Job* 104

McKern, Leo 40, 105–6, 116, 141, 152, 159

McKinnon, Kate 354

McQuickly, Dirk 266, 270, 279, 326, 329, 331, 336, 337, 341, 362, 363; *see also* Idle, Eric; The Rutles

media interviews/press conferences viii, xi–xiii, 46–7, 51–3, 66, 137, 247, 322–3

Meek, Joe 33

Melly, George 193, 239

Melody Maker 84

Mendelsohn, Jack 123, 189

merchandising 195–6, 330, 337

Mersey Beat magazine 18, 35, 36

merseybeat sound 145

Merseyside 2

The Mersey Sound 52

Merton, Paul 174

Michaels, Lorne 255–60, 262, 263, 268, 332, 341, 356

The Midniters 33

Miles, Barry 22, 65, 143, 166

Millar, Gavin 199

Miller, Jonathan 37, 187; *Bridge on the River Wye* 38

Miller, Max 150–1

Milligan, Spike: Associated London Scripts 56; and The Beatles 186, 315; *Bridge on the River Wye* 38; Cilla Black show 201; on Everett 138; The Goons 4–5, 10–13, 16, 186; Harrison letter 315–16; *The Idiot Weekly Price 2d* 14; 'I'm Walking Backwards For Christmas' 13; influence on Lennon 16, 19, 85; Lester on 77; *No One's Gonna Change Our World* charity album 219; *The Magic Christian* 224, 225, 226; and Martin 13; and

McCartney 315; mental health 14–15; problematic humour 88–9; *The Running Jumping & Standing Still Film* 40; *A Show Called Fred / Son of Fred* 14; television shows 14–15, 39

The Millionairess 31

Mimi, Aunt (Smith; aunt of John) 5, 86

Minoff, Lee: *Come Live With Me* 187; *Yellow Submarine* 187, 188, 189, 196

The Missionary 307

Mitch Benn Is The 37th Beatle 347

Mitchell, Warren 106-7

MMT see Magical Mystery Tour

Mona Lisa 308

The Monkees 128–9, 259, 344; *Head* 175; 'Randy Scouse Git' 129

Monkhouse, Bob 15, 96

Monroe, Marilyn 152

Monty Python: and Adams 241; Beatles as fans 229–31; as Beatles fans 247; Cambridge Footlights 235; 'Competing Documentaries' sketch 340; *The Concert for George* 327; *Flying Circus* 229, 230, 241, 248, 318; 40th anniversary 342; Goons influence 10; group dissolves 246; and Harrison 249–50, 251, 261, 288–91, 326; Harrison tribute 326; Hollywood Bowl film 291; *The Holy Grail* 231, 249, 250, 288, 336; influence of 296; and Innes xiv, 180, 248–9, 342; Lennon on 295; *Life of Brian* 288–91; 'The Lumberjack Song' 251, 326; and *Magical Mystery Tour* 175, 180, 231; *Matching Tie and Handkerchief* album 249; *Monty Python Lust For Glory* 330; Pao as designer 271; Presley as fan 130; The Rutles 231, 272, 341; *Saturday Night Live* 255; Scorsese on 110; and *The*

400